BETWEEN
GENERATIONS

THE Six Stages of Parenthood

BETWEEN
GENERATIONS

ELLEN GALINSKY

 **Times** BOOKS

Published by TIMES BOOKS, a division of
Quadrangle/The New York Times Book Co., Inc.,
Three Park Avenue, New York, N.Y. 10016

Published simultaneously in Canada by
Fitzhenry & Whiteside, Ltd., Toronto

Library of Congress Cataloging in Publication Data

Galinsky, Ellen.
   Between generations: The six stages of parenthood.

   Bibliography: p. 333
   Includes index.
   1. Parenthood. 2. Parenting—United States.
I. Title.
HQ755.8.G34   1980   649'.1   80-5132
ISBN 0-8129-0924-C

This book is for Lara, Philip, and Norman, with love!

Acknowledgments

There are two people who have been quite special in the writing of this book. They both possess that rare combination—expectations of excellence with the ability to reassure and support. They are insightful, honest, and wise. I would like to thank Caroline Shookhoff and Jeannie Boose.

I would also like to thank the Carothers family—Julia Carothers and two of her grown children, Suzanne Carothers and LaVerne Murray—for their knowledge and thoughtfulness, but mostly for being an example of what families can be.

In addition, I am very appreciative of the generous help from Karen and David Diamond, June Sale, Richard Ruopp, Seth Wolitz, Maritza Macdonald, Ruth Loud, Harriet and Gerry Nottingham, Debby and David Black, Penny Stirling, Florette Angel, Nancy Tolliver, Phyllis Louis-Dreyfus, Eleanor Lazarus, Sherri Nance, Jane and Ray Bernick, Barbara and Alan Wiener, Peter Kiers, Conrad Curtis, Lorin Driggs, Nancy Connors, Bernice Weissbourd, Melissa Bloch, Jill Shaw, Donna and Arthur Miller, Carol Darrow, Victor and Valerie Ostrower, Mary Alice Hayes, Judy and Morris Lampert, Vivian Weinstein, Mary Valley, Marjorie Goldsmith, Barbara Tanner, Nancy Sullivan, Jane Price, Kay Sardo, Peter Sauer, Sue Lewis, Bill Rau, and Margaret McCurry.

I am also grateful to these people for discussing the ideas of the book: Jacqueline Rosen, Suzanne Arms, Douglas Powell, Aristotle Anthony, Carolyn and Philip Cowan, Arlene Skolnick, William H. Hooks, Seymour Reit, Joanna Cole, and Judith Baumrin.

The following people have made an invaluable contribution by reading and commenting on various drafts of the manuscript: Edna Shapiro, Matti Feldman, Rochelle Mayer, John Munder Ross, Carline Shookhoff, Suzanne Carothers, Karen Sheingold, Mona Goldemberg, Anne Sturtevant, Frances Burck, Fay and Marvin Ellison, Martha Stuart, Jeannie and Andy Boose, Betty Boegehold, Rick Greenberg, Sally Ruth Rau, Robie Harris, and Norman Galinsky.

I am indebted to Roger Jellinek, Leonard Schwartz, John Gallagher, Rosalyn Badalamenti, Pat Sklar, Maria Temechko, and Jody Nolen from Times Books, and to my agents Ginger Barber and Mary Evans.

As I am to my mother Leora May and my sister Sally Ruth Rau.

Contents

III.   The Authority Stage   119

VI.   The Departure Stage

BETWEEN
GENERATIONS

Introduction

Parents grow? Parents go through stages? What does that mean?

Change in children is visibly dramatic: The newborn baby who just fits in the crook of our arm, measuring no longer than the distance between our elbow and our hand, will double and triple in size within the first years of life. We use expressions like "spring up" and "sprout" to describe children's growth, and though the process may often seem interminable, in retrospect it seems as if a projector has tripped onto fast speed and their feet, their faces, and their hands are soon magically as large as ours.

The changes in children's capacities are equally dramatic. The baby who is unable to grasp a bottle will, within a matter of months, be able to hold a spoon and drink from a cup. The toddler who walks as if he or she is tipsy will in a year or two be able to climb to the top of the jungle gym and hang upside down. The young child able to communicate only with shrieks and cries will soon have a large and proficient vocabulary, even be able, as a preschooler, to say, "I hate you means I love you because it's backwards day."

The underlying psychological changes that children go through are more subtle. It's less obvious why the young child seems to slide back and forth between dependent clinging—"You do it for me"—to demanding—"I can do it myself," even donning a superhero cape. In fact, these changes have been carefully studied. The young child, in this particular example, has become aware that he or she is not permanently attached to and protected by the parents, sees also that the world out there is fraught with hidden and not-so-hidden dangers, and feels vulnerable. This child in turn clings to the parents, warding off fear, then puts on a superhero cape, a shield, that transforms the child into the savior and the saved.

The cognitive changes that children make can also seem mysterious—not the more apparent growth of abilities, such as the acquisition of language and the capacity to compute, but the shifts in thinking itself and moral reasoning: the development of the capacity to abstract, to see the world in more than an egocentric framework. The six-year-old will have trouble grasping why his friend pushes him aside in a group, but at eight he will be able to empathize with the friend, to see that this child has trouble playing with more than one other person at one time.

Over three centuries ago, children were seen as miniature adults—smaller, yes, but not that different.[1] In the last century, Sigmund Freud's insights into the significance of the inner life of children have sparked a virtual explosion in the systematic study of childhood.[2] Most colleges and universities and some high schools now teach courses in child development, and the shelves of the bookstores and libraries are stocked with literature on the subject. In the last two decades, child development has been extensively written about for parents and professionals by Erik Erikson, Jean Piaget, Benjamin Spock, Bruno Bettelheim, Robert Coles, Selma Fraiberg, Jerome Kagan, Berry Brazelton, and others.[3]

But what about parents? Do parents grow? Do they go through stages? The first glimpse of such a possibility came to me not long after my first child was born, ten years ago. I was rereading a book that I had read countless times as a child development professional, a book, in fact, that I had often recommended to parents. But when I read it as a new parent, I found that it had soured. This book, in telescoping the child's world, had blocked me and other parents right out of the picture, leaving us in the shadows somewhere, monstrously powerful people, capable of doing damage to these young, fragile children. I closed the book tightly, determined never to recommend it to a parent again. Still, the smallest glimmer of understanding was there: I must have changed. The book certainly hadn't.

I wanted to talk with other new parents, to see if their feelings were similar to mine, but most of my colleagues at work had much older children, and my search for places where parents congregate in our town turned up no one. So I wrote to the local librarian, asking if I could start a program there, a place where young children could play and listen to stories and parents could talk. He called me immediately. He understood. He and his wife had just had a baby.

I ran that group for two years. There, and then at work (others had since had babies), I found people with whom to explore the thoughts and feelings that concerned me.

One winter Sunday afternoon, when my son Philip was two, I went for a walk by myself out to a woodland waterfall. I watched the water roaring down the stream, pounding over the rocks, splintering out like nails, then crashing against the frozen edges of the stream. The icy whiteness of the froth and foam was dazzling, the sound deafening. The sheer force of the waterfall reminded me of my two-year-old—the power of his drive to do things his way, his temper at being thwarted. Philip was struggling to figure out where his power began and ended: How much could he decide? How much couldn't he? How far could we, his parents, be pushed? Were we unified—or could he find a wedge between us? Would we stop him, save him from his own overwhelming feelings? He was growing up. And from my place by the stream, his struggles suddenly seemed as beautiful as the roaring, churning waterfall.

Churning. That's how I was feeling, too. Plummeted and twisted like those waters. He was figuring out how to be the child in our family. I was figuring out how to be the adult. As a professional, I had learned how to be in charge. Now as a parent, I was learning it all over again. He was going through something. So was I. That moment, eight years ago, was the beginning of this book.

The understanding that parents do grow and change opened the gates to more questions: What is the genesis of parental growth? Are there stages and phases? If so, what leads people from one stage to the next?

I searched the writings in my field of child development for answers, but there were few. So I turned to direct observation: listening to parents as they talked, always on the lookout for patterns in their perceptions, for common themes.

I joined a reading group at work some time later: a group to discuss the current research and writings about child development. Many of the members of this group happened to have children. Although all were professionals with similar training and work experience, I realized that parenthood had had and was having a substantial effect on their perceptions of any literature related to parents. Those who were pregnant were impatient with any mention of parents' lack of perfection. Those with young children had the opposite response. They were equally impatient, even angry with parents' strivings toward perfection. They described themselves as "realists" and saw the pregnant members of the group as "idealistic."

The same kind of differences in perception occurred in the six parent discussion groups that I have helped to organize and run since the birth of my daughter, Lara. From these groups (consisting of over seventy parents in all), I drew up a hypothesis of how parents grow and change, and then turned to a search of the studies on parenthood.

About this time, 1976, there was widespread interest in normal, as distinguished from pathological, adult growth, instigated by the publication of Gail Sheehy's *Passages*, and before that by Erik Erikson's seminal paper "Eight Ages of Man."[4] As I was writing this book, two psychiatrists published books on adult development: Daniel Levinson's *The Seasons of a Man's Life* and Roger Gould's *Transformations*.[5] What struck me about all these important books was their definition of growth. They concentrated on the adult's moving away from his or her parents into relationships with other adults and into a job or career. That other significant aspect of life—the adult's relationship to his or her children—was seen as a backdrop against which adults found meaningful or nonmeaningful work, and formed and broke bonds with mentors, colleagues, lovers, and husbands or wives.

The studies of life-span psychology, like those of adult development, have also minimized the place of parenthood. Parenthood, when stressed in adult development at all, as in *Women of a Certain Age*, by Lillian Rubin, and *In Her Time*, by Iris Sanguiliano, was more likely to be cast as something for women to be freed from in order to search for and find their own sense of identity.[6]

The research on parenthood itself has tended to concentrate on the transitions in and out of parenthood, on its beginning and end. Some of this work has been sociological, emphasizing the role changes that occur when the family goes from a two-member system or dyad to a three-member system or triad, and then the role changes that occur when the children grow up. This research is also concerned with the continuities and discontinuities in cultural norms that influence parents.

The preponderance of research on parenthood has been psychoanalytic, based on parents who were undergoing psychiatric treatment. Little of this research has been conducted on the general population. Psychoanalytic studies stress the changes in ego and the reemergence of unresolved childhood conflicts in parenthood.

Among the most influential thinkers and writers in the sociological study of parenthood are E. E. LeMasters, Alice Rossi, and Jessie Bernard. In the psychoanalytic field, Grete Bibring and Helene Deutsch stand out, as do two books: *Parenthood: Its Psychology and Psychopathology*, edited by Therese Benedek and E. James Anthony, and *Joys and Sorrows of Parenthood*, by the Group for the Advancement of Psychiatry. The work of Urie Bronfenbrenner on the family uniquely bridges both the psychological and sociological fields, as does an excellent summary of the research on parenthood, *Fathers, Mothers, and Society* by Rhona and Robert Rapoport and others.[7]

There have been a number of books by parents describing and analyzing the substantive experiences of parenthood. Most of these are about the first few years—for example, *The Mother Knot*, by

Jane Lazarre, and *The Growth and Development of Mothers*, by Angela Baron McBride. *Ourselves and Our Children*, by the Boston Women's Health Collective, shares the wisdom and feelings of parents with children of all ages.[8]

Since the overall growth of parents was just beginning to be studied, my question became: What should a first step in this kind of study be? It was, obviously, a soul-searching question. I eventually decided that the way I wanted to approach this overwhelming topic was to interview parents with diverse experiences in parenthood—married, divorced, widowed, step, foster, adoptive, and guardian mothers and fathers. They would be teenage parents and older parents, parents expecting their first child and those with large families. Their children would range from gifted to handicapped. They would be rich, middle-income, and poor, from different ethnic, racial, geographic, and religious backgrounds. From this welter of diversity I could search for common threads, the similar ways that different parents weave together their perceptions of parenthood. Put all together, these would form a theory on growth in parenthood. (See Appendix for the interview questions.)

To interview parents, I traveled across the United States. I went to a small farming village in New England and a revitalized city in the South. I went into the hills and hollows, and to a metropolitan area of an Appalachian state, then to a city in the Bible-belt South. In the Southwest, I interviewed in a city built long ago amid ranches, and in a modern, high-rise, sprawling megalopolis, interlaced with highways, the signs of construction everywhere. I went to the Far West, to a planned community whose uniformly planted yards rose up like steps against bleak canyons and brown mountains. I visited a large Western city and its outlying countryside, then went to the flat plains of the Midwest, to one city on a wide winding river and another that curved around the shore of a lake. And finally, I interviewed in a large Northeastern city and in some of its suburbs.

When I had finished, I had interviewed 228 parents with 396 children among them (from ten to forty children of each chronological year from *in utero* to eighteen). For the book I have changed their names and occasionally some biographical details to protect their anonymity, but I have not changed what they said.

I am fully aware that people tend to shape their stories, to present themselves as they would like to think they are. It is this psychological fact turned around, however, that led to one of my most significant conclusions.

Whenever parents describe a new event in the life of their family (an event as large as the birth of a child or as small as their child's reaction to a new toy), they used the words "should" or "supposed to" or "expected." I realized that parents had pictures in their minds of the way things were supposed to go, and of the way that they as parents and their children were supposed to act. I came to think of these pictures as images—because they were often fleeting, not fully conscious. This concept is similar to Bernice Neugarten's construct of "the normal, expectable life cycle" and to Daniel Levinson's "The Dream," though I see parents having myriads of images, filtering in and out of their thoughts, as opposed to one dream.[9]

I see images as being the adult legacy of children's play. Children explore; they try on the future by becoming it. The child who worries about robbers may pretend to be a robber or a cop attacking an intruder. Donald Winnicott, Barbara Biber, Millie Almy, and Eveline Omwake have for many years noted that through play, the child forms a rudimentary base of knowledge about what it feels like to be a mother, father, doctor, construction worker, or hero.[10]

By adolescence, the pretending has become more internalized. Teenagers, just like children, anticipate events to come, but they do so by taking mental forays, imaginative excursions out on a date with someone admired, or to a track meet or exam.

As adults, we continue this lifelong process of imagining what lies ahead. At transitional times when we are about to embark on something new—pregnancy, for example—our thoughts are filled with images.

Furthermore, we use images as a measure of our successes and failures as parents. If an image has not been achieved in reality, it is seen as a loss and can cause anger and depression. If an image is realized, it brings joy.

I see growth occurring at the points when parents modify an image to be more consistent with reality, or modify their own behavior to reach toward an image. This finding is similar to Klaus Riegel's idea that growth comes from the resolution of dissonance.[11] Roger Gould defines growth similarly, but specifies that the dissonance grows out of a clash between the view brought from childhood of a simple, beneficent world with a more rational, adult view of reality.[12] Where I differ from Gould is that I think that images stem not only from childhood but also from adult experiences.

If one examines the research on the highly problematic points in parenthood, there is certain evidence that severe depression and even child abuse follow from rigid adherence to an image which is conflicting with reality. For example, in some studies, child-abusing parents are found to believe that infants should act very grown-up and should be loving all the time. When the infants don't act this way, the parents refuse to let go of the image, turning the disappointment inward into depression or outward into rage directed at the child.[13]

The history of parenthood thus is a personal saga of images failed and achieved. It is a history, too, of passing through stages, led by our children's growth. Stages are periods of time in which one's emotional and intellectual energy is primarily focused on one major psychosocial task or issue to be resolved. These major tasks include many related tasks and themes, and each is present, embryonically, from the very beginning of parenthood. For the concept of stages and the tasks that people face within them, I am in debt to the thinking of Erik Erikson and Robert Havighurst.[14] Stages in parenthood differ from the stages in the cycle of life, however; as many parents have children of different ages, parents can be going through several stages concurrently.

The first stage is the *Image-Making Stage*, and it occurs during pregnancy. This is the time when prospective parents begin to cull through, to form and re-form images of what's to come, of birth and parenthood. They prepare for a change in themselves and in their other important adult relationships.

The second stage, the *Nurturing Stage*, goes from birth until the child begins to say "No," somewhere around eighteen months to two years. In this stage, parents compare their images of birth, of their child, and of themselves as parents with their actual experience. They become attached to the baby, and in that attachment, in learning how much and when to give, their conceptions of themselves become blurred and changed, often leading to identity questions: What are my priorities? How much time should I give to the baby and how much to the other aspects of my life?

The *Authority Stage* goes approximately from the child's second to the child's fourth or fifth year. In this stage, parents face the task of deciding what kind of authority to be, how rules are set, what the rules are, when they are enforced, and when they are broken.

The *Interpretive Stage* begins in the child's preschool years and ends with the approach of adolescence. The child's entrance into kindergarten or first grade usually prompts parents to review their images of parenthood, to ask themselves how realistic they've been. The task in this stage is interpreting. Parents are concerned with how they are interpreting themselves to their children as well as how they are interpreting and developing their children's self-concepts. Parents are also figuring out how they want to interpret reality, how to answer their children's questions—and what kinds of knowledge, skills, and values to promote.

The *Interdependent Stage* spans the child's teenage years. The issues that predominated in the Authority Stage rise back into prominence, often requiring new solutions. Parents form a new relationship with their almost-adult child.

The *Departure Stage*, the time when the children leave home, is characterized by evaluations. Parents evaluate their images of departure, when and how far away they thought their child would go. They evaluate whether they've achieved the parent/grown child relationship they wanted as well as taking stock of their overall successes and failures.

Growth can occur anytime, during any stage, whenever a parent resolves the clash between an image and reality. While obviously some parents resist or turn away from growth—by taking on the responsibility for a baby, or by facing the anger within or by figuring out how to explain the world to a child—people change. Parenthood is itself a transforming experience.

Parenthood is clearly complex in its innumerable variations. In this book, I have traced the development of parents in relation to the growing child. For example, the mother of a seven and a three year old, who is expecting her third child, would be in the Image-Making Stage in relation to her unborn child, in the Authority Stage with her three year old, and in the Interpretive Stage with her seven year old. The book is organized chronologically, one stage leading into the next. Circumstantial issues—such as wanting another child or facing the death of a child—can be located through the index. Within each stage, the subject matter is also organized chronologically, following the emergence of each of the tasks of parenthood.

A few people upon hearing that I was working on a book about parenthood were disparaging. "Why parenthood?" they said. "Haven't we moved away from the idea of children as fulfillment, children as the answer to all our problems?"

It is true that in the last few years we, as a society, have moved and that for a while we teetered on the other extreme, focusing almost exclusively on adults: their satisfactions, their fulfillments. At times, we talked about children as if they enslaved us. But I, for one, value parenthood, feel that it can be one of the most enriching experiences of adult life.

When other people found that I was working on a book about parenthood, they often asked very specific questions: Are divorced parents different from married parents? Are teenage parents different from other parents? Are fathers who have participated in the birth of their children different from those who haven't? What's the best way to handle teenagers? I replied that I had not done that kind of study, comparing one group with another. While I never set out to do a how-to book, with specific answers to specific questions, there is much that is practical throughout the book. Inevitably, the experiences of the parents quoted reveal solutions to common problems.

People that I meet also ask if writing this book has changed me as a parent. The answer to that question is yes. First, I no longer feel alone. Understanding about parental growth does not prevent it from happening—I still have the same moments of unabated guilt, anguish, and sky-high joy as I did before. My oldest child is about to be a teenager, and I, just like all other parents, wonder if I am ready, if he is ready, and how we will fare in these years together. When my youngest child goes off to spend the night at someone's house, common but irrational fears shoot through me—maybe these other parents won't watch her carefully enough, maybe she'll walk out into the street, untended.

Understanding parental growth doesn't prevent or even dim the influx of strong feelings. But I now know that parents all over are fretting, fearing, and rejoicing just as I am. In the matter of what I do with my feelings, I am a substantially different parent for writing this book. When I find myself caught in a bind, everything seeming to cave in on me, I look for an underlying image. I ask myself, "What am I expecting that's not coming true?" Then, when I uncover the image, I ask myself if it is a realistic one. If I decide it is, I look for constructive ways to achieve it; if it's not realistic, I try to replace it with a goal that's more workable.

This technique has been a great help when I'm having a problem with others. My husband and I used to have the same fight over and over, almost like robots, reacting to subliminal stimuli. The repeating conflict was caused because his image was short-circuiting mine, and mine his. Once we were clear about the problem, we could discuss it, and slowly we are trying to find a middle ground.

We also use this method with our children. Here the sources of conflict are also likely to be different expectations. I'm now more direct with the children about what they can expect of a new situation—and what I expect of them.

Understanding parental growth has also helped me as a professional, helped me know that parents at different times have very specific feelings and issues before them. Those of us who work with parents should start off by being mindful of their growth, and then communicate clearly about our own expectations while encouraging parents to examine theirs. It would be a great help if, for example, obstetricians spelled out the spectrum of parental response to birth or teachers told parents and children what will happen on the first day of school.

Understanding parental growth does not circumvent it. However, it does help parents manage their confusions so that instead of being entrapped or swept along, we can see where we have been, where we are, and make more deliberate and careful choices about where we want to go. That, I believe, will make parenthood more satisfying for us and for our children.

I.
The Image-Making Stage

"I see myself comforting a crying child, holding tight, until the tears dampen my shirt, until the child is happy again."
—A father-to-be

"I think about coming back from the grocery store with a baby who is just walking. It's a long way from where we park the car to our house and I'm balancing a bag of food in one arm, while the baby holds onto the other one, climbing up the path home."
—A mother-to-be

"I can picture myself in a vacant lot on a hot Sunday—playing a great game of baseball with all these freckled, dirty-faced, spunky little kids."
—A father-to-be

Everyone notices that expectant parents are at times unusually quiet. While they may look lost or vacant, their thoughts are often filled with pictures: perhaps pictures of sitting on a porch in the cool of evening, listening to birds settle for the night, rocking a baby; of being saddled with piles of laundry; of listening to music with a child close by; or of a fight at the dinner table, while a young child stares sullenly down at a plate, refusing even to taste anything.

Awaiting the birth of a child is strangely similar to the time before entering a new junior high, before moving, before getting married. Something is about to happen that will change everything. A new person, a mystery person, will enter the lives of these parents-to-be, and nothing again will be quite the same—how they use their time, their home, their money. Life will now be measured into eras: before and after this birth.

13

Parents-to-be prepare for this change the way that they have always prepared for the predictable and unpredictable future: by forming images of the future.

Images Are a Rehearsal

Pregnancy, whether it's the first, second, or sixth pregnancy, is a beginning, and expectant mothers and fathers get ready by culling through their images of parenthood. They look back at their own experiences as children with parents. They examine and analyze their friends', relatives', and neighbors' as well as their own experiences as parents. Throughout pregnancy, they cast out some images and keep others. Pregnancy is the Image-Making Stage. *The major task of this stage is preparing for parenthood. This includes preparing for a changing sense of self and changing relationships with one's partner and one's own parents. Parents-to-be begin to get attached to the unborn baby, begin to understand that the baby will be a separate person, and they ready themselves for the actual birth.*

The concept of dividing the life cycle into stages, each dominated by a specific task, grows out of the work of Sigmund Freud, Erik Erikson, and Jean Piaget, and has focused more on childhood and adolescence.[1] Growth is not simply a matter of becoming larger and being able to do more. There is a sequence of development which involves fundamental reorganizations in ways of perceiving and thinking. The three-year-old who puts himself at the center of the world and supposes he's responsible for everything that happens is very different from the ten-year-old who recognizes that people can have different points of view.

The stages in childhood are more rooted in biological development than in adulthood. Parental growth, in particular, is an interactive process with the development of the child influencing the development of the parent. In the Image-Making Stage, the ever-changing pregnancy causes parents to think about what kind of parents they want to be.

BRYAN JOHNSON'S IMAGE

Bryan and his wife, Vivian, are expecting a child in less than a week. They live in an apartment, high above a congested urban street in a large city. Bryan's image of parenthood is that he will be closer to his child than his father was to him.

"My father was twenty-three years old when I was born. He was very busy trying to carve a career in the middle of the Depression. I don't know why they started a family that early. The joke my parents always made was that they went on a trip, they were in a sleeping bag, and I was an accident.

"My father was very goal-oriented in his work. He just wasn't around. Then there was the war.

"I intend to take some time off from work after the baby's born. I'm going to take as much time as I can get from my boss—at least an afternoon and a part of a morning a week and say, 'Dock me if you want to, I don't care, I'm going to spend time with my baby.' I would like not to be as distant and as frightened and as squeamish of intimacy as I think my father is."

When Bryan thinks about becoming a father, he has decided "not to stop being the baby part of me. My father never let me see the adult-him or the child-him—only the parent part. I do not intend to give up the child inside of me. I think that would be terrible for a kid.

"I think that to be a perfect parent is to be an imperfect human being. The people that I see that want to be perfect parents really want their kids to be perfect. That's a dreadful burden. It's one that was laid on me. I'd come home with five A-pluses, an A, and a B-plus, and all I'd hear about from my parents was the B-plus.

"I don't expect to be a perfect human being or expect my kid to be perfect. If my kid has a problem, my kid has a problem. I'll ask myself what I've done to aggravate it and what I can do to alleviate it. I'm sure this is all very easy in theory. I'm sure that on a day-after-day basis, it's hard to stay on top. But that's what I'm going into it hoping."

MARTY OLSEN'S IMAGE

Marty and her husband, John, live in the country, in a large apartment with plush upholstered furniture. Eight months pregnant, Marty has just begun an indeterminate leave from her job in a county agency.

"I think about the kind of family life we will have. That's probably because of the kind of family life I had as a child. It was very hard, not having a father there. John and I will really have a nice, wholesome family.

"In a lot of ways, I want to be like my mother. She was always a very good friend of ours [Marty and her sisters]. She wasn't like our friends' mothers, who were very strict and authoritarian. She treated us with respect and admiration. I was always proud to have her as my mother, and the reason was that she was involved in eighty zillion things. She just wasn't home baking cookies."

And yet, because she had to work so hard, "Mother wasn't always there as much as I would have liked her to be," Marty says.

"We were always the last children to be picked up at school."

Although Marty likes the fact that her mother treated her as a friend and equal, she feels that her mother never seemed mature—at times she was selfish, impulsive, and unsure of herself. "I think Mother had a difficult time growing up. It's not an easy thing, to grow up with an immature parent. And when I conceive of myself as a parent, that's really one of the things I want to avoid.

"Now, that can be a very abstract thing. I mean, what makes you grow up? I think that a lot of the reason that Mom didn't grow up emotionally is that she didn't have rewarding relationships with other adults, particularly men, and she was a little bit bitter. That's something that I never want to experience.

"Knowing that I am going to have the care of a child, that I am going to be a mother, that—per se—makes me feel more grown up. Also that my body looks like this. I don't look like a sixteen-year-old anymore. I look in the mirror and I say, 'My God, I actually am a woman.' I feel more grown up."

Barbara Callahan's Image

In Barbara and Steven's Northeastern suburban home, Barbara has a workroom. Her bookshelves are filled with law journals and books. On her desk are boxes of tapes from a law review course. The teacher has given these tapes to Barbara so that she can learn at home and not go to class during the final months of her pregnancy.

"My mother was a martyr," Barbara says. "She would give up everything for us. I never felt guilty about that, because that's what gives her pleasure, but I know I don't want to do that. I would resent the kid. If I have any kind of flashing picture of what it's going to be like, it's of a kid who comes with me everywhere I go." Barbara plans to return to work in the law office where she is clerking four months after the baby's birth.

"My parents let us grow up the way we did, willy-nilly, and were supportive all the time. Every one of my sisters is different, and I give my parents credit. They didn't force us into little molds. So I hope I don't inflict my feelings of what I want the kid to be. I'm sure I will to some extent, but I just hope I appreciate the kid's strengths and weaknesses."

Images Are Based on Memories

First-time parents-to-be remember the child they once were, and then form images centered around the way they would have liked their parents to treat them. Bryan Johnson wished that his father had not been on a pedestal, but had been closer, more caring, more intimate. He would have liked his father to spend more time with him and to show his emotions. And so Bryan has decided to try to be the kind of father he wanted to have. Marty Olsen stands on the other side of the spectrum: She would have liked her mother to have shown less of her feelings, to have been more mature. She is ambivalent about whether her mother should have focused more attention on her. Barbara Callahan had the attention, which she appreciated, but it had a martyr flavor, which she didn't like. All three are struggling with the same issue: how involved to be in their future child's life. They all hope to treat the child with respect.

These first-time parents have formed images of themselves as parents by recalling their own childhoods, and as John Munder Ross's study of the development of ideas of fatherhood in boys shows, the image-making process begins early in childhood.[2] Images of parenthood are based on a multi-identification. These parents-to-be identify with the parent they will be and the child they were. It is *as if* they are the child they will have. That is not to say that prospective parents necessarily want their child to be like them—many want just the opposite. But they do identify with the child, or as Sigmund Freud said, the child represents the parent as a child.[3] It is important to note that most first-time parents' reminiscences are from the elementary school years on. Few people recall their earliest childhood experiences. And so they plan their parenthood based on memories of themselves as four or five or six or seven or eight years old.

Those expectant parents who already have children compound this process by reviewing their own experiences in parenthood and forming images that represent an opportunity to start over. They imagine the ways they would like to rectify their past mistakes; for example, they plan that they'll insist that the baby stay with them right after birth, or that they'll get help for those first few exhausting weeks, or that they won't get overly anxious when the baby cries or refuses to eat.

Images Are Influenced by Circumstances

Of course, the factors surrounding the pregnancy play an enormous role in shaping all parents' images. Was the child wanted or not? And if wanted, why? As an escape from a dead-end job or as glue for a marriage that seemed to be falling apart? Is the child conceived to reduce the pressure from one's own parents, who are saying, "Why don't you have a (or another) child?" Martin and Lois Wladis Hoffman have studied the reasons why people want children, and enumerate them as follows:

1. The validation of adult status and social identity. When people have children, they are valued in the social system.
2. The expansion of self. Children give adults ties to the future and some sense of immortality.
3. The achievement of moral values. One is doing something good by having and caring for a child.
4. The creation of a family—a bond that is larger than husband-wife relationship.
5. Stimulation, novelty, fun.
6. Achievement, competence, creativity. Having produced a baby, people can feel proud of themselves.
7. Power and influence. The baby will be under the influence and control of the parents.
8. Social comparison and competition.
9. Economic utility. A baby will grow into someone who will help in the family, bring in money, help care for the parents when they are older.[4]

Thinking about having a second or third child is different from thinking about having a first. Parents are much more aware of what parenthood is like, and they make this decision because they want to care for an infant once again, or they don't want their child to be an only child, or they want to be "more of a family."

Myra Leifer, while also not looking at specific images, related women's overall attitudes toward their first pregnancies with the reasons for having a child. Using extensive open-ended interviews and twelve personality measures, she found that those who were the most positive were those who had planned their pregnancies and wanted children for self-growth reasons. They viewed parenthood as an "opportunity for continued expansion of the self through the act of caring for a child. They anticipated that parenthood would be an opportunity to intensify and enrich an already satisfying marriage relationship."[5] Those women who were more negative about becoming a parent either had unplanned pregnancies or wanted children for escape, status, or security reasons. They felt that they should have a child because everybody does or because their current life was not satisfying and a baby might provide a new sense of purpose, give them new friends, or prop up their marriages.

Even though parents who already have children are more realistic about what parenthood means, some want another baby for many of the same reasons or because their other children aren't all that they'd hoped they'd be.

Images Are Influenced by Culture

It is obvious, too, that cultural expectations shade and color the images that parents-to-be form. The baby-products ads, showing a woman serenely holding her child, looking blissfully and mysteriously contented, or the television parents, wisely and humorously solving problems, influence parents-to-be. There has, however, been a recent outpouring of criticism against these one-sided pictures of parenthood.

The sociologist E. E. LeMasters has said that "parenthood (and not marriage) is the real romantic complex in our culture."[6]

Shirley Radl, writer and mother, begins *Mother's Day Is Over*:

> Everyone knows what a mother is.
> A mother is someone who makes you wear galoshes when it isn't raining. She gives you aspirin when you have a cold and reads you stories before bed.
> A mother is a happy, warm, patient person who effortlessly maintains a beautiful, spotless home. She plays games with her children joyously, teaches them constantly, and takes them to the doctor, the dentist, the zoo, the park, swimming and camping—sometimes all on the same day.[7]

And so on and on until Shirley Radl says, ". . . so much for the legend"—which has been "carefully fed and nourished for years by the mass media. Films, magazines, the women's pages of newspapers, and especially television have created a pervasive myth that victimizes every mother."[8]

Author Ellen Peck agrees. She feels we have been sold the ideas of parenthood like so much breakfast cereal.[9] Ideas with "sugar-coated descriptions," says Ruth Davidson Bell.[10]

These are interesting contentions. Have these one-sided rosy pictures been grafted onto prospective parents? Have parents been duped into buying visions of perfection in parenthood?

Partially yes, and partially no. A recent spate of books written by parents themselves picture parenthood in graphic detail. The sleepless nights, children's constant bidding for attention, temper tantrums, the wear and tear of being parents—all are evoked by Virginia Barber and Merrill Maguire Skaggs, by Angela Barron McBride, by Jane Lazarre, by Shirley Radl, by Eliot Daley, and by the authors of *Ourselves and Our Children*.[11]

Films also have changed. Children no longer exist angelically in the background, speaking only when spoken to. They burst in, they interrupt, they demand.

Many first-time parents-to-be, who have seen these films and read these books, are nonetheless impatient with what they see as the failings of these other parents. Somehow, they hope, they can be different. They build their images of parenthood around their own ideas of perfection, whatever their definition of perfection might be. These definitions can range all the way from "I'm going to do everything right" to "A perfect parent is an imperfect human being."

Prospective parents who already have children have a more tempered viewpoint, but many still view the coming birth as a new starting point, a renewed opportunity.

Thus for many parents the impetus for betterment is a part of the process of creating images in pregnancy. The specific form such images take can be greatly influenced by whether or not the child is wanted as well as by the cultural surround—that is, by the parents' particular ethnic background, their economic status, and by where they live.

Images Can Be at Odds

Very often, after the child is born, parents will say, "My expectations of parenthood weren't mine." They will say that these expectations came from their own parents or friends.

Images are always a blend of the personal and the cultural. People can take different mixes of this blend, taking in lesser to greater amounts from the outside. Those parents who later reflect that "I did what I was expected to do" are only partially accurate. They had an inner receptivity, small as it may have been. Later they have found that these various images were at odds and have had to discard those images that haven't worked for them.

The images that people have are not always harmonious. There can be several images, formed at different points in life, that coexist, but in an uneasy truce.

Here is where I differ with Daniel Levinson's emphasis on a "Dream." He states that men (for men were the subject of his study) form a "Dream" ("a vague sense of self-in-adult-world"). The task of adult life is giving this Dream "greater definition and finding ways to live it out." [12] I think that parents have many images, some with internal consistency, some that are conflicting. Occasionally images are shed, others are kept, while new ones continue to be formed.

Images Can Be Denied

What of the person who denies having an image? A few parents interviewed said things like, "I didn't have a thought in my head during pregnancy. Afterward it was a shock. I had no idea what being a parent was like."

In *Of Women Born*, the poet Adrienne Rich describes herself this way:

> In my own pregnancy I dealt with this waiting, this female fate, by denying every active, powerful aspect of myself. I became dissociated both from my immediate, present, bodily experience and from my reading, thinking, writing life. Like a traveler in an airport where her plane is several hours delayed, who leafs through magazines she would never ordinarily read, surveys shops whose contents do not interest her, I committed myself to an outward serenity and a profound inner boredom. If boredom is simply a mask for anxiety, then I had learned, as a woman, to be supremely bored rather than to examine the anxiety underlying my Sistine tranquility. My body, finally truthful, paid me back in the end: I was allergic to pregnancy.[13]

Adrienne Rich broke out in hives just before delivery.

No, not all people have fully formed images of the parent they would like to be. Some people dwell on such thoughts, others push them aside or mask them.

One mother I interviewed had much the same reaction as Adrienne Rich. "I was visiting a friend with a new baby," she said, "and this is terrible to say with one on the way, but I had to force myself to pick it up and say nice things about their baby." She told me that she never thinks about becoming a parent; she has shut it out of her mind.

An expectant father did the same thing. He said, "When we got married, I knew that my wife very strongly wanted children. It was a given: She wanted children. I wasn't opposed to it. But I gave it very little thought. I was apprehensive because I hadn't been around children, and I didn't know how I was going to react. That's probably my problem in approaching a lot of things. If I am apprehensive enough, I ignore what's going to happen."

But later, when his child was born, he said, "I am surprised at how much I enjoy her." Although he avoided thinking about the birth of the child, he still had expectations, so much so that he was "surprised."

Whether they are denied or sought out, everyone has images of parenthood. In some people, they lurk beneath awareness, acting as powerful but unforeseen determinants of behavior. The prospective parent feels and reacts in certain ways, but is unsure why. For others they are more conscious, but for all, images are the point of departure in the journey into parenthood.

ACCEPTING THE PREGNANCY

The task of the Image-Making Stage, preparing for parenthood, follows a developmental pattern as the pregnancy proceeds. *In the first days and weeks of pregnancy, whether or not it is a first pregnancy, the task is accepting the pregnancy itself.*

In her journal, *A Season to Be Born*, author Suzanne Arms wrote:

> I keep waiting for any sign that I'm pregnant, but my stomach looks flatter than it was at puberty. I can't feel a thing! If I could just feel something stirring. I'd even be glad to wake up sick in the morning. Then maybe I could really believe I'm pregnant.

After visiting the doctor and having her pregnancy confirmed, she wrote:

> I have the feeling that I brought a brand new body home from the doctor's office. I'm a new me. Nobody else would look at me and call me pregnant, but it's wonderful to know that I really am, and I look for every tiny sign to prove it's true.[14]

A medical confirmation doesn't necessarily make the pregnancy seem real. For instance, a young couple in the South: The day after her pregnancy is confirmed, the wife "knows" that she is pregnant and spends the day looking at photographs of embryos and fetuses, trying to picture her baby. Her husband hasn't accepted it. "I'm not positive yet," he says. "I'm not positive. It hasn't really hit me."

There is clearly a difference between the experiences of men and women at this point. While men can put thoughts of pregnancy aside for long periods of time, the woman's whole body starts to change. Some women have severe morning sickness, others don't. Some feel that their body has almost been turned inside out; they ache, feel exposed, and even fabrics rub the wrong way. Others feel more healthy than usual.

Arthur and Libby Colman write that the *symptoms* of pregnancy, "skipped periods, morning sickness, emotional lability, and fatigue can give reassurance (welcome or unwelcome) that the pregnancy is real."[15]

Accepting the reality of the pregnancy is not always a joyful experience, especially if the pregnancy is partially or totally unwanted. Then the physical symptoms can arouse apprehension and dread, a feeling of how dare this happen.

For most people, there is a mixture of contradictory, ambivalent feelings. One mother says that she'd be joyful one minute, while the next she'd be thinking, "I'm so young, I should have waited another few years."

The acceptance of the pregnancy is played out against the possibility of miscarriage. Some parents-to-be want to know exactly what to expect—perhaps they read statistics, they question others about when and how to know if a miscarriage is going to occur and what it would be like, they keep a chart of how many days old the fetus is. Others avoid such a concrete admission—but nonetheless the threat of miscarriage can flow beneath their thoughts, like an underground stream.

The First Trimester: Images and Realities

From the very beginning of this stage, there are times when one's images don't come true. Perhaps it was in the getting pregnant itself. Some people may have expected conception to be easy, then it took several months or years, requiring many tests, many medical hypotheses, many disappointments.

Or perhaps it was in the circumstances surrounding the pregnancy—it was unplanned or unwanted.

DANIELLE MITCHELL

Danielle is a sixteen-year-old unmarried student who didn't worry about the consequences of sex with her boyfriend because she somehow felt that pregnancy wouldn't happen to her. When it did, she wanted an abortion.

"My boyfriend didn't want me to have an abortion. And he didn't want to tell me that, because he felt like I had a right to my own body. He was supposed to pay for it, but he kept disappearing every time I had an appointment. I couldn't find him."

Then she turned to her mother "by leaving the results of her pregnancy test around so Mother could find them."

By then she was four months pregnant and legally needed her parents' consent, but her mother refused—"She said she wasn't going to sign anything—I think she had this vision of all of her grandchildren riding around in a station wagon."

Danielle had a different image, though. "I knew that when I had a baby, I wanted everything to be right, as much as possible. I wanted to be able to afford to give the baby much of what it needed without spoiling it. And to give myself some things too."

But, as a minor, she had no recourse. The decision had been made for her. Her image of parenthood had to be abandoned before it ever had a chance of being realized, leaving her prone to "having fits of temper, throwing everything on the floor," during her pregnancy.

MARY O'BRIEN

Mary was unmarried, a college student in her twenties, living with her boyfriend, and not being careful about birth control.

"When I did become pregnant, in December, I thought, 'Now what am I going to do?' I knew that I loved him, but didn't want to admit it, even to myself. I believe that the pregnancy didn't just happen. I allowed it to happen.

"I didn't tell Ralph—because I was afraid it would ruin his holidays.

"We were sitting together one January night—I knew I had to tell him. I was expecting the worst. He leaned over and gave me a big hug and a kiss. I was amazed. He said, 'What are we going to do about it?' I asked him how he felt and he said he didn't think he could handle becoming a father.

"So we decided to get an abortion. I set up the appointment. But I was miserable. I just knew there's no way I'd be able to go through with it—and live with myself. I was amazed at how quickly I had become attached to the baby.

"So I said to Ralph, 'I understand that you don't want this child. I respect that. But you also have to respect the fact that I'm not going to be able to live with myself if I have an abortion. I'll go away, have the baby, give it up for adoption.'

"Ralph knew if I left, I'd never come back. That's how we made the decision to get married and have this baby."

All of these people have images about having children: about the timing of this event in their lives, about the circumstances surrounding the pregnancy. For Danielle and Ralph, the timing of conception is off—too soon. The circumstances are also wrong—both wanted to be settled, to be financially secure, but Danielle is in high school and Ralph has a job which he considers temporary. He wanted to wait until he had found a job he liked, until he was earning more, to marry and have children. Yet continuing the pregnancy was the only way he could continue his relationship with Mary.

Both have had to go through the process of making a moral judgment about what to do, a process which Carol Gilligan's work has illuminated.[16] Danielle and Ralph have ended with decisions that contained the loss of their original images, a loss resulting in anger and sadness for them both. This loss will remain with them, undoubtedly with negative consequences for themselves and their children, unless they can reconstruct new images out of the rubble of the ones that are gone.

The images that prospective parents form are not static. Even in the first trimester of pregnancy, they are shaped and reshaped. Like the base of a building, these images are influenced by the ground they are set into, by the surrounding conditions. These earliest images are the foundation on which parenthood is built.

PREPARING FOR PARENTHOOD

The second trimester of pregnancy accents another aspect to the task of preparing for parenthood, and that is beginning the lifelong *task of accepting the separateness of the baby.* Separateness, as I define it, has two facets: one that concerns the emotional separation of the parent's identity from the child's and another that concerns their physical separateness. In pregnancy and the first years of parenthood, these two aspects of separation are interfused. Furthermore, parents seldom think about their separateness from the child without thinking of their connectedness.

In a 1961 report on an intensive, multi-discipline, psychoanalytically focused study of fifteen pregnant women at Beth-Israel Hospital in Boston, Grete L. Bibring, Thomas F. Dwyer, Dorothy S. Huntington, and Arthur F. Valentine found that women begin to think about separation at the time of quickening—the first soft, fluttering motion of the fetus that the mother feels.[17] Most changes in parenthood follow this pattern—they are instigated by the growth of the child.

BARBARA CALLAHAN

Barbara Callahan is at this point. It is not that long after her quickening. She says, "I used to dream that I would give birth to cats. Now I'm beginning to dream of actually having a baby.

"It hasn't sunk in yet that it's not going to be any old baby. I still picture having one of those things you see in the nursery. I'm glad that it's slowly coming because I was worried that I was never going to comprehend it.

"The baby kept forcing me to think about it. I'd be sitting in the law office, researching something, and it would kick me.

"I used to feel when it would kick me at work that it was intruding. Now I feel just the other way. I'm ready to leave work for a while and start thinking about my child.

"In the beginning of my pregnancy when I started to change shape, I was sort of embarrassed by my body. You are breastier and your stomach starts to grow, but it's not big yet and you look misshapen. I used to laugh and joke with my husband but I was really afraid that he'd tease me. Then when you start getting bigger, it looks right.

"I'm small-breasted and I always thought, wouldn't it be nice to be big-breasted. Then I discovered that I didn't like it. My breasts look like these very serious pieces of artillery sticking there. It doesn't look like me.

"You can't believe that there are things that have been common knowledge for centuries but you've never heard of them. Little things like your breasts leak when you're pregnant, or the pains you get. Common. Every woman who's been pregnant has had them. And then the language. Doctors talk to you about episiotomies and epidurals. They talk to you like you know all that stuff.

"The people who have gone through all this have all the information. They look at you knowingly, but somehow there's no method that they give it to you. I was shocked when I found out how much I don't know. There's probably a whole lot more I'm going to find out."

It is a changing self. A self who is pregnant. And as she awaits the birth of her first child, Barbara Callahan vacillates between wanting to push this new self back into the one she has always known, and being intrigued by what the seemingly secret society of parenthood will bring.

If this is a first child, preparing for parenthood includes the task of preparing for a change in role. Even parents who already have children realize, however, that the birth of another child will change the role they have assumed. A pregnant mother with a three-year-old girl says, "Our perceptions of ourselves are changing quite dramatically. Parenting seems more real: two adults and two children!"

Prospective parents have many questions: How will I be the same and how will I be different? Will I still be able to be spontaneous, do what I did before? How will this birth affect my work, my career, the rest of my life? Phyllis Chesler in her journal account of her first birth, *With Child*, describes herself as actually interviewing mothers. She writes, "Mothers must know what I need to know. I'm going to begin asking the mothers I know all the important questions."[18]

If a prospective parent (usually mothers, although as James Levine's *Who Will Raise the Children?* indicates, some fathers are now following suit[19]) is planning to quit or take an extended leave from a job, there are questions: Will I be bored? Will staying home with a child be enough for me? Will I be able or want to return to work later on?

If a prospective parent is not planning to leave work, there are also questions: Will the baby miss me while I'm away? Will it be all right for the baby to be cared for by other people? Will my work suffer because I'm devoting less time to it?

Most parents anticipate that the birth will bring a change in their economic situation, and money becomes a source of enormous concern. If the mother or father plans to take time off or leave work, earning power will decrease, prospective parents ask: Will there be enough money? The baby will bring many added expenses —doctors and delivery costs, food and clothing. Will I be able to afford the added expenses? What will I have to give up? Will one parent have to take on extra work? One woman said, "Sometimes big worries hit me. Oh, my God—what are we going to do? We don't have seventy thousand dollars in the bank. How will we pay for college?"

One woman who became pregnant soon after her marriage looked for something that she could do at home, or as her husband said, in her underwear, to make money. She responded to an ad in a magazine that said, "Do you like to work with your hands?"—and began making toy bunny rabbits.

"The thing was," she said, "that the advertisement said you could make up to a hundred and twenty-five dollars a week. Well, I found out, after I got into it, that to make a hundred and twenty-five dollars, you had to make a thousand bunny rabbits a week. I graduated second in my college class and was not prepared for cutting out velvet ears and gluing them on. You get up in the middle of the night and paste three hundred faces on bunny rabbits. And the one check I made over a hundred dollars bounced."

She got that straightened out, quit making rabbits, and began to look for another way to make money.

Along with beginning to accept the separateness of the baby and the self as a parent comes another task: forming feelings for the baby. The baby, from quickening on, does make its own presence felt. "It is concrete and abstract," Barbara Callahan says. "It is there. It is kicking you. You hear the heartbeat when you go to the doctor, and yet you can't picture what it is."

This is obviously a very different experience for men and women. Furthermore, this experience takes its meaning from people's feeling about the pregnancy. Some feel bleak, uneasy, afraid to begin to care about the baby. Perhaps they see the baby as an intruder, a monster. Psychoanalysts Lucie Jessner, Edith Weigert, and James L. Foy write of pregnant women who picture the fetus as a leech or jackal, devouring the mother, drawing off her food and energy.[20]

Most women and men fear giving birth to a deformed child, or as one pregnant woman said, "I dreamed that the baby was born and it didn't have any legs." Another said, "I dreamed that I went into the delivery room, and there was a lot of blood and gore. And the baby was dead."

There have been several hypotheses about the origins of such fears. Jessner, Weigert, and Foy write that they emerge from guilt feelings.[21] The psychoanalyst Therese Benedek thinks that the thoughts of monsters can represent the feelings about the badness or evil within.[22] Albert Solnit and Mary Stark think that prospective parents' concern with monsters is a rehearsal—in case there is something actually wrong with the baby.[23]

Whatever their genesis and meaning, these fears occur in most prospective parents. Myra Leifer, in her study of eighteen pregnant women, concludes that "high anxiety is a characteristic affect during pregnancy."[24]

The locus of concern, however, varies; it can be focused on the self, on the mate, or on the fetus. Leifer feels that focusing on the fetus indicates the beginnings of attachment. Development theorists used to speak of bonding to the baby as occurring at birth, but, as Leifer's research shows, it has its origins in pregnancy, if not before. Leifer found that those mothers who were the most attached to the fetus during pregnancy were the most attached to the baby immediately after birth.[25]

As people do begin to care about the fetus, they often give it pet names—sometimes real names or sometimes joke ones, such as "The Blob" or "Scrapper."

After Quickening: Images and Realities

In the second trimester, as in the first, there are times when one's fantasies do not fit reality.

Nora Ephron, in an article titled "Having a Baby after 35," describes such an experience. She had an amniocentesis test—that is, a sample of her amniotic fluid was taken to ascertain if the chromosomes of the fetus were normal. As a side benefit this test reveals whether the child is a boy or a girl.

"The call came through," Nora Ephron writes. " 'Your child is normal,' said the voice on the phone. 'It's a boy.' I shouted, hugged my husband, and jumped up and down several times. Immediately thereupon, we both became depressed."

Nora Ephron says when you don't know the sex of your unborn child, you fantasize about having a girl, then you fantasize about having a boy. "The minute you discover that your child is only one thing—a boy as opposed to a girl—you have to give up half your fantasies.[26]

The depression that these parents felt is a common response to the loss of an image. It can feel almost like a symbolic death. Roger Gould states that a mourning period usually follows the shedding of dreams.[27]

When people have medical problems during pregnancy, the collision between fantasy and reality can be very intense; the dreamed-for radiantly happy pregnancy and healthy child fades and the prospective parents are left with worry.

ISABELLE AGNEW

During the fifth month of Isabelle's pregnancy, everything, as she puts it, started to go crazy. Her doctor asked to see her every week, and when she asked why, he said that she was gaining too much weight (she was overweight to begin with) and that he could only detect a low heartbeat, perhaps due to her weight, perhaps not.

"Then, in my sixth month," Isabelle says, "they started to do tests every week. I got every test that there was. I really got scared.

"At that point, I just said, 'I'm not going to think about the pregnancy,' but it was impossible because I was huge. It was not something I could overlook. I wanted a baby really bad.

"And everybody kept asking me, 'How's the baby? How do you feel?' I always automatically would say, 'Fine.' Inside of me, I was dying. I was so scared."

Isabelle asked herself, "Am I going to be able to take it if there is anything wrong? Will I be strong enough to accept it?

"Some days, I thought, 'If I lose this baby, I'm going to go crazy.'

"And then other days, I'd wake up and say, 'No, I'm going to be a really strong person. Everything's going to be fine.' "

Isabelle's fear about and hope for her baby was tinged with sadness over the loss of her image of an idyllic pregnancy. That sense of loss stayed with her throughout the nine months, only ending when she gave birth to a healthy baby.

For those families in which a miscarriage does occur, the sorrow can be profound and is often compounded by the statements of friends as "it's no big deal" or "you should get over it quickly" or such as: "why don't you try to have another baby right away."

These statements belie the parent's feelings. It can take a while to recover, to give up the image that pregnancy means birth, not death. Parents often experience a mourning period after miscarriage.[28]

All through pregnancy, certain themes emerge. These act somewhat like a magnet in one's mind, exerting a force, pulling one's thoughts, monopolizing one's emotions.

Control/Loss of Control

One theme that emerges when images and actualities collide is control/loss of control. Parents like Isabelle feel responsible for the life growing within, but how much control do the mothers-to-be really have? They can eat well, stay away from drugs, try to stay calm, but what effect does it have over the child's personality, emotional state, physical well-being, and safety? The fathers-to-be can help their wives, but how much difference does that make?

Barbara Callahan's husband, Steven, says, "I worry—will the kid be all normal—have all its parts, be really bright, intelligent, and be a pleasure to get along with. But it's like worrying whether you've got cancer. I don't know if you can do anything about it or not."

Separateness/Connectedness

Another theme, much akin to control/lack of control, is separateness/connectedness. The baby is part of the parents and yet separate; is formed from them but will be unique; it grows within, feeding from the mother, but it has its own features.

Themes such as control/lack of control and separateness/connectedness, which arise at this time, are not resolved once and for all. Like waves in water, they rise up, cresting, bursting forward, only to draw back, subside, become almost still, and later swell up again. Each theme of thought that arises during pregnancy reemerges again and again in later stages of parenthood.

Pregnancy: An Inward Time

As prospective parents contemplate these themes, they often turn into themselves, wondering about the knowns and unknowns: that they are changing, but they don't know quite how; that the baby is made from them and yet distinct; that the baby will be an enormous part of their lives, but they don't know what it will look like; that they are anticipating the actual birth with excitement and fear. The middle months of pregnancy is frequently called an "inward" time.

JUSTINE SILVER

Justine Silver, six months pregnant, made a conscious effort to remove herself from the friction of everyday life.

"I've been reading scientific magazines for years and years and years on a million different things, and I sort of have my brain divided up into a million little file cabinets. I have all this trivial information stored away that just pops up. For instance, I know that chemical changes take place in a person's body when they have an emotion. If I got angry, hormones would pass through the placenta and there would be a direct effect on this baby. So it stops me from feeling—it stops me from giving full vent to my emotions.

"Not too many things make me angry, but when I do get angry, I have a physical reaction. If I knew that I was going to have a negative reaction to something, that wouldn't normally prevent me from plunging into a discussion about it or a fight or an argument. But being pregnant does prevent me—I think, 'Just wait two and a half months.'

"So I find that I'm more detached, which means I'm more self-involved. I won't let myself get touched in a way I would normally allow myself to be."

Whether or not one believes Justine's stance (the research evidence thus far shows that the mother's feelings do have an effect on the fetus, but do not cause harm [29]), many prospective parents—both men and women—pull more into themselves, become self-absorbed, narcissistic, dwelling on their bodies, their thoughts. The everyday world seems somewhat petty in contrast to what is happening within.

Evaluating the Relationships with One's Parents

One of the main things that mothers- and fathers-to-be think about is their own parents. They analyze their past and current relationship with their parents. *Evaluating, identifying, and differentiating oneself from one's parents is one of the tasks of preparing for parenthood, particularly first-time parenthood.*

Justine Silver had not thought much about her mother for a long time. After her father's death several years ago, her mother moved away. But, during this pregnancy, Justine began to evaluate the mothering she had been given.

"I grew up in the kind of household where if I said, 'I want to be a ballet dancer when I grow up,' my mother said to me, 'Yes, you can have everything you want. You can be a ballet dancer.' Well, maybe I could and maybe I couldn't. I now think it would have been much better if my mother had given me a genuine, honest response: that I might be a ballet dancer if I worked very hard.

"My mother thought these things were good things to say—to make me feel good. But just for the purposes of fostering some sort of amnesty of the moment, the parent is doing cumulative damage to the child. And the kid becomes a functional invalid by the time they get to the point where they think that everything should be dropping into their laps. When things don't work that way, the world, then, doesn't seem to hold much meaning.

"That's something that I've really thought about. Putting it into practice is another thing."

Evaluating one's parents can bring changes in the feelings as well as in the relationships that parents-to-be have with their own parents. Sometimes this involves the rekindling of old feuds, other times a circling back to the parents, a desire to renew or revitalize bonds that have gone slack.

Marty Olsen, eight months pregnant, notes that her mother told her she'd changed since she became pregnant. "I said to her, 'What do you mean?'

"And she said, 'You're just different.'

"She's right. I do see our relationship as different. Whenever I feel critical of Mother, I think, 'I hope my child is never that way with me.' So I value our relationship more."

The memories of the way she treated her mother when she was a teenager frighten Marty. Because she hopes her child is never rude or insolent with her, she has been making renewed efforts to draw closer to her mother.

Nancy Friday in *My Mother/My Self* writes that during pregnancy, many women long for an emotional reconciliation with their mothers.[30] And, as Marty is doing, these women push some of their more adolescent criticism aside and become more accepting of their mothers' idiosyncrasies.

For Bryan Johnson, Vivian's pregnancy doesn't "change my relationship with my father, it changes his relationship with me. I've felt good about myself for a while, but my father hasn't. In some ways, this pregnancy is a kind of proof that I am not a failure and that *he*, then, is worthwhile."

The response of expectant parents to their own parents is based on many factors, not the least of which is their own parents' reaction to the pregnancy. If it pleases their own parents, fulfills their own images, seems like a validation of their efforts, then it will have a different effect than if it presages growing old or contradicts an image.

Some expectant parents, in circling back to their own parents, want to be taken care of again. They remember times when they were sick, remember nighttimes, being tucked in bed, and they long for a return of those long-gone days. In *With Child*, Phyllis Chesler asks, "In becoming pregnant, am I hoping to find a mother rather than become one?"[31]

Some parents-to-be fantasize that their parents will pay more attention, give them the nurturing that they never gave them before. One pregnant woman who had such expectations dashed said, "I didn't get it—just because I was pregnant."

It may seem as if men primarily think about their fathers, women about their mothers. That was one of my questions initially—and it remains a question, one that I hope will be researched someday. I did find, however, with the people I interviewed, that the salience of the relationship made the crucial difference. A parent considered "remote" or "distant" was less likely to be thought about than one who was a pivotal influence, positively or negatively, in the parent-to-be's younger years.

If one's parent has died, there can be a resurgence of grief. That parent is remembered—little things he or she said or did come to mind, and there is often a wish that that parent could "see me now."

Nora Ephron says that her memories of her mother had faded in the seven years since her death. "For many years," Ephron writes, "it has been hard for me to remember what she was like before she became sick. It is still hard to remember, but for the first time in a long time, I feel connected to her."[32]

In addition to evaluating and identifying, prospective parents also differentiate themselves from their own parents. Differentiation may involve either thoughts or action, actually taking a stand in opposition to one's own parents.

When Justine Silver's mother found out about her daughter's pregnancy, she was "ecstatic." Then, according to Justine, "one day she called and started telling me that I should name the child after my grandfather. I had no relationship with him at all—very little feeling that he cared about me. Why would I want to name my child after him? My mother wants me to follow a tradition. I said, 'I've already thought of a name for the child.' She literally disregarded what I was saying on the phone. It was just as if I was a child again. I was starting to feel this tremendous resentment.

"I care for my mother, but I began thinking, 'I'm not going to get into that old syndrome,' because first it's your hand, then your elbow and arm—and the next thing you know, my mother would be saying that she was getting ill because of some minor request that I didn't seem to want to go along with. I think it's better to nip it in the bud now, and say *no, no*."

The wish that people have to be cared for during pregnancy is a delicate thing—if others cross the line, treat prospective parents as children once again, they often resent it. The first pregnancy makes many people feel as if they are on the verge of adulthood. In fact, in a large-scale study of 1,569 married women under forty years old, and of 456 of their husbands, Lois Wladis Hoffman reports that the majority of respondents did feel that becoming a parent was the demarcation, the initiation into adulthood.[33]

One's parents accept or don't accept these signs of adulthood. One woman says, "Sexuality in our family was far, far away. Tucked in a cupboard. Forget about it. It didn't exist. I was afraid that when I got pregnant my relationship with my parents would deteriorate significantly, because when you become pregnant, it's saying you are a sexual being.

"I had some real strong back-and-forth things in my mind, fearing that my mother was going to reject me. But it wasn't true—she didn't."

If one's parents do, however, actually reject, try to push the parent-to-be back into childhood patterns, they might respond as Justine did, and say, "No."

Another woman overrode her mother's wish to give her a gift of a new crib and mattress for the baby, and instead borrowed an old crib. It was, seemingly, a small matter, which to this mother-to-be was a landmark decision. She says, "It was important for me not to act like a kid because I'm having a child. I can't let people push me around. I'm supposed to be the adult here."

Giving/Getting

There is a dichotomy between the desire to be responsible and the desire to be taken care of. This is another theme of parenthood: giving/getting.

Polarities are characteristic of all themes: Two feelings, though opposite, form a continuum. One doesn't appear without the other. There is often a tendency to want to make things simple, to reduce the complexities of life to their least common denominator. But even in the beginning of pregnancy, it doesn't work. Contradictory themes emerge and exist together.

Prospective parents feel these divergent pulls, wanting to be cared for and wanting to be responsible, particularly with their own parents and with the person who will deliver the baby. Because of the medical personnel's unique role, their importance becomes magnified—if they play up the all-knowing or controlling aspect of their job, they can create relationships of dependency in which one or both prospective parents feel that they can't make a move without approval. For some prospective parents, such an attitude seems an affront and provokes severe resistance or anger. If the doctor or midwife is empathic and respectful, this kind of tension is less likely to occur. Whatever the relationship or role, the medical person is likely to figure prominently in the couple's thoughts and conversations.

Evaluating the Relationship with One's Partner

Parents-to-be have the task of preparing for changes in their relationships with their partners. Just as they evaluate their relationship with their parents, they also evaluate their partner, thinking about how he or she is managing the changes that pregnancy has brought and speculating how he or she will adjust after the child is born.

SAM MILLER

Sam Miller's wife is six months pregnant. They have known each other for only a year, and much of those first months was spent apart. When they were reunited, at a university where he was spending a sabbatical, she became pregnant.

"We had talked about the possibility of having a baby and even talked about timing, so that she would be pregnant when I returned from my sabbatical. We were in the first blush of feelings of getting to know each other. So that this pregnancy from a pragmatic and logistical point of view couldn't have been worse planned.

"We had no intention of terminating it. We both decided very quickly that it was something we wanted. That was a few-minute conversation, a kind of symbolic act of will, but it implied much more than the utterance of words."

In the beginning, Sam's wife, Neila, was quite sick. "She complained a great deal about morning sickness and nausea and extreme fatigue, and she spoke about this in earnest and compelling terms.

"And my reaction at first was to transmit my own reaction to a similar predicament. When I'm ill, I usually treat it in a sort of defiant manner, scornful of the condition. The defiance consists of not letting sickness interfere with the normal functions of my life, just to deliberately pretend it's not there. And fortunately my health has been good enough that only once in my life have I ever been floored by something." Sam thought that the best way for Neila to deal with her condition was "to put herself on a somewhat more disciplined regime, to try to get some exercise done." Because he hadn't known her very well before, he worried that the complaining and lethargy were a part of her character that he had missed.

"Neila was extraordinarily unsettled. She was disturbed by her own condition and unimaginably disturbed by my response to it. There were some fierce quarrels and misunderstandings. We behaved a little bit like children, like adolescents.

"Neila called me to account for a general lack of psychological awareness. She could point this out simply by referring to events that were in some sense real recorded events, but with a mode of perception and interpretation that was, I admit, quite novel to me. It made sense and it certainly altered my feelings about my own life and experience.

"I come from a very different background from Neila, who is from the metropolitan Northeast. I grew up in the West and had, without thinking about it, a macho orientation, and had attached a lot of importance to strength and endurance.

"My behavior, whatever my intentions, definitely aggravated the situation, at least for a time. We were in a new house, in a totally new environment. Neila had no friends, and that kind of reinforced from the beginning a very deep sense of alienation. We were living a relatively reclusive kind of existence. Almost convalescent. My contact with the university was minimal, just what was required for functional purposes.

"When colleagues ask me how I liked my sabbatical, it appears like it almost passed unnoticed. It was like riding across the landscape with the shades drawn, in a kind of limbo. In personal terms it was a tremendous period of emotional and psychological growth for me. Some experiences and feelings about life and about people in general were very deeply engraved during that period. I gained a heightened consciousness for Neila as a person; more sensitivity to her feelings.

Sam now realizes that what he calls a "lack of psychological awareness" was responsible for many of the problems he had with his first wife: "I was deeply absorbed in my work and I got married and had children without much reflection."

He feels that the ability to listen, to communicate, to show empathy, imply a level of respect and accord the other person dignity.

He regrets not learning this until he was in his forties. "I'm so grateful that I met Neila. She's the first person who's combined the interest and the will to do something about it with the ability. Once the message was transmitted, it was so sensible, so obvious, and so clear that I wonder only what took me so long to comprehend it."

Sam had many images that were contradicted by the timing and circumstances of this pregnancy—that he and Neila should know each other better before becoming parents, that Neila should ignore or conquer any weaknesses in body or spirit.

The first few months of Neila's pregnancy were extremely distressing, because so many of Sam's images were being knocked down at the same time. Yet his belief in these images was already faltering. He was ready for a change.

After he separated from his first wife, he "began to realize how much I missed my children and how little I knew them as people. It kind of appalled me. Just about myself. For much too long I had relied upon circumstance, upon the institutional implantation of people in each other's environment, and a lot of what held us together was only that. There was no reason for my children to seek me out as a person. In fact there were reasons not to—feeling of abandonment, bitterness after the separation."

Sam then supplanted one set of images for another. He accepted the pregnancy. He accepted Neila's emotional response as fairly legitimate. He began to change his overall view of how things work.

"I didn't fully understand the role of my own behavior in giving final shape to events in these later years. I've begun to understand that it's not as if there are these cosmic forces that fatalistically subdue us. It's that people have an enormous control of their own lives if they choose to understand and act upon it."

When people are able to replace an unworkable image with one that is more realistic, they describe such learnings as important turning points that lead to growth. "I don't pretend I've come very far," Sam says, "but at least in my own terms, I'm a very different person than I was a year ago."

Sam now worries about the fights that he and Neila had in the first months of her pregnancy, fearful about their effects on the baby.

"These worries keep coming back: that all the vital organs, all the superstructure of this creature, were laid in place during this period of absolute tremendous emotional turmoil.

"I read a book that gives a rather precise timetable of the formation of various organs. I remember trying to count days on the calendar [figuring out which organs were formed when] and then trying to date arguments that we had.

"Well, we'll see. We'll just have to wait and see what the baby's like."

It was out of isolation, the wreckage of a first marriage, and conflict with his second wife that Sam Miller has grown. It was also at the time, according to Daniel Levinson, that men reevaluate their lives and gain a greater comfort with what Levinson calls the feminine side of the masculine/feminine polarity: expressing their emotions, accepting the flux of other people's feelings.[34] Gail Sheehy states that men who have devoted their younger years to career often look around upon reaching the peaks of their professions and see that they have had to forgo many things to succeed. In their forties, these men sometimes begin to concentrate upon their families, or they establish new families.[35] These findings have made the important point that most men steer a wide path away from feelings early in life. Does this continue to hold true? Cross-culturally? These are questions which could use further research.

Nevertheless, adult growth does crisscross parental years, influencing it. Obviously a parent in his or her early twenties has a different experience from that of one at forty.[36] But are the issues and the patterns different? I don't think so. Growth in parenthood is predicated upon the growth of the child. Although one's station in life, one's age, one's health, one's personality, and the circumstances of one's life certainly affect the way the different times in parenthood are felt and are acted upon, the basic structure remains stable.

Pregnancy Brings Changes in the Couple Relationship

BRYAN JOHNSON

Bryan, like Sam Miller, found that his wife's pregnancy also called forth what he calls his "feminine side." "I was feeling bad that Vivian was going to have to do all the work in childbirth," Bryan says, "that she would suffer all the discomfort. Then we went to Lamaze classes and I started doing the breathing exercises instead of helping her do them. That's a subtle difference. But instead of helping her, I was doing it myself. I discovered that that isn't what it's all about. It's about coaching her, helping her. It's almost like the feminine side of me was trying to experience what Vivian was going through so that I would not feel guilty for her having discomfort that I didn't."

Psychoanalytic theories have focused on this facet of prospective fatherhood. Felix Boehm, in 1930, wrote:

Because boys imagine that conception and parturition are so complicated and uncanny, and because these processes are so mysterious to
them, they have a passionate wish to share in them or else an intense
envy of this capacity in women.[37]

Other theorists have called this womb envy: The man is jealous of
the power of a woman to bring forth a child and is jealous of the
unborn child's relationship with his wife.[38] Sometimes, pregnancy
pulls men and women closer together. They have created something together, and they feel joined by that act. One couple tells of
lying in bed together, naked, her stomach touching his, so that they
both could feel the baby's kicks.

Other times, pregnancy pulls the prospective parents further
apart. Perhaps the man draws away from the changes in the
woman's body, perhaps the woman turns into herself. A prospective father says, "When my wife became pregnant, I felt like there
was this alien thing that had come between us. Alien is just the
word for it. This alien thing got in the way, wiping away everything that was familiar."

One woman seven months pregnant says, "I'm a very physical
person and I usually get a great deal of pleasure from that, but I
don't want to be physical at all now. There is so much going on inside your own body and in your consciousness that you are physically involved twenty-four hours a day. And you don't need these
extra kisses and extra touches—you're getting plenty of it, inside,
and like, it's too much. In fact, it can be repulsive. It can be like,
leave me alone, don't touch me, leave me alone."

In *The Mother Knot*, Jane Lazarre describes an incident from her
pregnancy:

When I looked into that mirror at the foot of our bed and saw my
naked body next to James [her husband], my vaginal canal suddenly
felt as dry as an old sponge forgotten under the sink for months. I
couldn't believe the sight of myself, belly protuding and breasts huger
than they had ever been with nipples which had suddenly doubled
their size. No one had ever told me to expect such things. I was outraged.

 . . . I tried to pretend that upsetting glance had not occurred and
made heavy noises of passion. . . . I played the part well, grunting
and breathing for his pleasure, until I farted. And he laughed. That
laugh, which might once have been a comfortable sign of our closeness, was now humiliating, infuriating, the final confirmation of the
disgustingness of myself. I pulled away from him and began one of
those uncontrollable crying fits experienced by pregnant women.[39]

The changes that the pregnancy brings in the couple's relationship, in their sexual and intellectual relationship, are often given great weight by prospective parents because they are seen as an early indication of the changes to come. Little episodes or encounters are judged as clues. A woman who complains about morning sickness, as Neila did, may be seen as unable to cope with the rigorous adjustments and demands of parenting. A man who is not sympathetic may be seen as lacking the basic empathy and compassion to take care of children.

Independence/Dependence

The theme of wanting to be responsible and also wanting to be cared for is salient here. There are times when most parents-to-be want to curl up, almost like a child, and be waited on by their partner. For a pregnant woman who is alone, the question is: Who will help me?

It is important that these needs be met—the need for physical and emotional help, for comfort, understanding, reassurance, and approval. The psychoanalyst Therese Benedek has stated that when the pregnant woman's dependent needs remain unfulfilled, a sense of frustration can build, resulting in anger, hostility, and anxiety that can interfere "with the development of motherliness."[40] In a long-term study of twenty-two middle-class married women, by open-ended interview and psychological testing, John G. Loesch and Nahman H. Greenberg found that "in the few cases where the husband seemed able to provide a great deal of emotional support to the pregnant wife the pregnancy seemed to run much more smoothly."[41]

This focus on women's needs does not mean that men do not have such needs. It means that mothers have traditionally been the primary parent and have been studied most frequently.

The emphasis that our culture puts on self-sufficiency further clouds this issue. It may feel wrong to some people to show that they want to be cared for—that would indicate a weakness, a lack of independence rather than a genuine and worthy need. Yet the psychologist Mabel Blake Cohen writes: "Could it be more correctly stated that self-sufficiency consists in knowing how to get one's dependency needs met without blood, sweat, and tears?"[42]

Often the dependency need takes the form of fear. Just as parents worry about their baby's survival and having just the right amount of fingers and toes, they worry about their own or their partner's survival. Many fear the woman won't live through the delivery, or that the man will die or be killed.

Marty Olsen, for example, finds herself preoccupied with the thought that her husband might have an accident. "I keep thinking that I never am going to see him again. It's a very weird thing, but now we can't be away from each other. I don't know if it's irrational, but it is just complete, total attachment and the excitement and anticipation of making a family together." The need to hold on tight, to stay close together, is a guard against the feeling that their couple relationship is in flux. Prospective parents often fear that someone else will come in between them. They feel vulnerable, jealous of the slightest attention that anyone else pays to their partner.

In fact, someone else is going to come in between them—and that someone is a baby. If this is a first child, the change in roles will be greater—the twosome will become a threesome.

Forming Images of Future Roles

Prospective parents have images about their own roles and the partner's roles. They have expectations of how the responsibilities should be delineated. They imagine a family where the husband changes diapers or doesn't; they imagine a mother breast-feeding or not. Silent or spoken, conscious or semiconscious or unconscious, these images of child-rearing practice and family functioning are potent, for if one partner's images are in opposition to the other's, this can be a source of later friction. In a study of thirty first-time parents, Robert Fein found that those couples who did not talk to each other about their expectations were more likely to have a rough time together after the child was born.[43]

SUSIE AND EDDIE CARO

Susie and Eddie Caro are aware that they have expectations. She was raised strictly, had to tell her parents about every move she made and "was hit if I looked at someone crooked." She thinks she'll be equally strict.

Eddie was raised in a more permissive way, was allowed to do what he wanted to do. He sometimes felt that this laissez-faire attitude indicated indifference. "Still, I was never hit. I hope we can work this out where the kid won't have to be spanked."

He felt underprotected, she felt overprotected. Eddie says, "I think there has to be a happy medium between the two of us."

Interesting, hard, rewarding, exciting, anxiety-provoking, the act that cements two people together, conception, can put a wedge between them. Preparing for a change in the relationship is of considerable importance in pregnancy.

If there is already a child or children, the changes in the couple relationships are more understood. Expectant parents then tend to focus on how this new baby will affect their other children. A mother six months pregnant with her second child says, "I worry a lot about giving my first child enough time. She's been my whole life for three and a half years. I hope I'll be able to divvy up my time so that she won't be pushed aside. I don't want to hurt her in any way." Her husband agrees. "I think of a song that's been on the pop stations: 'Tell me I was the only one . . .' We asked ourselves: 'Is there enough love?' I hope so."

Evaluating Relationships with Friends

Relationships with friends undergo changes in pregnancy. Old friendships can cool when an expectant parent finds that this person is not interested in the pregnancy. Often friends are the bearers of stories—stories about delivery, about child-rearing—and some of these stories are weird and gruesome. One pregnant woman says that at first she listened, then she couldn't believe people could tell her some of the things they did, and she withdrew. There can also be a sense of competition among friends—as they compare which crib or carriage is best to buy.

New friendships are also formed, new closeness established. Parents-to-be often seek out people who will let them talk, who will listen and empathize. Many search for experienced parents whom they can learn from, models who will serve as mentors in this transition time.

Whether the circle of friendships is enlarged or closed down, prospective parents reach out farther, and pull back more intensely, webbed in by the strands of thoughts and fantasy that they continue to spin.

The issues which emerge in the middle of pregnancy—and which have their origins long before then—do not disappear in the final weeks. They continue. But the final trimester also brings up additional issues.

PREPARING FOR THE BIRTH

CONNIE FIORETTO

As her due date approaches, Connie Fioretto is fixing up her house, taking long walks, and waiting.

"As it's getting closer," she says, "I'm more anxious, both positively and negatively. I've been around babies, my nieces and nephews, for the past six or seven years. But I never really associated having one of my own. I mean, you think about it—but it's a dream. All of your life you think, 'Someday I'll get married and have children.' It's very beautiful but very scary at the same time as the faces start coming into the picture, as you find your husband and marry him. Then you are finally pregnant. You are going to have this child that's going to play a tremendous part of your life. And you have no idea what it's going to look like or what's going to happen.

"These feelings of panic just come upon me. I want to run and hide, but there's no way you can just remove this thing [pointing to her enlarged abdomen] and put it on the table for two hours. It must be so natural, these feelings of ambivalence, because there is no one in the world who is ever going to be closer to you, but nobody who can tell you now what this baby will look like, what color its eyes or its hair are going to be.

"Of course, I have these feelings of saying, 'Just give me two hours away.' But then I find myself hugging my belly. And I don't know if I ever want the baby to be born. It's so beautiful having it right where it is, so safe and secure. As soon as it's born, it starts moving away from you.

"I find there are times when I have this overwhelming feeling of melancholy. It's like when somebody you know has died. It makes you extremely aware of yourself and your life. And I think, if anything, being pregnant has made me aware of how quickly the time has passed. I think of my mother—she had me and then the twenty-two years she had me was up. I come from a large Italian family—my youngest brother has just left the house. Now there are no children left. That was sad, very sad. My parents always knew this time would come, but they never really believed it.

"I've been looking forward to being pregnant for twenty-eight years. And the time is going to go by so quickly. I wish there were some way I could just hold onto it. Already the pregnancy is nearly over.

"I have this wonderful, beautiful, sensitive husband and I see him working out in the vegetable garden and I know that one day we're going to wake up and it's all going to be behind us. I wonder how we're going to get through between point A and point Z.

"You do a lot of growing up when you're pregnant. It's suddenly like, 'Yikes. Here it is, folks. Playtime is over.' Sometimes I think I'm just a big kid.

"When I walk up the stairs to the bedroom I think there are going to be so many times I'll be walking up these stairs to get the baby, to feed him or change her or whatever. Walking up the stairs will be a whole new thing for me. Driving in the car is going to be a whole different thing. Suddenly, there's going to be a cradle, a crib in the bedroom, a high chair, a diaper pail.

"The house is going to take on a whole new dimension, just as my husband and I will.

"It's baffling. It really is baffling."

There are often extreme sweeps of feeling in awaiting a birth—joy, sadness, apprehension, anticipation, panic, calm, melancholy, excitement. Connie says that at times she cries for no reason. Other times, she dances with joy.

Nostalgia/Impatience

Though Connie Fioretto fears the change, the birth, she feels nostalgic about the pregnancy that is about to end. The final weeks of pregnancy often contain the dual feelings of nostalgia and impatience. This, too, is a continuing theme during parenthood. Parents don't want something to end, then just as quickly they want it to be over.

Prospective parents sometimes spend time, in those last weeks, getting ready, putting their homes in order, cleaning, fixing up a place for the baby. Sometimes massive home renovations are undertaken—repainting, remodeling. Others refuse to do anything until the baby is born.

The fetus, fully formed, takes on an even greater reality. Prospective parents' fantasies, as the researchers Marshall Klaus and John Kennell have noted, become more complete.[44] Parents-to-be dream and daydream of having a boy or girl, a child with blond hair and brown eyes, or a child with black and curly hair.

The final task of preparing for parenthood is preparing for the birth. Parents-to-be think about the delivery. From the very beginning, there have been thoughts about delivery, but they intensify as the time comes closer. Sometimes, expectant parents worry. They may have heard stories or have had a difficult delivery or they fear the pain. "Those hours loom in my mind," one woman said. Others see it as a performance. They may feel pressured by the prepared-childbirth courses, feel that they will be on trial. Will the woman be able to get through it without taking drugs? Will the man be a good coach? Others look forward to the event. Parents are forming images of the birth.

BRYAN JOHNSON

As Vivian approaches her due date, Bryan says, "My big secret is that I am so goddam happy and everything is going so well that I think that God is going to smite me down. I feel like when I was a kid and on the way home from Sunday school and I kept thinking, 'I can't think something bad about Jesus,' and then my mind would wander onto something bad. It's like trying to not think of an elephant. I keep feeling this all can't be real, this much good can't happen to one person. So I'll be relieved when the baby's born and Vivian's okay and the baby's okay.

"If someone said to me, 'If you could give me a thousand dollars, then I could guarantee you that everything is going to be okay,' I would write that check right now.

"Vivian is rather little. When I see her nude it alarms me. Now she's seen me look at her and she thinks that I'm looking at her like I'm not attracted to her anymore or like I think she looks grotesque. But it isn't that at all. It's that—how is that baby going to get out of there? I sometimes find myself wishing that Vivian would have a Caesarean. I cannot imagine something growing inside me. It seems abnormal to me and hence it's more scary to me.

"Sometimes in the middle of the night I think—there is something so absolutely biologically necessary about reproducing one's species. In other activities, in my work, I've always been good at what I was doing and I never had to take any chances. I've never had to throw myself into something that I didn't think I could handle or get out of. Here I am finally embarking on something that there's no turning back. You can't say I've decided I don't want a baby, certainly not after four or five months of pregnancy, certainly not after it's born. There's a sense of giving myself up to the fates of the universe, giving myself to something fully.

"Maybe for other people, having a baby wouldn't make them feel that way. Maybe it would be baring their soul in a novel or a poem. But there's something extremely basic here and it has to do with everybody lives, everybody dies."

No Turning Back

As the delivery approaches, there can be the sense of being on a sled that is slightly out of control, plunging high and low. One can't get off, but can just steer as best as one can. As another father-to-be said, it was the first time in his life that there was no turning back. If he didn't like college classes, he could cut them. If he didn't like a job, he could quit. If his marriage didn't work out, he could get divorced. But he could never undo the conception. He would always be a father to this child, about to be born.

A mother-to-be said that the first time she ever experienced the concept of inevitability was in her ninth month. "It is the first time in my life I can't say, 'Not today, tomorrow—or maybe next week—I'm not ready.' No one is going to care whether I am ready or not. The birth is going to happen regardless of how I feel, what mood I am in that morning. *I* do not matter. This is something that is just going to happen. I am going to have to do it, period."

Birth and Fears of Death

It is not accidental that the imagery of death appears in many of these prospective parents' thoughts. As they move closer and closer to the due date, they often think of death.

One woman says, "I was going to a group of people who wanted to have home births. In my eighth month, I asked to talk about death. Everyone said, 'We've been thinking about death for months. It's constantly here.' You're caught up in the miracle of birth, but I think there has to be some acknowledgment that sometimes this miracle doesn't work."

One father in his late twenties found that the coming birth of a baby marked a midpoint in his life. This event made the final ending, his own death, come more clearly into view, causing him to think more about his purpose in life. Because, as he put it, he was about to replace himself, he felt he should stop dabbling in different kinds of work and find something that was meaningful.

Others fear more immediate death. They have nightmares or dire thoughts about dying in a car crash or dying on the delivery table. Jessner, Weigert, and Foy tell about a woman who wrote out all of the names and addresses of the friends she wanted notified of the birth—in case she should die.[45] In many ways, these thoughts of death symbolize the coming separation. Death in birth. It seems alien. These events are at opposite ends of the spectrum, but like other aspects of parenthood, there is that continuum of feelings. The bringing forth of life brings a kind of death to the former self and offers the possibility of an eventual rebirth to a new self.

Image-Making

Feelings are very close to the surface all through pregnancy. There are highs, the sense that anything is possible, the conviction that they are going to be the most wonderful parents and have the most beautiful child. Although some people are predominantly euphoric and some mainly depressed, most experience highs and lows. Parents-to-be worry that they aren't up to the challenge, wish they could run away, fear that there will be something wrong with the baby. Angela Barron McBride writes of this mixture of feelings by describing two dreams. In one, "I stroked the baby's fuzzy cherub head and smooth yielding body. My hand melted into the velvety warmth of the baby." In the other, she dreamed "that the child was born without any hands and feet, and it refused to die."[46]

Pregnancy has been called a time of crisis by Grete Bibring, a time when the woman's defenses are loosened and old, unsettled conflicts appear. She writes that pregnancy is a "crisis that affects all expectant mothers, no matter what their state of psychic health."[47] By crisis, she means a biologically determined turning point which is characterized by new tasks, which leads to an acute sense of disequilibrium and the emergence of old, unsettled conflicts.

Crisis is a strong word, implying dramatic distress and discomfort. Other theorists, such as Alice Rossi and Rhona and Robert Rapoport, have preferred the word "transition."[48]

Pregnancy is a time of preparing for change, of rehearsing, of imagining. The concern with naming throughout pregnancy is a part of image-making—it is a fastening of parental expectations, made concrete, into a name. Names are turned over and over in parents' minds: Jennifer . . . Daniel . . . Katherine . . . Jack. But Jack reminds them of someone in grade school and Daniels all have a certain kind of personality. Maybe Emma, after grandmother, or Katrina, to recall the past, or something to signify the future.

And yet with this desire to mold the child's personality through a name comes the knowledge that one can't really do that. Pregnancy is a time when people explore, probe, even push, to see just how much they can effect.

It is a beginning or a time of starting over, of trying something different. Pregnancy is a time of image-making.

II.
The
Nurturing
Stage

One of the questions that I began this study with was: How does one stage lead into the next? While reading other theories of child and adult growth and development, I often felt that this transition seemed somehow magical—as if a stage sprang up, full-blown.

In the case of parenthood, it is the child who by his or her growth leads the parent from one stage to the next. The transition from the Image-Making Stage is abrupt: The child's birth is the demarcation, ushering in the Nurturing Stage.

The major task of this stage is to form an attachment to the baby. This encompasses the task of reconciling the imagined child with the child that is born. Accepting their new role, parents have to enlarge their relationships to each other, their other children (if they have them), and their own parents to include the baby, to redefine these relationships, and then to try to right the imbalance created by the birth, particularly to their sense of self.

Another question I had before beginning this study was: What happens to a previous stage when a new one begins? Does it disappear, fade away, remain, or become transformed? The major task of the Image-Making Stage, that of preparing for parenthood, becomes a base. Much of what happens throughout parenthood revolves around dealing with the images that were seeded and consolidated in the pregnancy, fitting these images with reality.

RECONCILING ONE'S IMAGES OF BIRTH WITH REALITY

The Birth: Images and Realities

The stories that people tell about giving birth reflect this process, one which recurs with every birth, first, second, or fifth. *This is, in fact, part of the task of forming an attachment to the new baby: reconciling the actual birth with the imagined birth.*

ISABELLE AND ARI AGNEW

Isabelle had had problems throughout her pregnancy. At first the doctor couldn't hear the baby's heartbeat, which he attributed to the fact that Isabelle was overweight. At eight months, Isabelle's cervix (the opening of the uterus, which remains tightly closed during pregnancy) dilated three centimeters, but labor, fortunately, didn't begin.

She was given a battery of tests, and her progress was monitored.

"The day that I became nine months pregnant, the doctor called me and said, 'We would like for you to come in and take another test.'

"It was funny. I had this dress that I had saved for going to the hospital to give birth. I put that dress on. I said, 'Forget it, baby, I'm not going to wait until you're born.' And I went to the hospital and took the test.

"At the hospital, I saw all these wonderful people who had taken care of me. They were all very positive. They said, 'Isabelle, don't worry. If it is meant to be, it is meant to be.'

"After the test, the doctor said to me, 'Call me this afternoon at four-thirty,' but I was so scared that I went to a movie and never called him. When I got home, the doctor was hysterical on the phone. He said, 'I want you to get over here now.'

"They could detect the baby's heartbeat, but it was so low that they just didn't know how long it would hold on. And the other reason was my hormone count. The reading from the placenta had gone from twenty-five, which is more or less normal, down to a seven. And the danger point is ten."

(The hormone Esroil is normally found in quantities of 10 to 50 milliliters per day in the urine at term. A sudden or progressive fall in Esroil levels presupposes that fetal life is in jeopardy.)

When Isabelle got to the hospital, the doctors waited to see if she would go into labor on her own. But as Isabelle says, "I never did. Then they found out that my pelvis was a mess. The baby could not fit through the pelvis." (By X-ray, the doctors saw that the opening between her pelvic bones was narrow in comparison with the size of the baby's head.) "So the doctors said, 'We have to do a Caesarean.'

"I really flipped out. Every bit of sanity that I had left. It was just out the window." Because her sister had had a sickly baby who died shortly after birth, Isabelle was very scared.

"When I woke up, they said, 'You had a boy.'

"The first thing I thought was *had*, past tense.

"Ari was crying. I thought there was something wrong. I said, 'Ari, what's wrong?' But he didn't answer right away.

"I just wanted to know that the baby was alive. I mean, I didn't even care if there was something a little bit wrong. I just wanted the baby to be alive."

Finally Ari said, "You gave me a wonderful boy."

Isabelle had known that she might have a Caesarean, had read and talked to many people about this procedure, and although she was frightened, she felt she was prepared and she felt the caring concern of the doctor and nurses.

"I find all these people who say, 'Oh, you had the baby. How was the labor?' And I told them I had to have a Caesarean section. And they say, 'Oh, what you missed—you missed this—you missed that.' I don't care.

"I would like to have other kids. I really would. I remember the bloodstains [this is five weeks later], but that's the only thing I really remember."

MICHAEL AND RENÉE HESS

Of her birth, Renée says, "I love retelling it. I love reliving it."

She begins, "It had been a very crazy day. Michael had had emergencies all day long at the hospital, where he's an attending doctor. I spent the day with a friend, shopping, going to the mall. I had my bag packed. Everything was ready and waiting."

"At eleven o'clock at night, Michael looks at me and he said, 'Have that baby whenever you want, but if you ever do me one favor, do me this one: Don't have it tonight.' Those were the words we went to sleep on.

"I woke up in the middle of the night, about one a.m.. I had to go the bathroom. As I was getting back in bed, my water broke. So I went downstairs and I called the doctor, and he said, 'Have you had any contractions?' and I said, 'None that I know of.' He said, 'Okay. Go back to bed and if you don't have any contractions by morning, call me.'

"I couldn't go back to bed—I wandered around the house—made Jell-O. I figured that from here on in I'm not allowed to eat.

"I went back to bed and started to feel contractions. They were very easy. I remember Michael telling me how tired he was, so I didn't wake him up. Then I dozed off."

Michael continues the story. "About two-thirty I woke up. I wanted to get something to drink."

Renée interjects, "When I opened my eyes, I realized Michael was up. I figured I'd better tell him."

Michael says that when he saw Renée, she seemed to be "surrounded by a halo of light. That's the impression I carry with me. She just seemed to be glowing."

Renée started her Lamaze breathing, and though they thought it would be a long haul, "things started getting hot and heavy."

Renée says, "I'm doing this breathing stuff and it's not helping me anymore and I said, 'I bet I'm in active labor.' And suddenly I started to have these really painful cramps.

"At three-thirty I looked at Michael and I said, 'This is it. I can't stand this anymore.' So Michael calls the doctor and he tells the doctor that I'm having pain and cramps. The doctor said, 'Get to the hospital and I'll meet you there.'

"Before we left, Michael gave me a gift [small diamond earrings] that he had bought, just for that moment.

"When we got to the hospital," Renée says, "they wheeled me upstairs. The nurses recognize people who are about to go into transition." (Transition is the time between the beginning part of labor when the contractions dilate or open the cervix large enough for the baby to pass through—ten centimeters—and the final part of labor, when the woman pushes the baby out.)

Renée says, "I wouldn't let anyone touch me or examine me at that point."

The nurses were helpful, Michael pointed out, in not bothering Renée with lengthy hospital intake procedures.

"When they examined me, I was eight centimeters dilated. The worst part was the pushing."

At six-forty, their son was born. As Renée says, "When the baby was born, Michael had his arms around me. It was the perfect way to do it."

It may seem unnatural to stop both of these birth accounts before the parents hold their babies, but parents' stories about giving birth fall into two parts. The first is about the birth itself, the second about their first moments with the baby.

Parents' accounts about giving birth are evaluative. Parents say, "It was perfect," as Renée did, or "I would do it again," as Isabelle did. Sometimes in their enthusiasm they think about having another baby very soon. Or they have more negative judgments: "It was the worst experience I've ever had," or "I couldn't wait for it to be over."

The difference between a positive and negative evaluation does not have to do just with the length of labor and the amount of pain. By that measure Isabelle would have been very unhappy—but she wasn't. At the core of this evaluation is the question: Did this birth live up to or not live up to prior expectations?

LYNN AND HAROLD TALBOT

Lynn and Harold were "in complete and utter shock" after Lynn gave birth. They thought it was going to be "the most wonderful, beautiful experience" to give birth, but it wasn't.

"The labor wasn't bad," Lynn says, "but the nurses were awful. I walked into the hospital at two A.M., into the labor room, and the nurses said, 'What are you here for?'

"Wasn't it obvious why I was there? And then the nurses never let Harold in because they were prepping me, X-raying me, and doing all this feeling to see how tight the baby was in there.

"When Harold came in, they said, 'Out, out, out, out'—which was horrible for him, absolutely horrible. He had to sit outside in the hall and overhear conversations and not know whether the staff was talking about his wife or someone else's.

"They finally decided that I was going to have to have a Caesarean because my pelvis was eentsy and the baby was sunny-side-up in the brow position [the baby's head was toward the pelvis but facing up, instead of down]."

"I said, 'Give me an epidural.' " (An epidural is a local form of anesthesia that numbs only the pelvic region.)"And they said, 'We don't have time. We'll give you a spinal.' " (Another local anesthesia.)

"Then they said, 'We're going to cut you this way"—indicating vertical abdominal incision.

"And I said, 'No, you're not.'

"And they said, 'Well, there's not enough room to do a bikini cut." (A bikini cut is a horizontal incision just below the pubic-hair line.)

"And I said, 'You find room.' I was finally getting spunky at that point. So they did a low bikini cut.

"When they brought the baby to me, I picked up my hand to touch her. I wasn't supposed to pick up my hand, and they screamed, 'This is a sterile area. Get your hand out of there!' And then I was out, they gave me a general [anesthesia]. Zap!"

Afterward they told her that the reason they had knocked her out was that she was becoming anxious. As Lynn says, "When I saw her, I wanted to touch her. But they didn't even give me a chance. I mean, they could have said, 'Why don't you calm down?' But they didn't—they just put me out.

"In the recovery room, I woke up and there was Harold. We weren't very joyful. I guess we were glad that the baby was all right—but the birth was so awful that it outweighed the joy."

ANN AND PHIL LEE

Ann had a vaginal delivery.

"I had a long labor, and although everything went all right, I felt pretty glum about it, which my husband can attest to. I was trying to be cheerful, but the birth was more difficult than I thought it would be. My contractions really hurt, and I felt like my body was out of control—like here comes another contraction and there's nothing I can do about it. I did all the breathing exercises, and that probably made it better—nevertheless, I was pretty down. And giving birth, too, I didn't feel any of the elation and exhilaration that I had read you're supposed to. At that point, I just thought, 'Ooh, at least it's over with.' "

Why is evaluating one's birth so necessary, why does having the birth fall short or exceed one's expectations matter?

Birth is one of life's important moments. Parents have often seen pictures, read or been told of births with radiant parents. Sometimes those parents who have difficult births feel cheated, they feel they have missed out, been deprived or robbed of what they might have had.

But, beyond that, parents see birth as an early indicator of what kind of parents they will be. They look at how they have handled the birth and judge themselves.

"Did I withstand or buckle under with pain?" mothers ask themselves, comparing what they did with their expectations of themselves. If a mother wanted to avoid anesthesia and ended up taking some, she may be disappointed.

Ann Lee, whose parents were formal, distant, and remote (she was raised in China by an amah, or servant), wanted to be cheerful at birth. But she found, in fact, that she reacted more like her parents, and that thought upset her.

"Was I helpful, supportive?" fathers ask. And again, depending on their prior expectations, their feelings take shape.

"Did we work together or pull apart?" parents wonder.

A husband said to his wife, during transition, "You're doing

well," and she replied, "Shut up. You can't know how I'm doing."
A comment such as this is weighed against the husband's expectation of being in control, helpful perhaps, or against another expectation—that women want to be left alone, not bothered, during transition.

Then, parents wonder, "Did we accept responsibility or do what we were told?" Again, parents have different expectations and judge themselves accordingly.

Prior to delivery, Lynn Talbot had seen birth as a chance to prove that she was mature, an adult. Then, during the birth, she and Harold were treated like children, bad children at that. Lynn doubted that a Caesarean was actually warranted, resented the treatment she was given, and was sad that she hadn't had the chance to be more in control, although she did feel a glimmer of pride that she finally was "spunky" and insisted on making some decisions herself.

Often parents look at their handling of the birth as a measure of their adulthood—can they remain in charge? As in parenthood in general, parents aren't totally in control at birth. The baby is breech or is premature or takes a long time to be born, or the doctor or midwife or nurse is disappointing. But yet, parents hope to hold up their side, do as well as they can.

The way that parents are treated at birth feeds, in a very formative way, into their own self-evaluations. If a doctor or midwife or nurse makes a disparaging remark or acts in negative ways it will probably penetrate deeply and be long remembered.

When the birth or the parents' handling of it meets their expectations, they tend to feel "elated," "on top of the world," "high," "floating in the clouds and unable to come down." When, conversely, the birth or their handling of it falls short of what they had hoped for, parents feel "depressed," "disappointed," "angry," "down in the dumps," or "in shock." They often feel that their first step as parents has been a misstep, and they spend a lot of time comparing their fantasies with the actual birth. Sometimes this discrepancy is reconciled and the feelings lose their sharp edge, become smoothed over, but other times they don't, they remain jagged and painful and leave a scar.

It is important for prospective parents to understand the crucial role that living up to their prior images plays in feelings of success or failure at birth and to become well educated about the range of possible choices in birth. People should spend time with the doctor or midwife, before the birth if possible, or talk to other people who have used this person so that they know what he or she is customarily like during delivery. If the birth is to take place in a hospital or a maternity center, visiting there can be helpful.

The professionals who deal with birth should be similarly sensitive to the way their words or actions can impress new parents. And if a parent has had a negative experience, the hospital or midwifery service should provide an opportunity for the new parents to talk about it and help them come to terms with it.

The New Baby: Images and Realities

Seeing the child for the first time is a moment equal to that of the birth, a moment that remains, whether or not it's a first-time birth, etched in parents' memories. And like birth, the stories parents tell about this event reflect whether or not the child fit their image. *For that is another task related to forming an attachment with the child: reconciling the image of the child with the actual child.*

Just as a couple can experience the same birth differently, they can have different expectations of the child and can experience this first view of their child in totally diverse ways.

MICHAEL AND RENÉE HESS

Michael and Renée had decided that if their child was a boy, they would name him Adam. Just after the birth, however, Michael turned to Renée and said, "I'm not sure about the name. I'm not sure about the name."

"I peered at this reddish thing, lying there," Renée says, "and I called, 'That's Adam. That's him.'"

"Renée knew the baby," Michael says, "but I didn't. He was a stranger. I was terrified. I thought something was wrong with him. His eyes were so squinty and swollen. I thought he was mongoloid. I was beside myself. I immediately opened his hand and he had no simian crease [an indication of Down's syndrome], then I noticed that the baby's nostrils were flaring. I called the doctor over, but I didn't want to say anything to frighten Renée, so I kept jerking my head and pointing to his nose. But the doctor said, 'The baby's fine.'

"I think the difficulty was that I was expecting the birth of someone who looked like me," Michael says. "I think I was kind of expecting my own birth. And when I didn't see my face, it was the first inclination that this was another person. This wasn't someone just like me."

An interesting point here is that Michael was totally unaware that he'd been expecting the baby to look like him. It wasn't until the moment that he saw his child and felt a sadness sweep over him that he realized what he had been hoping.

Renée, on the other hand, knew Adam. "I had dreamed about having a boy. . . . I had also dreamed that I had given birth to a chicken. When Adam was born, he was twenty-one inches long and weighed six pounds. He was a long thin person with these long skinny chicken legs—dangling from this little round bottom. From all those images and from those dreams—I knew him. And of course, by the ninth month, several elements of his temperament had made themselves more than clear. His activity level, his grunting and moving around constantly had been established. So I also recognized that squirming."

Other mothers report that they feel that they know their baby. They recognize the movements, the way that a foot jabs out, a turn of the head. But it is not always the man who feels the child is a stranger and the woman who doesn't.

DAWN SIEGEL

Dawn, the mother of a five-week-old, says, "I had expected to have a girl, a girl that looked just like me. With pudgy cheeks.

"I had lots of dreams about a baby coming out who physically was just a shrunken me. It wasn't a baby. It was a little person who looked like me.

"Nat [her husband] was at the foot of the bed, and he saw the baby first, and he kept shouting, 'Look what it is! Look what it is!'

"I couldn't see. The umbilical cord was hanging between the baby's legs and Nat was so excited that all he could scream was 'Look what it is!'

"So they brought the baby to me, and it wasn't a girl. I started screaming, 'Oh, he looks just like me!' But, of course, he looked like blood. He was all messy. He looked nothing like me. But what I really wanted was a little miniature me."

The desire to have the baby look like the parents is not a deviation or an unnatural wish—it is a carry-over from pregnancy when one builds images of parenthood *as if* the parent were the child. Adrienne Rich has written, "I wanted to give birth—to my unborn self."[1] Some people are more identified with the child than others. Beginning with birth and lasting throughout parenthood is the process of slowly differentiating oneself from the child.

Parents have many other expectations for their child, conscious and unconscious. At birth, some are fulfilled, some aren't.

CHIP SMITH

"We [he and his wife, Stephanie] wanted a girl for many reasons. One was a family reason. There hadn't been a girl in our family for a long time.

"Another reason has to do with the times. I thought it would be exciting to try to raise a daughter within this new social framework. A daughter, raised today, would have challenges to face and the opportunity of meeting those challenges that her sex had been barred from throughout most periods of history.

"I have always enjoyed being in the company of assertive women. My mother is one. Her friends are too. And naturally I wanted my kid to be my favorite kind of person."

Chip and his wife, Stephanie, did have a girl!

Parents also have expectations about the ways boys and girls are supposed to behave. For example, Chip expected girls to be assertive, and his daughter was. But what if she had been contented or quiet or fussy?

As in birth, when parental expectations, hopes, images for the child more or less fit reality, the parents are pleased. Isabelle Agnew, hoping to have a healthy child, couldn't sleep after her son, Micos, was born in good health. "I was in a high," she said. "Nothing could make me sleep. All I wanted to do was to tell everyone that I had had a baby. I had a hospital telephone bill of one hundred seventy-five dollars."

When one's fantasy is not fulfilled, there is a period of regret for what might have been, and this unhappiness can stand in the way of the parents' reaching out, accepting the baby. But it can also be the trigger point for growth—one can either stay still, hang onto the old feeling, or one can change. The psychologist Klaus Riegel, in his studies of life-span development, thinks that human growth occurs when an individual is caught in the middle of contradictory conditions and feels an internal sense of dissonance, which he or she attempts to resolve.[2]

Michael Hess, in retrospect, describes his disappointment in his child as an impetus to grow. "In a way," he says, "I found myself through that experience." He discovered qualities in himself that he didn't know he had: flexibility, the ability to handle problems as a parent.

This reconciliation of fantasy and reality can be immediate or lengthy, particularly if the baby is premature, is born ill or with a handicap, or dies after birth. The Yale pediatrician Albert Solnit, and Marshall Klaus and John Kennell, pediatricians from Case

Western Reserve, have worked with many parents who have just given birth to a baby with problems. Their initial reaction, these doctors report, is shock, disbelief, and denial.[3] This, Klaus and Kennell say, is an understandable attempt to escape the news so discrepant with usual parental expectations for a newborn "that it is impossible to register except gradually."[4]

A numbness, a bewilderment, seems to creep over parents, overwhelming them. They feel shaky about what's real and what isn't, almost unsure whether they are dreaming or awake. A mother after giving birth to a baby with a cleft palate said that she had to keep telling herself over and over that this had happened. When a child dies soon after birth, the professional attitude can often be that it's "for the best," overlooking the long and sorrowful mourning period that parents can go through.[5]

YOLANDA PHILLIPS

Yolanda had expected her child to be "wonderful." "I had stopped teaching, we had planned for Mark to have time off from his store—we had thought of everything.

"Then the baby was born very ill [his stomach was not fully developed]. They did surgery the night he was born.

"We had expected this child to be nice and healthy—but there was nothing we could do to make that happen. It was my first experience with feeling powerless.

"I said, 'Why did this happen?' I had been raised a Catholic, and I was just infuriated at the fact that if there was any God, why did this happen to me? My father is still a very religious man. The only way I could show my anger was to write my father, whom I knew was close to God, and tell him I didn't believe anymore. He became the real target of my anger. I wanted something to hold onto, and I couldn't find it. I knew my father had it. So I just wrote him every day—these horrible letters—as if he were God almost and it was his fault.

"But he wrote me back these extremely patient letters. They began to make me feel strong.

"Then I went through this guilt thing—of trying to think back on my nine months of pregnancy. What idiotic thing could I have done that could have caused this? I took an airplane trip when I was five months pregnant. Maybe I shouldn't have done that. When I had a cold, I didn't call the doctor. Maybe I should have called the doctor.

"I drove all the doctors in the hospital crazy asking, 'Do you think this caused it or that caused it.' There is still no answer. They aren't sure what caused it. Maybe a virus, early in pregnancy, but they can't isolate it or treat it.

"Then I thought maybe I should have stopped working and stayed in bed for seven months. Oh, why am I so selfish?

"The guilt was the second stage. The third one was—I'm never going to have any child. I'm sure I'm not meant to have children."

As Yolanda got to know her baby, her anger began to fade. She learned that she was capable of handling the medication he needed, of giving him oxygen, of taking him out—even though he remained ill for many months.

Bonding

Whether or not there is a substantial discrepancy between the imagined and the actual child, it is by getting to know the child that the parents can resolve these differences—by holding, touching, caring for the baby. The first time that parents do, in fact, hold their child can be a powerful experience. Perhaps they feel the baby's skin on theirs, nestle the baby against them, cover the baby's tiny fingers with their hand, rub their mouths over the fuzz of the baby's hair, and look into the baby's eyes. Perhaps the mother offers the newborn her breast and the baby licks the nipple. Or perhaps the mother or father gives the baby a bottle.

Klaus and Kennell, in observing many first meetings between parents and infants, have discovered that there is a ritualistic way that parents get to know their babies. First they explore the baby's hands and feet, moving inward toward the baby's back. If the baby is covered with a blanket, they reach under it and begin to rub or stroke the infant. The baby's eyes are very important, and parents gaze into them.[6] If the eyes are closed, the parents jiggle and talk to the baby, saying such things as "Sleepy baby, open your eyes—now—look at me."

If this meeting takes place just following birth, assuming that the mothers weren't given too much anesthesia, the babies are wide awake and alert. Wolff has described six states of consciousness in the baby from asleep to screaming.[7] Desmond and his co-workers found that the infant is in state 4, a state of complete attentiveness, both quiet and alert, for most of the first hour of life.[8]

Berry Brazelton has observed that the infant does respond to the mother and father in the first minutes of life, and a kind of synchronized dance begins to take place: The parents and infant communicate back and forth, using their eyes and their bodies.[9] Parents sometimes, though not always, feel high at this time; "in a remarkable state of ecstasy" is the description given by Klaus and Kennell.[10]

The word that the researchers Martin Greenberg and Norman Morris use is "engrossment." Engrossment is more than an involvement with the baby. The word means "making large." The infant seems to "assume larger proportions" for the parents, and the parents, likewise, seem to grow in self-esteem.[11]

Klaus and Kennell regard the minutes just after birth as the "sensitive" time for bonding or forming an initial relationship between parents and child. In a well-known study reported in the 1970's, they discovered that when thirteen first-time mothers were given one hour more time with the babies in the first three hours after birth and fifteen more hours in the first three days of life than were thirteen other comparable mothers (who followed the usual hospital schedule for being with their babies), the mothers who had early and extended contact were more likely later to stand near their infants and watch during a physical examination, were more soothing, looked at their babies frequently, and were more reluctant to leave them than were the mothers who had not had this additional contact. At one year, the extended-contact mothers spent more time with their children during the pediatric examination and reported themselves to be more preoccupied with the baby at times when they were away from him or her. At two years, the extended-contact mothers spoke to their children more, but used fewer commands than did the mothers who had had less time with their babies at birth.

Klaus and Kennell conclude from their own research and from reviewing others' that there is a sensitive period, a period that is a prime time for this initial bonding behavior between mother and child.[12]

But what of fathers? Do they from this initial bond with their babies or not?

Greenberg and Morris, the coiners of the word "engrossment," asked just that question. For years, most studies of birth had concentrated on mothers, and Greenberg and Morris felt it was time to include the fathers. In the 1970s they studied two groups of fathers, fifteen of whom had been present at the birth and fifteen of whom had seen their newborns soon thereafter. They used a questionnaire and an open-ended approach. The only difference between the two groups they could discern was that the men present at the birth felt they could distinguish their babies more easily and were more comfortable in holding them. Both groups of men became engrossed: They felt very attracted to the baby, drawn in, compelled to stay and stare at the baby. Fathers, too, Greenberg and Morris conclude, do become very involved with their babies.[13]

Then what of the parents who are unable to be with their babies right after birth? There are two kinds of separation. One is a short-term separation in which the baby is taken away for pediatric observation after birth, and then returned to the mother at scheduled intervals during her hospital stay.

Then there is a prolonged separation, the kind of separation that occurs when a baby has been hospitalized in the intensive-care unit for prematurity or for a congenital malady. Again, Klaus and Kennell have done the major piece of research on this subject. They found that often these children were returned back to the hospital with a syndrome called "failure to thrive." Nothing organically was wrong with the babies. They just didn't grow and flourish, which Klaus and Kennell speculate may be caused by parent's lack of an intense parent/child attachment.[14]

The research thus far, however, has only opened the way to further questions. It is well known by people in the midwifery, pediatric, and obstetrical fields that early contact at birth is not a magic pill; it does not guarantee attachment. Neither does a lack of contact prevent bonding. Parents of premature or sick children and adoptive parents, who obviously are not with their children at birth, can and do form profound and sustained relationships. Why? What factors make a difference? We have only just begun to know.

I think that one crucial factor has been overlooked. The idea that early contact is important for bonding has been incorporated into the mainstream of images of parenthood. And those parents who have a less than ecstatic first meeting or who have to miss that early time with their child because of the circumstances of their birth usually feel as if they have failed, feel that they are already remiss in their relationship with the baby. I am convinced that the loss of this image and the resulting depression over failing is much more likely to block parents from reaching out to their babies than the actual physical separation of parent and child.

Separation per se does not inhibit bonding. Thus I hope that childbirth professionals will be more sensitive to the power of images, will become able to spot a new parent in the throes of suffering over an unrealized image and help that parent understand and deal with this loss so that he or she can then reach out to the new baby.

Bonding and attachment are a complicated, lengthy, and uneven process. Attachment begins long before the birth of the baby and proceeds in a stop-start way throughout the postpartum period.

FACING THE FEELINGS OF ATTACHMENT

Is This Child Really Mine?

Just after the birth, it's hard for some parents to believe that this baby, whether or not it's a first baby, belongs to them. A mother, for example, the day after birth, when asked about her new baby, looked blank and said, "What baby?" A father of a new baby likewise said, "I had expected to love my child, to have this feeling 'This is my child . . . I'm his father.' It was all there in pieces, but the gestalt didn't occur."

For parents, the task of accepting that the baby belongs to them—that they are now parents—is a part of forming a relationship with this baby. This process can take varying amounts of time and can be prolonged by others who often edge in between the parents and child, often in the guise of helpfulness.

LYNN TALBOT

After her delivery Lynn reports, "I really didn't feel like the baby was mine. I was tired and in pain until the fourth day. Then I began having a good time with her.

"We came home to this baby nurse whom we had hired. She decided that it didn't matter what the pediatrician or Harold or I thought or what our ideas were about raising a baby. She was in charge. And I was tired and scared to have this huge responsibility. And I didn't like the baby. I really didn't like her.

"The first morning I woke up at home I had this feeling in my stomach—I thought, 'My God, I can't get out of bed and face this, I really don't want to at all.' And every day after that I would lie in bed and cry and Harold would call from the office and say, 'How are you?' And I couldn't answer the question because I would be crying so hard.

"I think a lot of it was that bitch of a nurse. She was undermining me about breast feeding all the time."

"You know what I started doing. I started thinking that the baby really belonged to the nurse and I started looking for physical resemblances between the nurse and her. I completely forgot the baby was mine—no, I never connected. It wasn't a matter of forgetting—it had never connected at all.

"I talked to some of my friends and asked them if they had loved their children from the beginning. One said she did—she really felt like this child was her flesh and blood. Well, I didn't at all. No connection.

"Then the nurse left. She didn't want to leave—she liked ruling our lives—but she left. And Harold left [on a business trip] and I was left with the baby by myself. And finally it seemed like she was mine. One day [when the baby was six weeks old] it clicked. Something happened. I fell in love."

GLORIA PATTERSON

Gloria is a teenage unmarried parent, living at home. She, too, doesn't feel as if the baby is hers.

"My mother wanted a baby real bad. She's got five of us but she wanted another one. And so when she found out that I was pregnant she was saying that she doesn't have to go through the pain, she just might as well go on waiting to be a grandmother."

Her mother takes the baby whenever possible, even puts the baby into her own bed at night. Then Gloria waits until her mother is asleep, "and I come for her and take her back downstairs."

"It seems like I don't have too much to do with the baby. I don't feel like it's my baby. I don't feel like I'm a parent at all."

It is obvious that not all grandparents or baby nurses act this way, but when they or others do, they can block the parent's acceptance of the child.

Even without such obstacles, however, new parents feel an inner ambivalence. One moment they are thrilled, then later they want to get rid of the baby. A new mother says, "Sometimes we have evil thoughts about the baby. We wonder why we did it and we joke about having her stewed, you know, suckling kid for dinner, so that we can get rid of her. But most of the time, we are thrilled."

Years later, parents tend to forget this initial reaction. They can't imagine a time when their child wasn't a part of their lives, and often they react to the new parents' hesitations with denial—"I never felt like that"—or disapproval—"How could you feel like that!" Their comments can make the new parent feel abnormal, like a freak. But, in fact, this initial tentativeness, moving in, moving out, is a very normal part of becoming attached to the baby.

Affinity/Dissimilarity

Another important ingredient in the early attachment is a feeling that parents have of affinity with or dissimilarity to the baby. This feeling is related to whether or not the baby fulfilled the parents' expectations, but it is not exactly the same. Parents (whether they have become parents by birth, by adoption, or by the foster-care system) either feel close to or distant from the new baby—they feel that this child reminds them of themselves or is different. There are any number of qualities in the baby that make a parent feel this way. Perhaps it's the baby's appearance—the shape of the face, color of the hair, color of the skin. For one mother it was size: "I am small. My whole family is small. And then this thing comes out and she's huge. And she's relatively independent. Her cries are not whimpers; they are demands. And so the result is that I see this large independent thing. I can't really identify her with me—even though I was awake at the birth and saw her come out of me."

For some people, the baby's personality makes a difference. A father responded to a newborn girl who was persistent as "like me." A mother felt that an infant daughter who was "stiff" wasn't at all like her.

It is important to note that a sense of affinity does not run along sex lines; that is, mothers don't automatically feel an affinity with daughters and fathers with sons. Equally important is that both parents or neither can feel an affinity with the same child. There seems to be no predictable pattern.

The sense of affinity does not necessarily hasten forming an attachment, nor does a sense of dissimilarity retard it. The crucial factor is how the parents feel about themselves. If the child, even at a few weeks, reminds the parent of a quality that he or she dislikes (a loud shrill voice or hyper movement, for example), then that parent may want to keep a distance, and conversely if the child is different from the parent in a pleasing way, the parent may move in faster.

Babies can also remind parents of other people—an aunt, grandparent, mother- or father-in-law. And the parents' reactions to the child become more or less colored by their assessment of these other people.

These feelings that parents have of affinity and dissimilarity to their child are normal. The parent, however, can stay stuck with the idea that "this child is just like me" and not look further, not look at the ways that the child is an individual. Or they can look at their response to their child, beginning to separate their fantasies and projections from realities.

Can I Take Care of My Baby?

As parents deal with the question "Is this child really mine?" another concurrent question emerges: Can I take care of him or her? In retrospect, the newborn seems to have been so safe, so protected *in utero*. Will the baby survive in the world? parents wonder. How can I make sure that the baby will survive? One Midwestern mother, the day after her child was born, had what she calls "this tremendous nightmare—it was like having a fever and hallucinating. I kept thinking, 'Oh, if I can just keep this kid safe from dire pestilence, from all the terrible things that can happen.' " *Answering those self-doubts, uncertainties, and worries is a more intense process for the first-time parent, but does recur with every new baby because this task is a part of getting to know the baby, becoming able to care for, provide for, nuture, and thus be attached to the new baby.*

CHIP SMITH

"You worry most about—'Can I find out what she [the baby] wants? And can I provide it?'

"It began the first time I fed her. Stephanie [who was nursing] had been the food giver; I hadn't. She had been up every two hours feeding the baby, and she was a walking zombie. When the baby was about two weeks old, I convinced Stephanie to let me have one of the late, dead-of-night feedings.

"I was scared. I went crazy that night making the preparations—like it was a five-course banquet for a person who was going to give me one hundred thousand dollars if she liked the dinner.

"Finally, the baby woke up and I went to get her. By this time I was used to handling her. I put the bottle in her mouth and she started drinking! It was about the most satisfying thing I've ever done. I was doing the right thing for her, and she was letting me know, just by eating."

Feeding is a frequent source of worry, even obsession, particularly for the first-time parent. Is the baby getting enough? Is the baby getting too much? One mother of a six-week-old said, "One day I'm convinced I'm underfeeding. Then I have her weighed, and she's gained a tremendous amount, so the next day I think I'm overfeeding." Some mothers and fathers at first question their commitments to breast feeding or bottle feeding.

Sleep, too, is a source of anxiety. One father worried that his baby wasn't sleeping enough. Then one night, the baby slept for seven hours, and the father was beside himself with anxiety that something was wrong, that the baby was sick.

There is also the question of what to do when the baby cries—pick the baby up or let the baby cry.

VANESSA COOK

Vanessa, an Englishwoman in America, initially as a student, now lives in the Midwest with her husband, also a student, and their six-week-old daughter. Soon after the birth, they were visited by her English uncle, who criticized Vanessa for picking up the baby so much. "You'll spoil her," he said.

"English babies cry it out for two or three months," Vanessa reflects, "then they never cry again.

"But Erik Erikson says that's destroying basic trust. Burton White and Frank Caplan and every other American-oriented child psychologist say that, too. There are differences between American and British babies, and I wonder, do I want her to be an English baby, brought up by a kind of nanny's rules, or do I want her to be an American baby?"

Whether or not parents have a dual culture, like Vanessa, first-time parents are barraged with conflicting images—from their childhood, from parents, relatives, friends, neighbors. They have to sift through the images until they find the one that fits, that seems right.

For Vanessa, it was: "My instinct says that when the baby cries, I should pick her up and console her. And so I'm going by that."

One reason that parenthood the second time around is so much easier is that parents have gone through this sifting process and have, for the most part, settled on images that feel comfortable. Yet even with a second child, there is worry, just because this baby isn't fully known, because he or she is different and the methods that worked with the first don't necessarily work with the second. Many parents, experienced or inexperienced, find themselves getting up at night to check on whether the baby is still breathing. If the baby hasn't cried or made any noise for a while, many parents wonder, "Is the baby still alive?"

And if the baby does get sick, a cold or a diaper rash, worry can intensify for even the most experienced parent. As one parent said, "The thing is that you worry because each baby is for a while an unknown quantity."

The question that new parents ask themselves again and again is, "Is this normal?"

One woman, now a grandmother, and the director of children's services in a hospital, says that when she had her first child she didn't know that babies' heads sit squarely on their shoulders; they have almost no necks. This woman, while looking at her newborn one day, panicked, thinking that her child had a misshapen neck, and rushed the baby to the doctor.

Another large concern is: Can I afford this baby? Birth can be expensive, and depending on their insurance coverage or lack of it, some new parents are saddled with staggering debts. Then there is the cost of clothing or equipping the new baby (if these are not borrowed) and feeding the baby. One new mother says, "We think about money all the time now. This concern about money is altering our whole life."

At the base of all these feelings is the question: How am I measuring up as a parent? And each new experience with the baby often seems like a test of one's ability to be a parent: mixing the baby food, curing the diaper rash, rocking the baby to sleep, getting the baby to the doctor or the clinic, taking a walk with a carriage.

One mother tells of such an experience. "The first time I took Andrew out in the carriage, I thought, 'Now, this isn't half bad.' I was going up the street, doing my errands. The baby was asleep and I felt normal. Then the wheel of the carriage fell off! Rolled down the street.

"So I had to go down the street balancing the carriage on three wheels.

"Finally, I said to this lady, 'Would you hold my carriage while I climb under this car to get the wheel for my carriage?' There I was, on all fours, getting the wheel.

"When we finally got home, we didn't go out again for several days."

Underneath parental questions is still a more fundamental one. How much leverage do I really have? Is what I am doing making a difference? What kind of difference?

A mother of newborn twins says, "I'm wondering about how much control we really have over them. How do we make them into the sort of people that we like, that we want them to be?" Being a parent is unlike any previous job—the results of any one action are not clearly visible for a long time, if at all.

While some parents go through this period of wonder and worry in a lesser degree, the fumbling advances and anxiety are a normal part of getting to know and working out a relationship with this new human being.

Getting to Know the Baby

Parents have always known that infants have different personalities. In the late 1960s, Stella Chess, Alexander Thomas, and Herbert G. Birch published a long-term study of 231 children in which they had begun to analyze and concretely describe some of these differences:

1. "Activity level." Some babies are physically more active, some are less active.

2. "Regularity." Babies differ in their own biological time clocks in whether they eat, sleep, and eliminate in a regular or irregular way.
3. "Approach or withdrawal as a characteristic response to a new situation." Babies greet *new* situations more or less positively.
4. "Adaptability to change in routine." This differentiation refers to how babies respond to change over an extended time.
5. "Level of sensory threshhold." There are variations in the way that babies react to bright light, noise, confusion, being wet, wearing clothes with different textures, and pain. Some babies are bothered by these experiences more than others.
6. "Positive or negative mood." Babies, too, have a range of characteristic moods, which this group of researchers rated as positive or negative.
7. "Intensity of response." Intensity means the level of energy expended.
8. "Distractibility." Distractibility refers to the baby's degree of concentration. Some babies concentrate without being distracted; others are more distractible.
9. "Persistence and attention span." The investigators say, "We observed great variation in the ability of different babies to continue an activity in the face of difficulty or to resume it after interruption."

The investigators call these nine qualities "temperament," which they define as the "how" of behavior, or the way in which behavior is expressed.[15]

The match between the temperament of the parent and the child is clearly enormously important. A live-wire baby and a slow parent, for example, will have to adjust to each other in a far different way than an active baby and an active parent.

The Parent/Child Relationship Is Interactive

The relationship between parent and child is interactive: What the child does affects what the parent does, which in turn affects what the child does. This picture of the parent/child relationship is far different from the view which proclaims that parents are totally responsible for the development of their child, who is seen as a *tabula rasa* or as a piece of clay to be molded. Recent research in human development has moved to this point of view, perhaps best typified by the work of Richard Bell, Sibylle Escalona, and Lois

Murphy.[16] Michael Lewis and Leonard Rosenblum write: "Not only is the infant or child influenced by its social, political, economic, and biological world, but in fact the child itself influences its world in turn."[17]

In the first weeks of life, parents begin discovering what pleases and what distresses the baby—what stops the baby from crying, how often the baby needs to sleep, to eat, to be changed. Parents learn the skill of paying attention, of being empathetic with and responding to the baby's cues and clues. This is the way that parents answer their own questions, reduce their anxieties, sort through their images, settling on one that fits, and strengthen their relationship with their newborn. This skill, one which often has to be learned and relearned, underlies the entire course of parenthood.

A father, before the birth of his child, had a fear: "I was scared that I would have a communication problem—that I would have this howling, screaming infant and be at a complete loss as to what to do. What I found, very early on, were two things that gave me great comfort. First, there weren't a whole lot of things that the baby wanted. She could be wet, she could be tired, she could be hungry, and that was about it. And then I realized, by the time she was two months, that she did different things for wet, tired, or hungry. And my realization that she could communicate with me, tell me what she wanted if I was just ready to listen, took away all my nightmares and give me a feeling of confidence."

Louis W. Sander, from his long-term observational study, has separated the mother/child relationship into different time frames. The first is "the period of initial adaptation," which covers from birth to the child at two and a half months. The measure of success of this period, he reports, are the two feelings that this father describes: a feeling of "knowing" the baby, and the moderation of anxieties about the baby's care.

The arrival at this state, Sander thinks, depends "in part, at least, on the balance the mother can maintain between her empathy with what she feels are the child's needs and her objectivity in viewing him as an individual apart from her own projections and displacements."[18]

The parent does bring many associations to his or her expectations of the child—both personal ("this baby is like my father-in-law") and cultural ("all boys are rebellious"). Responding to the babies' cues and clues is a continuous sorting out of fantasy and reality, paring away at conflicting images that don't match up to the realities of the parents' perceptions and the child's behavior.

The child's mode of communication is critically important. A child who howls constantly, no matter what is wrong, will be much harder to decipher. Success in responding to the baby's cues does not necessarily come quickly or easily.

Two other factors are important. One is a knowledge of the tricks of the trade: what else to do when the first thing one tries doesn't work.

"I lacked a repertoire of skills," one first-time mother said, "of what to do when my baby was unhappy and nursing wasn't enough. I didn't want to put her down, because she needed me. I didn't know about swaddling [wrapping a baby securely in a blanket], I didn't know about turning the baby over my knee, or holding her over my shoulder."

The second is a knowledge of child development and an understanding of what kinds of behavior to expect and what these kinds of behavior signify. Knowing that every baby needs differing amounts of sleep, for instance, is comforting to the parents whose child sleeps infrequently and yet for the most part is alert and contented.

The father of a child with Down's syndrome said, "I didn't know what was normal—I didn't know what to expect of a child with Down's syndrome. And that was the hardest thing of all." This father gained this knowledge of development for his child by getting to know some other parents of children with Down's syndrome.

Success at parenthood is a process of finding realistic images and skills, but most parents have to grapple, picking these up willy-nilly from their parents, friends, doctors, or books.

The lack of a realistic fund of images of parenthood is a large and unnecessary lack in our country—a lack which could at least be partially remedied by giving adolescents and young adults courses in child and adult development and by giving all children experience in caring for younger children so that they could establish an early inner sense of comfort and competence in nurturing.

Getting to Know Oneself

The other side of getting to know the baby is the opportunity to get to know oneself better. Parents' actions and reactions to the baby are self-revealing, for those who choose to try to understand. One new mother says, "Last night something was wrong with the baby. He didn't sleep. I was a wreck because I had been up all night with him. I couldn't figure what was the matter.

"The next day, I sat around numbly. Then I started to get angrier and angrier. I knew I wasn't angry at him.

"I finally figured it out about two hours later. I was angry because he was making me feel so helpless. Everybody has their weak spots, and I realized that's a weak spot of mine. Feeling uncertain and helpless drives me right up the wall. I just feel these tremendous surges of anger."

Fortunately this mother didn't turn her anger at her child but saw that it was tied to an image she had of herself: "that mothers should know what to do." When the image wasn't holding up, she felt depleted.

When parents are in the midst of this kind of turmoil, they also can feel depressed or guilty. At times such as these, parents veer from one point of view to another, bound and rebound. Contradictory thoughts seem equally valid and true.

Parents can also shield themselves from this kind of stress, by standing behind defenses. "It's not my fault—it is someone else's." They can deny the whole situation, or they can engage in magical thinking; if only such-and-such were true, then this wouldn't happen.

There is a difference between growth and change. Parents can pass through these stages and as such be definitely changed, but not necessarily grow. Growth comes from encountering a rough spot, a problem. Growth means wending through one's feelings, seeing what is actually happening, and what has been projected or wished. It means dropping some of the unworkable images that one had of oneself as a parent—perhaps being a supermother, having an immaculate home.

Finally, to grow, one must replace the defective image with a new, seemingly workable image. For instance, a month after his son was born, David Steinberg writes in *Fatherjournal*:

> Tonight I cried for the first time since Dylan was born.
> . . . I was going to be the perfect father: loving, caring, nurturing, soft. I was going to make up for all the men who leave children to the women, who back away from intimacy with children, who are cold and distant. I was going to do it right.
> Tonight I see how scared I am. There is so much to do for this little creature who screams and wriggles and needs and doesn't know what he needs and relies on me to figure it all out. I watch myself run away, leaving the baby to Susan and her woman's intuition and her breasts full of milk. . . .
> . . . Afterwards I had the beginnings of a new vision: I need to accept my fear, my reluctance, my instinct to flee. I have to start from where I am instead of where the model new-age father would be.[19]

This journal entry perfectly describes the shedding of images that don't hold up for those that are sounder, more realistic.

Separateness/Connectedness

Inherent in this process of an ever-increasing perceptivity about oneself and the baby is confronting the theme of separateness/connectedness.[20]

MARGO ANDERSON

Margo Anderson has eight-week-old twins. Her mother-in-law came to help her, after the birth.

"My mother-in-law brought this funny package with her. It was this mechanical swing. I looked at it and went, 'Oh, bad!' I had seen one in my sister-in-law's house, and I had thought, 'Why can't people hold their babies? Why do they have to stick them in a machine?' I gave this machine a dirty look and didn't open it up.

"Well, three weeks passed. Both of the babies are colicky. One day Jennie was screaming and screaming a long time and nothing worked. And finally we sat her in the swing. She stopped crying. She loved it! She loved it!

"I looked at my husband and he looked at me. I said, 'Well, we'd better get used to this. She's going to like a lot of things that we don't!'"

Parents weave back and forth, between the two extremes—that the baby is separate, that the baby remains connected. Both are true. *The task of becoming attached includes beginning to understand separateness.*

DAWN SIEGEL

Five weeks after giving birth, Dawn, a teacher, is caught in this dichotomy.

"My son seems so separate from me. He has a strong will and seems to know exactly what he wants. I mean, I can't even play and dress him up anymore. When he was a week old, he was kind of limp, and he would let me do it. Now he fights back.

"When he's given a bath, he seems like he's absolutely all my baby, and I can do whatever I want. I can mush him around, bend his arms.

"Here I have this kid who already seems separate and I'm trying to push him back in. I want him to be more of me. Today, I had this baby carrier on. I had the coat buttoned around both of us and that was the nicest thing, because he was almost mine again. I was almost able to put him back inside.

"It goes so fast I can't believe the baby is already five weeks old. I couldn't believe it when he was a minute old. The event [the birth] that I looked forward to for so long is already over."

The psychoanalyst Helene Deutsch says that birth gives women the fear that " 'I am losing the child,' but also that of 'The child is losing me.' "[21] It is perhaps for this reason that so many new parents talk about having another child right away.

A father, however, felt that birth was not a loss, but a gain. At first, he experienced being separate from his child. He said that when he put on a hospital gown and held the baby, he felt that he was "on the outside." Then later, as he got to know the baby, "there are moments when I hold him and close my eyes and disappear into this nice warm feeling. I am inside."

For other parents, the loss and gain coexist. A new mother said, "When I nurse the baby, for all intents and purposes he is still a part of me. I mean the amount of milk I have in my breasts depends on how hungry the baby is. The nutrition I require, the things I am hungry for, I'm sure are in large part determined by what he needs at the time. I am eating things that I would normally not eat at all." But, at other times, when she holds the baby, measuring him against her arm, he seems very much his own person, separate, individual.

Another new mother saw the situation slightly differently. She felt that the baby was more independent, more determined and persistent, than she had imagined and that she and her husband had become the dependent ones. "We are extensions of the baby—running in circles around her."

Jane Lazarre writes of the same sensation:

> Who was this immensely powerful person, screaming unintelligibly, sucking my breast until I was in a state of fatigue the likes of which I had never known? Who was he and by what authority had he claimed the right to my life?
> . . . After only several days of his life, we [she and her husband] both felt that the breast was his.[22]

These parents are talking about a transformation in themselves, a state of being joined and not joined to the baby. All of the words that traditionally have been used to describe this state—"symbiosis," "bonding"—denote total fusion of the self with the baby. But in fact, attachment is not only an uneven, lengthy, stop-and-start process, and it also implies both emotional and physical separateness and connectedness.

Attachment

Eventually, parents come to feel attached to the baby, either with "a sudden first gush of love" or in a more gradual way: "It took a couple of weeks until it wasn't like having an object in our home, this blob that we were trying to keep alive. It became organic." *Becoming attached to the baby is the major task of the Nurturing Stage.*

Once in a parent education group, I asked each person to describe when and how he or she had become attached, and the variation was wide, from before birth to months later.

The work of John Bowlby focused attention on the importance— in fact, the necessity—of the attachment relationship between mother and infant, a relationship which Leon J. Yarrow and Frank A. Pedersen define as "characterized by strong interdependence and intense affect."[23] Mary Ainsworth writes, "An attachment is an affectional tie that one person forms to another specific person, binding them together in space and enduring over time."[24] Marsha Weintraub, Jeanne Brooks, and Michael Lewis, in a recent paper, have contested the traditional definitions of attachment, pointing out that the infant forms a unique relationship with several people, that these are not necessarily enduring but change over time, and that using proximity seeking as a measure of attachment is not scientifically valid because this factor changes, depending on the place and age of the child. They propose a redefinition of attachment, resting on a theory of social network: "Man is a social animal who from the day of birth enters into social relationships with numerous people."[25]

I think that attachment is a passionate experience. Parents feel drawn to the baby. "I couldn't just look at her," a father says, "I wanted to touch her all the time." Another father describes his new baby as like a magnet—the smell of the baby's hair, the feel of the warm folds of fat, the intent eyes seemed to pull, to draw the father to his son. "It's a total sensual experience," a mother says. "The baby smells good, she feels good, she even tastes good when you kiss her." Attachment also has sexual overtones. "I was surprised at how sexy it feels to nurse my baby," a mother says. "My baby turns me on," a father says.

Attachment is a state of consuming involvement, of feeling joined and not joined to the baby. Almost all parents have forgotten their own earliest experiences, but they feel that this time of intense attachment to their new baby in one sense transports them back to infancy: Time slows down, colors become more vibrant, sounds more vivid, touch heightened.

JULIANNA DANIELS

Julianna and her husband had a daughter, their second child, six weeks ago.

Julianna says, "I would like to spend hours every day holding the baby. Everything else is an annoyance, an interruption. In fact, I think I want everyone else to go away—my husband, my four-year-old son. I'd like to get into a little burrow with this baby."

When Julianna does leave her baby, after a while, "I start to think about coming home. I feel like if I don't get home immediately I'm going to go mad. My image of myself is of an elephant mother charging through the jungle because she heard her babies squeal.

"The fact is that I am just as dependent on her as she is on me. I mean, I would wither away as fast as she would if we were separated."

DENNIS GREEN

"When Anna was born, they brought her to me. She was crying. I held her and she stopped crying. It was an epiphany. I suddenly realized that I had always thought of 'a father' as my father. Now whatever I would be to Anna would be what 'a father' will mean to her.

"I feel a really shocking kind of love, a completely unalloyed, non-quid-pro-quo love for her. The most perfect relationship you can have with another human being, in a marriage or friendship, always has some quid pro quo, or form of barter—like I'll love you if you love me, and we'll sort of work it out. But with a child of your own, that doesn't exist at first."

Fathers and Attachment

The attachment studies of the past twenty years have focused on the infant/mother relationship, but the increase of men in prepared-childbirth classes, present at the deliveries, and men who take larger roles in the infant's early years has stimulated an upsurge of interest in the infant/father relationship. In a study by Ross D. Parke and Douglas B. Sawin, trained observers watched and recorded a wide variety of parenting behavior in the first days after birth in a group of middle-class and lower-class fathers. It was concluded that "the fathers clearly were just as involved with their babies as the mothers—looking and smiling at them, holding and kissing."[26] Another investigator, M. Kotelchuck, takes this point one step further, concluding that infants' attachment to their fathers depends on the degree to which men interact with them.[27]

Parke and Sawin, as do other others, qualify this finding: "While mothers and fathers are equally involved with their infants, they are involved in different ways right from the start." Fathers play with their babies more whereas mothers take care of them. Parke and Sawin wondered if mothers took on caretaking roles because of a greater degree of skill in such roles. Assuming that the skill involved was a responsiveness to the infant's cues, they tested this hypothesis and found that mothers were only slightly more responsive, that fathers did very well at the tasks of child care.[28]

Their conclusion parallels that of several contemporary psychoanalytic authors. As summarized by Ernest L. Abelin, who, like most other child development theorists, looks at attachment from the child's vantage point, this position is: "The father's first role is to draw and to attract the child into the real world of things and people." Initially, the child has a two-way mother-child or "binary" relationship, and then the father is added, and "triangulation" takes place.[29]

The psychologist Michael Lamb has been conducting a long-term observational study of mothers, fathers, and their children in their homes, focusing on the father-child relationship. He does not rely on reports of fathers' relationships by mothers, as many researchers do, but observes fathers directly. The families are economically mixed, all white, with traditional marital roles (the mother is the primary caretaker). Lamb has reported that infants in the second half of the first year are equally attached to both parents, but that mothers were more likely to hold their infants to care for them while fathers are more likely to hold their babies to play.[30]

Michael Yogman and Berry Brazelton have videotaped five infants with their parents from two weeks to six months. They've found that the mothers and fathers in their sample spoke differently to their child. Mothers spoke in soft voices, imitating their infant's sounds. Fathers spoke less, touched more. Their play was more dramatic, while mother-infant play was more gradual.[31]

Most of the studies on infant-parent relationships have been done on families with traditional role patterns—that is, the mother, working or not, is the family member most responsible for the baby. There is a social justification for this kind of sample. Recent research, such as that by Lois Wladis Hoffman has shown that even families with shared responsibilities before a birth of a baby tend to revert to more traditional divisions of labor after the birth.[32]

Likewise, Philip and Carolyn Cowan, reporting on their long-term study of eight middle-class white couples, found that all couples planned to share some of the tasks of child care before the birth, but that six months later, the women were doing more of the child care than they originally thought they would, regardless of whether or not they were breast-feeding or employed.[33]

Still, I feel that studies of sex differences have only begun to skim the surface, as the investigators into this domain readily admit. It is not at all possible to rest with the conclusion that men are one way, women another, without studies of equalitarian families as well as cross-cultural work.

One initial difference between fathers and mothers is obvious. Women carry the growing infant within their bodies. They feel themselves enlarge, feel their own internal organs being pushed aside to make room, know that they are providing sustenance, become familiar with the motions of the baby, and finally go through the travail and pain of birth. Then, if they are breast-feeding, they establish that uniquely physical, nourishing tie.

One father says, "As close as I feel to my baby—I was there at her birth, I held her right after my wife did, I was as close to her as I could possibly be—but that's not as close as the mother is."

Women who become parents by giving birth have a prior physical, emotional experience that fathers don't have—and they start out at different places.

Dorothy Dinnerstein has written a persuasive analysis of the malaise that comes from not having fathers care for infants, as has Nancy Chodorow. Both argue that the lack of nurturance from the fathers in the early years is a loss for both men and women. In addition, there are serious ramifications for the child who becomes too dependent on one person, the mother, and is thus deprived of the richness of experience that comes from knowing two different kinds of adults intimately. The development of boys has a discontinuity. Boys have to renounce their identification with the mother and her nurturing attributes in order to identify with their fathers. This has consequences for the next generation of fathers.[34]

For those fathers who do become involved in their children, it can be a transforming experience.

CHIP SMITH

Chip, a father who is very involved in his new baby, does feel changed by this experience. He says, "On the day after Nell was born, I got onto the subway train and looked at everyone and started to envision that each of them had been a day-old infant once.

"It was a whole new way of looking at people and it makes you feel more of a piece with your family, with your roots, with all of life.

"I spent a great deal of time reading anthropology and thinking about the biological progression of humanity since Nell was born. I've gone back in the range of hundreds of years and tried to understand more fully how Stephanie and I can make love, how my sperm can pump into her womb, and how nine months later, it can result in this blond, blue-eyed little bit of humanity."

Adoptive and foster mothers and fathers start with an equal footing. After the birth, however, what any parent does, how much he or she moves in or away, depends on this parent, on a personal image of roles.

A father who spends a great deal of time caring for his baby says, "I knew that if I had wanted to, I could have had the traditional out. I could be a father who wasn't as familiar with the kid as the mother. The mother would be the primary caretaker. It's not what I wanted to do, but it was in the back of my mind that I had that escape route."

Another father admits that he did stay away after the birth, frantically working on trying to restore a car that had been junked.

John Munder Ross terms men's ambivalences toward the baby the "Laius Complex." The child reminds the father of his own mixed feelings toward his own father. "Anticipating that a son, or a daughter for that matter, will be similarly moved, a man may be secretly tempted to abandon or to hurt the baby."[35]

Women, too, can feel a similar ambivalence. The quality of the attachment relationship established between father and child depends not only on the father, but also on the mother. Many women take over, becoming what Jean Curtis calls "the psychological parent," or the one most responsible for the child. They shut the fathers out.[36] Still other parents feel uncertain about their roles, shifting back and forth about who does what.

Fathers, however, can become very attached to the new baby, as can mothers—but so can siblings, grandparents, other relatives, and friends. Attachment isn't the singular emotion that it is sometimes described as being—it can affect and envelop more than just the mother, and it changes as the relationship develops.

The Importance of Attachment

As with every task, the task of forming an attachment contains the possibility of a positive or negative resolution, or the avoidance of one altogether. Again the studies have focused on the outcome for the infant. A few babies never become attached. For the most part, they are the babies in foundling homes or institutions who have no permanent caring adults around. Even though they are receiving adequate physical attention, they become withered, apathetic, withdrawn, or they die, according to the studies of René Spitz.[37] Furthermore they don't form a sense of self or ego, according to the work of Selma Fraiberg.[38] Babies need people to care passionately about them in order to survive and grow well.

It is through this attachment relationship with their parent or parents that infants do learn to trust in the reliability of their environment, to develop what Erik Erikson calls a basic sense of trust in the world. As their parents respond to them, the seeds of their self-concepts, their egos, begin to grow.[39]

The Parent: A Changing Sense of Self

As parents become attached to a baby, they realize that this is a transforming experience. Jane Lazarre writes:

> As [my baby] drew the milk out of me, my inner self seemed to shrink into a very small knot, gathering intensity under a protective shell, moving away, further and further away, from the changes being wrought by this child who was at once separate and a part of me. Frightened that he would claim my life completely, I desperately tried to cling to my boundaries. Yet I held him very close, stroked his skin, imagined that we were still one person.
>
> I turned to that self inside of me, that girlwoman who had once been all I needed to know of myself, whom I had fought to understand, to love, to free—I turned to her now and I banished her. Into a protective shell tied in a knot, she retreated, four, five, six times a day, whenever Benjamin wanted to nurse. Soon, even when I sought her, she would not come, but began to stay out of reach longer and longer, sometimes not reappearing for whole days.[40]

A shrinking of self. A loss of self. A postponement of self—indeed, a changing self.

RENÉE HESS

"When you get on a schedule of waking up every two hours and you do it long enough" Renée says, "reality ceases to exist and then you cease to exist. You do what you have to do. There's no time for reflection. There's no time to sense the meaning of what you are doing. You just do it.

"I vacillate from this euphoria of feeling really successful as a person, as a woman, to feeling disgusting, sort of like a cow. All of these intellectual attainments, all of those years of education, seem meaningless. I am existing on a very primitive level, and I can't identify this with any other part of my life. It is a painful, uncomfortable kind of losing myself."

The baby cries, the parent answers. The baby is hungry, the parent provides food. The baby is awake most of the night, so is the parent. Parents feel as if their old life, their ability to plan, to have a reliable pattern to their days, is slipping away. If they are first-time parents they aren't sure from one moment to the next what they'll be doing. They don't know how to gauge themselves. The chores, the repetitious cycles of feeding, changing, putting the baby to sleep, seem endless. Night blurs into day. Time and their ability to control it, even count on it, seem far beyond their grasp, perhaps forever.

One mother says that every time the baby would go to sleep, she tried to get a few things done, "but by the time I would start doing whatever I wanted to do, the baby'd be crying and rooting again. I was devoting myself entirely to feeding her and I found I wasn't eating lunch until about four in the afternoon. I never got out of my night dress. I never had a bath—I mean, to take a shower was a major event. I had to find my husband to hang onto the baby."

Another mother of a new baby says, "However much they tell you that it's going to be hard work, however many books you read with dire warnings of what babies are like, there's no way that you can realize what's involved. No one can know what feeding a baby every two or three hours means until they've done it. You can't prepare people for that."

The changing sense of self which began in pregnancy, particularly a first pregnancy, when one's identity seemed blurry, unstable, continues after the birth. At first it mainly seems that the old self has slipped away or been dislocated and nothing emerges to fill in the gap. Parents feel that they are in flux, in transit from one point in life to another, but the routes and boundaries are still distant and unclear.

The intensity of this reaction varies, person by person, situation by situation. Having had other children, being knowledgeable about children, or spending relatively little time caring for the baby may lessen the force of these feelings. However, this is not an experience that hits only stay-at-home or nursing mothers; it affects employed parents, too, men as well as women, because having a new baby alters how a parent uses time, taking away time spent formerly on the self. One father who had a demanding daytime job and who wasn't getting up for night feedings still felt "like I was walking around on my eyelids."

The exhaustion, lack of sleep, plays a large part in these feelings.

"For the first seven days," one new father said, "I didn't sleep. It was hellish. I don't ever remember being that tired. And one of the worst parts of all the sacrifices I was making was, nobody appreciated it. I mean no one was really there to say 'Thank you' or 'Oh, how wonderful.' And here my wife was with these lousy stitches and this kid screaming and not sleeping and hungry and there was nobody to pat me and say, 'There, there.' As a matter of fact, I was expected to say, 'There, there.'"

An unmarried mother, living alone in a New England village with her son, says, "You are confronted with a twenty-four-hour-a-day job and that's it. There's nothing else in your life that you can't escape like you can't escape your responsibility to a baby. You can finish a job and go home. You can leave your boyfriend, but you can't do that with your new child. There's a lot of doubt about whether you can pull off what you want to pull off."

A mother who ran a business with her husband says, "In the beginning we really thought we were strong, independent, sensitive people [with a flexible work schedule]. We really thought we would cart this child everywhere. But I would wake up every morning and cry because I was so tired. I was nursing, so there was very little relief my husband could give me. I mean, he would get up, because our apartment is small, and everyone woke up when the baby woke up. I kept saying, why did I get myself into this mess. Since I like kids, I should have been a teacher. I wouldn't have to stay up all night if I was a teacher.

"I'll never forget one night. My husband came in and he said, 'What's the story with the eggshells in the refrigerator?'

"I said, 'What eggshells in the refrigerator?'

"And he took me by the hand and he walked me to the refrigerator and there was this egg carton filled with eggshells.

"What had happened was, that morning I was trying to get some breakfast-lunch mixed fast. I wanted to drink something nutritious so that I could nurse this child, but I didn't want to cook breakfast and I didn't want to cook lunch. So I had taken some milk and eggs and some vanilla and made this milkshake. I guess in my craziness I had drunk the shake and had very mechanically put all the eggshells into the carton. And put them back into the refrigerator.

"It was at that point that I realized I was completely spaced out, I was going cuckoo. That did it."

In a strange way, this state that parents feel somewhat parallels infancy, a somnambulistic, sensory, dependent state, with a lack of a clear sense of self. Of course, the adults do remain adults, but simultaneously, they are transported back to an experience which somewhat revives memories of their earliest years, an experience which can give the adults a partial understanding of what life is like for their infant.

Parents, particularly those home with the child full-time, feel an inability to think about anything but the baby. A new mother says, "I haven't even been able to read. I can't concentrate very well, and I can't retain what I read."

A father who is a writer says, "It's made it difficult to concentrate and work in the same way I used to."

Another mother said, "I am having problems with my memory. I can hardly remember anything for very long."

Parents, feeling tied down, engulfed, have the recurring desire to burst out, to run away from the responsibility.

A mother with a toddler and a new infant says, "Many days it's like a three-ring circus around here. One's up and the other's down. I literally wait on the doorstep for my husband to come home."

Some parents end up going to places they weren't that interested in before—long walks outdoors, treks through used-car lots, endless trips up and down the aisles of the supermarket. Lillian Rubin, in her study of fifty white working-class families, reports that one new father "cut out on work a lot." This father says, "I used to think I was already in the same place as my father, and here I was only twenty. I felt like I was old, and I couldn't stand it. I just *had* to do something to get away from that feeling. When I cut out on work, it was sort of like I could be a kid again, just hanging around, doing what I wanted to, like cutting school and just hanging out on the street."[41]

A mother recalling the postpartum period says, "I waited all day to go to the laundromat. My husband would come home from work and I would run to go do the laundry. I usually don't give a shit about doing the laundry except that I want to have clean clothes.

"Doing the laundry became one of the most wonderful things that could happen to me. It was because I could get out of the house without the baby. I could read. There were other adults. I could even sit and stare into space."

David Steinberg, in *Fatherjournal*, writes about running away, one night, to a coffee house—"fleeing the vacuum. The dread and the panic. . . . Somehow it is all related to having a newborn baby. . . . How shall I live without being who I have been?"[42]

The changing sense of self is manifested in women's concerns about their appearance. They have changed—perhaps they are still heavier, flabbier, their breasts more pendulous. Many wonder if they should look different. Should they dress in more matronly clothes, or should they try to look the way they used to look, as fast as possible?

"I used to see mothers as asexual people," a new mother says. "You know, they wore dowdy clothes. I remember thinking that once I have a kid, I'll wear this old cruddy stuff. [When the baby was born] I found myself very much wanting to dress up every day—even if it was to go to the grocery store. I had to take a shower, put on makeup, dress up—sort of prove to myself that I could still be an attractive person. I guess because of a big fear of loss of self."

New parents have stereotypes, positive and negative, of parenthood. Walking down the street, mother and father, hand in hand, pushing a carriage, was one mother's stereotype. One day, soon after the birth, she and her husband were out with the baby in a carriage. "We looked like the little American family," she said, admitting pleasure. Another parent felt, likewise, that they had jumped into the mold of a family by having a child and that their lives would be a preordained number of steps. She fully expected someone to "call up, wanting to sell us a burial plot."

Postpartum Depression

The postpartum time is a time of change. Many people, envisioning "postpartum depression," think of it as a single bizarre time of sinking into depression, of losing contact with reality. And for some, particularly women, that can happen—a massive letdown occurring some time from days to weeks to months after the birth.

In many others, men and women, during the weeks after birth, moods are cyclical, contentment alternating with despair.

JULIANNA DANIELS

Julianna says, "I have shifts in moods. I'm slightly euphoric and slightly depressed. When I'm depressed I feel like I'm on a lowered level of everything, slightly slower and sluggish. I don't think about eating. I don't eat. Then I suddenly realize that I'm very hungry, I'm ravenous, and I gobble down food and I feel this quick energy, this up feeling."

When the parents of a new baby feel up or euphoric, their thoughts center on many of the subjects already elaborated. For instance, they revel in the miracle of the birth, they feel successful as parents, they are drawn fully to the baby in a sensual way. The dejected moods perhaps concern parents' feelings that the birth, the baby, or the experience of parenthood hasn't lived up to their expectations, that their prior education and achievements seem worthless, that their other work might suffer, or that their relationship with the other parent is altered and they feel unloved or left out.

For Julianna Daniels, "all the depressed thoughts have to do with the future and with death. I have this feeling that I will go insane if anything happens to the baby. I worry that all the perverts [on a main street in her city] will snatch her out of her carriage. I worry about my older child hurting the baby, deliberately or inadvertently. About two or three times, he's gone over to pick her up and I have this vision—I see her neck getting snapped off.

"This morning she was in her crib and he went in there and I couldn't resist going in to see what was happening. He was just looking at her. But I felt terrible because I was looking at my own child like a murderer."

A Midwestern mother of one child also gets depressed thinking about what might go wrong. "I'm in a panic that something might happen to him physically or that he'll get leukemia or some other disease. I don't think I could handle it. I'm so wrapped up in him." Other parents worry about the inexplicable crib death. Becoming attached to the new baby brings fears of loss.

Attachment also brings fears about the self. New parents sometimes worry that they will die. Some reduce the chances they've been taking—perhaps not riding on motorcycles, swimming alone, flying in airplanes, jaywalking. They make pledges to give up cigarettes or sugar or food additives or saccharine. One group of young mothers in an Appalachian city set up a chain phone system. "We wondered what would happen if we passed out or keeled over. We worried that our children would scream all day and be hysterical. So we even got to the point that if no one heard from us during the day, we would check. We were always calling each other to check in."

The concern with one's own death, after birth, is perhaps also a reflection of the symbolic death one has undergone—in the temporary loss or lack of clarity of the self. Depression after birth is attributed to many sources: the abrupt hormonal changes, the lack of sleep, the change in the life-style of the family, and in the sense of self. The people who seem to suffer the most intense depression are those who have had an image unrealized: an image about birth (perhaps that it would be a transcendent experience), about their child (that the baby would be "good" all the time), about themselves as parents (that they would be a supermother or superfather), or about parenthood (that parenthood would make them completely happy, solve all their problems). Rather than give up the image, the parent feels that it is correct while the parent or the child is the failure. The anger at the self is experienced as depression.

For those parents who eventually modify unrealistic images, the depression subsides. They get back up on their feet, so to speak, and move ahead.

Many first-time parents spoke about mastering a skill, which seems to make their new lives a lot easier. As one mother put it, "I'm learning that I can still do the things I want to do, it just takes a longer time." This mother and other parents, particularly those at home with the baby, spoke of learning to juggle their other duties, leaving and coming back, even coming back to a conversation mid-sentence after an interruption, working in fits and starts, and of learning to ask for help from one's husband or wife.

But even the asking for help and the giving of it are a new kind of negotiation.

Parent/Parent Relationships

Couples find that the birth of a baby makes them feel as if they have been transported to another land. Different systems and customs seem to prevail. The birth of a child—particularly a first child—affects couple relationships profoundly.

DAWN SIEGEL

When she is breast-feeding her five-week-old son, Dawn says, "it is just the two of us and I feel very circular about it, like there's a little wall around both of us. Nat [her husband] always touches the baby's head while I'm feeding him. I insist that it is bothering the baby. It doesn't really affect the baby at all. The baby's just sucking away like crazy. But I don't want any intrusion into that little wall. Of course, after I've breast-fed, I say, 'Sorry—I know you want to be part of this wonderful thing that both of us are going through and next time I'll let you pat his head.' And the next time comes around and I still can't stand it. It's a feeling that I never thought I'd have. I thought I'd be very loving and giving about this baby, and I'm really really not.

"We've taken the baby for walks to the park and to the zoo with the carriage and I don't even want Nat holding onto the carriage. I want to kind of push him away.

"When Nat comes home after work, it's the worst time of day. I've just changed thirteen diapers and Nat comes in and the baby smiles and of course I don't care if the baby's smiling because he's having a bowel movement, I don't want him smiling at his father after I've been with him all day, doing all the dirty work."

Dawn is returning to her job of teaching part-time soon, and her husband has arranged his schedule as a psychotherapist so that he can take care of the baby then. "Those times are going to be difficult for me," Dawn says. "All the things I thought would never bother me are things that really are bothering me."

Push/Pull Feelings

The early attachment feelings often usher in concurrent feelings of possessiveness for both new and experienced parents. Part of possessiveness is the conviction, shadowy or stark, that "I'm the only one who can take care of this baby"—"The baby isn't safe with anyone else." This feeling does not just belong to women. One father tells of racing his wife for the baby every time the baby wakes up and cries.

The wish to push others away can affect the couple relationship. Many women report an initial withdrawal from physical contact with their husbands.

ISABELLE AGNEW

"The biggest change in our marriage is sexually. Nobody ever talks about that. Ari wants to have candlelit dinners and sex. The last thing I wanted to do is to have sex. 'Please,' I said to Ari, 'don't look at me. Don't even touch me.'

"Ari says, 'Yes, but it's me. I'm your husband, you know, the one that you were married to before Micos came home.' He understands, but he's also demanding. He competes for time. He competes for attention. And for affection.

"And it upsets him that I don't want sex. It busts his ego like nothing. I told Ari, 'Sex will hurt.' I even made up excuses. After a few weeks there was no excuse and we had to deal with the fact that I just didn't feel like it.

"I asked myself, 'Why am I doing this? Is it because it hurts?' I know damn well it does not hurt. And the question is, 'Do I love Ari or have I given all my love to Micos?' No, that wasn't it. It was just plain—I do not want to have sex. Why, I don't know.

"And I was the type before that I would chase my husband everywhere. Nothing could stop us. I could have had intercourse every minute of the day."

With the new baby commanding so much attention, some fathers feel jealous. One mother says that every time she nursed the baby her husband would prod her to make love with him.

In Lillian Rubin's study of the working class, *Worlds of Pain*, a new father says, "When we were first married, I'd come home from work and [my wife would] be kind of dressed up and fixed up, you know, looking pretty for me. . . . [After the baby was born] she was too busy and too tired to pay me any mind.

"I used to get mad and holler a lot. Or else I'd stay out late at night and get her worried about what I was doing. We had nothing but fights in those days because all she wanted to do was to take care of the baby, and she never had any time for me. It sounds dumb when I talk about it now—a man being jealous of a little kid, but I guess I was."[43]

Rubin cites Nancy Chodorow's theory as a plausible explanation: that the jealousy men feel when they have a baby goes back to their own attachments to their mothers, and the fact that they had to renounce this relationship when they accepted their fathers' primary relationship to their mothers and identified with their fathers in order to be "masculine." Marriage seems to reestablish the same kind of total and exclusive relationship; then the birth of a first child disrupts and destroys it once again, making the men feel jealous and angry. As Chodorow says, "Having a child recreates the desired mother-child exclusivity for a woman and interrupts it for a man, just as the man's father intruded into his relation to his mother."[44]

On the other hand, some couples feel closer after the baby's birth, joined by creation of this child.

Most couples readily admit that, after birth, they have much less time for each other. In their study of eight couples, Philip and Carolyn Cowan asked each individual to "divide the pie," which means that on paper each person segments a circle into the roles he or she fills: husband, breadwinner, friend, etc. "Everyone chose as many of the aspects of self as were applicable and divided the pie into pieces representing each aspect." This was done before the baby was born and again six months later. The Cowans note that for most of the respondents, the space given to "partner" or "lover" was smaller after the birth of the baby.[45]

A mother says, "At night, if you start talking to your husband while the baby sleeps, oh boy, you know you're going to have to pay for it in the morning, 'cause this kid already got four hours of sleep ahead of you.

"And you know that if you're going to have a decent relationship with your husband, you're going to have to schedule it."

One task of early parenthood is to move toward enlarging the man/woman relationship to permit the addition of the baby. I use the words "move toward" deliberately because this process takes time.

Birth brings new dimensions of distance and closeness. In addition to wanting to push one's partner away, new parents concurrently want to pull the partner back, to be taken care of.

Lillian Rubin quotes a new mother as saying, "All I wanted was to be a little girl again, real little, so that somebody would take care of me."[46]

Another mother that I interviewed had a similar reaction: "About the third or fourth week after the baby was born, my house was a disaster. I was in complete disorder. I would wake up and my day would end the same way and five days would go by, and I never got a chance to wash myself. And I thought my life was going to be like that forever—until this kid could walk."

This mother realized that she wanted to be "mothered" by her husband and that she was going to have to tell him. He listened and agreed to take over more household chores. "My husband would say, 'I'm doing the dishes.' I had to accept that he was going to do them—it didn't mean do them right after we ate—maybe he would do them that night, maybe on Saturday when we had a pile twenty miles long—but if he said he was doing the dishes, I accepted it."

Her husband began taking more care of the baby. "One of the hardest things was to refrain from saying, 'I know how to do it better.'" Now, she admits, she is no longer the family expert on children, but at first she felt she was.

Other mothers or fathers do not tell their partners of this need, or perhaps they complain rather than ask for help, or their pleas meet unyielding resistance. Just as in pregnancy, new parents do need to be parented themselves. When such caring is denied, it can be harder for that parent in turn to care for the child.

Does Birth Precipitate a Crisis for the Couple?

For most couples, the disequilibrium brought by the addition of children takes a while to be righted. Many researchers, thus, label birth as a time of crisis. The sociologist E. E. LeMasters in 1957 interviewed forty-eight couples with an open-ended technique and concluded that 83 percent of these couples underwent a crisis with the birth of their first child. Reuben Hill's definition was used: "any sharp or decisive change for which old patterns are inadequate." LeMasters concludes that "the arrival of the first child destroys the two-person or pair pattern of group interaction and forces a rapid reorganization of their life into a three-person or triangle group system." [47] This study has been replicated, although altered (by a random sampling method and a structured questionnaire), by Everett Dyer in 1963 and by Daniel Hobbs in 1965 and again in 1975 by Daniel Hobbs and Sue Cole. The later study found parents expressing less dissatisfaction than in the other investigations, and Hobbs and Cole refute the term "crisis," stating that "initiating parenthood may be slightly difficult but not sufficiently difficult to warrant calling it a crisis." [48]

Nonetheless, the birth of the first child causes substantial changes in the couple relationship.

Single parents, unmarried or divorced, feel the same stresses and tensions, but often have no one ready-made partner to turn toward.

STELLA TAYLOR

Stella is a twenty-seven-year-old single parent. "The baby's father and I broke up," Stella says, "before I even knew I was pregnant. And I had a difficult decision as to whether I felt I had the strength to do it myself, to bring a child up in the way I want.

"I just left it up to God. I prayed to know what I should do and finally, when I cleared the confusion out of my head, a very clear-cut thing inside me said, 'Follow your heart.' So that's what I did. And I never, never regret it, but it hasn't been easy.

"The responsibility is constant. If I get sick, it's not like having a husband there to help me. It has never been easy for me to ask people to help me. I don't want to be a burden on other people.

"At times I wonder whether I'm adequate, to give my child what he wants." Sometimes, she wishes, "If only I had a husband."

Many other single parents, men and women, echoed that phrase. "If only this child" had a father (or a mother), then things would be better. Stella, however, has decided that "this isn't true," that though having a partner would make a big difference, it wouldn't erase the problems she occasionally has with her son. These problems reside in her—they are things she has to deal with by herself.

When parents, single and married parents, can learn this ability to ask for help, they report that parenting becomes much easier.

At first, however, some parents feel that there are few people to turn to, particularly if their family is spread out or far away. That secret society of parenthood may still seem remote, mysterious, impenetrable.

Parent/Grandparent Relationships

The new parents' relationships with their own mothers and fathers, whether they are close by or far away, also undergo similar kinds of changes right after the birth of a baby, particularly the first one. The push-pull tension prevails in this relationship, too: Help me, but don't interfere; take care of me, but understand that this is my child and I have to make my own mistakes.

Adrienne Rich writes passionately of her feelings following birth:

> Emerging from the fear, exhaustion, and alienation of my first childbirth, I could not admit even to myself that I wanted my mother, let alone tell her how much I wanted her. . . .
>
> I wanted her to mother me again, to hold my baby in her arms as she had once held me; but that baby was also a gauntlet flung down: *my son*. Part of me longed to offer him for her blessing; part of me wanted to hold him up as a badge of victory in our tragic, unnecessary rivalry as women.[49]

"My mother was here for the first week when I got home from the hospital," a mother of an infant says. "And it was great because I was totally incapable of doing anything, I was so exhausted and tired. But as soon as I was able to do things for myself and the baby, I resented my mother terribly. Of course, by that time, she already felt that she was the mother of the baby. We were walking to the supermarket, and she kept holding onto the carriage. I remember physically taking her body and pushing her almost clear across the street and everybody looking at this crazy girl, pushing her mother away from her grandchild's carriage. What kind of daughter would do that! But I didn't care. I really just said, 'This is my baby.' "

Grandparents have, as one of their developmental issues, to understand that they are the grandparents, not the parents of their child's child, and to work out the dimensions of this new role. Most new parents want to be helped without being usurped.

When the grandparent denies the help that the new parent is craving for, the crevice in their relationship widens, the split often seeming insurmountable. One new mother who had a baby with congenital problems found that her own mother "was demolished, almost as if it was happening to her, as if it were her baby." This mother says, "My mother was not the person who gave me strength. It was like I had to take care of her. So I became very tough and strong to pull my mother through it. But the pain of needing her, of not getting what I wanted, of not being able to count on her, to hug me and say it's going to be all right, hasn't healed yet."

Women also speak of yearning to be taken care of by their fathers. One mother said that she was thrilled by her father's response to her baby's birth. He was fawning and fussing over her "like I was nine years old again."

Men, as well as women, can have these same desires to be cared for by their parents. One father expressed delight that his parents came and took over after the birth.

Beyond the ambivalences in their relationship with their parents, new parents can also have mixed feelings about the attention the child is receiving from the grandparents. One mother says, "In the beginning, this incredible outpouring of love and affection on the part of my parents to the baby made me jealous, very jealous. I resented it—that was my love they were giving the baby. And I have a brother, so it wasn't like I wasn't used to sharing." Others say they are glad that their parents' attention is not so riveted on them anymore, that it has been shifted to the baby.

This is all part of the task of enlarging one's family to include one's parents.

If this is a first child, parents may feel that parenthood is the key unlocking the door to adulthood. The new grandparents often reinforce this rite of passage by their treatment of the new parents. "My mother has treated me like an adult for a long time," one thirty-year-old mother reports, "but it took the birth of my baby for my father to see me that way."

Some new parents see the baby as an offering to the grandparents, an achievement to be lauded. When the praise comes, they feel pleased. But when the grandparents seem nonplussed or even rejecting of the baby, it can be an enormous blow. One father described how his own father had checked himself into the hospital the day the baby was born and how when he came to visit, the grandfather dominated the discussion, spelling out stories of his own aches and pains, ignoring the baby.

When one or both of the grandparents have died before the birth, new parents can feel, just as in pregnancy, an intensified yearning for them.

Sibling Rivalry

If there are other children in the family, the parents have the task of enlarging the family structure to include the new baby.

There is such a mass of literature on the older child's response to the birth of a new baby, on the rejection, jealousy, possessiveness, and insecurities that the older child passes through, that it may come as a surprise that the parent, too, can have changed feelings about the older child or children after the birth of a new baby. So-called "sibling rivalry" is not a one-way street—the child changes, the parent changes.

"It's not paranoia on the part of the older sibling," the mother of two children says. "Things really are different. It must drive children crazy if they hear people say, 'Things are just the same,' or 'Mommy and Daddy love you just as much.'

"I have changed in the way I see my son. He's now instant bigness. He was my baby six weeks ago. Now I see him as being enormous.

"It seems to me that it's incredibly easy to have an infant and the hard thing is to have a four-year-old. I find I'm feeling much kindlier toward her [the baby] than I am toward him [the four-year-old].

"I used to think that Joe was smart, sweet, fun, but now I have all these doubts about him—that he might be bossy, that he might not be smart, that he might not be socially well adjusted.

"I sometimes feel that he might turn out to be a fat, aggressive, bossy, know-it-all, obnoxious ten-year-old. I'd never thought of him that way before.

"In fact, I feel absolutely mean toward Joe sometimes now. Yesterday, we were having a fight and it popped into my head to say, 'Joe, I think I'm going to send you to someone else to live'—which is exactly what he is most afraid of. The reason that I thought of saying it [although she didn't do it] was that I wanted to hurt him right then and there."

It is a tug-of-war of feelings that the parents experience—personality traits and physical attributes can seem less acceptable, and the older child can seem bigger, especially compared to the newborn baby. The parents can feel confounded when this older child acts in a babyish way. The birth of a baby does often precipitate a return to more infantile behavior for the older sibling, who perhaps reasons or senses that if the baby is getting all this attention by crying and screaming, then maybe that will work for him or her, or who just succumbs to feelings of exclusion or craves to be reassured by being held.

Thus a vicious circle can be set into motion with the parent expecting more grown-up behavior and receiving less, and the child wanting more attention and not getting it.

Another mother of a four-year-old and a new baby says, "Though I was intellectually prepared for [her daughter] Katie's intense jealousy, I was horrified at my intense anger at her. I found it hard to be loving. For a while it was pretty bad. Katie turned to my husband for support—she was very flirtatious with him. He felt left out of the relationship I had with the baby and almost seemed to encourage the rift between me and Katie.

"I had always wanted a sibling myself, and that image was shattered. So was my image of being a good mother who could handle sibling rivalry."

That the birth of a baby alters parents' responses to their other children was shown in a research study by Muriel K. Taylor and Kate L. Kogan. In this study, eight working-class children ranging in age roughly from two and a half to three and a half were videotaped in an unfamiliar room interacting with their mothers before and again after the birth of a sibling. The researchers, using an observational technique to record the behavior, discovered that "there was a consistent decrease in the expression of warmth on the part of both mothers and children." They note that their findings are only a beginning—that they are not sure what this change is caused by or how long it persists.[50]

The feelings that arise around the siblings either dissipate or harden and become permanent as time passes. Years later, though, it may be hard for parents to remember that they ever went through these changing feelings about their own children.

Changed Relationships with Relatives and Friends

Anyone who is in the close circle—family or friends—may also be perceived differently after birth.

FRANCESCA HALL

Francesca is a teenage mother. She doesn't live with her mother, who has moved away, but with her two older sisters.

"My sisters take the baby off my hands when I'm trying to do homework, but one sister gets carried away. I mean, she tries to be the baby's mother. I have to set her [the sister] in line sometimes."

When Francesca's at school, she has a baby-sitter. "She's all right—but she's always talking about stealing the baby, saying, 'I wish I could take her away.'

"Sometimes I just take the baby up and take her away myself. I'll be playing with her—my own little special time with my baby —and here comes my sister. She'll snatch her up and run off with her. So I kind of have to say, 'Hey. Don't do that. This is my time with my baby.' "

The appeal of a new baby draws in other people—parents, sisters or brothers, baby-sitters, even strangers in stores. The families of a teenage parent, seeing the new parent as still a child herself, can feel a particularly righteous claim on the new baby, which in turn can promote the possessiveness that the new parent feels, can turn it to outright competition, to the point that it has for Francesca, who feels as if other people are "snatching" or wanting to "steal" her baby. Noting these patterns, some programs for teenage parents teach them responsibility for their child and counsel their families not to intervene in the parent/baby relationship without asking or being asked.

When a parent, teenage and older, first begins leaving the baby with a baby-sitter or care-giver, doubts come creeping in. Have I done the right thing? Will the baby be safe? Will this person love and pay attention to my child? Guilt compounds the doubts. After a while, criticisms usually begin to well up—the baby is taken outside without a sweater, or has a dirty face when the parent returns home. The parents begin to feel critical, as do the care-givers, who think the parent is dressing the baby too warmly, or doesn't give the baby enough breakfast, or is spoiling the baby. Feelings of possessiveness, of wanting to keep the baby for oneself, of wanting help but also wanting to push others away, are the normal feelings that go along with attachment in the postpartum period. These feelings sweep out, including everyone who comes within the new baby's orbit—the grandparents, relatives, other children, friends, and care-givers. If there is good communication between these people and a respect for the parents' ultimate responsibility to the child, the feelings of competition begin to fade. However, if one person elevates these feelings to a battle, they can rigidify into a most difficult, exhausting relationship.

There is an irony here. A parent does need help with a new baby, whether it's just for a few minutes to run to the store unencumbered, to have time alone or together with one's husband or wife, or to go to school or work. Yet these needs parallel the feeling of wanting to have a new baby all to oneself, an aversion to sharing.

Successes in the Transition to Parenthood

"Support" is the quality that many parents desire—they want the support of their husbands or wives, friends, parents. The ideas of the home as an isolated walled garden, presided over by a mother whose exclusive job is to care for children, a mother who is isolated, cut off from support, are, according to Jessie Bernard, "the worst features of all the ways motherhood is structured around the world."[51]

There have been a number of studies of parental adaptation to the postpartum period—and most of these studies likewise conclude that having "support" is an ingredient in a successful transition to parenthood. It is an interesting concept, because it connotes a middle ground: help without taking over, listening, an understanding acceptance of new parents' feelings.[52]

Frank Pedersen and Kenneth Robson, in a research project with four-week-old infants, found a positive correlation between mothers who were more adept at care-giving and the presence of supportive fathers.[53] Of course, the obvious problem in such a study is the chicken-egg question—were the fathers more supportive because the mothers were more able, or did their support make the mothers more competent? The interlocked, interactive nature of behavior is difficult to disentangle.

Robert Fein, in an exploratory study of thirty middle-income Boston-area couples, focused on the men. He states that there is evidence that prior to birth, some couples contemplate the ways they will divide postpartum responsibilities. Men in these families seemed to cope with stresses better than men who had never discussed child-care responsibilities. According to Fein the other factors positively related to postpartum adjustment were (1) preparation for parenthood; (2) the baby's health; (3) support from one's family; and (4) support from fellow workers.[54]

Richard Gordon and his co-workers in 1965 enumerated several variables which appeared to differentiate those individuals who had the greatest postpartum problems. Again, the absence of support, particularly from grandparents, tops the list, followed by complications of the pregnancy.[55]

Beyond support, parents need adequate role models, other studies conclude. F. T. Melges found that the women who had the greatest postpartum difficulties often had mothers they didn't want to emulate.[56]

Problems in the Transition to Parenthood

In a study of thirty-five women who were actually hospitalized in the postpartum period (broadly defined from delivery to thirty-six months later, although 50 percent of the women were within the first eight months after birth), compared with thirty-five women who were not hospitalized, Bertram J. Cohler, Justin L. Weiss, and Henry V. Grunebaum found that the hospitalized mothers were unable to admit ambivalent feelings. They "view the child-rearing process in a highly stereotyped manner and respond much more in accordance with what they believe the typical mother feels or should feel about child-rearing than in terms of their own feelings."[57]

This study suggests that the women who collapsed under the strains of parenthood were clinging rigidly to the images that they had devised or put on and were unable to release.

The images that one sets provide a beacon, guiding one toward the future, providing an opportunity for growth, but conversely, images can be the stumbling blocks that stunt and cripple growth.

Being aware of the power that these images exert on us, finding out what our own images are, working toward them, and adapting them when necessary are processes that begin in pregnancy and are fundamental to feelings of success or failure in the postpartum period.

REDEFINING RELATIONSHIPS IN THE EARLY YEARS

The birth of a baby creates a momentary sense of imbalance within a family. The parents, their other children, and their own parents are caught in the wake of unsettled feelings as they make room for and become attached to the new baby. *As the postpartum period passes, parents face a new task: the task of beginning to right this imbalance. They find that they now are redefining many of the relationships within their family, including their ever-changing relationship with the new baby.*

JENNY RANDALL

"I'm always two steps behind my son's development," says Jenny, a Midwestern social worker and the mother of a six-month-old boy. "I get to the point where I feel that I really understand this baby, and then he changes. All of a sudden I look at him and say, 'I don't know this child. This child is a stranger to me.'

"Part of me wants to hold onto the younger infant—part of me wants to let him grow. He develops much faster than I do."

After the first months of life, the parent-child relationship becomes increasingly more reciprocal, or in the psychoanalyst Donald Winnicott's phrase, more "mutual."[58] Louis Sander terms the time from approximately two and a half to five months the "Period of Reciprocal Exchange."[59] Margaret Mahler describes the child as hatching out of the symbiotic orbit between mother and child at about four to five months and beginning to move toward separation-individuation.[60]

The infant social smile is the milestone that the latter two researchers use as the sign of this emerging period.

Parents, too, have a tendency to choose key or "marker events," to use Daniel Levinson's term, as representative of each step in their changing relationship with their child.[61] The first smile is often this remembered event, but parents have different ones, too—the baby's first step, or first hurt, or when the baby's hair or breath loses that sweet, always fresh infant smell. One father recalls walking down the street toward home and seeing his wife and baby. The baby, from a distance, recognized him and began kicking with delight, seemingly trying to propel herself, in her stroller, forward to him. It was a magic moment for this father.

When growth seems stagnant, stilled even, there is an urge to stir things up, to rush ahead. Despite all knowledge to the contrary, parents, particularly first-time parents, feel stuck in time, feel that the phase that they or the child is in will go on forever. Then a forward thrust of growth occurs and the parents experience a backwash of feelings, a desire to slide back or stay put.

Every step of growth brings losses and gains for both parents and child. As the postpartum period passes, there is a slight decrease in the feeling of sensory union with the baby and an increase in the give and take of the parent-child relationship. The baby, as Daniel Stern's research shows, has the ability to attract, initiate, sustain, and turn away from social interchange.[62]

Changing as the Baby Changes

Parents learn another facet of reading and responding to the baby's cues and clues: being able to change as the baby changes. The establishment of this parental skill is of enormous importance to the child's development—for it is through a personal, sensitive responsiveness, through the mutual, stimulating, changing relationships, that children develop their capacity to use language, to think, and to learn.[63]

For instance, a child throws a rattle on the floor. The parent retrieves it. The child throws it again—and it becomes a game, punctuated with words. Then the child changes the game—hands the rattle to the parent for the next round of throwing. This interchange may not seem momentous, but it is as incidents like this occur on a day-after-day basis that the child increasingly develops thinking and learning skills.

This ability to change as the baby changes applies not only to playing with the baby, but also to caring for the baby. A certain way of comforting a baby may work one week and not the next. Techniques of spoon-feeding, of burping, changing diapers, putting the baby to sleep, cannot be adopted permanently. They have to be evaluated and reevaluated as the baby grows.

Novelty is an important ingredient in relationships. The researcher Richard Bell notes from his observations of mother-child interaction that a new kind of behavior tends to attract both the child's and the mother's attention, renewing both their interests, whereas a lack of novelty seems to diminish attention. Bell hypothesizes that "it is possible that a decrement in maternal attachment would occur were it not for general changes in infant behavior."[64]

STEPHANIE AND CHIP SMITH

When Nell was a newborn, she fell asleep in Stephanie's or Chip's arms and then they lifted her into her crib. As she grew older, they put her to sleep by walking her back and forth.

"I didn't mind doing that at first," Stephanie says. "It took a few minutes and it was okay." Then Nell got heavier and it began to take longer for her to fall asleep. Stephanie felt as if she were wearing a hole in the floor. "It had reached the point of no return. It didn't work anymore. And I was going nuts.

"So I took a poll: I asked all my friends how they put their kid to bed. I talked to my mother, to Chip's, and called the pediatrician."

"We finally came to the conclusion that we were going to have to put her down and let her cry," Chip says. "And the first time, she cried for half an hour and we felt like criminals. The second night, she cried for ten minutes and we felt like misdemeanors as opposed to felons. And since then, she's gone off to sleep very easily, so it was worth that first half hour of agony."

Chip and Stephanie felt all right about this decision because they were very responsive to Nell's crying during the day and because her crib was close by in an alcove off the living room where they sat while she went to sleep.

In figuring out such issues, parents have to listen to their own feelings about how their chosen course of action is affecting them as well as the baby. This requires another skill—for the parents to trust themselves and trust the child, not blindly, but based on an appraisal of their own and their child's abilities and weaknesses.

Giving and Getting

Many of the issues in the nurturing stage can be distilled to a singular question: How much should I give and how much should I be given to or get? Attachment is giving and receiving.

It is a hard question for parents to answer because the consequences of one or another course are not necessarily immediately clear. The Smiths were "giving" to their baby by picking her up when she cried; they were giving her a sense that the people in her world care about her, will feed her when she's hungry, comfort her when she's sad. They were giving her what Erik Erikson has termed "basic trust," and what Therese Benedek has called "confidence," or the assurance that her environment is trustworthy.[65]

But then they felt as if they had crossed an invisible line. They had gone beyond providing nurturance, and even their message, though perhaps not consciously, had changed. Rather than communicating that the environment is safe, they were almost saying that sleep is not safe—that they had to shield the baby from it. So they had to shift to get back to their original message.

Adrienne Rich writes:

> Most of the literature of infant care and psychology has assumed that the process toward individuation is essentially the child's drama, played out against and with a parent or parents who are, for better or worse, givens. Nothing could have prepared me for the realization that I was a mother, one of those givens, when I knew I was still in a state of uncreation myself. That calm, sure, unambivalent woman who moved through the pages of the manuals I read seemed as unlike me as an astronaut.[66]

Rich writes of early parenthood as being a "continually changing dialogue."

David Steinberg writes:

> As soon as I get oriented to one of [my son] Dylan's patterns, he changes and a whole new pattern begins to evolve. It's like standing up in a roller coaster. I'm finding that the more I accept this constant change, the more I can enjoy the dynamics of it, the constant growing. Dylan is deepening my sense of change as a way of life.[67]

Parenthood is a trial-and-error process based on reading one's own and the child's cues. It is working toward clarity and consistency, but also being able to admit one's mistakes, face one's weaknesses, and change as the child changes.

This is a time of parallel discoveries—the parents discovering things about themselves and their child, the child discovering new words, new ideas, new places, new people. Parents usually delight in watching as their child, for instance, figures out how to work the light switch, or chase a leaf spinning around in the currents of air as it drops from a tree, or crawl after an ant that is dragging a crumb across the floor.

Holding On/Letting Go

Change in childhood and parenthood always entails separation. The child moves away from his or her parents by the increasing physical ability to turn over, to turn away, to hide, to sit up, to hold food, to use language.

The mother of an eleven-month-old says, "The issue that I'm dealing with right now is giving my daughter space, not being on top of her all the time. If I'm in the dining room and she goes crawling down the hall, I have to tell myself not to run after her. I want to give her the space to move out and yet to make sure that it's a safe place for her to move out into."

Toward the end of the first year, the baby is a study in contradictions. At one moment, she or he seems totally fearless, scooting or crawling out of sight or to the top of steep stairs or the edge of the bed, or yanking a tangle of electric wires, or trying to topple a floor lamp. The next moment, this same baby seems full of fear, clinging to the mother or father, face buried, refusing to budge. This is the time of "stranger anxiety." The baby, previously undaunted when handed from person to person or tickled under the chin by strangers at the supermarket, now may scream or cry or turn away from a stranger or less well-known person, particularly if that person intrudes into what Daniel Stern calls the "psychological bubble," the invisible barrier that people erect around themselves, the distance they keep between themselves and others.[68]

Parents of this age children do sometimes feel as David Steinberg does, as if they are "standing up in a roller coaster," buffeted between being desperately needed and being ignored, wanting to push the child toward more independence, wanting to keep the child a little baby. The trapeze act of holding on and letting go, knowing when to lean which way, dealing with the dichotomy of feelings, is a theme of the separateness/connectedness relationship.

This theme can become even more pronounced as the child learns to walk. When the child goes through the phase of grabbing onto the parents' finger, pulling forward, one foot swinging out, then the next, the parents can feel as if their child is glued onto them, a permanent wind-up toy, ready to go. Then the child masters walking and goes everywhere, streaking or stumbling away, without looking back, in department stores, perhaps dangerously near the edge of the sidewalk. Then, just as resolutely, the child, hands up, refuses to walk, won't budge, wants to be carried everywhere.

Holding On and Letting Go: Images and Reality

As with every phase of parenthood, for some parents this time can contain half-hidden barriers, tripping them over an image of themselves.

ROSALIE DIXON

Rosalie, a woman in her mid-twenties, felt totally overprotected as a child. "My father did everything for me. He made me feel I wasn't capable. I fought him every inch of the way. I didn't want to have things done for me, but he always did anyway.

"When I was seventeen, I ran away from home. I felt like I had no perspective on who I was and what I wanted from life."

For a while, Rosalie sang in a coffeehouse in a large city, but felt lonely and went home, getting a job as a nurse's aide and eventually ending up as a member of a religious commune.

She has, in effect, moved from one protective environment, her home, to another, the religious commune. In her home, her father dominated; in the commune, the leader does. Nevertheless, Rosalie has decided not to be overprotective with her son, fifteen months old, an ideal which she is now finding difficult.

"I can see why my parents protected me. I can see why they didn't want me to get hurt because I now have the same feelings. I don't want my son to get hurt. But because I saw what happened to me, I have to watch myself constantly so that I don't make my son feel like he can't do things. It's a constant walking on the fine line of not protecting him too much and yet protecting him enough."

As children venture out into the world, as they explore, they are learning to turn the trust they felt in their parents and care-givers back to the self, to gain a sense of autonomy vs. shame or doubt in Erik Erikson's developmental schema.[69] The same issue that faces parents, holding on or letting go, faces the young toddler.

When parents feel a lack of confidence in themselves, it may be more difficult for them to pass confidence on to their children. For this reason, many psychoanalysts have focused on parenthood as an opportunity for adults to deal with the still-painful issues left over from childhood. For instance, as a parent Rosalie has to face the fact of her own temerity; at times she even has to conquer it because she doesn't want her son to suffer from the same fears.

Connections to Grandparents

Parents continue to work at the task of enlarging their relationship with their own parents to include the baby. They are also involved in the task of redefining their relationships. But now, their judgments have been tempered by the experience of parenthood. This often brings new levels of empathy for emotions that formerly seemed unreasonable.

ISABELLE AGNEW

"I always told my mother, 'You worry about us too much. I don't know why you worry. You know that I'm fine, so stop worrying.'

"Now I understand that you never stop being a mother—even when your children grow up. My mother came to see me— and I was shy to tell her, but I did. I said, 'Now I understand why you tell me that you worry.' I told my mother, 'It's like we're on the same level now—it's no longer that you're up here and I'm down there. We're on the same level.' "

JESSIE GREEN

Jessie, Dennis's wife and the mother of year-old Anna, says, "I think about my parents in an entirely different light. I now realize that they went through the exact same things with me that I'm going through with Anna. They changed my diapers and carried me around and hugged and kissed me. They felt the same way about me that I feel about Anna—had that same incredible rush of love.

"As much as I love and respect my parents, it's a completely different sort of feeling from the one that I feel toward Anna. So I know now that they have *always* felt differently about me than I have about them. That's very eye-opening."

Becoming a parent gives people more understanding of their origins, more understanding of their parents as people who have themselves passed through different phases of parenthood. Becoming a parent also seems to enable people to comprehend the rush and tumble, the foibles of humanity, with more compassion.

Jessie's husband, Dennis, says, "After a year of being a father, I find that I've changed in a sense that's very hard to describe, but there seems to be more resonance to my life. I do suddenly feel connected to the past and the future. I never felt that before—in fact, all of my feelings were feelings of being cut off, both cut off from my parents, the immediate past, and the future."

Part of the sense of a connection to the past is that seeing the grandparents with their grandchildren, seeing the way the grandparents talk, what they do, brings back memories for the parents. And for some, despite an increased understanding, the grandparents' behavior may still seem unacceptable.

ETHAN FRANK

Ethan is a commercial artist who has separated from his wife. He is the father of a two and a half year old, Jonathan.

"I took Jonathan to see my mother last week and got an enormously intense dose of what it was like for me to be a child. I sat back and I watched her with him and I saw myself as I was mothered. It was frightening to me, and it sort of clarified a lot of the reasons why I was doing what I was doing.

"My mother has no empathy for what it's like to be a child. She couldn't get into Jonathan's mind and think, 'How is he feeling in this situation?' She was all rules, without thoughts.

"We were there for two minutes. Jonathan hadn't seen her for six months. And she asked him if he wanted to go off with her while I parked the car. He said that he didn't want to be separated from me—after just two minutes. She thought, then, that I was pampering him too much.

"My parents are extremely negative—not in a cruel way. It's so subtle that I'm not sure they are even aware that they are being negative. I mean, they say, 'I love you. You are wonderful.' Then there's always a *but* at the end of every sentence.

"The first thing she said (after exclaiming over him) was, 'But you're still in diapers.'

"Then she says, 'You don't eat. What's wrong with you?' She's never satisfied with the situation.

"I discovered another thing from that visit—my mother never gave to Jonathan. There was always a barter involved. She had promised to take him to a store for a toy the next day. When he was getting ready for bed, he was fussy and she said that if he didn't stop crying, if he wasn't a good boy, they weren't going to the store.

"It is like you're going to the store only when you've earned the right to go to the store.

"It's like I'll only give to you if you give me whatever it is that I want—being a good boy, loving me, being a good piece of display for the neighbors.

"The overall effect is that I don't trust anyone. When someone wants to give to me, I expect that there's something that they're going to take away."

One way that his upbringing has affected him was in nurturing Jonathan. He feels that he overdoes it, especially when Jonathan was first born, "where because of my fear of not giving enough, I gave him too much, I gave a hundred and fifty percent."

Prospective and new parents often fear that they will, by some ironic twist of fate, turn out exactly like their own parents. It seems as if parenthood is automatically accompanied by an unwanted personality implantation.

This fear is reinforced because parents, unwilling or not, can step into using the very same words, the same gestures, the same behavior as their parents did.

In reality, parents do not necessarily replicate their own parents' problems. Often those issues that affected the parents also affect the children as parents—and the problem-laden aspects of their own growing up are rekindled as their children reach these same points of development. In an effort to right what they see as their parents' wrongs, parents can go too far in the other direction—as is the case with Ethan Frank. His behavior is, temporarily at least, an overreaction to his parents' behavior.

But parents, particularly if they have support in doing so, can become different, even different in a moderate way, from their own parents. Many can and do succeed in living up to their images.

Grandparents can hasten or retard this process. If the grandparents are complimentary, this usually gives the new parents sustenance, it seems to fill them up with an emotional nourishment. If, on the other hand, grandparents are critical, displeased, it can be difficult, an added source of tension for the new parents.

GLORIA EAGLETON

Gloria and her husband have two very young children. They live in the rural South.

"My parents," she says, "feel guilty because *I* do things differently, and my in-laws try to make *me* feel guilty that I'm not doing things the way they did."

Gloria says that in many ways she is like her own parents. But if she veers from their ways, they take it as a negative judgment of their own parenting.

Gloria finds she has substantive differences with her in-laws. They are uncomfortable when she lets the children run around the house naked. Her father-in-law once roared at her, "If you don't get a diaper on that child, I'm going to leave."

"I got furious," Gloria says. "He could have just said, 'Look. It's bothering me.' I would have respected that—rather than make my child feel that there's something wrong with his body.

"My husband had that kind of hang-up when we got married. He'd blush from head to toe if I walked in on him in the bathroom.

"My first reaction was that I didn't want my father-in-law back in my house again. But I finally have decided that I'm going to keep the children dressed when he's around.

"My in-laws are not open. I wish we could talk about this, but we can't."

These are complex problems. It is customary in our society for adults to carve out areas of uniqueness, to differentiate themselves from their own parents. And the grandparents, as one of their development issues, have to come to terms with their grown children's individuality.

These issues—such as whether to let the toddler run around without diapers, how many toys to buy, how to respond to a crying baby, how much to feed, when to introduce solid foods, when and how to wean—can cause conflicts between grandparents and parents as well as between the mother and father.

The reason that Gloria's own parents "feel guilty" when she does something differently is that their behavior was predicated on images and Gloria's new route is not only challenging what they did, it is also challenging what they believe—or their images of parenthood. The loss or weakening of an image can be very painful.

Gloria, on the other hand, has drawn some of her images in opposition to sexual repression of her husband as a child. And when she sees her father-in-law attempt to reinstate this style, it is likewise battering away at one of her strongly held images.

Reestablishing Couple Relationships

The disequilibrium that shook the couple relationship after the birth of the baby, particularly a first baby, continues to reverberate in the infant and toddler years. *Parents continue to work at the dual task of including this new child in the family while reestablishing their relationship as a couple.* The cause of turbulence, when it occurs, can often be traced back to conflicted or conflicting images.

MARGARET AND ROBERT GAINES

When Margaret Gaines met her future husband, Robert, he was seventeen years old and feeling very bitter about his father—a man who refused to eat with his family and who often said, "I should never have had children." At twenty-three, Robert and Margaret married, and when they talked about having a family, they both agreed that they wanted Robert to be a very involved father. Yet, when their first child, Andy, was born, Robert literally turned his back on him. "I had trouble giving to Andy," Robert says, "because I was never given to as a child. My father never gave me anything—no toys, no time, not even the car when I was a teenager. I wanted to be a different kind of father, but I couldn't—I began to resent Andy for having so much more than I had."

Robert and Margaret had discussed their images of parenthood, they shared an image, and yet when they had a child, they found their behaviors didn't match up to this belief.

They decided they both were still committed to their image and that they would work on it. The first way was for Robert to have some of the things that he was deprived of as a child: time, attention, some material things. Secondly, they set up a time to talk together in the evenings, a time in which they could talk about what went right and wrong in their days, discuss their feelings about each other and their son, and try to solve problems as they arose.

All new parents have to resolve this issue of responsibility—who is going to do what, when. Those parents who have stepped outside of a traditional, woman-centered system of responsibility for the children may find themselves having problems at first.

Philip and Carolyn Cowan, with John and Lynn Coie from the Becoming a Family Project at the University of California at Berkeley, have developed one of the few parent discussion groups that includes both parents.

The Cowans found that the couples did not share their images of parenthood. Philip Cowan says, "I get the picture sometimes of two people who may be very much in love and very much together, having private dreams that shape their lives, but not letting each other know the content."[70]

In their group, the Cowans and Coies tried to help the partners bring their pictures of becoming a family into the light and eventually to find ways to handle change and resolve differences.

For many, parenting young children means that their own adult relationships are relegated to backstage. The mother of two young children says, "If you had told me when we were first married that we would go for two weeks without making love, I wouldn't have believed it. Now we just can't find the time. Often we're so exhausted we just collapse into bed and we're asleep."

The mother of a two-year-old says, "He's working. I'm working. He gets home about seven. Then there's the time with our child. After that, we collapse. I sometimes feel that we mechanized our lives so that when it's time to go to sleep, we've done what has to be done. But there's a price. My husband and I have lost sight of each other."

Another mother of a twenty-two-month-old says that after she and her husband put their child to bed, they "sit like zombies and look at TV. We're both crazy about our son and that makes us feel warm toward each other, but he's our focus right now."

Some relationships unfortunately deteriorate after the birth of a child. As Carolyn Cowan writes, "The babies themselves, in our view, do not *cause* the difficulties for most couples. Babies come into an already-established relationship between the parents; their arrival can shed light on differences in partners' expectations about family life." [71]

ETHAN FRANK

"Amanda and I had been married seven or eight years before Jonathan was born. Things were always rocky—bad and good, good and bad. We separated for a year and we got together and things really got good. We felt that we had somehow gotten ourselves on solid footing and we decided to have Jonathan. We felt we were ready to have a child.

"But, the fact of the matter is that the footing was so soft, the foundation on which it was built was so weak, that the pressures of Jonathan collapsed it. Jonathan was a difficult baby. He had trouble sleeping. He cried all the time. He was incredibly hard work.

"We didn't give each other any support. We spent most of our time being parents, giving all of our support to Jonathan. We always had the feeling that we were never giving him enough; at the same time we resented him enormously for the demands he was making on us.

"We had decided before Jonathan was born that we were going to share fifty-fifty in the responsibilities of taking care of him. We would argue about who was doing more. I can remember an argument where she thought she was giving sixty percent and I was giving forty percent, but I thought I was giving sixty percent if not seventy percent.

"The answer was that we were both giving a lot, and it was a drain.

"To be simplistic, Amanda became the aggressive blamer and I was the guilty withdrawer.

"We never did the simplest things to give ourselves time together. We never got a baby-sitter, never went out together. Our lives together just ceased to exist."

When their son was two, Ethan made the final with-drawal—against Amanda's wishes: He left.

Now, six months later, he says, "It seems too simple in retro-spect. It seems that if I were to become a parent now I could do it better."

But even that knowledge hasn't changed the quality of his rela-tionship or even his attachment to Amanda. He is still battling with her over time with Jonathan. She continues to blame and punish, by threatening to move far away. He still feels guilty that he isn't giving enough, that the separation has hurt Jonathan.

For others, the birth of a child improves their relationship.

MAXINE AND JACOB ROSS

Maxine and Jacob waited a long time to have a child. Maxine says, "A lot of my excess mothering needs went into taking care of Jacob. I think that it was good that Jane [their baby] intervened to help us interact more as adults to each other rather than as a parent/child thing."

Jacob also feels that the birth of Jane, now over one year old, has improved his relationship with Maxine. "I tended to have a bad temper and was difficult to live with. I'm not a believer in the cliché that if you repress your temper it will boil up in another area. I think that temper is a muscle. If you use it, it gets stronger. If you don't exercise it, it goes away.

"My parents were screamers. They always fought with each other. Before Jane was born, we tended to have bad fights about once a week.

"After she was born, I felt that it was my responsibility to stop raising my voice, since I was the one who previously brought that into the relationship.

"Since she's been born, we've only had one bad fight, and even that wasn't as bad as the kinds of fights we used to have. Jane has been sort of a moral conscience, like those cartoons where this little angel sits over your shoulder and says, 'Ah, ah—don't do that.'

"You suddenly see yourself from her point of view. Whenever I feel myself beginning to lose my temper, it's a moral cost accounting that goes on. But it's worth it to give Jane this vision of life."

Finding a balance in giving to the baby, to oneself, and to one's partner is a task in the nurturing and subsequent stages. Giving is only really possible in a sustained way if one is getting at the same time. If that has been a problem since childhood—that is, if one wasn't nurtured as a child—it is often more difficult to be able to give as an adult. In parenthood, the volcanic issues from one's past—perhaps quieted, perhaps almost forgotten—begin to rumble and bubble up. Parenthood gives people deeper, more complex, and more complete views of themselves if they can or are able to look, and an opportunity, although often a very difficult one, to reach back to old feelings.[72]

Friends and Mentors

Because giving and getting are so important in the nurturing stage, friendships, too, are affected and become elevated to a station they have perhaps not had since adolescence. In the first years of parenthood, friendships can be like lifelines out into the world.

Marilyn French, in *The Women's Room*, writes about new, suburban mothers:

> They spent most of their free time in each other's kitchens and yards. They sat over coffee, hot or iced, and a home-baked, packaged coffee cake, watching the children
> . . . Their daily conversation drew them very close. Most of them would never again know with such detail and intimacy the elements of others' lives.
> . . . They gave, through good humor and silent understanding, support and affection and legitimacy to each other and to the concerns they shared.[73]

These friendships do not exist for everyone—some people find that they are isolated, locked into their apartment or home, knowing few people. The customs and traditions for new-parent friendships vary by region, community, and neighborhood. In an industrial, highly transient neighborhood in the Midwest, new parents stay to themselves. In a Southwestern suburb, there is a ritualized meeting: coffee on Tuesdays. In a Northeastern town, the kaffee-klatches are more spontaneous and informal. In a Northern city, new parents meet day after day in the playgrounds and parks. More often than not, these friendships are the dominion of full-time mothers.

But employed mothers and fathers have the same pulls.

"I find," an employed mother of a two-year-old says, "that since I have a child, I'm much more drawn to other people with children.

"With my friends without children, I just can't give them my undivided attention. I feel guilty that I'm depriving them of my time.

"It seems that the people with children understand that when conversations get interrupted, you're still paying attention to them even when you're looking over to one side, trying to feed a child."

"The best thing that's happened since our child was born is getting to know people with children," a father says. "A year ago we knew one couple that had children. We've met literally dozens of couples with children two years old or younger. It's expanded our horizons immensely."

Competition can creep into these relationships. Whose child

walks or talks the best? Whose child is the biggest or smartest? Then rather than being supportive, these relationships can become undermining.

When new parents spend time together, they often probe for common feelings—whether or not other parents are experiencing life as they are, and whether other children are going through this or that phase. Some parents use each other as backboards—dribbling out their worries, bit by bit, and letting them bounce back. Parents also use each other for specific help in the solving of problems. They ask for and dispense advice. Ultimately, these friendships provide the guidelines in the new game of parenthood, helping parents through the fumbling toward an understanding of the subtle principles that prevail. Often it is in these friendships that parents try to establish what is normal, what isn't.

These friendships can also exist for the children. People notice that it can be very pleasant to be with their child when other young children are around. The children sustain each other. Even as infants and toddlers, they notice and play together, handing toys back and forth, climbing up and down on the couch, hiding together behind a door. The growth of parent discussion groups and play groups represents a formalization of a long-standing informal tradition of parents seeking out other parents for themselves and children for their children.

These friendships, whether formal or informal, are a link for the new parent—feeling in part that they have postponed the adult part of themselves in becoming a parent, they, with their friends, move back toward recouping the loss. There at least they are able to traverse in both the worlds of adulthood and childhood.

New parents also look for mentors, other parents who do things seemingly the right way. They seek these people out, to emulate, even to serve as a guard, who, by example, will protect them from their more negative feelings.

Because, too, new parents often worry and question their own adequacy—Am I doing the right thing?—they can fall prey to a dependency on "experts," either other parents or professionals. In some cases, these experts, undermine the parents' own sense of adequacy.

Parents in the nurturing stage eventually find the necessity of achieving a balance in giving and receiving. They find that they are connected to others in many powerful ways. But this point seems to contradict the cultural picture of motherhood—the mother alone, contentedly with her baby.

Away on the Job

Traditionally, attachment theory has assumed that it is the mother who raises the children. This is not true for mothers at home—all have other people to help—husbands or relatives, or neighbors or baby-sitters who help them. This assumption, furthermore, bypasses the reality of the large increase in households headed by single women and of working mothers. Recent figures from the U.S. Department of Labor show that 35 percent of the mothers with children under three worked in the labor force. These figures, despite a tight job market, show no downward decline. In fact, the largest labor-force increase since 1960 has been for women with children under three.[74]

But then, what happens to the mother's attachment to the baby if she has a job? This trend has never been studied from the parent's point of view, only from the child's.

I have found from interviews with many parents—fathers and mothers—that when the mother of an infant or toddler returns to work, both parents initially feel a powerful surge of guilt, of questioning. Am I or are we doing the right thing? Will the mother's not being at home hurt the child—now or later? Will I or we be able to find adequate child care? Will the baby be safe? Will the baby be loved?

If there is no ready-made baby-sitter, if parents have to seek out child care, this search can be fraught with feeling—of annoyance at getting entangled with the bureaucracy of the outside world much too soon in the child's life, of guilt, of fear and repulsion when less than adequate child care is seen. Finally, if an acceptable care-giver or child-care program is found, parents feel relieved.

When the mother begins her job, she (as do fathers) finds it difficult to say good-bye to her child in the morning. The early push and pull feelings return in full force. Parents want help, want the child care, and yet they fear it, want to shove it away. Questioning and reassuring themselves, they feel hopeful and doubtful. Unwelcome fears streak through their minds—what if the child is hurt, rejected, cries all day, eats something unsafe, falls off a swing?

The change of routine can be difficult, too. Parents have to shift their own tempo, moving from an adult pace at work to a child pace at home. They have to make this transition at a time of day when both the parent and the child are tired—when the child may be especially demanding, when the parent may be worn down. Although they can get used to making the transition, for many it remains the hardest part of the day.

Furthermore, in the first few weeks, as the care-giver or baby-sitter becomes attached to the baby, normal feelings of competition, jealousy, resentment arise, both on the part of the parents and on the part of the baby-sitter or care-giver.

These feelings can become difficult—the parent and the care-giver can become competitive—or if problems are dealt with and solved, and communication lines are open, they can cooperate.

The parent's image is paramount. If the couple wants and expects the wife to be employed, and if the child-care arrangement lives up to or exceeds the parent's expectations, parents feel happy, even exhilarated. If, on the other hand, one or both of them expect the mother to stay home full-time, but she wants or needs to go to work, there can be an uneasy truce fraught with defensive rationalizations or denial, which may or may not be easily resolved.[75]

Child Care: Effects on the Parent-Child Relationship

It is important to remember that child care is not by nature bad, parenting good. There can be all shades of both—ranging in quality. But the quality of child care is a social, political, and policy issue. Because of the increase in numbers of working mothers, there have been many calls for research on the question of what happens if the child care is not adequate, if the young child is cared for by an uncaring, unresponsive person, or if the care is not consistent or not of high quality.

The research that has been done so far, such as the Infant/Toddler Day Care Study by Abt Associates, suggests that large group size and untrained care-givers are not beneficial.[76] This, too, is the contention of Selma Fraiberg in her book *Every Child's Birthright*.[77]

Much of the research that has been done has focused on model infant/toddler centers. "Model" means that the staff is caring and emotionally responsive to each child, that there is a low staff/child ratio, small group size, and a consistent, relatively unchanging staff, and that the program is stimulating, intellectually and physically.

The research has looked at the effects of infant/toddler day care on the child, asking whether day care weakens the child's attachment to the mother. To test that, researchers have generally used the method developed by Mary Ainsworth. The child is brought to an unfamiliar room for approximately twenty to forty minutes. The mother, the care-giver, and a stranger or family friend are there. The adults come in, perhaps exchange seats, and leave. The child's response to each of the adults is carefully watched, particularly affiliative behavior (whom the child smiles at, approaches, or plays with) and attachment behavior (whom the child turns to for comfort in distress). These results are compared with those obtained from a control group of children and parents, matched for age, sex, social-economic group, and ethnic background.[78]

In 1970, Bettye Caldwell and some of her colleagues at the Syracuse Children's Center reported on a study comparing eighteen thirty-month-old children who had been in good day-care programs since they were between six and fifteen months with twenty-three children who were not in day care. These observers found no difference in the children's attachment to their mothers between these groups of children.[79]

The most often quoted study was headed by Jerome Kagan of Harvard University. He studied thirty-five Chinese-American and Caucasian children at twenty months old who had been in a good day-care program since they were between three and a half and five and a half months old, comparing them with an equal number of children without day-care experience. Kagan found that there were no differences between the groups; the children all preferred their mothers when they were bored or distressed, and the same proportion of each group cried when their mothers left the room. The researchers concluded that children in day care were no less attached to their mothers than children without day care.[80]

There have been several summaries of the research on day care and attachment.[81]

Henry Riccuiti, author of such a report for HEW, concluded that "the research thus far is based for the most part on children in day care facilities set up to demonstrate high quality infant care." But with that in mind, "there appears to be little or no persuasive empirical research evidence thus far indicating that infant day care experience is likely to have unfavorable developmental consequences."[82]

These studies, in my opinion, are just a first step. Most look at a child in a highly artificial environment, rather than in the home or the child-care setting. They exclude fathers, they disregard the opinions of parents and care-givers, and most don't look at the broader or long-term effects on the child.

Child Care: Effects on Parents

There is also a comparable need for a study of the adults: What effect does full-time child-care responsibility or full-time employment have on fathers' and mothers' relationships to their children? What are the effects of part-time work or flexible work schedules? Though these options are not yet common in the United States, other industrialized countries, notably Sweden, are moving toward longer and shared parental leaves at birth, ample time off for taking care of sick children and making school visits, and shorter working hours for both fathers and mothers. Sheila Kamerman from the Columbia School of Social Work feels that this route can counter the effects of industrialization, what Urie Bronfenbrenner calls "the isolation of children from the world of work," by bringing these two aspects of life closer together.[83]

Though part-time work or flexible hours are an unlikely possibility in the lives of many new parents, the conflicts, compromises, and pleasures of employment and family are not. They are a theme of thought running through the first years of parenthood.

Parenthood does not happen in a vacuum. Other influences impinge on the parents from conception on: the treatment by doctors, nurses, employers, neighbors, friends, strangers. Parents are affected by everything—from the weather to the state of the economy to the current, topical social attitudes. All are mainlined into parents' perceptions as they shape and reshape their images of themselves as parents.

Identity in the Nurturing Stage

In the Nurturing Stage, parents continue to deal with the questions of identity that were seeded in the Image-Making Stage: What kind of parent do I want to be? What kind of parent am I being? Who am I apart from being a parent? Often they fantasize about themselves in the future—with question marks: Who will I be when all of this is over?

Eleanor Johnson

Eleanor Johnson describes herself as an average person. She lives in an Appalachian city, in a new development, where identical houses dot the spiraling streets in regular intervals, like a patterned tape sewn into the landscape. She was a teacher, is now happy to be the mother of a twenty-two-month-old son.

"I think I'm going through an identity crisis," she says. "Who am I? When I was growing up the goal was to get married, have children, live happily ever after. I believed that. You know, it's not quite that easy."

Yet, she feels that even this identity crisis is normal. "Everybody goes through it. It's nothing unusual—just something I have to cope with."

ALEXANDRIA THOMAS

Alexandria lives in a similar development, red brick houses punctuating the green squares of grass, yet where Eleanor's development is all-white, Alexandria's is all-black in a city in the South.

Alexandria enjoys her children, yet she too is feeling "discontent. I feel like I've kind of lost my identity and I don't know where to find it."

CAMILLA GOLDMAN

Camilla lives in a renovated Colonial house in an expensive Eastern suburb. She, too, has a young child. "When we used to drive through the country, we'd pass through towns and we'd see these people, sitting at their windows, looking out. I used to wonder what kind of lives they had—what could have led them to these windows looking out like that.

"Well, now I'm one of those people who sits at the window. I didn't know it would be so hard—these questions of who am I and who am I going to be that you deal with."

These women, all full-time mothers, have made large changes in their lives. The questions reflect these changes: Was what I did right? What will I do when the children begin to grow up, move away? And if having a child was seen as a solution to other problems—problems in a marriage or with a job—parents begin to see that children are not a forever solution, that they will eventually have to deal with the problem itself.

With the birth of a child, parents feel as if they give up or postpone or lose part of themselves. The child changes how they allocate their time. The child also changes how they make decisions.

Often, when the child is alternatively clinging and adventuresome, parents begin to see a glimmer of the future. This is when issues of identity arise.

ELIZABETH TOBIN

Elizabeth lives in a large city in a postage-stamp-sized apartment with her husband and two-year-old daughter. She has a very busy schedule, between teaching and pursuing graduate studies. Suddenly she is confused. What does she want to do? How much time should she put into taking care of her child? How much time into her work? What kind of mother does she want to be?

ANTHONY LEFCOURT

Anthony lives in a house he and his wife share with several other couples. He has modified his schedule as a community organizer and leader to spend time with his two-year-old.

"It feels like I'm doing something quite right, but it puts me into conflict with my old, leftover image of what it is to be a man.

"Sometimes, when I'm with my daughter, the thought comes crowding in on me that I am not pursuing my career. And so I go through all kinds of changes about my identity as a man.

"I have a feeling that I could be quite content as a house husband, taking care of the house, being with my daughter. I would still have to have something else for myself, but I could get into that. But then I feel that I'm not allowed to be that. I have this other stuff about what it is to be a man. It plagues me a lot.

"Being a father, devoting a lot of time and care and loving to a child, can tighten the screws on that whole identity thing—what am I supposed to be doing as a man?"

DONALD HATHAWAY

Donald works full-time as a writer for a national magazine. Yet his child, also two, has brought identity questions to the surface for him. He wonders how much time to spend at work, how much time at home. He wonders what his priorities are.

The questions that parents feel have to do with achieving a balance of identities, as a parent and as an individual—as a giver to the child and as a giver to the self. The larger the excess, the further away from a balance that parents start at, the more pitched the upheaval seems to be.

MAXINE ROSS

Before Maxine had children, she devoted herself to her husband and her teaching, to giving to others, and waiting. When her daughter was one year old, Maxine was quite content to give and give, channeling the giving she used to do with her classes and her husband to her daughter. At the end of that year, she felt depleted.

"It just came over me," she says, "that I couldn't do it anymore. I had to get some time for myself, but by the time I realized that, I was already desperate.

"I realized that over the course of the year I had given up all sorts of mental activity. I started getting depressed about that. My self-esteem began going down so fast that I figured that I might as well give up everything else. It sent me into a depression that I've never, never had before.

"There has been no other period of my life when I've felt so consistently terrible. It's a completely unfamiliar feeling. I don't recognize myself.

"Because I've been with my daughter so much up until now, it's asking too much of her to leave me abruptly. But I'll have to have some time to myself.

"All of the things that used to seem like strengths now seem like weaknesses—for instance, my willingness to put myself second to other people's needs.

"When I realized how much of my actions were governed by this need and this training—of living on someone else's behalf—I saw signs of this behavior in everything I did.

"It was like a loss of faith, a religious loss of faith, because it was so sudden. When this faith disappeared, there was nothing. It wasn't like I could pull my socks up and say, 'Yes. This is my situation. I'm going to deal with it.'

"There is this incredible feeling of guilt, too, for feeling this way. What's the matter with me? Millions of women around the world for eons have dealt with being a mother. What's the matter with me that it's sent me into such an incredible decline?

"On the positive side, at least I recognize that I have to start figuring out what I need and how I'll get it. I know the first thing I need is time, and that seems very far away."

The plight of Sylvia Plath comes to mind—that torturous conflict between the self and the child. Maxine feels that she was "trained" to give to others and neglect herself. Eventually, this way of behaving began to take its toll in unrelenting depression. Anthony Lefcourt feels that he was taught only to give to himself, not to children. Arlene Skolnick, a University of California sociologist, says that one of the problems in our culture today is that the norms are changing, that it is acceptable and expected for both men and women to have their own lives, apart from their families and also with their families. Yet there are few models. Many parents of today grew up in a different culture, a culture where the woman's domain was primarily the family, the man's the outside world.[84]

It is impossible to determine how much of this conflict is cultural and how much is developmental. These days the onset of parenthood brings a sense of a changing identity—one that causes some a great deal of conflict, others less.

One task of the Nurturing Stage is to begin to reconcile this identity confusion. Such a resolution comes when the parent has found a workable balance between the self as an individual and the self as a parent. For some, finding such a balance happens during this stage, for others, much, much later. For all, it is a delicate balance, one that requires renegotiating time and time again.

A part-time teacher and single mother of a two-year-old says, "I reached a point just about the time my son was two where it all clicked together. I realized that I could still do what I wanted to do, that I didn't have to give up my life by including him. I think I really came to a point of accepting that I was a mother."

In the first years of parenthood, parents gain a clear sense of themselves as parents. Concurrently, although not necessarily at the same exact time, the child begins to explore and establish the perimeters of "me" and "not me," what he or she can effect, can change, can do. It is the psychological birth of the child and of the parent.

Becoming and being a parent, as Alice Rossi has stated, is different from all the other jobs adults undertake. There is little preparation, an abrupt transition, and a need for substantial change and skill. In our society most jobs have clear expectations—parenthood doesn't. For most jobs there is a feedback system—but the feedback in parenthood is tenuous, often delayed.[85] As one father said, "No one hands you a report card with an A on it." And the job itself, parents feel, is undervalued in its importance to society. Yet parenthood brings profound pleasure and satisfactions—the unparalleled pleasure of caring so intensely for another human being, of watching growth, of reliving childhood, of seeing oneself in a new perspective, and of understanding more about life.

In the Nurturing Stage, change is the byword.

"I must have read about two hundred pregnancy and childhood and parenthood books," one new parent says. "But none of them said that you will be a different person.

"It's unbelievable. It is like a force, and if you are not strong enough or if you don't have someone strong with you, it's like a wave and it can break you.

"Some people say, 'Oh, having kids. It's as easy as opening up your legs and out they come!' There's more to it than that, more to it than nursing, than the sleepless nights. Nobody told me about the changes you go through."

III.
The Authority Stage

The Authority Stage sets in more gradually than either of the two preceding stages. The theme of control/lack of control has been present in the Image-Making Stage; it approaches a crescendo in the Nurturing Stage, until it reaches a peak and predominates: Then the parents are in the Authority Stage.

The major tasks in parenthood thus far—preparing for parenthood and establishing an attachment with the child—become tinged with questions of authority, as if a color transparency had slid over them, changing their hue.

The parents know that they are parents—in fact, their identity is so sure that they usually can't imagine a time of not being parents. But their question becomes: what kind of parents?

The parents know, too, that they are fully attached to their child, but ponder the nature of the attachment: When do I say yes? When do I say no? How do I know the effects of my decisions? How do I enforce them? When do I give in, backslide, shift?

There are changes in the child which precipitate and predate the Authority Stage. First the child gains an increasing command of the ability to communicate. Obviously, communication is always intrinsic in the parent/child relationship. Even in pregnancy, the child, by its fetal movements, communicated to the mother (and father). From the moment of birth, the child has been making himself or herself understood with rapt, attentive eyes, with averted eyes, with cries and gurgles, with a stiff or relaxed body, with hands that push away or pull toward. The child and his or her parents have

119

engaged daily in complex and subtle communications, but toward the end of the first year and into the second, these communications become more varied and verbal. The parents and child develop their own code for talking—and included in what each child says, either verbally or physically, is "no."

Children, as they become more mobile and more aware of these expanding abilities, want to try them out, to test their prowess. "I can do it" and "I want to do it myself" are familiar refrains coming from young children. Parents have to decide what to do when the child jumps up and down on the bed or pulls the pots and pans out onto the floor, or throws lunch off the plate or knocks another child over in a dispute over "my sand bucket."

Another change that precipitates the Authority Stage is that children are moving into a wider world. Not that other people haven't had an impact on the child's daily life from the beginning—the baby-sitter, the neighbor, the doctor, and so on. But now, in addition, there is the lure of candy next to the checkout counter in the supermarket, the ads for super toys on television, the sneakers that another child has. Perhaps the child begins a preschool program. He or she is reaching out farther, perhaps being away for longer periods of time.

In the Nurturing Stage, the parents, by assuming responsibility for the care of their dependent child, put, even push, many of their own needs aside. In the process, their sense of self changes; they have the opportunity to grow and mature. Though this is not necessarily an easy stage, parents can, at least, feel that what they do—the nights they stay up, the days spent in comforting a fussy baby—are for an obvious good, the care and nurturing of their child.

In the Authority Stage, that feeling changes. Is it for the obvious good of the child to say "Stop" or "No"? Sometimes it clearly is, but other times the distinction is hazier. The parents' action can feel hurtful and thwarting.

In the Authority Stage, parents confront the issue of "power" in a way that they have probably never experienced in their lives. In most other encounters there are preestablished rules, procedures, and conventions for resolution. In parenthood, there are no such systems, no easy step one, step two plan to follow. Not only that, the child will probably test any strictures to see how steadfast they are, if they'll sway. The child wants and needs to know what the real ground rules are and how his or her parents react to pressure. The parent's response is to feel transported back to childhood—to anger or even humor.

Within this context, the parent has the major task of accepting

*this new dimension of responsibility, accepting his or her authority
over the child. This entails determining the scope of authority,
communicating, then enforcing what has been established. In the
process, parents begin to feel more separate from their child, begin
to understand that the child is not really an extension of them.*

It is a transforming experience to understand that the negative
impulses which exist in everyone—the well-meaning parent as
well as the most innocent child—can be put into the service of nurturing and care.

DEVELOPING AUTHORITY

Just as children differ at birth, they continue to differ in their
modes of communication as well as their level of activity. Yet
whether the child is quiet or active, verbal or physical, older
toddlers or preschool children are usually inveterate explorers.

A mother of a child almost two says, "He gets into everything,
including the garbage which he threw out of the garbage can. He
was shaking his head, saying, 'No—no—no' while he was throwing
the garbage to the right and left. Then he went for a plant and dug
all the dirt up."

Another mother, of an older child, speaks of her delight in seeing
her child become "a mobile little person who has needs and can
express them" and her frustration when the expression of the
child's needs interrupts her. "The times that she knows that I'm
most vulnerable, like when I'm on the telephone, she says, 'Give
me a cookie.' "

A four-year-old's father describes the highlights of a day:

"When she woke up, she was so upset that her older brother had
gotten dressed first that she refused to put her clothes on.

"She climbed onto my desk, took a stamp, took one of my best
pieces of stationery, and asked me to spell [so she could copy] 'I
love you, Daddy.'

"While riding in the car, she asked, 'How does my mind work?
Who tells my mind what to say? How does my voice work?'

"She didn't want me to leave her at school, so she said she
wanted to read to me, then picked a long, long book, telling de-
tailed stories for each page.

"In the evening, she found a tiny scratch on her finger and she
fussed and fussed because we didn't have the right kind of Band-
Aids.

"She called her brother a stupid idiot. Later she shared some old
birthday candy that she had hidden away with him.

"When I look at her, finally asleep, I can't believe that bundle of energy is really quiet."

Children pass through a number of developmental hurdles in these years: the acquisition of mobility, of language, toilet training, weaning, feeding themselves, moving into a "big bed," perhaps the birth of another child, perhaps entering a preschool program. There are the magic moments of childhood—often those moments when the child learns something new. And then there are the problem-laden parts of the day—early-morning awakenings, getting dressed, perhaps boredom or tiredness before naps, nap time itself, just before dinner, and bedtime.

Each family reaches and passes through these events differently. For some, toilet training is a breeze and the child trains himself or herself, while other parents have children who pull down their pants and go to the bathroom on the floor. Some children snuggle into their covers after a nighttime story, while others fight sleep, fuss, whine, calling their parents back again and again.

How the parent responds and communicates affects the child. Then the child's response, in turn, affects the parents. In the course of their interaction, children, randomly at first, hit upon something sooner or later that is their mother's and/or father's Achilles' heel, a kind of behavior that especially upsets, offends, irritates, or embarrasses them. One parent dislikes name-calling, another teasing, another food eaten sloppily or smeared on the face, another bathroom jokes. For the parents, this behavior may have ties back to their childhood, may have been something not allowed, stamped out, forbidden, and when it appears in the child, it causes a high-voltage reaction in the parent.

Illusory Images

Most people approach parenthood with expectations about the kind of disciplinarian they are going to be. They themselves have been disciplined, and long ago may have sworn to themselves that they're never going to "hurt" the child, or "be mean," "be unreasonable."

Furthermore, before they had children of their own, they have been confronted in public places with parents punishing children. At amusement parks, circuses, carnivals, and zoos, places that are presumably set up for families to have fun together, they have seen parents slapping their children, screaming at them, demeaning them. They have seen parents with a stranglehold on children's arms, dragging them down the street. They have seen parents insult and threaten children at restaurants or wheel them wailing through supermarkets.

Before they had children, they have spent time with what they have often regarded as "obnoxious" children, children who monopolized adult conversations, who were rude, insolent, demanding, who seemed to have a remote-control switch on their parents, monitoring their moves.

Before they had children, many parents have built their images of themselves in opposition to this kind of parenting and in favor of a humane, respectful, peaceful relationship.

Then, as their children grow, many people find themselves transported back to the scenes they played as children or that they have viewed played out by other parents and children. Now they have the role of the parent—they have the child whining at the circus, demanding crackers, cookies, candy, gum at the supermarket, jumping off the curb into the street, interrupting when they are in conversation. And almost by surprise, some hear themselves speak their own parents' words or act the part of the resentful, angry, or complaining parent.

The aggression of children can transport parents back to childhood. Since they've grown up, they may not have had to deal with tantrums or the other behavior that children, because of their lack of controls, use to express feelings. Unceasing tears, screams, slaps, or childish logic can stir up a long-ago childhood response— parents can feel like screaming or hitting back. Or they can feel like laughing, joining in the vacuousness, like being a child with their child.

The Image of No Anger

The aggression of children can unleash powerful aggressive feelings in adults, and with these feelings, for some, an image of themselves comes crumbling down.

JUDITH O'BRIEN

Judith is a West Coast mother of one, formerly a preschool teacher, now a writer whose books and articles are about children and parents.

"I find it interesting," she says, "that someone who spent so much time thinking about children, working in nursery schools, teaching children, someone who has been so concerned about the way people treated their children, someone who was such a child advocate, should find difficulty in parenting.

"I'm a person who feels things very, very deeply, an easily frustrated person, so I suppose that I should have expected that I'd be quick to anger and quick to love.

"I expected that I'd be quick to love. *Period.* And because I was quick to love, that love would override all anger.

"I found that the anger was as strongly felt an emotion toward Meg (her daughter) as the love was. And so was hatred.

"If Meg didn't seem to get satisfaction from what I had to offer, if it didn't seem that I was enough for her, it was a terribly frustrating thing, and just on the other side of the frustration was anger.

"I had no training to deal with this. I had been raised in a family where anger was unleashed inappropriately at all sorts of times when you could least prepare for it—that was one of my parent's faults and the other always tried to repress anger, push down the lid, make sure that nothing bubbled out. So I didn't have many skills handling it, and I didn't have a realistic sense of what I could expect and what was all right, and that led to a lot more anguish than I needed.

"In my neighborhood, people didn't talk about how angry their children could make them. So I thought I was the only one who felt this desire to do harm to someone I love.

"I remember one incident. I had invited three or four friends over for dinner. I was trying to put Meg to bed and she wouldn't go to sleep. She had a little bed on the floor. I'd put her down and she'd pop up. She did a lot of crying. I felt badly because when she cried before sleep, it pushed an old, old memory in me which said: 'A child should never go to sleep sad.' I remembered how lonely that could be. Children should go to bed happy.

"I stormed out of the room, burst into the dining room, looked around at the entire group of people, and said, 'One of you had better take care of Meg 'cause I'm going to kill her.'

"They looked at me like I was crazy. They didn't have children, so they didn't know. All I needed was someone to go sing Meg a song and rescue me. I'm dramatic and maybe I use those words when another parent might say, 'I'm awfully angry at her today.'

"I can picture hurting a child. All I ever did was shove Meg into the bed. But I did want to grind her into the floor."

Adrienne Rich writes that "every mother has known overwhelming, unacceptable anger at her children."[1]

"Unacceptable" perhaps because such anger is often unexpected and unwanted. The strictures on aggression have been tighter for women, but that first flush, that red-hot flush of anger that parents feel toward their children, can come as an unwelcome shock for both parents.

Then there are the aftershocks. Is it true? parents ask. Am I really capable of such angry feelings, of such destructive impulses toward my own child?

The Image of Unconditional Love

Adrienne Rich also writes: "I was haunted by the stereotype of the mother whose love is 'unconditional.' "[2] Other parents have had that image, too, of "unconditional love."

DAVIDA KAUFMAN

Davida is the mother of a four-year-old son.

"There is something I've been thinking about a lot: that even though in my experience of growing up, my family was not *totally* caring, open, giving, and warm, I expected the family I made to be that way. I guess those were my unfulfilled childhood wishes. And when I didn't meet those standards, I have been very hard on myself.

"I didn't want to be the kind of parent my parents were. I wanted to have a different kind of availability. I thought of myself as very nice, very conciliatory, very easygoing, and then I found out *I wasn't like that at all!*"

When Davida found that she wasn't *always* "emotionally available" to her son, that she in fact resented him following her into the bathroom, interrupting her when she was talking to other people, seemingly bossing her around, she "saw red."

"I wanted to kill him, but, of course, I wasn't going to do that."

Davida found that she initially avoided her angry feelings and self-knowledge. "I wasn't able to face the issues squarely—so my anger turned to depression. I had a year in which I was terribly depressed."

The Image That I'm Different from My Parents

Other bits of self-knowledge can also be painful, or as Judith O'Brien said, "Consciousness is definitely a double-edged sword." Another image that many parents such as Davida find shattered is that they are going to be radically different parents than their own parents were.

One parent says that when she was a child she used to think of one or both of her parents as "The Big Bad Wolf." Now she sees that she is often "The Big Bad Wolf" to her children.

If as a child a parent liked his or her own parents' manner of authority, the parent often plans to repeat it. A father of a four-year-old says, "I don't remember any restrictions on me that were odious. I don't have any violent objections to the way I was brought up, and I'm raising my son the same way." Then he adds, "Sometimes I feel like an oddity—feeling the way I do about my parents—because most of my friends talk about nothing but their problems with their parents."

Those parents who hope to be different from their own parents may find that they are prone to the same problems.

BARRY ROSEN

Barry, a playwright, is the father of a toddler.

"For a long time, I was very much afraid of having a kid because I was afraid of being a model. The image in my mind of a father was fixed somewhere behind Clarence Day in *Life with Father*. Being a father meant you had to have a mustache, live in the latter end of the nineteenth century, have a stable job, and preside at the dinner table with no nonsense.

"Growing up, I was very much aware that my father was not the authority figure that a father should be, mostly because he was a rebel. He would tell me that Marx is great and Rockefeller bad and I'd go into school and say that and get into a lot of trouble. So, since there were more of them out there than there were at home, I accepted society's models.

"Also, my father tended to be completely nonauthoritarian, even to the point where if I asked him for advice, he wouldn't give it. He didn't want to be responsible for my doing anything that I might regret.

"My father believed in Rousseau, that people are born free and get screwed up by the world. He didn't want to give me any direction because he didn't want to screw me up.

"I felt that my father had not been a father. He'd been a good friend, a companion, actually more of a good crony. But he wasn't a father in what society told me a father should be—an authority figure. I think that society's right—parents have to give direction.

"So, in reaction, I wanted to be the kind of father who could 'have everything together' for my child. But I am a playwright. And being a playwright—you can write conservatively, but you're still a bohemian to some extent. Definitely, it's not secure.

"And so for a long time, the economics prevented us from having kids. I wasn't prepared to give up my work and take a job I would hate for a kid. So we waited. Thirty was the watershed year. That year, things were working out well in my profession. I could support a family.

"I think, in essence, I was afraid. Even if everything else had been perfect, I would have been afraid of not being a good father."

His mother, too, was not the kind of model he wanted for himself. "My childhood was filled with dealing with her power games. For instance, if I was going out, my mother would suddenly say, 'You have to clean your room before you go!' Why she couldn't have said that earlier in the day, I don't know! Then there'd be a huge battle and she'd say, 'Well, you just can't go!' At that point, I'd break down in tears and she'd start comforting me and let me go—it was a matter of her proving that she could stop me from going if she wanted to, she could break me, even make me cry.

"So I wanted to be an adult, not to be like her, not like my father.

"Then our child was born." During her second year, Barry found himself with a struggle.

"I don't want to be a progressive, permissive parent. I want to be strict, but I'm not." When he sets a rule, he simply tells his wife, rather than his child. "I put my foot down and then leave it in my wife's hands.

"That's the exact kind of thing that I guess my father did. In trying to escape from recapitulating all those things I disliked about my father, I backed into his role. He *was* my model. I can't escape that."

ABIGAIL KIRK

Abigail is a businesswoman, the mother of a child two years old, Lisa.

"Lisa was an easy baby, responsive, never crying or colicky. The first year was like a honeymoon for me. There are reasons for that. My mother was very loving to me when I was an infant. In addition, I was twelve when my youngest sibling was born, and I had assumed a lot of the child care. I knew how to take care of babies.

"But the second year has been something else. The last month has been full of really rough things. One night, at dinner recently, I felt that I had really had it. Lisa was making demands on me. Finally, I picked up my dinner plate and just threw it on the floor and broke it. I am not this way, normally. . . .

"One day, we had gone out for a drive and had gotten a flat tire. Lisa and I were sitting in the back seat [while her husband was changing the tire]. Lisa began to make demands on me, and I said angrily, 'Lisa. What do you want?' She looked at me and she was frightened—this tough little kid was frightened.

"A couple of weeks ago, we were at dinner and she sat on my lap again and started to provoke. By the way she was sitting, I couldn't eat. I finally spilled some food and I put her on the floor and I calmly said, 'Lisa, I'll hold you later, but right now, I want to finish my dinner.'

"She started whining, demanding. I just said, 'Shit!' It frightened her. I could see the little shaking red face."

Abigail's mother had followed the same pattern, an easy time with infancy, but "when I began separating from my mother, the shit hit the fan. By the time I was two or three, it was so bad I didn't want to live with my mother anymore.

"She [Abigail's mother] didn't handle anger well at all. She had tantrums, outright tantrums, very uncontrolled.

"Now, although I've made quantum leaps from her, I'm still like her in my temper."

Scenes between parent and child usually begin with a minor incident, but an incident that nonetheless rubs at the parent's old wounds or eats away at the parent's sense of self or makes the parent feel, as Judith O'Brien did, that "I'm not enough," or flagrantly defies or tests the parent's authority. There can be a reciprocal escalation of the little things, a back-and-forth that leads to a flare-up. If parents are open to it, these encounters can provide them with a surfeit of self-knowledge and knowledge about the child.

The Image That Children Are Always Nice

Not only are their images of themselves as parents being countered, parents may also find that they may have images of children that don't hold up.

The first times that the child seemingly turns against the parents can be a shock. Perhaps the child refuses to be held and scrambles out of the parent's arms, pushing the parent away, or the child strikes out against the parent. These moments are often remembered. A mother recalls her two-year-old pinching her nose. For a father, it's his four-year-old saying, "I hope a witch bites off your head." "I'm going to stick knives in your stomach," a four-year-old said to her mother. "You're ruining my life," another four-year-old boy announced.

One woman, living in a Northern mill town, who had her first child at seventeen and now has three children under seven, says, "I thought my children would be nice.

"I thought they were going to be quiet and once in a while they'd be awful and you'd say stop and they'd stop. I wasn't prepared for the way they are."

A father who is the foreman of a ranch, used to working with horses, had certain convictions about "training" children. "I was thirty when I had children. I had seen a lot of obnoxious children and we [he and his wife] had ideas about how we did and did not want to raise our children. I mean really down to the last detail—we had a mental list. We were very excited about raising children—we refused to have obnoxious children that drive people crazy.

"Now, I know that my children can be obnoxious. I know that if you don't have an obnoxious child, you don't have a child. All children get carried away with themselves sometimes and get the dumbs or get the smarts."

The Image That My Child Will Stay the Same

Although parents know intellectually that children are constantly changing, they also expect their child to stay the same. When children in the normal course of development do change, parents usually react to this loss. The mother of a son who was a placid, contented baby began pulling other children's hair in his first year. Even though she realized that "most babies do this," she felt angry and depressed because she didn't want to lose her "happy baby."

Another mother clearly dates the change in her child. Her daughter as a baby was "perfect"—she slept and ate on schedule from three weeks on, until the child was two years old and the family moved. The child was picked up by her grandparents in her old house, spent the night there, and was brought to her new home the next day. After that, the child began waking up at night. The mother became upset fearing that she had handled the move wrong, missed the "child I had known," was tired and angered by the child she now seemed to have. To her, it was the loss of an image about her child that was the hardest to take.

The loss can be equally hard if a child who had been a difficult baby improves, and then momentarily regresses. Often parents fear that all their progress will be swept away, and, in one parent's words, "I overreact all out of proportion."

There can also be expectations created by a first child that a second child doesn't meet. Or expectation of an event: that it was going to be a "fun-filled" family reunion, or "peaceful" family dinner, a "joyous" trip to the zoo. In the parent groups that I have participated in, when parents of young children describe a problem they are having with their child, if they probe, they usually find that an unmet expectation is at the core of the problem.

These images that prove illusory do stem from what Roger Gould calls the childhood consciousness: "a whole network of assumptions, rules, fantasies, irrationalities and rigidities—that allow us to believe, on a nonrational, emotional level, that we've never really left the safe world provided by omnipotent parents."[3] Gould outlines a very clear sequence for the shedding of this earlier consciousness: Certain assumptions are given up in the twenties, others in the thirties, still others in the forties. I question this age sequence; the parents quoted earlier are all different ages, from early twenties (the woman who had her first child at seventeen) to late thirties (Davida Kaufman). Gould's theory does not ascertain the effects of having or not having children on the process of growth.

I also don't think that images come exclusively from childhood. They are shaped by the experiences we have as adults, and they are altered by what happens in daily life.

Circumstances Can Affect the Loss of Images

A bad day, feeling tired, edgy, depleted, troubles with other aspects of life, a death in the family, the loss of a job, a divorce, can affect the parent, just as these events can affect the child.

AMANDA FRANK

Amanda and her husband, Ethan, have been separated now for eight months.

"Ethan and I split up when Jonathan was almost two. My thinking about being a mother, thinking about Jonathan, ended abruptly when we split up.

"I was emotionally absent. I was totally preoccupied by the other situation, feeling deserted after a twelve-year relationship, feeling despondent, feeling depressed, feeling confused, and very obsessed with trying to reconcile the situation with Ethan.

"It was what I thought about all the time I was awake. I was driven by it. Essentially, my care of Jonathan was limited to changing his diaper, feeding him, getting him to the baby-sitter's, and picking him up.

"During these months there were a number of times when I was abusive. I think the worst part of the abuse was neglect.

"If Jonathan were building, he would say, 'Come and build with me,' and I would make an excuse to leave the room—that I had to check on dinner or I had to do this or I had to do that. I was aware that it was fake, but I just couldn't stop because I didn't want to be with him.

"Our marriage started falling apart when Jonathan was born. So I went for a long time during the separation of feeling like I traded Ethan for Jonathan. I wasn't able to tolerate that at all. If I could have had my choice or reversed the whole thing, I would have done it in a second.

"Also, when I look at Jonathan, he reminds me of Ethan. He looks like Ethan, and that's very hard on me.

"I lost my temper really easily. When I lost my temper I was verbally insulting. I was out of control—there is no other way to describe it. I hit Jonathan for the first time, and the kind of spanking that took place was the kind I didn't want to take place. Like my hand would just come out. That made me feel nuts. Like this hand would just do it. That never happened before, and all the resolutions I made to change were worthless.

"Jonathan was afraid of my anger and my sadness. Jonathan talks about sadness a lot. He projects sadness onto inanimate objects—a car can be sad, a room sad, a lake sad if no one's swimming in it.

"That scared me. I couldn't believe how I treated Jonathan for a number of months. Compared to my expectation of what I want for myself, the kind of parent I want to be, it was awful."

Amanda sustained a double blow—the ending of the relationship with her husband and the loss of her positive image of herself as a mother. "I had wanted to be nonmanipulative, noncontrolling—giving my child plenty of space and alternatives, available as much as possible, honest."

What ended this period of withdrawal for Amanda was the termination of her relationship with Ethan. For six months, they saw each other off and on and Amanda retained the semblance of a hope that they would reconcile. "The lingering doubt kept me really obsessing about the situation.

"For the last two months, I've started to notice Jonathan in my life again. There are times when I'm aware of feeling a lot of love for him. I can now project the two of us into the future together, and I feel good about that.

"I've started to care about doing it well again, instead of getting through the days. I started Jonathan in therapy so that he can have someone to talk to about this.

"One of the main feelings I now have is guilt because I'm still not altogether all right and I probably won't be for a while. I feel like his life is still far from what I would like, and that's another terrible pain that I live with.

"I still don't like the person I am right now. I don't think Jonathan has seen me laugh—hardly ever. I'm still not happy.

"I feel like in a way I'm just waiting for time to pass, I'm moving through time, waiting for the healing to take place."

One longitudinal study of forty-eight divorced families and forty-eight intact families by E. Mavis Hetherington, Martha Cox, and Roger Cox corroborated Amanda's experience. Many techniques of study were used—such as interviews with parents, parents' structured diary records, observations of the parents and children in the laboratory and at home, a behavior checklist, and several personality measures, each administered at two months, one year, and two years after the divorce. This study concluded that "mothers and fathers encountered marked stresses in practical problems of living, self-concept and emotional adjustment, and interpersonal relations following divorce. Low self-esteem, loneliness, depression, and feelings of helplessness were characteristic of the divorced couple."

Divorced parents, according to this study, tended to show less affection and to have less control over their children's behavior. And notably, the children were more disruptive and disobedient than the children in intact families; that is, the divorce engulfed both the parents and the children, causing reaction in both and in their relationships. "A peak of stress in parent-child interactions appeared one year after divorce," but marked improvement occurred thereafter.[4]

Divorce is a complex condition—and as thorough as this study is, I think more studies are necessary. For instance, what difference do the parents' perceptions and evaluations make in their experience? Do those parents who see the divorce as a positive step fare better than those who see it as a loss?

Nonetheless, in such cases as Amanda's, where the divorce was unwanted, it diminished her ability to be the kind of authority she hoped to be.

So can illness. One mother began bleeding profusely in her second pregnancy and was sent to bed by her doctor. The worry expressed by the mother was: Will I be able to carry this baby? The worry expressed by her three-year-old was: What has happened? Why has my mother changed? Where is the fun-loving mother I had? What has turned her into this sad, bedridden, fearful person? These feelings began to eat away at their relationship, making them lash out destructively at each other.

Similarly, a father who returned from summer vacation to find that his job had been terminated became depressed and his relationship with his daughter deteriorated. Again, I don't want to imply that job loss will necessarily break down the parents' control—just that it can, as can frequent moving. One mother says, "I have moved so much, and every time I have to sift things out, figure out everything again. This winter has been just grueling for me—watching my husband go out the door every morning and me being left with one screaming infant and one active toddler. It just wasn't fair."

She has become quite angry at her husband over this, and the anger has sifted down to the children.

"My husband's life would be peachy keen right now if it weren't for me. He loves his job, loves his house, is a great father when he's with them. I'm his needle.

"The only power I have is negative. I can say I'm not going to do this or I'm not going to do that. It's like a two-year-old. That's what I am. I'm a two-year-old many times. And I don't like it.

"The other day, my son called me a fucking asshole. 'Cause he hears me and my husband fight and that's what we throw out at each other. Lovely, isn't it?"

She remembers long ago hearing friends talk about spanking children and couldn't imagine ever doing it to her first child, an infant at the time. Now she does spank him. "I don't know why I do it—why I lose control. Almost a day doesn't go by when he doesn't get whacked."

This mother doesn't see any out for herself—except perhaps a part-time job, but her initial attempts haven't proved fruitful.

Mainly she feels isolated. She sees her husband feeling purposeful. She watches all the doors in her neighborhood open early in the morning and men and women striding off busily while she remains on the threshold.

Even without moving or without marital conflict, some parents do feel isolated and lonely. They sit in their apartments or houses waiting for something to happen, drowning out the silence with the soaps on TV or the radio. As women, they feel that what they are doing is undervalued. One woman tells of doing the ironing every day because that made her feel she had accomplished something. She said she suspected she had been taught that ironing was more important than child-rearing.

Another mother missed adult company. At the end of the day, she felt she was "talking Mickey Mouse."

The sociologist Jessie Bernard notes that isolation in the job of motherhood can be a powerful eroder of control. She writes:

> The way we institutionalize motherhood in our society—assigning
> sole responsibility for child care to the mother, cutting her off from the

easy help of others in an isolated household, requiring round-the-clock tender, loving care, and making such care her exclusive activity—is not only new and unique, but not even a good way for either women or—if we accept as a criterion the amount of maternal warmth shown—for children. It may, in fact, be the worst.[5]

Jessie Bernard is referring to a study of six cultures done by Leigh Minturn and William L. Lambert which found that in cultures characterized by isolation in child-rearing, mothers expressed less warmth, were, in fact, more hostile, more out of control with their children.[6]

This is a point which some recent books, such as *Mothering*, by Elaine Heffner, are trying to redress, speaking out for a higher social valuation of the act of parenthood.[7] The growth of parent groups has also begun to counter the isolation for some parents.

Isolation can wear down control, as can having several young children at the same time or having conflicts between husband and wife or between grandparent and parent.

The hostilities between grandparent and parent are complex. A grandchild can remind a grandparent of the parent as a child and stir up old battle wounds, or the stage itself, one of the child asserting independence and separateness, may have been a difficult one for the grandparents. Some parents use the child's aggressive behavior as a way to shock, upset, or get the grandparents. For others, differences in child-rearing styles are threatening.

One mother of a preschool child had a recurrent dream. She dreamed that she was in a reviewing stand, watching a parade pass by. Before her were beautiful Victorian women, dressed in lace and ruffles, cradling doll-like perfect children in their arms. As she watched the parade, she thought, "Why can't I be a mother like that?" Then she left her distant seat, came closer and closer, only to discover that the marchers weren't real people at all. They were cardboard cut-outs.

Her dream symbolizes the transforming nature of this stage— parents see that some of their images are illusory. They realize that they live with their child in the real world, the love-filled, strife-filled world. They realize, in a way that they never have before, that adulthood is not gliding through an unencumbered stream whose course is set—there are rough spots but these can lead to growth.

Establishing and Enforcing Limits

The question then becomes how to resolve the problems which occur. Parents face this question consciously and deliberately or they muddle through, day by day, situation by situation. *This is the major task of the Authority Stage: becoming an authority.*

A related task is determining the scope of parental authority. This means that parents are deciding what they are in charge of and what their child is in charge of—who decides, for instance, what the child wears or how his or her possessions are kept. In handling issues of authority, most parents feel alternating desires. They know they need to set limits, yet they want to give the child latitude; they want to provide an atmosphere of order and respect, and yet they don't want to squash the child's spirit. It is at this time, according to Erik Erikson's theory, that children are building the foundations of a sense of initiative.[8] Parents want to promote this burgeoning ability—but without having chaos, or anarchy. It seems like a tenuous balance to achieve, and parents, particularly first-time parents, wonder, "Am I coming down too hard or hard enough?"

"My question," the mother of a child just two says, "is how to be a disciplinarian. This really didn't come up until now, but there are times when my daughter wants to do things that I simply don't want her to do. And I have to face myself and ask—is it just that I don't want her to do it? Am I really being fair?

"I have no trouble with certain things, like 'No, you cannot go out onto the street without holding my hand' or 'It's dark outside, it's your bedtime.' But there are other things I'm not clear about. And I don't understand myself well enough yet. I don't want to be an intimidating parent—I don't want to be stifling.

"I'm also in a position to know that she needs limits—but I'm still a little murky about what those limits should be."

Children, as they grow, will test parental limits. A refrain familiar to many parents is: "You're not the boss of me," or "You can't tell me what to do," or "I can take care of myself."

Children also have extremely accurate sensors and can often tell when a parent is unsure of a limit and then will muster all of their force to dislodge it. Parents sometimes find themselves halfway through an argument about whether the child is going to wear a sweater outside, and realize that they don't care—thus they know themselves better the next time the issue is raised.

Another task of becoming an authority is choosing how to communicate. Is the child told what to do? Is the child told the reasons behind the limit or is only the limit itself stated? In what tone of voice? When? Is it in anticipation of a problem? "Before we go into the supermarket, I want to tell you the rules. You can buy one thing—and that thing can't be candy." Or is the limit set at the time of a problem, when the child sees the candy, for instance, and begins to clamor for it?

Still another task is choosing how to enforce limits. If the child does not listen, accept the restriction, what is done? Is the child given a warning, threatened, yelled at, scolded, punished? What kind of punishment? Ultimately, this means, what happens when the child loses control? And what happens when the parent feels like losing control?

If there is more than one child, the parent has another task to deal with: choosing how to handle conflicts between the children. Are different children given differential treatment (because of their age or personality) or are they treated the same? Is there a concept of "fair," and what does it mean? And finally, what about those disputes when siblings are off by themselves, no parent close by, and the parent hears two different (and sometimes conflicting) versions of what happened?

When tasks are spelled out in the way I have done, it may seem to imply that parents figure all these out, apply their conclusions, and move on. But living with children is not that simple, as parents know full well. A conclusion reached one month may no longer seem sound the next. Becoming an authority for most is a process of making mistakes and rectifying them.

Images That Work

The images that people have play an enormous part in this process, for they spell out the kind of authority that parents want to be.

STANLEY BARON

Stanley and his wife have one son, eighteen months old. Stanley is a doctor. "In my family, growing up, when someone got angry at someone, they'd stop loving them—which made me feel abandoned as a child.

"When my son gets angry, the easiest thing for me to do would be the same—walk out and slam the door.

"But when you've suffered that yourself you don't want to see it repeated. What I do is to stay and let the rage go through my ears and try to think clearly about what's going on.

"I tell him that even though I've said no, I still love him. I hold him while he's having a temper tantrum, and I tell him it's okay for him to be angry with me.

"Being able to do this is recent, new, and learned, and it's hard work. In the past, I couldn't see beyond my own feelings. What I've now learned is that I have to see past them.

"Another thing I've learned is that if I've gotten angry at my son or if I've done something that I feel I shouldn't have, I'm not the Loch Ness monster or the worst person in the world. I learned the reparability of a mistake."

SOPHIE BRANDENBERG

Sophie, a graduate student, and her husband have two children, a daughter, eight, and a son, four.

"I know that I have troubles expressing myself. My words aren't good enough, come out in a jumbled way, in an avalanche, in an unorganized way. I have trouble writing. I have to work at getting to what I want to say.

"And that's what I have to work on with my kids. The most essential thing is first for adults to take children's behavior, reactions, and words as legitimate.

"Like my four-year-old. When he's confronted with something that he thinks is ridiculous—like a classroom which is too noisy, or bedtime—he reacts. Straightforward. He shrieks or runs around. He's expressing himself in the best way he can, and I think adults have to take it as legitimate and help the child learn words to use.

"My childhood didn't have any—I use that word again—legitimacy. I was *not* permitted to react. If my mother didn't hear anything from me, she was happy. So what I did all my life was read, learn how to think about things, and never talk about them.

"I never thought about the way I was brought up until I had children. I didn't have to face it."

These two parents have been able to meet the goals they have set for themselves, and they both feel an overall sense of pleasure and accomplishment. In fact, Stanley says, "I have at times experienced myself as almost an old sage." This is not to say that these two parents don't have their difficult days.

Images Denied

For others, some of their images of themselves and their child prove less obtainable. What then?

Some of these parents justify the loss, building up barricades of reasons. One woman, the parent of three children, had been severely beaten by her grandmother as a child. She wanted a different kind of discipline for her children, but when she hit her children, she rationalized that maybe her grandmother was right, that maybe beatings did build character.

Other parents try to hide the loss of an image from themselves, or as one parent says, "Every part of me wanted to deny this."

But whether a loss is denied, rationalized, or admitted, sorrow, anger, and guilt usually follow. Guilt is, in fact, the harbinger that an image has been abandoned.

Such feelings can be turned inward, leveled at the self, or turned outward and aimed at the child, who is seen as betraying the parents' efforts. As one parent says, "I conceived this baby with the man I love, carried her inside my body, bore her—and now she's ruining my life."

Images That Are Revised

In the wake of these feelings is stultification or growth. The impetus for growth is often the realization that "children learn from the way they are treated." Although this insight seems quite trite, and is stated everywhere from greeting cards to posters in baby nurseries, many parents rediscover its meaning.

For one mother, the insight came when she and her daughter happened to be in a department-store dressing room. The mother was framed in one mirror, the daughter in the other, and both reflected in each other's mirrors in diminishing proportions. For this woman, the split views of herself symbolized the past, the views of her daughter the future.

This vision made her determined not to be the kind of disciplinarian her parents were, to break the link.

Another impetus for growth comes from a realization that the kind of authority the parent is becoming is hurting the child. Judith O'Brien while shouting at Meg realized that "she was afraid of me. That's what brought me up sharp. The pain of that."

Abigail Kirk

Abigail at first denied to herself that she was following in her mother's footsteps, losing control with her own child just as her mother had done with her. She denied that an old childhood problem—her own short temper—had resurfaced in parenthood.

"I finally had to acknowledge my anger. I had to do it because I knew it was important. The only motivation I had was I didn't want to hurt my child. Everything else in me screamed, 'No! I don't believe it! I don't want it!' It was just a big 'No!'

"But in order for her to grow, I have to grow.

"I read somewhere an article saying that if parents stop growing and developing, then their children catch up with them, and bypass them.

"My father is going through his death ritual at this point. He has a tumor. We know it will kill him, whether it's now or ten years from now. If he fails to show me what death means and how to deal with it, then I'm somehow stunted.

"That's how I feel about raising Lisa. There's a push in me to continue to grow. There's this little kid, right behind me, breathing down my neck. She needs me to deal with anger. She requires it. I have to. She has been—a mandate for me to grow, to admit my anger, and to find ways to control it."

Parents who rise up beyond the anguish, the denial, the depression, who face the raw issues that may have been with them since childhood, find that they have complex inner negotiations facing them. They have dialogues of thought: Should parents get angry at their child? Is that human nature? Should children learn about human nature right from the beginning, from their own parents? If so, how should parents express the anger in a way that isn't frightening and overwhelming to the child?

Judith O'Brien decided it was normal to feel anger but not to express it in a way that was harmful. So when she becomes angry, she says, "I call for help. I find that I need to get a distance, be away from Meg for a while to get a perspective on what to do."

Davida Kaufman had a similar solution. She realized that she was far more capable of being "emotionally available" if it wasn't all the time, if she had some time to herself. And after a long and arduous search, she found a part-time job. Her search was long because part-time jobs are not that easy to come by; and it was arduous because she had lost some of her self-esteem by what she at first deemed as a partial failure in motherhood but later decided was a justifiable need for time for herself. Interestingly, her part-time job is working with battered women, child-abusing women, and their children.

These parents began with images of an idyllic world, in which the harsher aspects of life were encompassed by the more tranquil ones. In fact, what they found was that these harsher qualities are a part of everyone and that, rather than being something to brush away, to deny, these harsher feelings had their own particular beauty. They are not the antithesis of growth—they are, in fact, the stimulus for it. That realization, one which everyone has to learn again and again, is nonetheless transforming.

A Skill: Understanding the Child

How *do* parents then figure out what to do? Parents find it most useful to look at the child's behavior and try to assess what the child is trying to say with his or her actions—in other words, using the skill of looking at the child's clues and cues.

People have personal interpretations of any one type of behavior, interpretations that are colored by their own backgrounds and experience.

At one parent discussion group, for example, all the parents discussed an actual incident:

A girl, aged two, watched a boy of the same age take a stuffed animal off a shelf. The girl ran over to the boy and grabbed hold of one of the animal's furry legs, attempting to pry it out of the boy's hands. When that failed, the girl knocked the boy to the ground and ran out of the room with the toy.

Every parent present at the discussion had a different analysis.

One woman thought that the girl was "a fighter" and should be immediately stopped.

Another woman disagreed, saying that this child was assertive and that children, especially girls, needed to retain the ability to be assertive.

A man thought that the girl knew that she would get attention from the adults by causing trouble.

A different man thought that children of this age don't know the difference between "mine" and "yours" and that the child was exploring, without understanding adult/societal rules of possessiveness.

This discussion is useful, for within it are all of the diverse elements that make up parents' reactions to behavior.

The first is that any behavior of a child produces an emotional response in the adult. It is not hard to figure out how the adult who claimed the child is "a fighter" really feels. The first job for parents, then, is to stop and consider their own reaction to a child's behavior so that they are clear about their own feelings.

Secondly, these statements that the child is a "fighter" or "assertive" represent different social values for girls. Equal to understanding one's feelings is understanding one's cultural vantage point, so that actions on the part of the parent are not just adopted but are thoughtfully chosen.

Thirdly, the responses to the child's behavior contained assumptions about the child. If these adults were the child's parents, these assumptions might be based on whether the adult felt a sense of affinity or dissimilarity to the child. For example, here are several different parents talking about their own children:

THEODORA GRANT

Theodora, a hospital worker, is the divorced mother of a two-year-old who lives on the West Coast. Her son is "into everything."

"The other day, he went into the refrigerator and grabbed two eggs and just dropped them on the floor. Then shortly after that, I decided I'd feed him a little something and I gave him some soup. And he was awful quiet. Whenever he's quiet, I have to check on him. I went over and he had his hand down in the soup like he was trying to make a handprint, you know, instead of eating the soup. Then he turned the bowl up, over his head.

"He reminds me of his father [her ex-husband]. He has that same stubbornness, like if you tell him to zip, he's got to zap. That's the same thing his father did. And he doesn't know his father's ways—he was just a baby [when they split up]. But to me, he's just like him.

"I think about his future. Like how he would be toward his wife or children.

"People tell me that I'm just making myself see this in him. But I do see it."

KATE McCREDY

Kate had three children while she was still a teenager. She feels that the behavior of one of her children is a prophecy come true.

"I was pretty wicked as a child. I was a witch. My mother used to say, 'What you're doing to me, your children are going to do double to you.'

"My daughter [her second child] is a witch. You can't say no to her. The minute you do—it's the moaning and crying.

"I said to my mother, 'This is what you meant, this is what you wished, wasn't it?' She said, 'No, no,' but I think it was."

JONATHAN LOBEL

Jonathan, now a doctor, was shy as a child. He is pleased that his daughter isn't shy but is adventurous. He says, "She is living out what I would have liked to have done as a child."

A parent's feeling that a child is "just like me" (or like someone else) can have positive and negative outcomes. It can give parents a pipeline into understanding their child, an empathy perhaps unobtainable another way, a deep sense of what the child is going through. But it can also blind parents to their child's individuality, can cause them to project a personality onto the child (a projection which can become a self-fulfilling prophecy). Finally, it can enlarge a jealousy between parent and child or cause parents to live through their child's advances while neglecting their own.

It is significant that both Theodora's friends and Kate's mother were warning these women that they were seeing their children unrealistically.

A third step, then, in interpreting children's behavior is for parents to think about their analysis of their child's affinity or dissimilarity to them. If the child reminds them of someone, they should reexamine that idea, looking at how the child is different, a unique personality.

Often interpretations of a child's character are based on time assessments: that this child is "demanding" because he spends most of his time doing that. Yet, an informal experiment at a day-care center found that parents tended to overestimate the amount of time their children were being difficult and underestimate the time they were being cooperative. Having a more realistic sense (for instance, that a scene which seemed to last endlessly only went on for ten minutes and constituted a small percentage of the time that the parent and child spent together) helped parents get through the more difficult moments.

Whenever a child is going through a particular phase, parents can feel stuck. They imagine their clinging child, grown up, refusing to go anywhere new, a passive, frightened person. Or they see mental pictures of their defiant child cheating on a test, ripping off stores, swindling others, involved in gangs.

A knowledge of child development is enormously useful. Although such a knowledge can't completely dispel parents' negative fantasies, it can give them an intellectual solace and understanding that this behavior is a phase. Furthermore, it can elucidate the meaning behind the behavior—that the clinging child may have just grasped the idea that he can't always be protected by his parents and is denying that knowledge by holding on tighter, or that the defiant child has accepted the degree of separateness from her parents and is stressing it.

Ultimately, the advantage of understanding child development is that it gives parents more realistic expectations. Often, when there is a conflict between parent and child, at its very hub is an expectation that the child *should* be acting differently. Sometimes these expectations run counter to what is known about children's growth. They stem from remembering oneself, but usually at a slightly older age, and they are perhaps memories culled from any unpleasantries. Perhaps parents remember that they were capable of playing alone, of being self-sufficient, of listening to and obeying their parents. Their children don't exhibit these traits because they are too young. Child development can give parents more age-appropriate expectations.

Furthermore, understanding child development takes the emphasis away from the child's character—looking at the child as good or bad. The emphasis is put on behavior as communication. Discipline is thus seen as problem-solving. The child is helped to learn a more acceptable manner of communication.

While I was interviewing one father, his four-year-old daughter burst in, announcing a phone call. The father's first impulse was that his child was interrupting; his second was that she was acting in a responsible way by answering the phone all by herself, taking a message, and coming to relay that message.

A father who has custody of his three-year-old daughter says, "My daughter, Jessica, went on her first two-week visitation with her mother.

"The minute her mother walked out of the door, after returning her, Jessica stuck out her tongue at me and said, 'No.'

"Jessica doesn't usually act that way, saying 'No' in such a defiant way. I hadn't seen her in two weeks, and I had missed her like crazy."

This father could have taken his daughter's reaction as a rejection, which he momentarily did. He could have taken it as bad behavior picked up from his disliked ex-wife, another thought which occurred to him.

He concluded that his daughter was "testing my authority and she was also asking me if I still loved her."

Another interpretation is possible: that the transition back from the first visit with the mother, after a long-drawn-out custody fight, is a painful one for the child, full of churned-up confusions, anxieties, and losses.

This father responded to his child's "no" by putting his arm around her, telling her how glad he was to see her, but that he didn't like her to stick her tongue out.

It is often hard to think as rationally as this father did when a child is acting aggressively. This mother's story is such an example:

"My daughter was about three. We were in the car, and I insisted that she could put her own seat belt on. She kept fumbling with it, acting as if she couldn't do it. I thought she could do it, that she was out to get me.

"I started telling her how angry I was. Then I was shouting at her—telling her that I wasn't going to hit her, but, by God, I felt like it. In fact, I said I wanted to hit her a lot of times and she was lucky because all I intended to do about it was shout.

"Well, I shouted at her, and then she cried, a full fifteen or twenty minutes.

"Now, I wonder if she really was unable to put the seat belt on because of her motor ability or because I made her so nervous that she couldn't do it."

A Skill: Avoiding Battles of Will

This mother resolved to try to consider her child's point of view next time and to employ another parental skill: avoiding a battle of will.

JUDITH O'BRIEN

"One of the few things that has really helped me was a message that was given to me by some adult a long time ago. The message was: Never get into a battle of egos with a child. Never. It will be a fight to the death.

"I learned as a teacher that if you fight with a child over things that are ego—'*You* won't,' 'I must'—the child's need to be a person will cause that child to play without any rules and to fight to the death.

"The other day, at the Motor Vehicle Department, I saw this big football-hero-style guy who is pinching this little kid who is two years old. He wants the kid to stand up, military style, and pay attention. He's giving him painful rabbit punches. But then this kid would start wriggling around. It seems hard to believe that the kid would keep doing it again in the face of the violence he knows he's going to get. But this child is fighting for his own survival and identity. It's up to the parent not to get in a situation where he is pitted against his child."

Two contradictory expectations sometimes stand in the way of avoiding a battle of wills. On one hand, some parents feel that if they don't exert control at all times, the child will take over. These parents feel they must win. On the other hand, some parents think that if they do exert control, they are setting out on a lifelong conflict. One mother said, "I just don't want to fight." So she always gives in. In actuality, neither of those positions has to be true. It is possible to find a middle ground.

A Skill: Changing as the Child Changes

And this involves another skill of parenthood: solving problems as they arise and changing as the child changes.

CHRISTOPHER KIRK

Christopher, a minister, is Abigail's husband and two-year-old Lisa's father.

"Last Saturday, I took Lisa to the museum. No sooner had we gotten in the door, paid the fee, and started to head toward the big animals when Lisa said, 'I want to go outside.' My first reaction was: I just paid one-seventy-five for myself and seventy-five cents for her and we just got in the door and she wants to go out! But we were supposed to come to the museum for her to have fun. So we left and spent half an hour playing on the steps, climbing around, and went back in the museum later.

"What I try to do is to be sensitive to her emotions and to avoid power struggles. Now sometimes 'No' means 'No,' even if she has a tantrum. But usually I try to find an alternative that suits us both.

"I think everyone brings their childhood to parenthood, the things that hurt you that you hope you don't repeat. For me that was situations of 'Yes' or 'No' and never a third alternative that was mutually agreeable. It was either somebody wins and somebody loses, and it's a loss of face for the one that loses."

The ability to communicate with children—for it is an ability which both parents and children learn—can involve moments of poignancy. A father watching his son shout at a small kitten suddenly had a different perspective on how his own actions looked and felt to his child. A mother had a comparable insight. She says that one evening after dinner, her four-year-old cut up some fruit to make a fruit salad. Proudly, she brought the salad to her mother, insisting that she eat some. The mother said no, that she was still full, but the child insisted. "I suddenly realized how my daughter feels when I make her eat," the mother said.

Communicating also contains moments of pure satisfaction. A mother found it most gratifying to watch her son handle an aggressive young child in the playground by saying, "Use words!"

Communicating can be funny, too. One four-year-old, when told that she had to take a bath, refused and stomped out of the bathroom saying, "I'm not going to. And I don't care," only to return and ask in a semi-whisper, "What does 'I don't care' mean?"

Many parents said that their children "cracked them up so much" that they had trouble remembering to set limits. Seeing a four-year-old sprinkling baby powder and saying, "It's snowing," or finger-painting in the sink with the toothpaste, can be funny.

There is the urge that parents have to join right in, join the chanting of "me first" or the tickle fest. Children love to see their parents do this, as long as the boundaries between children and adult don't slip too far to be frightening to the child.

Authority and the Other Parent

Becoming an authority has still another task: Each parent has to find ways to work with others in an authority relationship to the child, particularly the other parent.

Do both parents want to be the same kind of authority? For some people that answer is yes, and that is an enviable position. If not, do they accept the differences between them, do they attempt to work out a middle road, or do they undermine, ridicule, and criticize each other?

What happens when one parent says, "It's time to get ready for bed," and the other says, "You can stay up and watch TV with us"? What happens when one parent says, "No new toy," and the other buys the child the toy? And what happens when one parent hits the child and the other disapproves?

Do these discussions take place when the children are asleep at night, behind closed doors, or in front of them? How much are the children shielded from the discussion or brought into it?

Parents (whether married or divorced) have found that trying to understand the other's image, the other's reasons for wanting to be a certain kind of authority, is a successful first step. Parents have also found that a certain amount of accepting the other's differences and compromise was necessary.

As the children grow, some parents change the patterns they have established for solving problems with each other. One man and woman who enjoyed long and pitched battles found that the noise of their encounters, though not hurtful, still frightened their child.

The "conspiracies"—a term used by the psychologist Roger Gould—that a couple have forged may surface at this time.[9] One couple had established a pattern in which the man used the woman to voice his hostilities. When he was upset, he would provoke her and then sit back while she sounded off. The woman gradually became aware of what was happening because she disliked exploding in front of her child.

Authority and the Non-Parent

Parents also have to figure out how they are going to handle grandparent/parent authority relations. This is another task in becoming an authority. They have to decide what they are going to do when a grandparent, knowingly or unknowingly, contradicts one of their precepts. If the parents permit the child to get dirty and the grandparents refuse, what are the parents going to do? Assume that different rules prevail, or hold the grandparents to the parents' rules?

These authority relationships, between mother and father, between grandparents and parents, do not just begin in the Authority

Stage. They have been present since the child's birth and will continue, but such issues do peak during the children's preschool years.

Parents also have to work out their authority relationship with the others who are involved with their children: teachers and babysitters and neighbors. They have the same kinds of decisions to make—how much difference in their own methods is acceptable, and at what point those differences become confusing, even hurtful.

Finally, working out the authority relationship with one's child does not just happen in the so-called "haven" of one's home. A parent faces situations in stores, on the street, when he or she is picking up the child at a center or preschool program, or in friends' houses. *And parents have to decide how they are going to handle these more public situations, as still another facet of becoming an authority.* What are they going to do if their child hurts or is mean to another child? What if their child throws a fit in a store, refuses to cross a street, dawdles when it is time to leave a friend's house? What if another child is mean to their child? And what if passersby or friends or teachers stare or offer advice?

The Mentor Relationship

These can be difficult situations to handle, particularly because parents often assume, "I am the only one who ever had to go through this."

"Why is it," one mother asks, "that everyone else seems so calm and I am the only one who gets flustered?"

"When my child cries," another mother says, "everyone else's children seem like angels."

One mother says that she always found some other mother whom she would assume was perfect ("not like me at all") and would idealize her. Eventually the veneer would be cracked and this woman would see that the admired mother had faults. "But did I stop looking for the perfect mother? No. I'd just find someone else to idealize."

Just as young people form a mentor relationship in the beginning of their work life, a process that Daniel Levinson and his colleagues emphasize, many new parents form mentor relationships either with slightly older parents or with parents in their age range whom they consider exemplary.[10]

Eventually the knowledge that these mentors have rough spots, hard times, comes filtering in, and some of these relationships dissipate. Occasionally, the breakup is difficult. One woman says, "I finally realized that my friend was using me to make herself feel superior."

Everyday events can also tell parents that they aren't the only ones. One mother, about to leave a nursery school with her four-year-old son, heard another child shriek and stood at the door so she could watch. "I find it so reassuring," she said to a friend. "I seem to need to be told over and over that other four-year-olds can act like this."

Parents' relationships with other parents can have all the complexities of the friendships that formed right after birth—jealousy, competition, and support and understanding.

Gossip is an interesting part of these relationships—it can be used in diverse ways. One way is to prop the gossipers up, make them feel that they are above the people they are talking about. An opposite use is to share perceptions. Gossip can be a way that people try to fathom a confusing, contradictory story, to gain meaning from something that initially seems senseless, to piece together a version that fits their realities.

Successes, Failures, and Growth

Although almost all parents seem to have ups and downs in this stage, some emerge with an overall sense of success and some don't. What seems to make the difference?

Again, just as in the Nurturing Stage, a feeling of success stems from having lived up to one's image. For some parents, that is easy —perhaps because they approve of their parents' manner of disciplining and are able to replicate it. For most others, however, living up to their expectations is not so easy and involves the mutual process of adjusting their image to including their own and their child's foibles and of modifying their behavior, too. That is growth.

Growth is never easy. Looking more closely at how growth happens, at what factors facilitate it, I found that a dramatic experience was often the impetus: something that gives the parent a new perspective on his or her behavior. Usually this insight comes from something the child says or does. For one father, it was the breakup of his marriage. He realized that his "shying-away-from-responsibility-in-family-matters" was the cause of the failure of his marriage, and he was then able to establish a better authority relationship with his children.

However, by far the most often mentioned ingredient in growth is *support*. It is with the support of one's husband or wife or one's friends that parents can dare to and even succeed at being different. It is, occasionally, with professional support, therapy or analysis, that one can perceive one's patterns and work at changing them. And finally, for some, it is the support of a system—a laid-out method. It is following or adapting the child-rearing plans of Rudolph Dreikurs, Thomas Gordon, Haim Ginott, Lee Salk, or Jean Illsley Clarke, or the nutritional plans of Ben Feingold or Lendon Smith, usually with the help of others involved in working with the same method.[11]

One mother summarizes the importance of support: "You feel that you are the adult and you ought to be cool and handle problems. But sometimes you can't. Sometimes a child can reduce you to a state of total lack of control, or powerlessness. That's really scary and upsetting. You need someone to listen to you, to say that you're all right as a person and as a parent. That's what's always helped me. It would be nice to figure out ways for that to happen more easily."

There is one very interesting report about those parents who by society's standards are the failures of this stage, those who become child abusers. Brandt F. Steele and Carl B. Pollock spent five and a half years studying sixty such families who were referred to their care in a hospital (that is to say, this population was not gathered by any statistical procedures, but still happened to represent a cross-economic population). In searching for common behavioral patterns, the investigators found that such parents have unreasonable expectations of their children, that they deal with them as if they were much older, and in the process misperceive the child's own needs. "It is hardly an exaggeration," the investigators write, "that the parent acts like a frightened, unloved child, looking to his own child as if he were an adult capable of providing comfort and love." These parents feel a sense of righteousness about what they do. "From early in infancy the children of abusing parents are expected to show exemplary behavior and a respectful, submissive, thoughtful attitude toward adult authority and society." The difference between the parent who abuses and the one who doesn't is a staunch adherence to these principles at an inappropriately early age. Furthermore, all of these parents were raised similarly. Whether actually beaten or not, they all had experienced "a sense of intense, pervasive, continuous demand from their parents."[12]

These are the people whose images stand in the way of growth; the images are like shields held in front of the eyes, severely limiting their vision, if not blinding them to the humanness, the developmental needs of their children.

GAINING DISTANCE

"Perfect" is a word that figures prominently in the stories of parents in the Authority Stage. They say that they started off wanting to be perfect parents, but now fissures are appearing and widening in that expectation.

The desire to be a perfect parent can be translated to mean that the parent wanted to be the kind of parent he or she wished for as a child. These are the hopes garnered during one's childhood and then in the early years of parenthood. They are based on the *as if* relationship: Parents think of the child *as if* they themselves are the child they will have.

The Child as Ambassador

As the child grows, the parent/child relationship goes through several phases. The first is the state of being joined and not joined, a state in which the identities of the parent and child mingle, blend, and yet are separate. Then, toward the end of the toddler years, when parents have secured their sense of identity as a parent, though they may be reevaluating their own personal identity, another change in the parent/child relationship occurs. Parents now expect their child to be their ambassador out in the world. What the child does reflects upon them; they are responsible for the child's behavior. *The task for parents is to gain more distance in their relationship with the child.*

ELAINE YUSOFF

Elaine is a free-lance writer, married, the mother of a preschool and a school-age child. One of her children, following Elaine's father's death, is refusing to go to school.

"My daughter says, 'I hate school,' every morning. She used to like school, so what I'm hoping is that the core of all this comes out of her sadness and fears about my father's dying. If he could leave her, so could I—'Maybe Mommy will die, too.'

"Despite understanding this, I still feel terrible. On the bottom line is this terrible guilt. I still feel that anything miserable that happens to my kids is my fault. I keep thinking that if I had handled it better, somehow she wouldn't be so unhappy, that I should be equipped to make problems go away. I mean, I want my kid to glide through life, to have everything come easily, to have experiences that I can sit and talk to them about and they'll say, 'Gee, Mommy, that's right.' When I can't make that happen, it's painful.

"When I was in the eighth grade and I got the highest grades in class, I thought to myself: 'I am the best at what I do.' I think that's what I've translated to mothering.

"I reduced my work to part-time and I thought to myself that if I was doing mothering, I had to do it real well. That's why if a baby is supposed to get an airing, I had to make sure I got that walk in. I was going to work real hard at doing a good job. That's what I'm thinking about this year when my daughter is having a hard time. Part of my guilt or unhappiness is that I'm working so hard at being a mother, I want to do it well."

Of course, not everyone has such a sad event as the death of a father to cope with during these years. Other parents experience these same feelings in different ways. Although they may know that every child has nightmares, when their child wakes up in a sweat, screaming in the middle of the night, talking almost incoherently about being chased by a monster, the parents think, "What did I do to cause this?"

Similarly, parents may know that sibling rivalry is normal, but when their child teases, hurts, or holds grudges against a brother or sister, the parents wonder, "If I had just done this or this, we wouldn't have had this outburst."

When the child has a temper tantrum in public or hangs onto the parent or butts into the parent's conversations or is rude in front of the parents' friends, parents feel, in the words of one, as if "people are looking at me to see what I am doing right or wrong. Every time my kid acts obnoxious, it means that I'm doing wrong."

Guilt! Once when I was giving a speech about parenthood, a woman raised her hand and asked, "Do parents ever stop feeling guilty?" "Probably not," I said. Guilt is one of the most frequently felt emotions. It is a signal that an image has been denied. Frequently at the very center of the guilt, a parent harbors what I think of as a secret transgression—the ultimate betrayal of the image of the self as a parent. For one mother, it was that she had kicked her child. For a father, it was that he had said, "I wish I didn't have children." These transgressions, because they remain secret seem to become infected, grow in size, spread, and are recalled, guiltily, whenever the child reaches a problem phase of growth.

During this stage another image may come to the surface: that the child will exceed the parent's accomplishments.

The mother of a three-year-old, a full-time student completing her doctorate in psychology, says, "I buy the idea that children live out the unfulfilled expectations of their parents. No matter how much I can accomplish in my own life, it's impossible to do everything as well as I want to, especially considering the fairly defini-tive capabilities I was born with. And even if I become more secure in who I am and what I am doing with my life, there still isn't enough time, and so my kid has to do some of it for me."

Angela Barron McBride writes of these feelings:

> I expect my children to be like me, *only better*. I want them to be dis-ciplined and steady in their work habits, even though I work in spurts. I tend to complain and indulge in tears when I am hurt, but I expect my children not to whine or tattle on their friends. I am prejudiced about all sorts of things, but I expect to raise daughters who are free of bias. I don't want my children to be tormented by the guilt feelings I have, yet I resent it when they don't seem sorry enough for some trans-gression of my will. I seduce my friends with cocktails and dinners, but I resent it when my child "buys" a friend's attention with apple juice and animal crackers.[13]

Many child-rearing books and articles rail against this viewpoint: One's child is not, should not be seen as, an extension of the self. Thus parents may admit to these feelings with a sense of com-pounded guilt. As a father said, "I know I'm not supposed to talk this way."

And yet, these feelings do exist, in a greater or lesser degree, in parents. I suspect that these feelings represent a phase in the devel-opment of images, a phase which for some remains permanent, for others is more transitory although never entirely eradicated. Like most of the psychological processes of parenthood, this state has dual and seemingly contradictory possibilities. On the positive side, it provides the impetus for parents to care about their child's future. But at their extreme, the same feelings can prevent parents from accepting their own child's separateness.

Time for Self, Time for Children

Questions of involvement in the Authority Stage remain a daily negotiation. Should I read a magazine or read to my child? Should we do something together as a family on this beautiful Sunday or should I catch up on some work?

Even though parents may have already outlined the way they use their time, many find themselves still wondering, worrying.

A mother who had decided to work questions whether she has done the right thing, as does another mother who is staying home: "Sometimes I feel like there's something wrong with me because I want to spend these early years at home with my child. Do I lack ambition? Will I smother my child with too much attention? Will she become too dependent on me?"

Our society has been moving through a transition on this score, and sides have been formed—those who support mothers' working and those who oppose it. The advice of experts falls on both sides, and their opinions are thrown about as justifications, hard and fast, often putting parents in the middle of these volleys. Whatever internal questions parents may have, they can be intensified by the outward confusions.

Men face similar questions and confusions about how much time to spend on their families and their work. The amount and degree of role-sharing has to be determined: what is done by the father and what is done by the mother. As always, parents' images of their roles play a large part in the decisions they make.

ELAINE YUSOFF

"I remember when my daughter was born, I thought that my husband, Allen, and I would really share parenthood. We talked about sharing feeding schedules, and 'You're in charge Saturday and I'm in charge Sunday.' I had a friend who decided not to nurse so that her husband could help feed. I thought that was going one step too far—but just *one* step. We were really going to be parents together.

"Then when Amy was born, I didn't go to work right away and I fell, to my surprise, into a traditional motherhood role, which was most unsettling. I didn't feel that I had achieved the equal shared parenting that I had idealized. It has a lot to do with economics: Allen earns more than I do, and it's very hard for me to say, 'You be home at three and take Amy to that birthday party this afternoon.' He just cannot, will not, take time away from his work. So after a short time of that, a year or two, I stopped asking, and I became the primary parent."

Elaine is still "unsettled." Her husband, although he helps more, does not live up to her expectations. And she doesn't live up to his of being a high-powered writer.

When images are lost, they leave a wound unless new ones are built.

RONALD CHRISTENSEN

Ronald, a businessman, is the father of two children, ages one and three.

"We've tried the route of total sharing, of you do the dishes Thursday and I'll do them Friday, and it didn't work. My wife can't do it. I can't do it.

"So we've gone to roles that are not based on a fantasy of what we expect the other person to be, but on a very hard-nosed sort of basic understanding of the strengths and weaknesses of both of us."

By this, Ronald means that they've talked through what each other's likes and dislikes are, and have been able to negotiate and compromise. He doesn't like to get up at night; she doesn't mind, so she does it. She doesn't like to go to the park; he likes it, so he does that. He works full-time, she part-time.

This couple have been able to achieve a workable system. That they are economically able to compromise should be noted. Other parents have fewer choices.

Push/Pull Feelings

In the issue of separateness/connectedness, the push and pull that parents feel toward their child is a thread that can either lie dormant or be pulled taut by circumstances.

A foster mother is in a triangular position with the child's actual mother, who is institutionalized (and was before the birth). Even though there are no indications that the mother will be released, she is worried and thus pulls her child closer to her. "I worry that someday someone will come and take my child away, and if they ever try to, I think I'm just going to leave the state."

A single mother, upon finally meeting someone whom she cares about, has a sudden and unexpected wish to push her son away. "I've read about how children respond to a new man in their mothers' lives," she says. "I've read about their jealousies. But I didn't realize that I would be jealous, too. I find that there are times when I am actually jealous of the attention my son's getting from my friend and I'd like my son to disappear."

Possibly sensing his mother's feelings, this child "acts more obnoxious or outrageous to get attention."

Parents do experience the full range of human emotions toward their children: love, hate, envy, resentment, sadness, joy, fear, excitement. The more negative feelings (such as jealousy) may come as a surprise, but they do exist and have to be dealt with. The single mother decided not to put herself in a competitive situation but instead to spend time alone with her boyfriend and with her son.

Feelings Around Preschool

Enrolling a child in a preschool program is an event that can pull taut this thread of push/pull feelings. Although the child may have already gone to a child-care program or been cared for by a baby-sitter, entering a preschool program is a societal landmark.

As parents think about where to send their child, they begin to reminisce about their own school days, thinking about what they liked and disliked, and in what ways they benefited from school-ing. They form images of the experience they would like their child to have. If they want children to have the same kind of education they had, these images tend to be more securely anchored in expe-rience, more grounded, than if the parent is choosing something substantially different from what he or she has known.

At this time parents also evaluate their own parenting. Have they prepared their child for this new venture? How will their child fare? How will they be judged as parents? Such transitions always trigger evaluations.

A social worker, who has frequently observed parents arriving with their children on the first day of school, says, "They dress them up. It's like a presentation. I know they are feeling that we [the teachers and administrators] are looking at them to see how they've done."

Now this woman has a three-year-old and is getting ready to send him to school. "I'm feeling just the way all those other parents felt."

In part, these thoughts are a ramification of parents' identifica-tion with their children; they feel that their children represent them in the wider world and that they are responsible for their successes and shortcomings.

Enrolling a child in a preschool program is both a severing and an enlarging experience, an ending and a beginning.

Any separation can stir up anxieties. Parents worry: Will my child be safe? These concerns may be vague and generalized, just barely felt, slightly troubling pinpricks on the emotions, or they may take the form of flashing pictures: the teacher forgetting the child, the child falling from the top of a jungle gym, the child get-ting sick from contact with other children.

Each parent has his own cluster of worries. One man worried about his child's head getting hurt, while a mother feared her child's getting lost. These fears lie fallow, only to enlarge with tran-sitions throughout parenthood, to the point that they are like dis-liked relatives, familiar but unwelcome.

Then comes the actual beginning of school, a beginning which can be positive or negative for teacher, child, and parent alike. The strength of one's passions can blind one to the other people's per-spective in these transitions. For example, in one school a teacher, thinking of her own need to get to know the children and the children's need to begin school in an orderly and peaceful way, scheduled a short school day for the first few days. She asked the parents to stay until the children were adjusted. She interpreted the parents' distress as selfishness—as an indication that parents nowadays don't have the time for their children. But one of the parents explained it differently.

LINDA CHASKIN

Linda is the mother of a three-year-old daughter in this group. She teaches in a college, as does her husband.

"I didn't expect to have any very important feelings about sending Becca to school. She's my second child. I've been through this before, and Becca was in a play group last year. But then I began having these dramatic feelings, as did the other parents.

"On the surface it looked like the parents couldn't wait to leave, couldn't wait to get rid of their kids. They seemed to want to walk away, run away, do anything to get away.

"But at night some of us were crying, others were coming as close to nervous breakdowns in our own minds as we had ever come.

"I would come home, take these long showers, dress, and redress myself until I liked the way I looked—pampering myself. I was exhausted all the time.

"I think that we all had to be self-indulgent.

"Why? For a while it didn't make sense. What I came up with was this:

"Each of us has a lot of pressure to perform as independent people. Bringing our children to school was supposed to be a transition that we could go through smoothly—we weren't supposed to be missing our children. We were supposed to be progressing, and our children were supposed to go along with the plan.

"For this period of time, someone was laying a guilt trip on us: that we couldn't walk away from our responsibilities. We had to stay with our children.

"The more I thought about it, the more I decided what was happening was that we were losing control, not of our children, but of our own lives, through our children.

"We realized that in the process of getting our children involved in school, the school was saying where we could be and when—whether we could go to work or not.

"We were trapped—absolutely trapped. For our children's sake we couldn't defy the system.

"It was a loss of control, and most of us have worked so hard after the child's birth to gain control of our lives again."

Obviously, not everyone has this same experience with enrolling a child in a preschool program—not every school has this kind of child-centered policy of asking parents to stay with their child for the first few days. Not every parent (particularly men, although they did at this school) gets involved in this event.

However, I still feel that Linda Chaskin's experience is significant, for several reasons.

First, she used the words "expect" and "supposed" over and over. "We hadn't fully anticipated," she says; "we weren't told." She had an image of what this experience was supposed to be like for her, and when it didn't work out, she was upset.

I am reminded of parents' stories about birth—also a major life transition—and how important it was for them to have their images actualized. Like birth, school entry involves loss and gain. And when parents are treated like children, when they feel stripped of control during an important passage, that loss digs deeply

Thus, the schools and centers that prepare the parents with realistic descriptions of what they can expect, that treat the parents as responsible adults, have a better chance of achieving a cooperative relationship with parents. "Cooperative"—a term that is bandied about with numbing frequency in educational programs, but, in my experience, is not always achieved.

If children do go to a preschool program, be it nursery school, kindergarten, or day-care center, this program constitutes only one part of the parents' child-care system. This changing, sometimes growing, sometimes diminishing system includes all the other baby-sitters, neighbors, and relatives who help care for the child.

Separations and Reunions

Life with children involves frequent separations and reunions. At various times these go smoothly or roughly.

Leaving the child with a new person or in a new place can cause parental anxiety which then diminishes as the separation becomes more routine. If the length of the separation is unusually long (for example, the child spends the night or several days away), these anxieties resurge. Parents speak of almost specter-like phenomena—the phantom child. It is as if their child, ghostlike, is somehow present, yet unseen, as if the child's absence were burning a hole in space that is as vivid as the child's presence. Particularly if the parents are at home without the child, a stuffed animal on a kitchen chair, a children's book on the floor, seems poised, waiting, and the child seems just around the nearest corner.

Parents have expectations of how these reunions should go. While the child is away, he or she grows more and more beautiful in the parents' minds. Then the parent sees the child again; the child may be tired, or he or she may have stockpiled any difficulties that occurred during the absence and may express them at this point. The child may be angry at the parent for leaving and punish him or her accordingly. Reunions aren't always what parents and children hope they'll be.

The Child in a Widening World

The child's world is enlarging. He or she may be going off to school, to "spend the night over," to play with new friends. Parents frequently look to the other adults in their children's lives for overt or covert judgment of: How have I done as a parent?

This feeling is particularly aimed at teachers, who by training and by experience are expected to be evaluators of the child's development.

"I remember the first months of school," the mother of a three-year-old says. "I wanted to be told in no uncertain terms that I had a fabulous child who had been raised to be a delight in school.

"I didn't hear that. It was crushing. I took it all out of proportion that there were things that my child needed to work on.

"I was coming to the teacher for an A-plus in parenthood. She was supposed to give me that A-plus, and she didn't. And that hurt. That really hurt."

The parent of two young children slipped and called a parent conference an "interview," and then laughed, saying, "I guess conferences are like interviews. I always feel like I'm being interviewed for the job of mother. Maybe if I don't do well, I won't be able to keep my kids!"

Many teachers, while realizing that they are being evaluated by the parents, lose sight of the fact that parents, too, are feeling judged. Teachers don't always realize the power of their words. In leaving out the positives or concentrating on what's wrong about a child, a teacher can devastate parents, can in fact shape parents' pictures of their children.

One parent, after a negative conference with a teacher, says, "I went home and looked at my daughter and I hated her. Ugh. I looked at her and I thought, 'You shit, you unpleasant, arrogant, disgraceful person.' Then, the next day, I turned against the teacher and hated her, too."

Another parent found it useful, after several bad experiences, to exercise some control over the interchanges with the teacher. She set herself and the teacher on equal footing by asking, in a friendly manner, about the teacher's out-of-school interests, and then asked to hear about what the teacher liked about the child.

This feeling of being judged as a parent is not new, but it takes different forms now because the child is in contact with more people, even some that the parents don't know.

This widening world brings many positive feelings to the parents. A father working in his office once glanced out of the window to see his three-year-old son walking down the sidewalk in front of the building with his day-care group. Proudly, the father watched his son, a sturdy, beautiful child, stopping to inspect dandelions growing beside the sidewalk, then skipping off, almost strutting as if he were leading the band. These glimpses of the child's separate spheres (the child receives a phone call or runs off to the corner to mail a letter or draws a picture for Grandma)—these glimpses can bring pride and joy.

Growth. The baby's face, once slightly amorphous, has taken character. The hair, once wispy, is now thick. The relationship, once mainly physical, now includes conversation. The child asks such questions as: "When were the olden days?" "Were you alive?" "Will babies grow up to be people?"

The child can use words to express his or her more dire feelings. "I wish you could have found a different brother for me," or "Pretend that I wasn't your baby, that you just found me under a bush."

Parents marvel that the once small, dependent baby could turn into a child with his or her own thoughts and feelings, angers and pleasures, perceptions.

The child's growth into the wider world also brings influences that parents dislike. Parents may object to the violence of cartoons, the characters being flattened like cardboard, beaten until stars ring around their heads. They may wish they could eliminate the temptation centers—the displays of Easter, Christmas, or Thanksgiving candies right next to the checkout counters in stores. Parents may deplore the fact that all of the family-centered places—the zoos, museums, parks—are filled with stands where vendors hawk cheap toys and junk food. Those products most disliked by the parents can become the most desired by the children and thus a bone of contention between them. One four-year-old girl defiantly looked at her mother and said, "When I grow up I'm going to be a TV man and a candy woman."

Furthermore, parents find that many places are not set up to accommodate children. Parents feel as if their babies, so admired and fussed over by the public, have been transformed, almost by fairytale magic, into menacing figures called children—children in the public's mind now equal trouble, equal spilling things on table-cloths in restaurants, putting grubby hands on merchandise, making noise, causing confusion.

These unspoken barriers, these silent "keep-away-children" signals, do not exist uniformly, community by community. Some places and subcultures are fortunately quite welcoming to children.

Then, of course, other people do not always act the way parents wish (again a factor which has been present since the baby's birth). A doctor may trick children by distracting them and then without warning plunge a syringe in their arms. A baby-sitter may set up new and highly arbitrary rules. The parent of a friend may punish or scold the child in a hurtful way. Even strangers may channel their violent feelings toward children. One dark Hispanic woman, married to a white man, was crossing the street with her four-year-old perched on her shoulders. A man approached them, seeing the fair-skinned child atop the dark-skinned woman, and took his lit cigarette and held it against the child's arm, shouting to the mother, "You shouldn't have a child like that."

This woman cried for days and days. It wasn't just the racist elements of society, a fact she had been at least accustomed to if not numb to for herself. It was that the racism could hurt her child and she had been powerless to stop it.

David De Sisto

"There are moments in being a parent," says David, a school psychologist, the father of a three-year-old, "that are anger, total anger.

"My daughter had to have a tooth pulled, and we sought out a dentist that worked with children. We searched, found two or three, then discussed in detail what we would tolerate or allow. We finally picked one. He led her off, and lo and behold, we find out that this person decides to put her in a straitjacket to fill her teeth. And we not knowing this until after it took place. Angry! I'm still angry."

Abigail Kirk

Abigail had an equally devastating experience with her daughter, Lisa, age two. She had searched for the best child-care program, found one she liked, and enrolled her daughter. Then one day at pickup time, she found Lisa in tears because a teacher had yelled at her.

"I put my daughter in a place I trusted," Abigail says, "and then I discovered that the trust wasn't totally justified.

"My sense of it was that the Garden of Eden had been violated.

It's like someone has opened you up and all of your raw organs are exposed and you can't control it.

"I remember picking Lisa up and holding her and feeling that I wanted to put her back in the womb. That's just the way I was feeling.

"What I learned was that I can't relinquish my role as a responsible parent, just because I am eager for her to have other attachments.

"That's also part of my learning to deal with my own anger better. Okay, this is the reality. Teachers are sometimes wonderful, sometimes not. Now what do I do? How do I become an active parent in my child's situation? It's really lobbying for your kid, all the while being understanding and reasonable.

"But that death of Eden is really painful."

Through these experiences of "meeting the cold cruel world," many parents find, sometimes in painful ways, that the imperfections in others, in society as a whole, do touch their child. There is no sea wall strong enough to hold them away. And the problems one sees in oneself (for Abigail, it was a quick temper) can be the hardest to accept in others.

Reevaluating Perfection

In the Authority Stage, many parents find that their images of being a "perfect" parent, of having "perfect" children, and of creating a "perfect" enclave for them to live in have been eroded. They find that there are flaws in them, in their children, in the others that affect their lives, and in society as a whole.

Of course, all parents have different definitions of perfection. It would be fascinating, for instance, to do a long-term study of the kind of parent who starts out by describing perfection as "an acceptance of the self as an imperfect human being." How do such parents change? Do they have other expectations they don't realize they hold?

The Child Is Not Really an Extension of the Parents

As the child's and the parents' world expands, as the child grows up, and as the parents reevaluate perfection, the stage is set for another task: the beginning of the parent's realization that the child is not really the parent's ambassador.

Sometimes, parents have a dramatic experience which symbolizes this distance. One mother was at a birthday party with her four-year-old son when a game of musical chairs was announced. As a child, the mother had always hated party games, and she was feeling sorry for her son. Her son, however, rather than standing on the sidelines as the mother expected, dashed into the center of the group and, when the record was turned on, played the game eagerly.

"That was a very significant event to me," she says. "I now see clearly that my son is separate."

JANET SANTOS

Janet lives in a mill town in the Northeast with her husband, her in-laws, and her daughter, age five.

"I had always felt that my daughter was a copy of me. She was going to behave exactly as I wanted her to, especially when there were other people around. She was going to be a proper little girl and not get chocolate on her dress and stuff like that.

"Then a real important thing happened to me. I was listening to a comedian on the Merv Griffin show and he was talking about going to a restaurant and having a young couple sit next to him with a three- or four-year-old little boy. He said that he had heard the mother make such a ridiculous remark that he had to turn around. She had said to this little child, 'Would you please sit like a young man!'

" 'That *is* ridiculous,' I said to myself. A three- or four-year-old isn't an adult, it's a child.

"Then I said, 'Not only is my daughter a child, but she's her own person. She's not an extension of me. She has a mind of her own and she's going to use it!'"

The understanding that "my child is not an extension of me, though we are very connected" is the next phase of the parent/child relationship. People reach this phase at different times, some early, some much later.

Independence, however, does not come during these years of parenthood. In actuality, to the surprise of some parents, the opposite is true. Even though the children are clearly more separate, they "stay right up under you," the mother of a three-year-old says. "Look at me" could be called the theme song of preschool-age children.

"My children are no longer babies," the mother of a six- and a three-year-old says. "I'm not feeding them six times a day. If one of them wants an apple or a cookie, I don't have to go into the kitchen and get it. Their physical care is less. But they don't need me any less, and that's been a revelation to me. They still need me as the supporter, the confidante. I'm expecting that someday they'll need me less, but right now, that seems a million miles away."

This time seems to be a kind of critical juncture for parents. And they, as Margaret Mahler and her associates have documented, do have different responses to this change.[14] Some look back on the closer, more nurturing relationship with nostalgia, yearning for it again, missing the public attention they received as the parent of an infant, while others are glad that the more constricted, more demanding period has passed. For others, there is a mixture of both of these sentiments, and sometimes, within a family, there is a split, with the husband and wife on opposite sides.

People's culture plays a part, too. For instance, a woman who lives in a large city, two blocks away from her parents and fifteen blocks away from her grandparents, feels that families should stay close, the middle generation taking care of the young and old, and is already talking to her four-year-old son about this. The father of a four-year-old in the Southwest who has moved frequently holds just the opposite view. "You teach your child not to need you. If at the end of X period of time you can say, 'My kid doesn't need me anymore,' you've done it. That's being a parent."

Wanting a New Baby

It was hard to know where to place the subject of having another child within this book, because people obviously have them at many different times. But I did find that the subject of "new baby" came up over and over as the child grows and seems more separate. At this point, some parents begin to try to conceive, while others have just the opposite reaction. Women go on diets, determined to lose all the weight they had retained from the previous pregnancy, to regain their former figures.

Another time the urge to have a baby comes is when one's friends are expecting. Women particularly talk about an almost physical force, drawing them in, making them desire to have and hold a baby once again.

People's images of family are influential in their decisions (if they in fact make a deliberate decision) to have another child. Parents see "family" as many children or few, closely spaced or with years in between them. Often they are responding to what they see as lacks in their own upbringing. A woman who was much older than her younger brother decided to have her children close in age so that they would be friends. No matter how much the other mothers she knew told her that age-spacing didn't determine friendship, she did get pregnant again soon after her first child was born.

Perhaps the poignancy of this desire to have another baby is most deeply felt by parents when their "last" baby turns the corner away from babyhood into childhood. Putting or giving away each piece of equipment—cribs, bottles, car seats—are a "last," and parents think about the fact that a certain phase or season of their life has passed.

Parents do sometimes avoid or postpone this realization by keeping in the back of their minds that maybe they'll have another child, someday.

How Protective Must a Parent Be?

All of these issues culminate in a part of the task of becoming an authority, and that is: how much to shield or protect the child and how much to plunge the child into the realities of life.

Parents find many solutions.

DORIE VAN HOUGHTON

Dorie, a graduate student, married, has a daughter, three years old.

"Somewhere, I know from my own life that you have to go through difficult times in order to really grow up and mature. But every time my daughter gets in the middle of a difficult time, it doesn't seem like something which is just developmental, a part of growing up, but instead seems like, 'Oh. What's wrong? What's the matter? What can I do to help her?'

"I've begun to change within the past three months. I've gone into a new phase—it's not to make life tough for her but to concentrate on allowing the difficulties that she is facing to exist. I try to help her over problems rather than protecting her from them.

"The thing that comes to mind immediately is that Catherine is afraid of monsters at nighttime. Before, I wouldn't have seen that as normal. I would have blamed myself: Have I not allowed her to show enough anger? Is she projecting her anger? Have I been too angry with her? Now I still wonder those things, but I take them less seriously.

"I am moving away from taking the credit and blame for who Catherine is. She is who she is. I am moving away from trying to make life perfect for her. I'm becoming more accepting of her and of life."

Dorie's conclusions place her in the next phase of the separateness/connectedness relationship between parent and child. She has realized that "my child is not an extension of me." While not all parents reach this phase at this point, there are many elements in the relationship that are ripening and readying for it now.

Donald Winnicott, in writing about women, says: "The good enough mother . . . starts off with an almost complete adaptation to her infant's needs, and as time proceeds she adapts less and less completely, gradually, according to the infant's growing ability to deal with her failure." [15]

In the Authority Stage, the parental task is twofold: to provide the structure, the customs, the rules by which the family is governed, and then to help the child learn to deal with frustration when it occurs.

DEALING WITH SEX ROLES AND IDENTITY

There is some research evidence that from the very earliest days, boy and girls are treated differently.

In research for a doctoral dissertation by Hannah L. Frisch at the University of Chicago, fourteen-month-old infants played with two different adults in a laboratory setting. Once the child was introduced as a boy, once as a girl. This technique made it possible to observe how adults treated the children, simply based on their notions of "boys" and "girls," apart from the actual behavior of the child.

The observers (who weren't told the nature of the study or the actual sex of the child) recorded what the adults did with each child. When these results were tabulated and analyzed, Hannah Frisch found that the adults were nurturing to girls and encouraged activity in boys. [16]

There is a widespread belief in the research and in the popular mind that when parents are "liberated" or their "consciousness is raised" they will no longer engage in this kind of sex stereotyping, or, as one parent told me, they will raise their children in a culture-free situation.

I think that these assumptions need a more careful look. It would be interesting to compare adults who consider themselves nonsexist with those who espouse more traditional roles. Parents—all parents, I am convinced—have expectations and images about sex roles. Perhaps a parent thinks that girls shouldn't rough-house and get dirty—or perhaps a parent thinks girls should be adventurous and exploring. Both of these are expectations.

Parents have the task of communicating sex-role expectations to their children. Just as in all aspects of parenthood, sometimes parental expectations are flexible, sometimes hard and fast; and sometimes they are met, and other times they aren't, causing the parent to hold on tightly or to grow.

Because our culture has shifted rapidly in this area, many parents have been raised differently from the way they are trying to raise their children. They face a degree of discontinuity in what they feel and say.

A mother is bothered because her daughter refuses to wear dresses. The modern strain in her says that that's okay—but is it really? She wasn't allowed to wear jeans as a child, and that makes it harder to know what to do. This much she does know—if she tries to change her child's behavior, she'll probably create rebellion in the child, set her on the path of resistance.

But what if she goes along with her daughter? Is this just a phase? Is her daughter rejecting femininity? Do clothes mean that much? There hasn't been a generation raised this way. The results aren't clear. She also knows that two plus two in parenting doesn't always equal four—that is, the results of any one course of action are not straightforward and immediately discernible.

Furthermore, will the child be able to read the parent's hidden feelings if the parent pursues a course that doesn't feel comfortable?

Perhaps this example seems petty, but underneath it, the parent confesses secret worries: Does this child want to be a boy? A mother and father picture their daughter "dressed up" in the mother's old miniskirt slip "knocked up at thirteen." The parents of a boy who likes to dress up in girls' clothing, despite the teacher's assurances that many boys like to do this, suspect that this is the first sign of homosexuality.

These are the kinds of concerns that face parents—whether they feel that they should have them or not.

The mother of a two-and-a-half-year-old says, "I feel in a way that my son is emerging as a type, not particularly athletic but very thoughtful, very verbal. So I'm sort of wondering how I feel about that type of child. I guess I've always wanted a child who was terrific at everything, and I have a child who is terrific at some things. I'm also scared about thinking of him as a type and treating him that way and then seeing my behavior toward him as fostering the type of person he's becoming. I mean, I am reading to him rather than running around with him—does that make him want to run around less?"

And so, at best, it is a continuous process of looking at one's image against the glare of what one feels and thinks and what one's child says and does, and when there is a clash, working from there.

Communicating About Sexuality

The same process governs the parent's response to sexuality. *Parents also face the task of responding to children's indirect or direct queries about the origins of life and sexuality.*

MAYA NEWMAN

Maya, a dancer, and her husband have two children. "I saw my mother naked too much," Maya says. "I saw her naked all the time on the toilet and had a sense of being assaulted by this giant defecating, pissing female body.

"I never saw my father naked in my life. My parents never told me anything. They didn't tell me the facts of life, and up until I was seventeen I thought that a penis was like a long cord, like a spaghetti that got wrapped up in a strange way. When I noticed all the different shapes of men's fronts, I decided that each man had his own style of winding up this incredibly long thing, of wrapping it up and tucking it in his pants before it all collapsed. I didn't know anything."

Maya feels that she both had too much and too little sex information. Her own solution was to let the children see her and her husband naked, but not to overwhelm them. "I was surprised at how soon I realized that it was too much for the kids, and I stopped.

"My daughter was five and a half when I told her about menstruation. I told her all about special women's blood, told her the whole wonderful story. But I didn't want her to actually see the blood. When she hears about it, fine—but I know about the power of the visual.

"It was important to me to get in the story of sex before anybody else did. I did not want the first time my children heard about a man and a woman making love to each other to be said in some awful way by another kid. It was important to me to say it nicely and to say it was about love.

"I remember that my daughter—when I told her at four and a half—she was astonished.

"She had most of the facts then. One day after our son was born, she said, 'But how does the seed get to the egg?'

"And I said, 'Well, it goes from the daddy to the mommy.'

"And she said, 'But how does it go from the daddy to the mommy?'

"So I said, 'From the penis into the vagina.'

" 'How does it go from the penis into the vagina?'

"I said, 'The penis goes inside the vagina.'

"She said, 'What?'

"I remember her face—it was that wonderful pink, it was round, and her dark eyes were wide and her mouth dropped into an O. She looked absolutely like Columbus who had just discovered America. Astonished.

"But somewhere it really made sense to her. Then I sort of explained it: that the penis got longer and harder and that's how it could go in. It made sense to her. And I've had a stake in following up every one of her questions.

"I didn't masturbate as a child. I didn't even know there was such a thing. I didn't know what those terrible feelings of sickness, nausea, and disgust, grief, and agony in my body were. It was like I was horny, horribly horny all my life until I was finally with someone.

"My daughter used to have her hand between her legs a lot—I sometimes kissed her on the top of her head and said, 'Honey, that's for your own room.' Her sexual life is very private now.

"I said the same thing to my son when he was about four. He's had erections all his life and would play with himself. Finally, I said, 'That's for when you are by yourself,' and he would go into his room.

"The other day he told me that he couldn't draw himself because there was 'something all sticking out, sticking out to there' and it was too difficult to draw.

"And I said, 'I know. That happens with boys a lot.' I approved of myself for having said that. I also approved of myself for not saying anything more.

"Another day he was playing with himself and I said, 'Does your penis hurt or is it really feeling good and like it wants you to pay attention to it?' And he said, 'No, it doesn't hurt. It's just hard.'

"And I said, 'I know. That's part of life and love.' I didn't plan to say that, but that's terrific. I'm glad I said 'love.'

"Usually I'm critical of myself—anything I've said to the children is rot. But later I figured out that those two remarks I really like. But sex is an area of life I really like, so it makes sense to me."

Maya seems able to hold to her image—stress privacy of sexual behavior—with a comfortable, yet terse communication about sexuality. Perhaps she is able to do this because she is herself comfortable with sex.

What is so interesting is that, as she describes it, "both of my parents had a very unhappy sexual life." Furthermore, Maya disapproves of the way they dealt with sex as parents. Yet Maya has not found that their behavior has affected hers.

Parents might disapprove of discussing sex with children as young as Maya's, or disapprove of the way that Maya introduced sexuality to them. This is a subject about which parents have intense feelings and convictions.

And sometimes these convictions are hard to carry out, for when the child brings up the subject, the parents feels embarrassed or stymied.

For instance, the mother of a son faced the same series of questions that Maya did:

"We got past the fact that the seed grows in the uterus and how the seed is fertilized.

"My son asked, 'How is the seed fertilized?'

" 'The seed is fertilized by the daddy.'

" '*How* by the daddy?'

" 'By his penis.'

" 'How by his penis?'

"I saw that my child was snickering, so I know that he was testing or he had already heard something; this wasn't new information, but he wanted my view.

"Then we got to how does the man get his penis inside the woman. At which point I panicked.

"I ran upstairs, grabbed a book by Lee Salk, and consulted it in the bathroom so I could try to find an answer. But Lee Salk didn't address that question in this book.

"So I just said to him, 'I'm sorry I don't have any more time to talk about this and I've got to go to my meeting.'

"How *do* you answer that?"

Children can ask questions that are difficult or upsetting. One son said to his father, "Can I touch your penis?"

"No," the father answered.

"Why not?"

"Because it's private," the father said.

"But you let me touch other parts of you."

Or two sisters, four and two, were playing the following game: One child opened her legs, while the other looked and then ran away.

Then the game turned into "smell me." The mother told the children that she wasn't comfortable with that.

"You do what you want with your vagina and I'll do what I want with mine," the child retorted.

These same situations would be hard for some parents, not hard for others, depending on whether they stir up unacceptable feelings or not.

Explaining the facts of life poses slightly different issues when a child has been adopted.

CASSANDRA TYLER

Cassandra, a full-time mother, and her husband have three adopted children, a four-year-old son and two-year-old twin boys.

"We had been telling our oldest son that we were trying to adopt another child, and then with a week's notice we got twins. We were concerned that a week wasn't enough time to prepare Jesse [the oldest], but he never questioned that there were two babies.

"Oh, the day after they came, he did say, 'Can we take them back?' But that's normal.

"I just said, 'No, they're ours now and they're going to live with us, and be part of our family.'

"This adoption really blew the sex education on this block. A neighbor was pregnant. All the children [in the neighborhood] couldn't understand how we could get babies without my being pregnant.

"We've talked to Jesse about adoption all along. We've tried to make it a word that's in his vocabulary, but when he saw a pregnant woman, he was disturbed a bit.

"He said, 'Did you grow me in your tummy?'

"I said, 'No, I didn't. We adopted you.'

"He refused to believe it, and that disturbed me, so I tried to bring it up several times, but I didn't want to argue with him, so I dropped it.

"It was several months later when he said, 'I didn't grow in your tummy. I grew up in a strange lady's tummy.'

"This upset me, too, because we'd been trying to get across the concept: Don't go anywhere with strangers, don't accept anything from strangers.

"He had gotten the idea that a stranger was someone to be afraid of, and I didn't want him to feel that way about his biological mother. I didn't know exactly how to handle it, but I said, 'She was only a stranger because I didn't know her.'

"That seemed to satisfy him, but I would like to pursue it further, get to the heart of it."

Questions of sexuality do touch a central nerve. Parents, in watching their own reactions, can, if they are willing, learn much about themselves.

One woman who was controlling about sex was unaware just how many strictures she put on physical expression until her young son—who was less controllable—made her aware of how she felt when someone wanted to cuddle and hug her.

Children do arouse a sexual response in their parents, but many push it aside—feeling that it is just too dangerous to admit. A few, unfortunately, act on this response, while others recognize it but keep these feelings under control.

Siblings, sometimes to the parents' surprise, do stimulate sexual feelings in each other. And parents have to decide what the boundaries of these relationships are. Do brothers and sisters bathe together? Undress in front of each other? The parents have to figure out what to do when, for example, a preschool brother and sister play "doctor" or "sandwich" (lying on top of each other).

Parents also find that their children have sexual feelings about them. Do they, then, undress in front of their children? Do they invite the children into their beds? How do parents express their physical love of their children?

"I want to give my kids a wholesome, open feeling about sex," a parent says, "but not overwhelm them." She found her best guide to knowing what to do (whether to take baths with her young daughter, for instance) was to watch and listen for the child's reaction.

The Oedipal Relationship

Children do, in the preschool years, become romantic and flirtatious with their parents. In the Freudian and psychoanalytic schema, this begins, in infancy, when both boys and girls make a primary identification with their mothers. The boy in the preschool years competes with the father for the love of the mother, but eventually realizes that he is no match for this bigger, stronger man, and drops this courtship instead deciding to take on his father's qualities, identifying with him. The girl child wants her father, but realizing that her mother has already won him, remains identified with the mother.[17]

How does this schema fit parents' perceptions? I wondered. The fathers and mothers of preschool children I interviewed talked about being alternately loved and hated by their children. The child "splits" the parent into these two beings and finds them almost unreconcilable. The child wants to think the parent is all good and when the parent disappoints him or her, the loss is enormous, the anger great.

The parent who is with the child the most (usually the mother) tends to receive the brunt of this alternating current of feelings. The parent who is there less may be seen as what one father called "the knight in shining armor, coming to rescue the child."

Fathers talk about their daughters of three, four, five, and six as flirting with them, or "all over me." Mothers speak that way about sons: "He wants to jump into bed with me."

Then gradually the child begins to look up to (identify with) the parent of the same sex.

Many parents reported that the flirtations did not fade away as Freudian theory supposes and that the child's interest in sex continued in the school-age years (or latency period). This whole subject needs more study: Is a different definition of latency, for instance, called for?

When the child turns toward one parent, admiring him or her, there can be a strong reaction in the other parent. This behavior causes many parents to reevaluate their partner as a suitable model of masculinity or femininity.

NANCY O'FARRELL

Nancy stays at home with her child, John, five. Her husband, Robert, is a West Coast businessman.

"I started trying to raise John in a nonsexist, pacifist way when he was a baby.

"If you ask me if there was one thing I would change about my husband and any number of men that I know, I would say that I would like to see them be more nurturing. So I thought I would add this quality to John. And I thought that having a doll would allow John to be nurturing. When I brought a doll home, Robert said, 'Gee, I'm not sure I want him to have a doll.'

"I said, 'It's not going to hurt him.'

"But John never played with it.

"I also didn't want John to be violent, so for a couple of years I wouldn't buy him any guns. John became obsessed with guns. So I allowed my mother, his grandmother, to buy him a gun, though *I* never have bought one.

"I don't know that I've been successful—although John is very affectionate. I guess, in part, that's nonsexist.

"He's also been taught that it's okay to cry. Now sometime, somewhere, Robert said to him, 'Don't cry when you're out in the neighborhood.' I know that for a fact. Because a friend told me that John's feelings were hurt. And I said, 'Didn't he cry?' And she said, 'No, he did not.' And I thought, 'That's strange.'

"So somehow, Robert has snuck this thing in there that you don't cry if you're out in front with your buddies. I felt like there goes all my years of trying to teach him that he can cry.

"So I thought, well, if our society wanted to teach our men children not to cry, then to have my child crying might be a little freaky, in terms of what society expects. I have never seen my husband cry—not once in the fifteen years I've known him.

"I mean, it's hard to teach a child things that go counter to society. Unless you are off living on a ranch somewhere. When you are here, you have to teach your child to adjust and survive—hoping that perhaps you can make just a slight change in the way he would go about things—maybe my child would wait longer, try more options before getting violent, before hauling off and whacking someone."

Nancy says, "I really thought you could mold your child. Now I'm not so sure." To her, her husband represents the larger society. He is trying to conform to society while she has been trying to resist it. From the doll onward to the crying in public, her husband has been winning out.

Now John is identifying with Robert even more. As she says, "His mannerisms are suddenly just like his father's. Some of his more learned skills and interests are mine, but the real basic core of him is Robert." Nancy sees that even one statement by her husband can undo hours and hours of her teachings.

Nancy is conflicted. A father, she feels, has a right to influence his child, but how much? What if his values contradict hers?

"My husband spends a lot of the hours of a week at work. In his free time, there is social pressure for him to do other things like go out with the men—play tennis, join clubs, play racketball. These things take him away from home. And he is so caught up in this routine that he doesn't often think about what really matters.

"I have all day around here to think about what really matters. I'm alone a good part of the time, and the mindless work I do allows me to think. You know, it really comes down to one thing: Family love to me is the most important thing. I don't care where I live as long as we have that.

"But Robert, on the other hand, thinks, 'Gee, the guys at the office assume that I should live over on Peacock Hill.' In order to be admired in the economic business world, we have to have a house over on Peacock Hill. At this point in his life, he's motivated by economics. He's finally achieving what he's always wanted to achieve. And he doesn't have time or doesn't want to think about what's important."

At the center of the maelstrom in this family are different images of "fatherhood."

"I view Robert against the standard of my father. I think my father is the only way to be a father. My father is not a successful businessman. He is a working man. He spent a great deal of time with us. I basically learned high school physics at the age of five underneath my father's car.

"Now Robert was brought up by a different father, a father who was more intellectually oriented. But I would like to see Robert take apart the car in the garage so that John could be under there just like I was with my father. And when he doesn't do these things, I become critical."

There are many differences that all are converging at once in this family: the parents have different, competitive, and conflicting images of their roles. They have different expectations of their child. When the child moved away from an alliance with his mother toward expressing more of his own individuality, and toward a greater identification with his father, these differences became even more exposed. In such a case, the child can become a pawn, to be won or lost, in the competition. Many parents who have been divorced have similar feelings—they didn't like certain qualities in their "ex," and it is disturbing to have their child reinstating them. But if they look at the situation from their child's point of view at all, they will see how distressing it can be for a child to be a pawn, to have the parents that he wants to look up to torn down. Nancy and Robert are stuck, each holding onto a separate image.

"We're riding this out," Nancy says. "I don't dare talk to Robert about it. Probably we'd just end up in an argument and then we'd get personal."

She has pinned her expectations on Gail Sheehy's premise that when men reach their goals of success, they change. "I think that in about three years, Robert will start thinking about what's important."

In many ways, this family has come to a point that Nancy Chodorow of the University of California has been speaking out against. She feels that when both parents are not fully involved in the child from infancy onward, the male child then has to break off from, denounce, and devalue his mother in order to identify with his father. Girls, too, suffer by being all too connected to their mothers.[18] Perhaps Robert, Nancy's husband, had to cut off the thoughtful, nurturing, caring side of himself when he identified with his own father and now the same process is happening when his son identifies with him.

This example may make it seem that it is impossible to raise children in a nonsexist way. That is, of course, not true. It has been particularly difficult for Nancy because she is isolated; no one around her seems to agree with her, she has no support.

Support, as always, is critical when parents are trying to change.

Yet, Nancy's example is instructive. For no matter what the tenet that parents hold, their children's individuality, their need to be slightly different, comes shining through. And parents find, just as Nancy did, that they must accept their child's differences.

The Child's Emerging Identity

Every stage of parenthood has within it the possibility for growth. In the Authority Stage, growth begins when parents face those images which prove untenable; for example:

- "I expected that I'd be quick to love. Period. And because I was quick to love, that love would override all anger. I found that the anger was as strongly felt an emotion as the love was."
- "I thought of myself as very nice, very conciliatory, very easygoing, and then I found out I wasn't like that at all."
- "In trying to escape from recapitulating all those things I disliked about my father, I backed into his role. He was my model. I can't escape that."
- "I thought my children would be nice . . . and quiet and once in a while they'd be awful and you'd say stop and they'd stop. I wasn't prepared for the way they are."
- "I had always felt that my daughter was a copy of me. . . . That is ridiculous."
- "It's hard to teach a child things that go counter to society."
- "I really thought you could mold your child. Now I'm not so sure."

Many of these parents had childhoods which belied these assumptions. Many were self-aware people. A few have had therapy; others have had a great deal of experience working with parents and children prior to giving birth. Nevertheless, they all had started with a dream that they could do it better, a dream which is intrinsic to the Image-Making Stage. In the first years of parenthood, parents are frequently revising and refining their images, which in the Authority Stage often center on their own and their children's imperfections and limits. It is truly transforming to understand that despite one's foibles, and in fact because of them, one can grow.

There is no question that the authority relationship is worked out with one's first child. But what about the second, third, or fourth time around? Despite the folk saying "I wish I could throw my first child out and begin using what I've learned with the second," the research shows that it is possible this trial-and-error, mistake-ridden process can have many positive outcomes. First children (perhaps because more attention is given them, more is expected of them, and they then have to differentiate themselves from the younger children) are frequently the most successful, the highest achievers.[19]

But just because a parent has figured out an authority stance with the first child, it doesn't necessarily prove unshakable with the second or third. In one family the first child was persistent and demanding—the parents realized that they should be consistent with her and have very clear limits. The second child was compliant and obedient—and the parents felt that he should be encouraged to break some rules to test his prowess. In another family, the order was reversed. The first child was reasonable, the second not so.

Often parenthood is written about as if it takes place on a stage set, isolated from the rest of life. But life, with its ups and downs, very much affects parenthood. A woman who is having trouble with her subordinates at work will become a different kind of an authority than she otherwise might. One woman, an academic, says that she had always believed in the mentor system—that is, if she pleased those in higher positions, she would be protected. It didn't work. She was denied tenure. She attributes this denial to the fact that she didn't fight for it—she expected it to be handed to her. Now that her daughter is four, this mother is encouraging her persistent, aggressive qualities. And what she (or others) might have once defined as negative traits are now seen as "good."

Perhaps the most crucial element of this stage is how parents define their children's behavior to them—for in that process, they are feeding into the child's emerging identity.

In families, children tend to take on stock roles, as if there were hats hung up in some secret place, visible only to the children. Each succeeding child selects a hat and takes on that role: the good child, the black sheep, the clown, and so forth. There is psychological justification for this. If one child is very good, perhaps the only way the other child can differentiate himself or herself and become noticed is to be disobedient. Most adults, in describing their childhoods, will readily describe their parents' evaluations of

them. And it is those evaluations which affect children's definitions of themselves.

In the Authority Stage, parents are grappling with fundamental
issues of power. Out of the welter of these issues, self-concepts are
beginning to be shaped—both for the parent and the child.

IV.
The
Interpretive
Stage

"Parenthood has really changed for me. It's much more than taking care of my son; more than saying yes and no. Now I have to figure out what I think and what I know so that I can answer his questions and explain things to him."

—The mother of a five-year-old

Children from five through the elementary school years are pushing even further out and away. No longer is their experience bounded by the walls of their home or classroom or where their parents take them. They begin to take themselves—they walk, they ride on their bikes, they climb onto buses and wave good-bye. They may make friends that their parents don't know, may go places that their parents have never been. They listen to the radio, watch TV, go to movies, look at and learn to read magazines, newspapers, and books. The children are becoming citizens in their own children's world and initiates in the adult world.

Parents begin this stage by evaluating the past and preparing themselves for the changes to come. Their major task is to interpret the world to their children, and that entails not only interpreting themselves to their children and interpreting and developing their children's self-concepts, but also answering their questions, providing them access to the skills and information they need, and helping them form values. As such, parents also continue to define the separateness/connectedness of their relationships and to figure out how involved they want to be in their children's lives. The Interpretive Stage ends with the approach of the teenage years, and parents once again evaluate the past and prepare themselves for this new era.

Parents find that their children's questions cause them to reexamine and then to test their own implicit theories about the way things are, about the world and the way it works. This process in and of itself changes parents.

In the Beginning: Evaluations and Anticipations

The Interpretive Stage begins with parents facing the task of evaluating their own beginning years of parenthood to reinterpret, and where necessary revise, their own theories of child-rearing and parenthood, and then of forming images of the future.

The researchers who have probed development in the adult years have discovered that evaluation is a recurring phenomenon in the life cycle. Daniel Levinson and his co-workers draw these conclusions from their study of forty men:

> [The life structure] consists of a series of alternating stable (structure-building) periods and transitional (structure-changing) periods.
>
> The primary task of every stable period is to build a life structure: a man must make certain key choices, form a structure around them, and pursue his goals and values within this structure.
>
> A transitional period terminates the existing life structure and creates the possibility for a new one. The primary tasks of every transitional period are to question and reappraise the existing structure, to explore various possibilities for change in self and world, and to move toward commitment to the crucial choices that form the basis for a new life structure in the ensuing stable period.[1]

Levinson and his colleagues put a time frame on this pattern. A stable period lasts for six or seven or up to ten years. A transitional period usually runs for four to five years.

Since the publication of *The Seasons of a Man's Life*, a certain aura of controversy has surrounded the authors' contention of such a predictable sequence. I myself have found by studying parenthood that the times of evaluation are not programmed into the individual. They are a response to newness; a dramatic or not so dramatic change: a shift in the child's behavior, a move, an illness, a divorce.

The Interpretive Stage begins with an evaluation, not because it is predetermined but because it is triggered by the maturational shifts in the child, by the child's entry into a new school for kindergarten or first grade, or by the societal stress on this era of childhood as the one in which children are expected to begin to acquire the skills they will need in the adult world, particularly reading, writing, and math.

"Evaluate," as I define it, means to look back, review, and revise
in order to move ahead. It means to assess old images and to form
new ones.

School Is Often the Trigger

If their child is entering a new school, parents wonder: Will my
child be okay there? Will he or she be liked, be smart, learn?
They hope that their child won't be rude to the teachers, won't feel
shy about going to the bathroom at school, will be able to hold his
or her own on the school bus.

Certain facets of a child's personality may cause concern:

- "I worry about [my son]—his innocence and naïveté, that he
  doesn't have that toughness that seems necessary to get along
  in the world."
- "I worry about [my daughter] because she has absolutely no
  self-discipline."

Other qualities of a child may create optimism:

- "[My child] seems to love to learn."
- "[My child] gets along well with people."

Parents also think about the school and teacher: Will this school
be a good place? Will the teacher care, teach enough, teach well, be
a good influence?

Because parents obviously can't go to school with their children,
can't fight their battles for them or do their learning, they can only
hope that they have given their child solid enough underpinnings
to meet the days ahead.

There are also joyous anticipations: being able to sit and read
together, to discuss ideas, to have a more complex relationship
because the child is older.

As the beginning of the school year approaches, especially if the
child is going to a new school, parents find that many familiar feelings return—those flashing pictures of disaster, those grating worries about separation.

For some children, beginnings are difficult. They have fears,
which may exist as hazy apprehensions or clear concerns: Will I be
with my friends? Will I make new ones? What is math? What is
reading? Will I really be able to do the work? Will there be a rest
time? What will the teacher be like?

Children's worries are often expressed as resistance or as regression. Somehow knowing that he or she will be asked to grow up soon, to take a large step forward, the child slides back to the safety of trying to be younger, wanting to be carried, fed, or the child rebels, perhaps saying bathroom words over and over and over.

The children's behavior the summer before school starts can accentuate and amplify the parents' discomfort. I have been in several parents' groups during the summer when parents of five-year-olds or six-year-olds come in and ask, "Is five (or six) an especially difficult year?" It becomes clear as these parents talk that their children are vacillating between assertion of timidity and prowess. And that the parents are vacillating too—between wanting and not wanting the child to grow up and go to school. "I don't know if my husband and I are ready to cut the apron strings," one mother says.

When the actual beginning occurs, parents find themselves reconciling images with actualities, just as they do after the birth of a child and after the child enters a preschool program. The beginning is judged—it was better or worse or the same as expected, leaving the parents feeling unhappy (if it was worse) or happy (if it was better).

The start of school does not necessarily mark the end of this evaluating/anticipating period. Some parents think as far back as pregnancy; they look at their successes and failures, tally their scores, outline what they've learned, and prepare to move forward.

It is interesting and significant to me that many of the firsthand books about motherhood have been written at this juncture, when the author's children are approaching or have entered kindergarten or elementary school. Examples are Angela Barron McBride's *The Growth and Development of Mothers*, Jane Lazarre's *The Mother Knot*, and Shirley Radl's *Mother's Day Is Over*.[2] These books are evaluations, the author's early experiences are described, and their images (or myths) are threshed out from what they see as realities.

INTERPRETING ONESELF AS A PARENT

Evolving out of these evaluations is a feeling that parents have of knowing themselves better. They know how they are going to react to tears and threats, to fighting among the children, to a dawdling child, to a child resisting sleep or awakening in the still-dark morning. They know how they feel when a little hand reaches over and takes theirs, when they are handed a child's colorful drawing, or snuggled against. They know when they get tired, what refreshes them, how far they can be pushed, and what gives them pleasure. Many of the parents I interviewed said that they felt "realistic" about themselves, by which they mean they have a concept that corresponds fairly closely to the way that they behave with their children. These concepts have ratings: "I think I'm basically a good parent" or "I'm not such a good parent."

Evaluations Are Based on Images

In pushing beyond these ratings, I found that they were based on images.

LYLE STEVENS

Lyle has two sons, seven and eight. She is a full-time mother.

"I am beginning to feel," she says, "that I may not be the best parent in the world, but I am a pretty good parent. I am all right. I am doing a pretty good job."

The basis of her judgment rests on her children: "I look at my children and I say to myself, 'They're okay; you know, they are okay.' "

She is also judging herself, primarily on the fact that she has changed since that time, long ago, when she was first pregnant: "I had all the insecurities that I'd had all my life. Whatever the doctor told me to do, I did. I'd go in there with a thousand questions to ask and he'd have me in and out in two seconds. I'd find myself on the street, not knowing a single thing more than I had when I went in. I'd be furious with myself, but never furious with him.

"I had wanted to have natural childbirth. I had taken classes and had talked about it with my doctor, and he was very positive. He agreed with me that it was a wonderful thing. We were going to do it. Together. He would help me. He would be there.

"Then I got to the hospital. He wasn't there. I was in a tremendous amount of pain, but doing all my breathing. Robert [her husband], of course, went to sleep in the bed next to me, making me absolutely furious. I can hear myself saying, 'Oh, you poor thing. You've been up all night. Please go to sleep. I know how you must feel—I'll be all right.' Ever brave.

"Finally, the doctor came in and I was so relieved to see him that I broke down and said, 'Oh, I'm in so much pain. It hurts so much.'

"I really needed him to be supportive, but instead of that, he said, 'Oh, you women! I don't know what you are trying to prove. There's really nothing to having a baby, and you should just let me put you out.' He went on a tirade.

"And I gave up. There was Robert asleep on the bed next to me. There was this doctor, the one person I could depend on, doing this to me. So I let them put me out.

"And it wasn't until I was pregnant with my next child and I made an appointment with that doctor that I realized that I could not go back. I couldn't do it. I called his secretary and said I wanted to cancel the appointment, and she asked me why. And she began to yell and scream at me and I ended up in tears, but determined never to let it happen again."

Her determination was shaky at first. When her oldest son was in preschool and her second child was a toddler, she was "in such a state of exhaustion" that she tended to follow other mothers' leads in making decisions.

Now, Lyle has reached a point where she thinks through her own decisions, and though she often turns to others for suggestions, she ultimately makes up her own mind. "Being responsible for my children and realizing that I was good at it has made me feel more self-confident."

When parents come close to living out their images, they report feeling more self-confident and more relaxed about parenthood in general.

"I'm at ease," the mother of three says. "If we were to have another child, I don't think that even the two-o'clock feedings would bother me—anymore."

Parents who have a negative concept of themselves have, thus far, been unable to live up to their images or modify them. They speak of themselves in guilt-stricken ways. And the guilt, which in a mild form can be informative if parents look for its sources, becomes cancerous, spreading everywhere, crowding out and destroying most of the parents' good feelings about parenthood.

Most of the parents I interviewed had mixed self-appraisals. They realize what they are good at and have come to an acceptance, grudging or not, or are working on aspects of themselves that they admire less.

"I really enjoy being a parent," one mother said. "I love my children and I think that that comes across as being my predominant feeling. When I'm acting in a way that I don't want to be acting, I think, 'Well, gee, this is not the way I feel most of the time and I think my children know it.' I know that realistically speaking, I can't really change my basic personality—and when I'm down, I'm down.

"I used to think that if there were a problem you could just handle it in the accepted way—whatever that happened to be, according to whatever book I was reading. Now I know that's not true. The way you know you should handle problems intellectually is not always the way you can emotionally handle them. You can't just make up your mind that you're going to do something some way, because your personality doesn't let you. I'm not nearly as good a parent as I thought I would be, but I'm reaching a stage where it's not as important to me. I can see that you don't have to be perfect to survive or have your kids survive.

"You make mistakes and you learn to accept your mistakes, to accept yourself a little more."

Parents Interpret Themselves to Their Children

As parents face the task of rethinking their role as parents, they are deciding, consciously or not, how they want to behave toward their children, and similarly how they want to interpret themselves to their children. Certainly these thoughts slide directly over from the preceding years, particularly as parents consider the kinds of authorities they were or were not becoming. But now, there is a slight difference. The end of parents' child-rearing years, which once seemed remote, even imponderable, slides into the picture, though perhaps it remains a bit out of focus. Time, at least in an overall sense, seems to be passing quickly. The children are approaching their parents' size. Their shoes are not that much smaller. Their hands, too. A child's socks may fit his mother. They can share personal belongings—records, a badminton set, belts, shoelaces. The father of two school-age children says, "These years are going so fast, and I know that some day we're going to look back with nostalgia and longing. I really know that more as each day passes."

Now parents think about such things as what kind of impression they want to give—and leave with—their children.

"I want my children to have fond memories of me," one mother of two girls, ages seven and ten, says. "That's a new insight for me. I realize that when I snap at them, when I say something that I know I shouldn't say, I wonder if I'm really worrying about it afterwards because it's going to ruin them or if it's because I don't want them to think ill of me."

Sharing/Withholding

Primarily, the issue or theme is how much of themselves to share with their children—or as one parent put it, "how real" to be. If a parent has had a bad day at work or a disappointment, does the parent share it? Many parents report trying to strike a balance, albeit a difficult one to achieve. On one side they don't want to be withholding. Children can sense parents' feelings, and when no mention is made of something that is clearly going on, children's imaginations can run rampant. They can see themselves as responsible when they are not at fault. On the other side, parents don't want to overburden children with more than they can handle.

One mother tells a story about her attempt to find this balance. She and her husband were supposed to go to a dance. At the last minute, the baby-sitter canceled and they were unable to find another.

"I was really psyched up to go out—because Bill and I hadn't been alone for over two months. The girls were in the living room. When I went in to take off my gown and put on my jeans, I got all filled up and ready to cry—I was just so anxious to go out and so angry at what had happened. The girls came in and Melissa said, 'Mommy, are you crying?' And I said, 'Yes.' She said, 'Why?' And I said, 'Because I really wanted to go out tonight.' Then I started to think about it and realized that though I wanted to share my feelings with them, I didn't want to make them feel guilty—that because of them, Mommy couldn't go. So I told them that—and then we all went to McDonald's.

"I can never remember my mother sharing her feelings with me. This was not part of her makeup. Maybe that was typical of her generation—that they played the role of mother. I don't want my daughters to see me only in the role of mother. I want them to see me in a wider spectrum than I saw my mother in."

The decisions of what to share and what not to is trickier if there is family animosity. How much should the children know?

A divorced mother of two who is remarried to a man and has custody of his children faces this situation with her ex-husband and her present husband's ex-wife.

When they sent the husband's children down to visit their own mother, they usually paid their airfare, sent clothes, and gave the ex-wife spending money. One summer they were unable to afford the spending money because they had paid for orthodonture for both of the children.

"Before the boys left, we called them down to talk, because I didn't want them to go home and hear their mother complain about us—and then they would wonder what the truth was. So without attacking their mother, we just told them that the extra money this year was going for braces."

INTERPRETING ONE'S CHILDREN TO THE CHILDREN

Parents also evaluate their children. The nature of children's growth, its backswings and forward spurts, its tumultuous and calm times, seems less alien now. "I know that each stage is not going to last forever," a New Jersey mother with an eight-year-old says. "I used to think that when he was little. Whenever he was in a bad stage I thought that he was going to be like that for the rest of his life and that I'd better do something to shape him up. When he was in a good stage, I thought he was going to be the perfect child and I would never have to worry; he was always going to stay that way."

Parents are also more realistic about their child. They have a good idea what he or she is going to say upon awakening in the morning. They know what might bring on tears and what might stop them. They know what the child will want to eat for lunch, and how the child will respond to the time spent with a grand-parent or friend. They know what their child is like with a stubbed toe, a mosquito bite, a cut, or in bed with a fever. They know what TV programs, books, or movies their child likes. With closed eyes, they can envision their child with pajamas on, just before sleep or leaving for school in the morning. The script is more routine, the scenes known, because most have been played over and over. A bath, brushing teeth, sitting down to a meal, the endless round-robin of clean clothes to dirty clothes to clean clothes again, seem to have happened forever. Despite the surprises, the child con-tinues to grow and change—and parents have to get used to dif-ferences in their child. But each phase lasts for a longer time than in the beginning of the child's life, and so for the day-in and day-out time, most parents are accustomed to their child's behavior.

There are reasons for this sense of greater understanding beyond the years that the parent and child have spent together. The child has entered a period of childhood which many parents clearly re-member. Previously parents gained empathy toward their child from what I think of as normal regressions (the sense of self-dif-fusion that one feels after the birth of a baby gives parents an appre-ciation of their baby's state of being). Now their empathy stems from another source: their own recollections. They can remember what it felt like to be bored on a hot summer afternoon or excited by the prospect of going to a carnival or scared to walk home alone in the dark or mortified by an unjust remark made by a teacher or proud to have done one's work well or jealous of a compliment given to a brother or sister. They can even remember the words of jump-rope chants, knock-knock jokes, and "ob" or pig-latin lan-guages.

Evaluations Are Based on Images

Whenever asked to describe these children that they know so well, parents do so with many value judgments affixed. Their child is "competitive, insecure, and aggressive," or "a very loving, sweet, delightful, happy child, very easy to please," or is "agile" or "clumsy."

The actual behavior that prompts these descriptions could be interpreted in any number of ways. For example, a child asks his parents repeatedly for a guitar. He could be described as "persistent" or "spoiled," as "demanding" or "musically precocious." Perhaps he is "sure of himself, knows what he wants and tries to get it," or maybe he is "on a power trip, trying to see what he can get away with."

In listening to parents' open-ended descriptions of their children, I heard the word "expect" over and over. Parents' judgments of their children were in large part a reflection of whether the child has met, surpassed, or failed to meet their images.

The children have entered the stage in which, according to Erik Erikson, they develop a sense of industry or inferiority. Erikson writes that the child "now learns to win recognition by producing things."[3] Parents have many images about academic achievement. They expect the child to do well, to excel, or just to get by. They expect the child to favor certain aspects of school—reading, writing, math, science, the arts, physical education.

They also may have some expectations that they wish they didn't have.

A father says, "We have a tendency to expect an awful lot from [our oldest son, ten years]. We know we're doing it and yet it's difficult to stop. Many times, it's almost automatic. When he's working with me and he's on the power mower, I'm almost expecting what a twenty-one-year-old would do."

Frequently parents spoke of pinning their most stringent expectations on the firstborn. "I'm much easier with my other kids," this father says. A mother of three girls, eight, seven, and six, says, "I expect very little of my younger children. I want them to be happy, but the oldest has to achieve. She has to prove herself. I'm overstating this a little bit, but not that much." A father of two boys, nine and five, says, "We expect the most of the oldest, make the most demands on him."

Other parents spoke of expecting the most from sons (usually the oldest boy child). A father with a son nine and a daughter thirteen says, "I expect more from my boy certainly. Subconsciously, maybe—but I do expect certain standards."

Sexism, or different expectations for boys and girls, is a subject that warrants much more analysis and study: Does a heightened awareness necessarily mean changed behavior? What are the effects on the children?

Evaluations Are Also Based on Comparisons

Parental judgments are also based on comparisons—how the child acts in comparison to siblings or classmates or neighborhood children.

DIANE JONES

Diane lives in a medium-sized Southern city, with her husband and two sons, ages eight and six. In describing her six-year-old, Lawrence, she says, "If you say, 'Lawrence, don't do such and such,' he'll do it, even if he has to wait three hours, until you've gone to bed. You'll hear him mumbling in the room 'cause he's getting that last word in. He's very negative and stubborn. But at the same time, he's almost like Dr. Jekyll and Mr. Hyde, because he can be so affectionate and sweet. You can't believe that these same negative qualities are coming from this child, this same child that five minutes ago was hugging and kissing you.

"Franklin Jr. [age eight] is more independent and sophisticated.

"The hardest thing is realizing that you have two different personalities. Frank is very fast, picks up things fast. Lawrence is slow. I haven't decided whether Lawrence is slower than normal or just slower than Frank.

"It's been hard for me. Everybody says, 'I don't care how many children you have, they are all going to be different.' But I always find myself comparing them just because Frank was there first—which I know is bad, but it's just something that I do unconsciously."

In this family, as in most families, parental judgments are based on their feelings of affinity or dissimilarity with the children. "Frank is very much like me and Lawrence is like my husband's family. Frank is sophisticated, and I'm not just saying this because everyone says it. He's smart, academically inclined.

"And Lawrence—he just doesn't care, like my husband. Now, my husband is a smart person, but he doesn't put any special effort toward it."

The message is coming to Diane from her friends. Each of your children is unique. But though it is coming from others, it does strike a resonant chord and reverberates within her.

The acceptance of children's individuality is a perennial process in parenthood, a part of every major task. It involves examining and discarding one's projections, the motivations that parents attribute to their children that really come from and reflect the parents themselves. It involves accepting a degree of distance between parent and child. And it involves reconciling one's images of the child with the actual child.

The mother of an eight-year-old is dealing with just this process when she says, "My child is an individual. He is not entirely the child that I anticipated or expected, but he is his own person. And as much as I may want him to do this or be good at that, to excel in this, I can't make him.

"I wanted him to be intellectual. I wanted him to be Mr. Popular. I wanted him to be athletic. I wanted him to be musical. But he can't be everything."

Parents Interpret Their Children to Their Children

Parents have judged their children from the moment of birth on, but what makes parental evaluations of special significance now is that children are more consciously than ever before forming self-concepts. *Parents have the task of deciding how to describe their children to their children.*

Books, articles, and papers about child development may make it seem as if parents hand the child a self-concept like a paper-doll cutout, ready-made. This is not the case, as parents know. Children form their own self-concepts, taking into account their parents' opinions, the opinions of their brothers and sisters, friends, relatives, teachers, and grandparents, and their own assessment of themselves.

BENJAMIN AND MARGARET REEVES

Benjamin, a career naval officer, and his wife, Margaret, are the parents of two daughters, ages nine and six. The older child, Virginia, was born with a cleft palate.

"Virginia," Benjamin says, "doesn't like herself as much as we would like her to. I think she's having a rough time now with her self-image—especially in relation to her sister." The sister has a slight but barely noticeable birth defect—a marking on her face.

"Virginia's first year at school was disastrous. I couldn't believe how cruel the children were. They were physically abusive to her. A bunch of guys pushed her off the sidewalk into the mud. Took her books and things and jerked them away.

"She had never experienced physical abuse before, and it scared me—because I didn't know what direction it would turn her.

"We've always let her know when we weren't sure of ourselves, and we told her we weren't sure what to do then. I think she feels more confidence in us because we're honest to her."

Margaret, Virginia's mother, continues that they did decide

"what to do." They moved Virginia to a school where the children and teachers were more accepting.

"One time," she says, "at the doctor's office, Virginia accidentally saw slides of how she looked at birth—before her first surgery—and it really threw her. She had never seen herself before her surgery—so when we came home and she was talking about it, I took advantage of the fact that she was already discussing it to try to tell her just how pretty we think she is.

"I love Virginia and I really don't think I see her as a birth-defect child. She does have a problem—the cleft palate—but she also has problems with math—but I don't think of her as a math-problem child.

"It's only when it comes up that I think about it. But Virginia does see herself in that way—as a birth-defect child."

Parents realize that they are not the only ones influencing their child's self-concept. In fact, Margaret pointed out to Virginia that the abusive children were giving her a hard time more because of her own attitude about herself than because of the way she looked. "I told her that she was cheating other people as well as herself [if she only sees herself negatively], and she seemed to understand that." Thus Margaret is helping to reshape Virginia's feelings about herself.

Parents' opinions are enormously important. One has only to think about one's own parents and recall: What did they think of me? What did they *really* think of me—despite what they said? As children, we were adept at ferreting out our parents' true feelings, whether camouflaged or clearly stated.

Parents Have Images About Their Children's Self-Concepts

From their own experiences parents have formed images about the kinds of self-concepts they want to foster in their children. The mother of two school-age children says, "I came from a family of shouter-downers, yellers, fighters, and I remember hearing such things in my childhood as 'I wish I'd never had children.' And so I have been intensely protective of my children's self-image, and I cry inside every time I'm mean because I want to ego-boost."

If parents have been demeaned as children, they may work hard not to repeat the process or they may go too far on the other side and "ego-boost" when the child's behavior doesn't warrant it (only to be told so by children—"You're just saying that because you are my parent").

If, on the other hand, a parent has been given self-esteem as a child, it may be seen as a gift that he or she wants to pass on. "My mother always made me feel good about myself," one woman said, "and I want to do the same for my children."

Yet parents find that an abstract idea. "Giving a child a positive self-concept" is a daily negotiation.

HERB AND HELEN WESTHEIMER

Herb and Helen, both doctors, are the parents of an eight-year-old, Charles, whom they describe as "competitive" and "insecure." In addition, they have two other children.

Helen says, "I think we tend to see more negative in Charles [than in the other children], but I don't think that that is really a function of him. I think it is more a function of us and how we related to the first and what we expect of him. We tend to pick up much more on his negative qualities than we do on the other children."

Herb says, "There's a vicious cycle involved. It's obvious that Charles uses behavior which will be disapproved of as a way of gaining our attention."

Suspecting that Charles was being negative not out of the desire to drive his family crazy but as a way to make his mark, to be noticed in his family, his parents attempted to ignore the negative behavior (though they knew this pattern was set and would be difficult to erase) and to try to find other ways to give Charles more pleasurable attention.

Parents Reconcile Their Own Judgments with the Judgments of Others

Parents are not only rendering judgments of their children at home, but receiving them from others, particularly at the child's school. Teachers are judging children all the time—on their behavior, on their social skills, and on their academic achievement. *Parents have the task of assimilating and reconciling other people's perceptions of their children.* Sometimes the opinions of teachers are at odds with those of the parents.

- What if the parent appreciates the child's whimsical, colorful drawings and the insight these drawings reveal, but the teacher thinks that drawing is an unimportant skill and dwells only on the fact that the child is shy?
- What if the parents have always thought of their child as

smart because of his quick questions and extensive vocabulary, but he tests average to below average on achievement tests?

- What if a parent sees her child as adventurous because she skips off eagerly to play with friends, and likes to go to new places and once there seems comfortable, but the teacher says that at school the child hangs back, refuses to look the teacher in the face, resists following directions?
- And what if one's child is "on the bottom of the class," or "a behavior problem" or "isn't motivated," or "seems preoccupied" or "is a daydreamer" or is "hyperactive"? Or on a positive side, what if one's child is "smart" or "gifted" or "motivated" or a "pleasure to teach"?

Parents have to deal with these other judgments of their children first by understanding them.

If the child is acting in a very different way at school and at home, why? What factors at home and at school are influencing this? Parents can confer with the teacher and can go to see for themselves.

For instance, the mother of the child who was "on the bottom of the class" spent a day in school and saw that the teacher was giving terse, highly abstract directions for workbook pages which the child didn't understand. The mother suggested to the teacher that after giving group directions, she might explain the task to the child. The child improved and began to be considered as "pretty smart" by the teacher.

This example omits the emotions of the mother—worry, anger, guilt, despair, and embarrassment. And it presupposes a cooperative teacher.

After figuring out why there is a discrepancy, parents have to try to assess the effect that the teacher's opinion will have on the child and on the parent. If the teacher sees the child as "aggressive" and comes to expect that kind of behavior, will that become a self-fulfilling prophecy, and what can the parent do about it? Sometimes a friendly conversation with the teacher will clear up the problem. Sometimes the child should, if possible, be switched to another teacher who can work with the child's more positive abilities. Or sometimes, the child or parent needs counseling or therapy.

The parents have other people's judgments of their children to deal with, too—grandparents, relatives, neighbors, clerks in stores, doctors, Sunday-school teachers, the parents' own friends, and then, importantly, the child's own judgments and self-evaluations.

Parents Reconcile Their Child's Self-Evaluations with Their Own

ELIZABETH BROWNELL

Elizabeth is a nurse, married, the mother of two children, a son, nine, and a daughter, seven.

"My son, Jack, has always had a tough time reading. And he started to feel real bad about it. He'd come home and say, 'I know that all my teachers think I'm stupid. I know they think that maybe I'm one of those retarded kids. They don't say it yet, but they think it.'

"I said, 'What do you mean?' And he said, 'Well, I just can't keep up. And I have to keep bringing stuff home, and even then, I'm always behind.'

"I said all that reassuring stuff—'We don't think that and we love you.'

"And he said, 'Yeah, but that's the problem. You don't see it because you love me.'

"I sat there thinking, 'What is he saying?' You know, you're so used to thinking that you can make the booboos go away by kissing, that you can make the bad things disappear by love and reinforcement, but something else was going on here.

"And then one day he was watching television, and there was an ad for a speed-reading course where you get your first lesson free. And Jack wrote down the address and brought it to me and said, 'Will you take me over there? The first visit's free. And then maybe I can get better.' And I thought, 'My God. How many more clues do I have to have? Here's a kid who's now writing down where he wants to go for help.'

"When he was in the first grade and having trouble, and the second grade and having trouble, and the third grade and having trouble, I would go to the school and talk to them and they would say, 'Well, he's bright enough but he's a daydreamer—or he's not motivated.' So I would tell him not to daydream or to pay attention.

"He had always been my golden child. He was the best little boy you have ever met in your life. He did everything right, said all the right things, never gave me a hard time.

"Then everything started to go. I took him to a psychologist who gave him a whole bunch of tests. She said that he had a high IQ but that he had pretty severe dyslexia. She said that when the child is smart enough, savvy enough in the system, he can compensate for these things, but the price of compensating was in his feeling about himself.

"He goes for therapy once a week—it's a combination of psychotherapy and educational therapy. The therapist works on comprehension skills with a story and the story leads into a discussion of feelings.

"A lot of things have come up that have been hard to deal with. My husband works until ten o'clock every night. He's only here on Sundays. So I've become the real authority figure. And not being shy or retiring, I have a lot of power. So it came up again and again that Jack defers to me all the time: 'My mother knows,' 'My mother decides,' 'My mother is it!'

"I wasn't even aware of it. But he would come to me over and over: 'Does this shirt look okay with these pants?' If I said 'No,' he wouldn't wear it.

"Jack drew a picture of his father as a robber hiding behind a rock.

"And I think it's back to the same thing that he was saying before: 'I know you love me. I know you think I'm important, but you don't see the problem.' "

Looking at the child's cues and clues is a skill needed just as much with bigger children as it is with infants. Parents find that they learn a great deal by taking their children's perceptions into account, as in Erikson's well-known phrase: "A family can bring up a baby only by being brought up by him."[4]

And that process isn't always easy, as Elizabeth Brownell has realized. Because of the therapy, Jack is standing on his own two feet for the first time. "He now talks back to us, and he never used to do that. I'm not used to dealing with him on that level. My daughter [age six] has talked back to me since the day she could talk. I'm used to it. But not from the kid who never talked back. So I stand there and part of me is happy because I think, 'Yes, that's what was wrong; he wasn't doing that before.' But it makes things more difficult in terms of raising him."

Elizabeth now has a changed image of parenthood. "This has knocked us over," she says. "We were so sure that love was enough, that verbal support was enough, that being a unified family was enough. But it isn't. Jack wants more than that."

This experience illustrates the nature of growth in parenthood. As her son grew, Elizabeth found that the images she had no longer fit. Although it wasn't always easy, she was able to listen to her son and to form new images.

Children Now Have Images of Parenting

An interesting phenomenon begins to take place in the middle years of childhood. Not only do parents have images of parenthood, but children are beginning to create their own images of what parents should be like, and some of their images are in opposition to those of their parents. It is by differentiating themselves that children become individuals. Margaret Mead has termed this striving that children have to be different from their parents as the immigrant personality.[5] If the grandparent has been strict, then the parent might decide to be more lenient, only to be told by his or her child: "I think you let us get away with too much." They hear their child espousing just the attitude that they once resisted. Despite parents' wishes for unity and closeness, in our culture a certain distance and differentiation between parent and child is inevitable.

SEPARATING AND CONNECTING

Defining the increasing separateness of their own and their child's identity while holding onto the connectedness has been a task of every stage and remains so in the Interpretive Stage. Inherent in the process is the realization that comes with increasing frequency as the child gets older: That "my child is not me."

More Separateness

LYLE STEVENS

"I have to tell myself over and over that my children are different from me. Something that might have upset me as a child is not necessarily upsetting to them.

"Shawn [her seven-year-old] has a teacher who yells at him. I asked him how he felt about it. At least I was smart about it. I didn't tell him how *I* felt. He said that it made him *sad*, and I thought, 'Well, that's interesting.' Because it would have enraged me.

"I was at the school the other day, and I found Scott [her eight-year-old] sitting out in the hall. I asked him what he was doing out there, and he said that he hadn't finished his math work and was doing it in the hall. I said, 'Work away.'

"I went into the office, but I could see him talking to himself, so I went out again. He showed me the problem he was doing. It was a problem that had to do with a lot of zeros, only the teacher hadn't told him the zero trick and he was trying to do it in his head.

"When I explained it, he whipped right through it. I was furious with the teacher. But he wasn't upset at all. So why should I be upset?"

One difference between this stage and earlier stages is that the child is now carving out a slightly separate domain: by being more independent, by spending more time with friends, by finding his or her own interests. Many parents find that their children are drawn to interests that are similar and yet clearly different from theirs: a mother interested in classical music, a daughter interested in rock music; a father interested in old-time movies, a son interested in science-fiction movies; a mother interested in animals but afraid of snakes, a son interested in snakes.

THOMAS MERRILL

Thomas Merrill is a schoolteacher in an inner-city school. Eschewing the acquisitive, materialistic society in which he was raised, he and his wife live simply in a working-class neighborhood with their two adopted children, a son, nine, and a daughter, two.

"We are going into a whole new phase with our oldest son. James wants a Ferrari and a BMW. That doesn't fit our values. I think that he's choosing to figure out parts of the world that are different from the parts we have held as most important."

Thomas now sees that parenthood follows a pattern: periods of harmony, of getting along with each child, followed by periods of disharmony when he and the child are out of synch. He has just gone through such a time with James.

"There were a couple of months of discomfort when things were not clicking, when he seemed to be angry all the time and he got under our skin—beyond what seemed reasonable. We finally realized that we were in a whole new phase. He was needing different things from us, and we were having to adjust."

This example illustrates the opportunity for growth in parenthood. Changes in the child call for parents to give up old images and form new ones. The psychoanalyst Judith S. Kestenberg states it well:

> Each transition from one phase to the next presents a challenge to both parents and children to give up outdated forms of interaction and to adopt a new system of coexistence. The ability of a parent to meet his side of this challenge depends on his inner preparedness to accept the new image the child forms of him and to erect a new image of his child.[6]

Parents' Psychological History Is Influential

Christine O'Shea, a full-time mother, recently went through such a transition with her eight-year-old son. It was very hard for her to allow her son to be himself.

She then realized that it was equally hard for her to let her husband do things his own way. "I now see that when I ask him a question, I'm not asking, I'm controlling. Like I'll say, 'What day are you leaving for your business trip? Don't you think that you ought to call up the airport and make a reservation?'

"I never thought of myself as a manipulative person. I'm quiet—not outwardly bossy. But I do see that I manipulate in my own quiet way. I like to have things done *my* way.

"My father does it, too, which I've just recently noticed. He controls people. I'm sure that in growing up I wanted to please him. It has always been important to me to find out what he thought I should do, and then do it."

Christine now doesn't try to please her parents if it goes against her better judgment. "My mother was just here, and my son was dawdling on the way to school, and she said that I should handle it in a certain way. I didn't agree. And so I didn't do it." Parenthood has brought an issue from Christine's childhood back into the forefront of her thoughts. She has taken steps to understand it and then to grow. This has made it possible for her to feel more separate from her children. "I don't want my kids to feel that they have to please me at all costs."

Circumstances Are Influential, Too

The circumstances of one's life play a powerful part in affecting the way parents face the issue of separateness/connectedness. Whether or not both parents are full-time working parents, whether the parents are divorced, whether one of the parents has died are all important.

MARY ELLEN HILL

Several years ago, Mary Ellen and her husband and their two children were returning from a vacation when a truck crashed into their car. She and the children were injured, and her husband was killed. Mary Ellen wants her ten-year-old son to identify with his father but fears pushing him too much.

"Joe is very much like his father. And people tell him and it makes him happy. He loves to be told this.

"Joe joined the Scouts at our church and he said, 'Mommy, do you think Daddy might have been in my troop—because it's the oldest one in the state?' And I said, 'He probably was. We'll look in some of his old Scout stuff.' So we started looking, and he was! Joe was thrilled—he really could identify with him. Joe found out that his father was an Eagle Scout, and he looked at the roster at the church and his father's name was on it. Joe told the scoutmaster, and he wore some of his father's old scarves. And Joe found his father's old handbook, and he took that to show his scoutmaster."

The issue becomes aggravated when Mary Ellen thinks of Joe's future. "Joe's father and grandfather and great-grandfather were all lawyers. I do not want Joe to feel that he has to be a lawyer.

"They all went to the university, and I don't want Joe to feel that he has to go to the university.

"Frequently people ask him, 'What are you going to do?' And I know what they're expecting. And recently he has been saying that he wants to be a lawyer and go to law school at the university. And I've tried to be very casual, to say, 'You do whatever you want to do. If that's what you want, I'd be happy, but don't think that you have to.'

"I've tried very hard not to pressure him, because I think that's a mistake that many parents make."

As for herself, she says, "I am much freer with my children than if there were the two of us. I do not want my children to grow up with the idea that they only had a mother and she was so protective that she wouldn't let them do this and she wouldn't let them do that. Sometimes it's hard, but because I don't want them to have that image, I have tried to let them do things that I would never have let them do before."

New Connections

With the increased sense of separation comes new connections. Many parents said, "We're further apart and at the same time closer together." Parents find that there are many more activities that they can share with their children. They can cook, photograph, or collect stamps together. They can go fishing in the morning, sitting side by side as the sun comes up. They can scream and yell and cheer at a ball game on TV, play ball in the backyard, the schoolyard, or the street together. They can sit through a movie passing popcorn back and forth, swim laps, or jog together. They can walk quietly through a museum, too. They can read and then talk with each other about a magazine or newspaper article.

INTERPRETING THE WORLD TO THE CHILDREN

Out of this myriad of experiences shared or apart, parents are often asked to or feel called upon to explain, to interpret, to analyze, and to moralize. *The major task of the Interpretive Stage is for parents to decide how they are going to interpret their children's existence to them; what facts they want to share, what behavior and manners they want to teach, and what values they want to impart.*

I have used the word "decide" in descriptions of tasks, but that is not meant to imply that the actions parents take are always deliberate and thought out. Sometimes decisions are fallen into, and sometimes they are chosen.

Providing a Life-Style

Parents have *the task of deciding what kind of life they want to and can afford to provide.* Parents may live in the community that they grew up in or they may live where their jobs have taken them, but many think (and these questions have been pursued for a long time): Do I want to raise my children in the suburbs, the country, or the city?

They daydream about the kind of family life they would like. Maybe it is living in an apartment where their children's friends are just an elevator ride away. Maybe it is having a home where each child has a room. Maybe it involves Sunday family barbecues with the good smells of food cooking. Or maybe it is living in the country with an organic vegetable garden.

LUIS SANCHEZ

Luis teaches at a college on the West Coast and has three daughters, eight, four, and three.

"My family was very important in my and my wife's growing up. For we [Mexican-Americans] are very interdependent. Part of it is probably a factor of income—you need to pull together when there's less to pull with.

When it came time to look for a job and [the other students in graduate school] asked me where I was going to go, I said, 'Home.' They thought I was crazy. 'Why don't you try to get a big-name school?' they asked. For my discipline, the Midwest is where the strongest schools are. But I'd rather teach at a junior college here than at a major university someplace where I didn't know anybody."

For Luis and his family, the image reflected a known. They were coming back to something very familiar, and their choice has given them contentment: that his brother-in-law is close by and will come over to help him move a couch, that birthday parties are for the whole family "and you stay and talk to your cousins," and that his elderly father-in-law will soon come to live with them.

For others, the images are more unknown, and sometimes when they are translated to reality they work, sometimes they don't. A middle-class father who wanted to raise children in an inner-city neighborhood says, "I got annoyed at my son's not using correct grammar, and I was really surprised that it bothered me." One family who wanted to farm found it fulfilling, while another found it drudgery.

The same process is true for schools. Parents may send their children to the neighborhood school without thinking much about it, or they might move to a certain neighborhood because the public schools are supposed to be good. Some search for a private school.

Parents have images about their children's schooling—that school will be a place that will nurture children's curiosity or a place where children learn how to succeed in the wider world, a place that will civilize the child, teach them, or help them learn. These images can be realized to a lesser or greater degree, causing the concomitant tensions or feelings of achievement.

Both neighborhoods and schools are not abstract institutions, but collections of people. And parents do have convictions about the kinds of people—adults and children—that they hope their children will associate with; although, as they know, their children make their own friendships.

Giving/Getting

The issue of providing is one manifestation of the theme of giving and getting that predominated in the first years of parenthood. Now questions of giving and getting are often focused on material things. Parents have to decide when to say yes and when to say no to children's requests for new clothes or for toys. Do they give the child an allowance or spending money? Does the child do chores to earn money?

These issues often have ties to the parents' past. One couple, both factory workers on the night shift, had hoped to be able to give their children everything they had lacked as children. But as their oldest child entered school, they realized that he wasn't caring much about anything because he had so much. They began to limit what they bought for him.

A doctor who had grown up in the affluent Hollywood milieu came to the same conclusion, but by a very different route. He decided that the reason he had been able to grow into a purposeful and productive adult—and many of his contemporaries hadn't—was that as children their every whim was indulged. They couldn't survive in the less indulgent world outside of their families. And he, too, decided to limit what he provided for his daughter.

Providing also extends to the out-of-school or extracurricular activities. Parents think about what experiences they want to give their children—ballet lessons, Little League, art, music, sports instruction, summer camp, scouting. These decisions are usually linked to the parents' own childhood. Were they given art lessons? Did they envy others who had them, or begrudge the time that organized activities took from "hanging around"? With the provision of special activities, what are the responsibilities? If the children don't like an activity, do they have to stick to it or not?

Interpreting Facts, Skills, and Experiences

In adjunct with providing is interpreting. *Parents have the task of deciding how to interpret life to their children.*

- A five-year-old child wakes up saying, "I had a bad dream—a witch was chasing me."
- She comes into breakfast wearing shorts and a T-shirt on a windy, brisk day.
- The child reacts to the morning's news and asks: "Why are there robbers? Will they come here?"
- She says, "I don't want the kind of cereal we buy! Why can't we have the kind Katie has?"

Fifteen minutes in the morning with a five-year-old, fifteen minutes rife with invitations for the parent to interpret.

Take an eight-year-old boy:

- He comes home from school announcing that his teacher isn't fair. She always yells at kids before she even knows what has happened.
- He becomes outraged by the way a neighbor treats his dogs and says that the neighbor shouldn't be allowed to have pets.
- When his younger sister comes home from school announc-

ing that she is learning to read, he shoves an adult book at her and says, "Let's see you read this."

Or a few minutes with a ten-year-old:

- She calls a friend to play, but the friend is busy, and then this child mopes because "I always call her first, she never calls me."
- She decides to read a magazine and comes in to ask what "incest" means.
- Later she has a plan for making money—she is going to sell the books and toys she has outgrown.

In almost every encounter with a child, parents are asked, verbally or nonverbally, to explain. Parents may choose not to or feel unable to answer. But if they do respond, they find themselves explaining facts: where the water in the sink comes from and where the water in the toilet goes, what happens to the sun at night and how bridges are built over rivers, why there are more right-handed people in the world than left-handed. Parents also pass on skills: how to solve the problem if there is one stick of gum and three kids, or how much change the child should get from the market if he brings one dollar and the milk costs eighty-nine cents, or how many inches the children have grown and how much they weigh.

Parents interpret the social world: why the man next door is always yelling, why a teenage baby-sitter said, "Shut up," why a neighbor is moving, and why people get divorced. They warn their children of possible dangers—of not putting their hands into electric sockets or leaning out of windows or crossing the street without looking, or taking something without asking, or going somewhere with a stranger.

Parents deal with fears, from the fantasies of monsters in the dark corners of the room that younger children have to the fears of older children—of crazies on the streets, of spiders scurrying across the floor, of pesticides, of prisons, war, nuclear radiation leaks, and eventual death.

Children's questions and concerns can be profound and disturbing. Essentially, parents find themselves being asked to describe their version of the world.

One day as a mother walked with her two young children out of school, she saw a crowd gathering. She walked to its fringes and quickly picked up some facts: that two men had just tried to rob a fast-food store on the corner (one which she occasionally stopped at with her children), that the manager had pulled a gun, that the assailants had countered with gunfire, and that the manager had been wounded, perhaps critically.

Her children did not understand what had happened, but sensing the tension, they began to clamor for information.

What should she tell them? she wondered. Should she give them an idealized picture—tell them that everything was fine? But that was clearly untrue and would make them feel distrustful. Should she give them an ultra-real picture, tell them everything to warn them about the dangers in the world? But that might be frightening.

This mother told her children the overall facts. They began to ask questions. She concentrated on helping them figure out what to do if they were ever mugged and how they could take special care to lead safe lives (dogs at home, locks on the door, not walking on dark streets alone, etc.).

Parents have just passed through a parallel process: from the idealism of the beginning years of parenthood, through tumultuous and quiet times, to what they now feel is a greater realism about themselves and their children. In the Interpretive Stage, parents turn toward the world to define and articulate realities as they see them: why someone would want to rob a store; why people injure each other; how they can and do protect themselves in the face of danger.

Telling/Listening

Besides interpreting or telling, parents are listening. Their images help to set their course of action. Images about listening and telling are also shaped by one's adult experience.

WILLIAM WIECKE

William at one time was a high school teacher. He now has a government job. He and his wife and their three school-age children live in a large Eastern city.

"A couple of years ago, I got a call from a boy I had taught. He was going up for his draft hearing. His board was maintaining that he had just made up the idea that he was a pacifist to avoid going to Vietnam. He asked me if I remembered an essay he had written in the tenth grade about going out in the woods and shooting a deer and finding the deer dead and deciding never to shoot anything ever again.

"I did remember that essay. Indeed I did. It was one of the worst written, punctuated, and spelled documents that ever came across my desk. He was a very nonverbal kid who wrote in tiny short sentences.

"I was able to write a letter [to the draft board] and had it notarized and that helped keep him out of jail.

"But the impact on me personally—I'll never forget it! This guy in the tenth grade writes something of deep, deep importance for the rest of his life, and I look at the goddam spelling. The only reason I remembered it was because he wrote it so badly. And I was furious with myself—miserable."

From this experience William decided that he wanted to be the kind of father who listens.

But listening is not always as simple as it sounds.

Mary Ellen Hill

Mary Ellen says, "I want my children to be free to talk to me, freer than I was, but there are times when I go back to the way I was brought up. Some of my old tapes are still playing in me."

Mary Ellen, in the course of living with her children, has found that she has redefined her image of being "free to talk to." She doesn't like it when her children, in saying what they feel, are "excessively rude."

A fine line exists between encouraging children to say how they feel and letting them take out these feelings on the parent, making the adult the brunt of the child's sadnesses, angers, jealousies.

Furthermore, children don't always want to talk about everything with their parents, as Mary Ellen has also discovered. Her son, Joe, was unable to talk about his father's death for a long time. As painful as it was for both of them, Mary Ellen kept the subject open, by mentioning the death every so often. She didn't make Joe talk—she just waited until he was ready.

School-age children often say, "I don't want to tell you" or "It's a secret." There are some domains of their life that they are beginning to keep to themselves.

Elizabeth Brownell

Elizabeth had just the opposite upbringing from Mary Ellen Hill's. Where there was little talk about feelings in Mary Ellen's home, in Elizabeth's there was too much.

"I grew up in the era when parents had learned that you could talk things over with your children, to avoid any kind of physical discipline.

"The teachers [in the school she went to] were always meeting with the parents and teaching them key words. One of the key words in 1945 was 'steady.' You looked the child straight in the eye and you said, 'Steady.'

"The whole time I was growing up, I was never spanked. Never. We would have talks that were enough to drive me over the wall and through the hills and up the trees. I would stomp around, slamming doors. And my mother would follow me around saying, 'Steady. Now let's talk about it. I'm so happy that you're acting out because now it's out of you. You're expressing anger and that's good. Now we can sit down and talk about how you feel about it!'

"So when I got to be a parent, I thought this stuff is for the birds. It's okay to discuss feelings in some areas, but not over every little thing."

Elizabeth, after Jack's dyslexia problem, has had to modify her position, however, and listens more to what her children are saying to her.

As children reach each new phase of growing up, parents cast back to their experiences and form images, which in the cases of Mary Ellen and Elizabeth have been successfully modified as they live with children.

It can be particularly difficult to achieve one's image if others, especially family members, disagree with either the image or the way to achieve it.

DIANE AND FRANKLIN JONES

Diane and Franklin both have the same expectation of their children: that they learn skills and manners. But because of their diverse backgrounds, they have different ideas on how to do it.

Franklin says, "I come from a—I wouldn't say a poverty-stricken background, but a very low-income background. My father worked in a cotton mill and he died when I was nine, and my mother and grandmother brought me up. We just didn't have any money. My mother dropped out of school in the ninth or tenth grade and cooked in a boardinghouse.

"Diane was brought up in a totally different environment. Her mother has a formal education.

"We argue, Diane and I, about habits that the kids got. She wants to teach them things that are right—like eating habits. I know they are right, but I think it puts a lot of strain on them right now.

"I didn't have much education, but I have constantly progressed, with the help of the Good Lord. I went from good jobs to bad jobs to good jobs. I think I got a real good job now. I feel that I bettered myself.

"I think that it's because of the wit I have. I taught myself. Not ever would my mother sit down and say, 'Son, your fork goes over there and you keep your hand in your lap.' I was never taught that, but I picked it up. And I think I could sit down with the President and be just as nice and respectful as he."

Diane says, "Well, what I feel is that you can't depend on picking these things up. You have got to start at home. Show children the right way. That's our responsibility. Not everybody has the kind of common sense to determine this is right and this is wrong. You have to get a foundation at home. You don't have to be a drill sergeant—and I'd be the first to say that I'm guilty of that sometimes."

Diane and Franklin are disagreeing not on the fact that they want their children to have manners, but on the nature of learning, on the relative importance of training and what Franklin calls "wit" or one's genetic endowment.

When parents disagree on how to raise their children—and they do disagree—they have three possible routes to take: They can continue the rift, digging it deeper and deeper; they can search for common ground and work out a compromise; or they can agree to disagree, that is, accept—without demeaning—the other parent's different approach.

Interpreting the world stretches beyond just telling.

Setting Behavior Standards

Parents at this stage have the task of deciding how they want their children to behave. That task which began much earlier continues in the Interpretive Stage and beyond. Parents think about such questions as: Should the children stand up when a grown-up enters the room or stay seated? Do they call adults Mr., Mrs., Miss, or Ms., or by their first names?

Parents think through their expectations about family organization. Are the children expected to make their own beds? Do they help with meals? Are they supposed to share in the care of the younger children if there are any?

The children's aggressions, resistances, disobediences, remain an issue in the Interpretive Stage, and, in some cases, can become more of an issue. Jack Brownell, for example, changed from a "golden boy" to more of a "behavior problem," and his mother had to cast aside the relationship she had established with him in the Authority Stage and establish a new one.

Children can and do change. A quiet child following a divorce becomes rebellious. A pugnacious child following a move becomes quiet. An easygoing child, without an overtly apparent reason, becomes demanding. If circumstances cause a change in the parent or

the child, or if the parents are dissatisfied with the authority relationships they have established, they can make changes.

Redefining the Authority Relationship

THERESA DUFFY

Theresa is a single parent who now trains teachers. She has four
children—three girls who are grown, and one son who is nine.

"In my childhood I wanted twenty children. I wanted to love
somebody. I wanted and needed to be loved, and I wasn't. When I
was a child, I was very abused—and I wanted children, enough
children to come out of the wall.

"It's always been hard for me to understand why—from nine
days old—adults hated me. The only thing I could rationalize is
that my grandmother blamed me for my mother's having me. I
couldn't have done anything at that age to make them hate me.

"My grandmother raised me. She would make me take care of all
the other children—and if I didn't do it, I would get beat up. And
so I guess you would say that I shouldn't want to have my own
children, but I did. I did.

"When I was eight I left my grandmother and came by myself to
find my mother [250 miles away]. My mother sent me back, and my
grandmother, of course, was waiting for me—to kill me.

"Then I started playing hooky from school, and the school said
that since my grandmother wasn't my mother, my mother had to
come get me.

"She didn't. She just said that she'd be waiting for me to come to
her. But when I got to the station, she wasn't there. I got from the
station to her house by myself [several miles away]. Nine years old.
My mother was home. She didn't do nothing that day—but she had
a habit—she would whip me for anything. It was her frustration.

"My mother had no time for me. I was always jealous of the
white kids she worked for because when they came to our house, it
was okay if they jumped up on the couch. It was okay for white
kids not to have any manners, but not for us black kids.

"I had children because I wanted to be loved, but I almost ended
up the same person as my mother and grandmother."

Theresa had three daughters when she was quite young. Later,
she went on welfare.

"My frustration came from taking care of my children in my
home and never being alone. I had wanted children all my life but I
didn't want them twenty-four hours and I didn't know what to do
about it.

"James [her youngest son]—I didn't want him, but I didn't believe in abortion. I had it in my mind not to take care of him, but he wouldn't eat and they called me and said he would starve if I didn't come. He was the only child of mine that I loved. I fell in love with him. If I was trying to bathe him, he would grab onto me. It was hard for me to try to ignore him.

"The strength that I have now—it comes from my children. My daughter made me get off of the welfare. She came home and told me that she'd be just like me—stay home, have children, be on welfare. I just had to get off."

Theresa started a small day-care center in her neighborhood and eventually began to work toward a college degree.

"I went to a black child development conference, and at this conference I realized that I could have been labeled as a child abuser. I had almost abused my girls to death. That made me want to change.

"And that's what I did. I learned from different workshops not to take my frustrations out on James. I'd rather tell him that I need to be alone than to abuse him. We sit down and talk about problems.

"I haven't put my hands on James for years. He was my guinea pig, my experiment."

The excesses of frustration can spill over to violence and abuse— but the denial of anger can also cause problems in parents.

JOAN WESTON

Joan, the mother of a nine-year-old, found that the way she initially resolved her authority relationship with her son wasn't working for her. As a child she had been the good one in her family— her sister was the bad one. "My sister was everybody's badness. She was my father's temper. She was mine."

As an adult, Joan was terrified of anger. She learned to be less afraid during her second marriage, "because I married a man who was Spanish, who had no trouble at all with temper tantrums. And he taught me."

The biggest source of her learning, she feels, was bio-energetic therapy.

"The guy I worked with actually taught me. He'd ask me to say, 'Give it to me.' And I couldn't say it—for about two months. 'Give it to me'—'I want'—whatever. Couldn't say it. Whispered it. Begged. And he finally said to me, 'You don't have to beg—you don't have to plead—you don't have to whisper. All you have to do is say it. 'Cause you have a right to say it.'

"What happened when I was through with this therapy was that I was able to yell and stomp. I have a couple of rules. If I am going to get mad at Josh, I never back him up against a wall, physically or psychologically. I never stare him in the eye. It's like, 'I'm going to blow this out now. I'm not going to hurt you. I'm not going to make you lose face. I don't want to shame you. I just want you to know that I'm really pissed and enough is enough.' "

In parenthood the issues from the past that have been painful can return. The way her mother and her grandmother handled their own anger was terrible to Theresa Duffy. The way Joan Weston avoided anger as a child was equally untenable to her as an adult. Both established authority relationships with their own children that replicated their childhood patterns. Their children had re-triggered childhood conflicts in the Authority Stage which re-mained unresolved in the Interpretive Stage. Finally, with help, both of these women were able to create authority relationships that worked better, that came closer to their images. They were able to grow.

Kenneth Keniston describes human development as "a very rough road, pitted with obstructions, interspersed with blind al-leys, and dotted with seductive stopping places. It can be traversed only with the greatest of support and under the most optimal con-ditions." [7]

Many metaphors have been used to describe development. Cath-erine Chilman describes it as a spiral staircase, with arduous por-tions, and landings where one can rest. [8]

As I have talked to parents and thought about parenthood, the analogy of traveling on a stream has seemed an apt one for parent-hood. This trip is at times calm. The stream is wide and mirror-smooth. The sun lights up the waters. All seems secure and tran-quil. Then rocks crop up, some hidden, some piercing the surface. The water churns around, and one has to be careful to steer around the rocks or be grounded or injured by collisions and out-of-control spins. Certain danger spots are inevitable—though they differ for each traveler.

This analogy is apt because in parenthood the very same themes recur, like waters that crest and fall. One solution of a task might not hold and must be resolved again. The critical factor always is the parent's images—of where he or she wants to go. When a par-ent can resolve the dissonance between an image and reality, then growth occurs.

Responding to Children's Concepts of Fairness

Then, along the stream of parenthood, there are always new vis-tas. Children are continually growing, changing. During this stage they are developing new mastery in reasoning. A parental dictate might be met with a countercharge of "It's not fair."

The research studies of Jean Piaget and Lawrence Kohlberg have shown that children's ideas of fairness (or morality) pass through stages. At six, the child thinks that what's fair is what he or she wants. At eight or nine, the child has a fixed and literal concept of fairness—everyone should have the same.[9] The psychologist Patricia Minuchin says, "It is emotionally important and intellectually necessary for children to go through this period of rigidity. They move from adult protection to the protection of a rigid social code."[10] By the time children are twelve, most have reached the concept of equity, that what's fair for one person might not be fair for another.[11]

Children also become adept at, almost legalistic in, reasoning. One nine-year-old, whenever he wanted his mother to take him somewhere like roller skating or bowling, would start out with "Do you like children?" followed by "Do you like doing things with children?" Parents have to figure out how to deal with such issues.

Responding to Sibling Combat

Another use of this sometimes sharp-edged verbal sword is in sibling combat. *Parents have the task of dealing with conflict between their children.*

Eliot Daley, in his book about fatherhood, *Father Feelings*, has a bittersweet description of teasing:

> In teasing, everybody loses. A lot. . . . This is a vicious tournament. It usually starts at the top, and trip-hammers its way down to the youngest. What seems to detonate this chain of fireworks is someone's feeling left out or upstaged. Someone feeling low looks for someone to put down even lower. They inevitably find their prey.
> . . . I know the fray has started by that particular kind of soaring, wounded howl that arches over my normal threshold of obliviousness to children's wrangling. This piteous cry pierces walls and windows, even shatters my heavy Saturday-morning sluggish slumber. I am suddenly bolt upright in bed, wide awake.
> More than that, I am fierce with rage. I cannot stand to hear one of my children tease another.
> . . . Why should teasing turn me into a roaring, grown-up temper tantrum, luring me to the brink of committing mayhem on my own children?

Eliot Daley finds that teasing makes him feel "helpless."

I lack the power to impose control on the uncontrolled impulses of a child. Nor am I able to stimulate their self-control.

So I lose my own.[12]

Control/Out of Control

Feeling helpless (that "I am not enough") or out of control has been a theme that has run through many parents' darker moments. It is the antithesis of what many parents expect of themselves as parents: control, responsibility, maturity.

Teasing does have more emotional connotations for parents—particularly those with siblings who were, at one time or another, teased as children and have a residual stock of feeling about teasing. If the teasing was by their brothers or sisters, their own ordinal place—oldest, middle, youngest—will make a difference in their reactions, as will their feelings of affinity or dissimilarity to their children.

Finally, parents' images of "family" and "family life" come into play. When one child in a family says to another, "I hate you so much," or when they all turn into a writhing, squealing mass of pounding feet and arms and shrill voices—it's hard for parents not to feel, "I must have done something wrong" or "It's my fault." But if they have separated their own identities from those of their children, and they see family life as having ups and downs, they tend to overcome their initial discomfort more quickly than if they see family life as television sit-coms picture it—parents always home in the magazine-fresh living room reading the paper, in the spotless kitchen stirring one pot which miraculously turns into a full-course dinner, with endless time and patience to listen to their children's minor scrapes and hassles (which happen conveniently one at a time) and judiciously resolve these problems (in a half an hour's time).

Parents have to continue to figure out how they are going to handle the intrafamily skirmishes, the competitions, the accusations and denials, the put-downs.

Transmitting Values

None of these situations is distinct from value-building. When one child in a family takes another's possession without asking, the parents, in mediating or offering an opinion, are transmitting values and morals. In fact, in most dealings between parent and child, values are being communicated.

- At a birthday party, a child opens a present and says, "I already have this." The parents, by what they choose to say, are telling their child when and how to express honesty and directness.
- A child comes home with perfect math papers. Later, it is discovered that he hasn't been doing his own homework. Here the values in question are the difference between cheating and getting help.
- Some kids decide to see what they can get away with and pocket a pack of gum from a drugstore, without paying. When confronted, they say, "That guy who owns it always rips us off by giving us the wrong change." Parents have two value-laden issues to confront: the children's action and the adult's.

Thus another task of the Interpretive Stage is for parents to decide what morals, values, and beliefs they want to pass on to their children.

As children approach the teenage years, parental emphasis on values intensifies.

LESLIE DAVIDSON

Leslie and her husband live in the South with their daughter, twelve, and their son, eight.

"I am more afraid now of making mistakes than I have ever been, even as a brand-new mother. Every day, every decision seems so vital. Now we're getting into the area of morals—the biggies. We're not just talking about saying 'How do you do?' and 'Thank you very much.' We're talking about this child's character."

Jerome Kagan writes:

> Raising children has another psychological benefit: It offers parents an opportunity to validate the value system they brought to adulthood. Sometimes it is similar to the one they took from their families two decades earlier, sometimes it is a radical transformation, struck from intense childhood pain and carried to adulthood in a vow not to visit upon the next generation the destructive practices and philosophies that scarred their lives. Each parent has a chance to promote a hard-won set of ethics and to test the utility of standards that took many years to create. In a sense, each parent is a scientist testing a personal theory of human development with each child.[13]

The parent is a scientist of sorts—in unraveling all the complexities of each situation he or she has to deal with, in figuring out the underlying meanings of the child's behavior, in discerning what's right and what's wrong, and then in deciding what to do.

The mother whose son was not doing his own homework found that it was better if she didn't respond to the situation at that moment because her impulse was to blame ("You should never have done that") and to moralize ("That's cheating yourself"). After she let her own feelings cool off, she could sit down with her son and ask him why.

He told her that he didn't understand the math assignments and felt scared. He wanted to do well.

The mother was then able to be understanding while conveying her moral beliefs: "The homework is really designed for you to practice what you've learned." She figured out that her son did need help, not the kind of help in which the math problems were done for him, but help in teaching him how to do them himself. She was able to find a college student to tutor her son. Figuring out what one thinks and believes in order to deal with this kind of situation is a transforming experience.

DECIDING HOW INVOLVED TO BE

Determining the right amount of involvement clearly stretches back to the first days of parenthood. Yet now parents find that earlier relationships have to be altered. *Parents have the task of deciding how involved to be in the children's lives, at home and away from home. This, like issues of identity, revolves around defining the areas of separateness/connectedness to their children.*

The children have changed. They can dress themselves, clean up their rooms, get food, and during the elementary school years, they become independently mobile—they can ride their bikes, walk, or use public transportation to get to many of the places they want to go.

In fact, the child's going off is often one of those "key events" that punctuate parenthood—parents retain such memories as the first time the child boards a public bus, money in hand, and framed by the window rides off until the bus disappears into the distance.

The children can also keep themselves entertained for long periods of time, though "I'm bored" and "There's no one to play with" or "I don't know what to do" are often repeated refrains.

The children are involved with their own friends much of the time. They form and re-form clubs, and make clubhouses in their rooms, or off in the woods. They hunt for buried treasure, they check the phone booths for unretrieved change, frequent ten-cent stores, and drugstores or soda shops. They look for fossils, go fishing. They go bowling, play miniature golf, ride dirt bikes or skateboards through obstacle courses that they set up. They talk in grandiose terms about making and spending money. In pairs, they discuss and analyze their other friends. And although they can be nonconformists, if one has a special new kind of sneakers, the others are likely to want them, too.

The children are moving out.

- The mother of a ten-year-old: "My daughter is spending more time away from the family than she ever has before. She took a trip for a week, to visit friends. She's talking about going to overnight camp. And she was a child who feared separation from me terribly a year ago."
- The mother of a nine-year-old: "[My son] has stayed at friends' houses since he was little. It's not the amount of time we are apart that's different. But he is now relating to the world in some ways that we can't touch. I have an image of having him tied to us in certain ways. He's got ten umbilical cords. Maybe five of them just got cut. Whereas before, they were all there. They were flexible but there."
- The mother of a nine-year-old: "I don't know where my son is all the time and I realize that we can't constantly keep tabs on him. He went and had dinner with some friends down the block and came home about ten-thirty. It's not new for him to be over at other people's houses—but now he's beginning to arrange these things all by himself."

Parents Have Images of Involvement

The involvement of parents becomes less dictated by the child's physical needs and more determined by the parents' decision to "do things together."

These decisions are usually affected by whether their own parents spent time with them when they were children and how they felt about that time.

JOANNE HOWARD

Joanne is an art designer, married, the mother of two children.

"My mother was never involved in me. I don't remember wishing that she would be, but I do remember feeling left out and not knowing why.

"I was an outsider at school because the school was not in my community. We lived in the country. I was bused in. My mother made absolutely no effort to have people over or to take me to people's houses."

Joanne is now very involved in her children's lives. She is there for them when they come home from school—she sits with them and hears about their day. Their house is a gathering point for children in the neighborhood—all of which pleases Joanne. But in rectifying her mother's "mistakes," she finds that she has to be careful not to become overly identified with her children and to move into their lives too much—arranging their social life for them, solving problems for them.

JILL HARRISON

Jill, a teacher, lives in sparsely settled mountains in the northern United States with her three children and her husband.

She describes her mother: "She was always ready and willing to take me to any of my friends, to any activity that existed. It was always my mother who drove the gang of us. When there was a production to be put on at school, my mother would do the choreography for it or write the poem or find the costumes—never in a pushy way. But whenever I would come home and ask her to do something, I never got a negative reaction."

Jill wants to be similarly involved in her children's lives. "I feel like I'm getting closer to my children now that they are older, there are so many things we can do together."

Both of these women have fulfilled their images, though both find that it is a tenuous balance—as Jill says—to be involved without being pushy.

Parents Have Images of Their Partner's Involvement

Both of these women have images of how involved they want their husbands to be.

JILL HARRISON

"My husband is involved in the children. He's one of those people who is a natural. He doesn't have to think about it very much. When a child comes up to him and says, 'Can I do some woodworking?'—he stops what he's doing and works with the kids. They'll go to him before they'll go to me for something 'cause they know he'll do it.

"It's part of his general personality. If we're walking down a street in a city and there's a building going up, I'll all of a sudden turn around and I've left him behind. He's just standing there, looking and watching. He's the same way with the children. He's slow. He goes at their pace.

JOANNE HOWARD

"As far as my husband is concerned, his parents did absolutely everything right. And, in fact, they did. They really did. They gave their children everything in terms of love, in terms of time, in terms of involvement, and they still do.

"But my husband isn't willing to do the same."

The involvement of one's parents in one's life as a child doesn't necessarily mean that one will be able or eager to do the same. One man, an actor, used to being given to, used to being center stage, found himself unable to move over and give some room to his children. Another man whose only involvement with his own father, as he remembers it, was "I got to wash my father's car on Saturdays," found it difficult to become involved with his children because he had been given so little time.

There has been some research on this subject from the children's vantage point. John Condry and Michael Siman studied 766 middle-class sixth-graders. Using a questionnaire that obtained information about their perceptions of their parents, themselves, and their peers, as well as how and where they spent their time, they also used the Dilemma Test, questioning the children about values. They were able to group the children into those who were "peer-oriented" and those who were "parent-oriented." The peer-oriented children felt they had less support from their parents, were more likely to spend time with peers, and were more likely to engage in illegal acts, without feeling remorse. The adult-oriented children had higher self-esteem. They reported that their parents were involved, nurturing, providing both companionship and discipline.[14]

The issue of involvement brings up those omnipresent themes of parenthood—giving and getting, how much time to spend with one's children, on oneself, on work, and with one's husband or wife or adult friends.

Time for Oneself

When parents are in the midst of balancing their needs with those of their children, time off can seem like a luxury, a luxury, however, that is often a part of their daydreams. Parents imagine themselves all alone, lounging in the bathtub or in a cozy chair reading magazines or books for hours. They fantasize that they are drifting on a sailboat, or sunning at the water's edge. One mother has what she calls an "airport waiting room fantasy." She dreams that she is stranded all alone at an airport for a day, with nothing to do.

I found that when parents were able to act on these wishes and do something for themselves, they reported that they felt and acted better. This is an area that should be studied, looking at the continuum of time spent on oneself (from none to a large amount) and seeing how this affects parenthood.

Time for Work

MARCELLA SANCHEZ

Marcella is the mother of three girls. She has recently completed a teacher education program and has been certified as a teacher. Now she must decide whether to go to work or not.

"An opportunity for a job came up that I'd really like, but I'm not sure. The children would have to have a sitter for an hour every afternoon. I would be twenty-five minutes away. These last few days, while I've been considering applying for the job, I've been tormented by the worst fears of what could go wrong with the kids.

"I was brought up to think that the woman stays home and takes care of the kids. My sister-in-law went to work, and we thought it was the worst thing in the world. We all look down on her.

"Now it's necessary for me to go to work. But what if one of the children got run over or molested? What if there's an accident on the schoolbus? I don't feel safe."

"My mother was a very neat person—and that's the kind of ideal I started with, to be a good housekeeper and homemaker. I started out with all these ideals of what a mother should be, but now I've reevaluated them—but it's still hard."

For this mother, the opportunity of a new job has triggered this turmoil. A new event or opportunity is often the catalyst for renewed concern about the dividing line between time for work and time for family. Although this is usually seen as a woman's issue, I found men frequently voicing the same kind of feelings.

A father of three, a researcher, says, "Sometimes I worry that I work too much. I feel a responsibility as a minority person. I was allowed opportunities that previous generations were denied. I was singled out for a scholarship. So I kind of feel that I have set a contract with my people—an obligation, a responsibility to put as much back into the community as I can, to use my education for the greatest good. It's hard to say no to a speaking engagement, to an offer to write. But that takes away time from the kids. So I try to write late, when they are in bed, but that means that I get up tired the next morning.

"I don't know the answer, and it worries me. I don't want to be one-dimensional. I want to be a father and a son and a professor and a brother-in-law—not just Mr. Professor.

Although other parents might have different circumstances to cope with, the question is universal: when to say "yes" and when to say "no." *All parents continue to face the task of parceling out time for their family, for themselves, their work, and their partner.*

Time for One's Partner

How much time do single parents spend with their new men or women friends? How much time do married parents spend together alone? When the child was first born, the parents' relationship with each other receded—for some briefly, for others longer. As a couple, they have passed beyond the time which Anne Morrow Lindbergh compares to the Double-Sunrise Shell and reached the Oyster Bed Stage—sprawling out in all direction. She writes, "In the midst of such a life there is not much time to sit facing one another over a breakfast table"—as a couple, both are "looking outward" and "working outward." [15]

Leslie and Arthur Davidson

Arthur says, "I can't remember what it was like not to have kids."

Leslie says, "I feel that we are losing touch with each other as husband and wife, even just as people."

Arthur: "They are important to us, our children, but by the same token, I'm kind of looking forward to when they are grown and we can have our lives to do other things."

Leslie: "The kids are the main part of our lives right now. They are top priority—not in a possessive way, but in an enjoyable way. They're what we're devoting our energies to."

Parents who have minimized their own relationships have all kinds of feelings about it. Some, like Arthur and Leslie, are willing to wait for time together, others aren't. They feel jealous, resentful, or become rutted in their relationships. The strain between time for children, time for adult relationships, can be more pronounced if, for example, a single parent has met someone he or she likes and is in the beginning phases of a relationship.

It is always a matter of balancing. After going too far in neglecting their marriage, Eric and Ann Nelson found a middle point which suits them.

ERIC AND ANN NELSON

Eric is a salesman, Ann a housewife. They live in an Eastern suburb with their children: three foster girls, all teenagers, and their sons, nine and two. In a matter of days, they are expecting a baby.

Ann says, "Our first son was born with a slight birth defect. Both of us had an inherent fear of what the next child would be. It was very strong. We didn't want to be a one-child family, but the fear was there, and we didn't know how to verbalize it to one another."

Eric says, "When you first get married, you think about the other person, you appreciate her. You talk to each other. Then comes working, the house, children. You stop talking about each other, and you start talking about everything else. Husband and wife are no longer husband and wife. They start becoming roles. And then we begin to measure each other in terms of how good a role. If all I'm doing is being a provider, well, it's a piece of cake. I can come home and say, 'Why isn't the house straightened up?' The kids are her problem. I'm doing my job. I sit back, watch TV, drink a can of beer. I'm no longer in a relationship with anybody. I'm doing a job.

"That's what happened to us; we found ourselves caught up in what everybody around us, the world, sees as husband and wife, mommy and daddy."

Six years after the birth of their son, they attended a religious retreat.

Eric says, "It was a weekend where you turn off the world. It gave us a chance to step outside and look at each other. We realized again what it was we saw in each other when we first got married."

After this experience, they decided to try to retain their own relationship.

Ann: "We now take time out every day for us—not to talk about the kids or the job, but just the two of us."

Eric: "Usually we talk at night, but sometimes it can't wait till night. This afternoon, we needed time together—and that means that the kids can't come around asking for a soda."

Ann: "At first, it was difficult for our son. He had been used to being included in everything. He had a hard time. He was jealous.

"Sometimes we get out of balance. We forget. For a period of two days to a week, we forget and we go back to the pattern of 'I relate to the kids and Eric relates to them.' Then we realize: 'Hey—this is falling apart. Everybody's fighting. Nobody's feeling close.' "

Eric: "We've found an awful lot of insight into each other by doing this."

Their painful feelings about their son's birth defect was one issue that came out when they began talking to each other. They eventually decided they still wanted a large family, and began by taking in pregnant teenagers who needed to be away from their own homes during the pregnancy and birth. Then the Nelsons decided to have more children of their own.

Ann says, "We didn't think it would be a good idea to have unwed mothers here who might be wrestling with the idea of adoption while I was having a baby. Then social service [the local social-service agency] put the arm on us and asked if we'd be interested in taking a girl on a permanent basis."

They now have three foster teenagers in addition to their two-year-old son (who did not have any birth defects) and one soon to be born.

Just as Eric and Ann have carved out a regular time to communicate with other, they see dinnertime as a time for their whole family to communicate.

Eric explains, "There are very, very, very few exceptions why anybody in our family is not here at dinnertime. It's not that we don't want somebody else to make their meals. It's that all day long Ann and I are going our separate way, the kids are going their own ways. We see dinnertime as a home base. Everybody comes together.

"Each of us starts by saying what our day has been like. Not so much what we did, but how we felt. Like, I just went to Cincinnati on business. I didn't talk about what I did and who I saw but that I felt uncomfortable there because I had never been there before."

Holding On/Letting Go

The task that parents have of determining the right amount of involvement has two sides. *One side of the task is deciding when and how much to step in, to do things with one's children. The other side is when to let go, to encourage the children to do things independently.*

The mother of an eight-year-old son says, "He's getting more independent. He thinks he can do lots of things that I don't think he can do. That's my biggest problem: knowing when to let go."

Parents in the Interpretative Stage are frequently making decisions about holding on or letting go.

- A girl says, "I want to play outside after dark."
- A boy says, "I want to walk to my friend's house all by myself."

- A girl says, "I want to ride my bike across the highway."
- A boy says, "I want to go to the ten-cent store myself."
- A girl says, "I'm old enough to stay at home without a baby-sitter when you go out."
- A boy says, "I can go down to the pond and swim [without any adults]. There are lots of other kids there."

Children's requests for more independence are often backed with "everyone else does it." Yet when do parents hold on, say no, and when do they let go and say okay? And what kinds of feelings do they transmit to the child in the process? That he or she is not trustworthy, or that the child is simply not old enough yet?

All of the children quoted above were pushing out. But every parent faces the reverse, the times when the child clings, doesn't want to go, wants to stay home.

- A girl says, "I don't want to go to school today. I need a vacation."
- A boy says, "I don't want to take swimming lessons. Just why do kids need to learn to swim anyway?"
- Another boy, while his parents are out, telephones them to come home because he doesn't like the baby-sitter.

Parents in these incidents find it important to determine if there are any unstated causes behind the reason given—for instance, if the girl who says she needs a vacation is really worried about a class trip planned for that day.

But sometimes no reasons can be unearthed. The growth of children contains times of surging forward as well as times of staying put or even holding back.

The phrase "making mistakes" appeared again and again as parents talked about this issue. A father of two sons, nine and five, summed up several hours of talking about his children: "I realize my children are going to make their own mistakes. But sometimes it hurts. They make the mistake and you cannot say, 'I told you so.' "

When to let one's child make a mistake—and when to try to prevent it—is another way of asking when to hold on and when to let go. These questions cut across all aspects of the child's life—at home, out in the neighborhood, and at school.

Parents' Involvement with Other Significant Adults

I found in my interviews with parents of school-age children that they spent a large percentage of time talking about the child outside the home. In fact, they were talking primarily about their own relationships with the other significant people in their children's lives. *This is another facet of the issue of involvement, another task of the Interpretive Stage: Parents are deciding how involved to become with the other significant people, children and adults, in their own children's lives.* This has been an issue since the nurse, midwife, or doctor handled the baby at birth. Yet, it differs now because there is potentially more distance between the parent and these other people. One mother who has a two-year-old and a nine-year-old summarizes the change: "The two-year-old is still living in a world that we create for her. The nine-year-old is out in the world himself."

Many parents talked about this distance. They spoke about the other parents on their block as "those other people." They had the same tone in referring to the parents of school friends or teachers.

THOMAS MERRILL

"The bind for me today was that I went to register my nine-year-old, James, in his new public school. School begins Monday. This is Friday, and they wouldn't tell me who his teacher was. So he couldn't meet her. He couldn't see his room. I was told, very sweetly, 'just call early Monday morning.'

"I have this relentless feeling that there are all these people who are going to be affecting my kid. And I know, from their point of view, that he's among hundreds. Whether it's the doctor, the teacher, or whoever. But from my point of view, I know all the things the kid is going through, the concerns and questions he has. It's just a constant agony around bridging that gap between us and the people who have to take care of him."

Support/Lack of Support

In *All Our Children*, Kenneth Keniston and his co-authors write of the historical shifts that have brought about the new roles of specialists and experts to take over some of the family's previous functions. Parents today, they say, have a new job: "choosing, meeting, talking with, and coordinating the experts, the technology, and the institutions that help bring up their children. . . . Parents today are in some ways like the executives in a large firm—responsible for the smooth coordination of the many people and processes that must work together to produce the final product."

The book argues that parents are the true experts, because unlike the specialists, they know their child completely and are not beholden to outside bureaucracies. "But as an executive, the parent labors under enormous restrictions. Ideally, an executive has firm authority and power to influence or determine the decisions of those whose work needs coordination. Today's parents have little authority over those others with whom they share the task of raising their children. . . .

"Teachers, doctors, social workers, or television producers possess more status than most parents."[16]

Parents' stories about their involvement with those other people were of two kinds. One was the "executive without authority," stories that recounted injustice, stories filled with futility. The other was the "executive with authority." Parents told of overcoming misunderstandings and problems, of creating cooperative involvements with these other people.

CAROL LASSER

Carol, an educator, has been working to change neighborhood life for her two children and her husband.

"People here [on the West Coast] live isolated in their little houses. You don't know the people out there and you fear them because you don't know them. You don't have a sense that they are going to care about or watch out for your child.

"We're lucky, though, because this is a target neighborhood for some community organizing. The Urban League is setting up block organizations. The neighbors are getting to know each other and to feel that there is that kind of caring to some extent here.

"We organized an eating group with some families in the neighborhood. We all eat together so that the kids can get to know each other. That helps, too."

BETTY LEE WALKER

Betty Lee is a full-time mother of four children, eight, nine, eleven, and twelve. Two of the children, the twelve-year-old and the eight-year-old, were adopted recently by Betty Lee and her husband. She is another parent who has taken things into her own hands and has been very active in an adoptive parents' group in the Southwestern city where she lives.

"You hear all these stories about the child who sits in the corner and never smiles. And then they're adopted and two weeks later they're smiling and happy and bubbling and everything is great. Parents tell that kind of story after they've had a child a number of years, and they've forgotten or they don't bother to tell you what came in between the smiles. When people tell about their children, they tend to forget the most unpleasant parts and cling to the most pleasant ones.

"That's one thing our adoptive parent group tries to do, to be honest, because we want people to be able to face these things.

"I find the thing that disturbed me most was the way the twelve-year-old adopted child used a toothbrush. You'd buy her a toothbrush and two weeks later it's in shreds. This is something very minor but at the time it was upsetting. It's the little things in parenthood that eat away at you and break down your resistance.

"With adoption, your best friend is not necessarily the one to talk to. They'll say, 'Send the child back.' In fact, some professionals have said that to me, too. And that's not what you want to do; you need someone who will support you and say, 'Oh yes—we were there. Give it some time.' Time being months or a year—not two weeks."

Parents who are trying to maneuver the course of parenthood without supportive people (husbands, wives, parents, friends, or groups) often describe the loss.

An older mother of three children, a seven-year-old and four-year-old twins, says, "We [she and her husband] don't know any parents that have young children. The ones that do have young children are so much younger than we are that we don't even move in the same circles. We kind of feel like oddballs. Nobody understands what we are going through. I have no one I know that I can say to, 'How'd you work it out?' Nobody's in this fix."

It is often by transforming "those other people" into what one father calls "kith" that parents become executives with clout.

This particular father tells a story which illustrates his point. One of his children, a daughter with Down's syndrome, had just transferred to a new school.

"Helen went to this new school and she was coming home and you could tell that something was not right. So after about a week, I stopped in to meet with her teacher, Mrs. Harvey.

"Mrs. Harvey said to me that Ellen seemed to have the spirit gone out of her.

"And I decided it was really time to build kith. So I went back the next afternoon for a conference. I asked her about her family. We talked about her children and her baby-sitter. Then I told her about me and my work.

"Then I, in a nice, positive way, explained that I thought that it was really important that the teacher learn Helen's name—that it was Helen, not Ellen. I thought that would improve their relationship."

The relationships that parents have with other adults can greatly affect their feelings about parenthood. If they can find friends to listen and help them think through a problem and if they can find or create positive relationships with the professionals and other adults who work with their children, these relationships seem to encourage and empower them.

When there is a significant change within the family, the need for support stands out in even bolder relief.

SALLY BRENNAN

When Sally's children were three and four, her husband asked her for a divorce. A year later she met and married David Brennan, who was the divorced father of two boys. They began trying to gain custody of David's boys, because his former wife was, as Sally puts it, "unstable." David's ex-wife refused to give up custody, but did send the boys up for long vacations.

Two summers after they were married, "we got a phone call from David's ex-wife. She said, 'You can have them. They will be on the next plane.'

"Oh, what went through me that moment. Now, I would never admit this to anyone—until now—but I was probably very eager to have them come to live with us because I knew they wouldn't. It's not that I didn't want them. But I didn't think I could handle it. And I didn't think it would be fair to my own children.

"David, being a very rational person, said, 'No. They won't be on the next plane. They're coming, but first I want you to sign custody over to me.'

"So that was done quickly, and they were here and I was over at the school enrolling them before I knew what had happened.

"I became very nervous. I was probably taking too many tranquilizers. I was probably drinking too much. I don't mean during the day or anything, but I was escaping.

"I resented those kids. It didn't make me turn against David, which is I guess what saved us. But I never thought of them as anything except nuisances. Oh, the public would say, 'Sally, you're a wonderful person. You must be a supermother, doing this.' And I would say, 'Oh, it's just working out wonderfully.' But underneath, my stomach was going flop, flop, flop.

"The resentment grew. I felt like I never had time with my own children alone [on the weekends, Sally's children went to her ex-husband's home].

"I felt like the boys were visitors imposing on my time. They were taking from me. And they weren't easy children. They had been defensive all their lives. They had to fight—and they were not good students.

"I resented that when Mother's Day came, they wanted to send their own mother a card. I resented the fact that they were anxious to talk to her when she called. Which was all perfectly normal, of course. I resented my son's having to share a room with them, and it mattered that these were my husband's children with another woman.

"You're probably wondering how I got out of this—right? If David had not been the person that he is, it probably would have been a disaster for our marriage. I was very depressed at times. We went on a vacation alone, but I cried all the way back because I didn't want to return home. I remember saying to him, 'I can't stand to see three o'clock come because they all run off the school-bus at the same time, and they all come in and they're all four wanting my attention at the same time.'

"As soon as I opened up and got some of this out I was better—though I never let him know that I resented his children.

"David listened to me. He didn't know what to say, but he would listen and not get mad at me for telling him.

"Then I read an article. Maybe it was in *Ladies' Home Journal* or *McCall's* or something. At the top was a big 'You Don't Have to Love Your Stepchildren.' And I thought—'Ah-hah.' I read the article and in essence it said exactly what I was thinking. Isn't it funny that it takes an article to tell you that it's okay to feel the way you are feeling?

"The article said to me, 'You don't have to love these children as much as you love your own. You love them in a different way.'

"I had really been in a tailspin trying to force myself to love them in the same way and not getting anywhere. The only place I was getting was in a complete quandary, and they were, too, because they could see this person trying to be supermom, running around doing everything, doting on them, a hollow doting, very hollow. The emotion behind it was nil because I was trying to concentrate on how do I make it seem this way.

"The article said that whatever rapport is going to happen between the stepchildren and the stepmother is going to happen in spite of you and it will probably happen faster if you just relax, be yourself, and let them accept you as yourself. These kids have been through an upheaval too, and they have rights to their feelings too.

"I began to relax, and then the boys relaxed. They also were getting more mature. I quit doting on them—fixing what they wanted to eat and then resenting that I was fixing something special.

"Now they seem part of the family. And, by the way, I can get past three o'clock okay now."

When two children were added to her family (and even despite the fact that she had two children of her own already), Sally went through all stages of parenthood. Sally started out with an image: that she would love her stepsons and they her, that she would make up for the unsettled life that they had thus far lived. As soon as the phone call granting custody came, her image was eroded with the kinds of self-doubts that parents feel following birth: "Can I do it?" Sally upheld her image to the point where it became hollow and she became shaky—as she nurtured them and then established an authority relationship with them. The first instance of becoming an authority was when one of the boys smashed her son's Christmas present. Then Sally had to set down rules. Finally, Sally loosened her grip on her image. It was a magazine article that revealed the distance between what she actually felt and what she thought she should be feeling. Just like parents at the beginning of the Interpretive Stage, Sally described herself as more "realistic" about herself. She was able to form a new image of being more relaxed and accepting of her stepsons. Thus she was able to grow. Finally, like parents in the Interpretive Stage, she is now defining her relationship with her four school-age children, figuring how much to communicate and be involved with them.

A Changing Relationship Between Parent and Child

Throughout the Interpretive Stage, parents are moving into a new relationship with their children. They are moving from the greater inequality of the authority relationship with a five- or six-year-old to the lesser inequality of a relationship with a twelve-year-old. *Parents have the task of deciding how to define this changing relationship.*

The mother of a ten-year-old and a twelve-year-old is grappling with this definition when she says, "I try very hard to let my children know that I want them to be my friends—that is, I want them to be able to tell me anything and everything. Yet I don't want to be so much the friend that I'm also not the mother. Because I think you can go too far and then your children don't respect you or want to consult you as a mother."

The Changing Physical Relationship

Toward the end of the Interpretive Stage, the transition in the parent/child relationship has accelerated, and nowhere is it re-

vealed more than in the task of defining the physical relationship between parent and child. How much do parents and children hug, hold, cuddle, and kiss?

These are not new questions for parents. One mother says, "My own mom, bless her heart, is a supermother, but she never really hugged us. I perhaps needed this above all. She was always embarrassed about showing affection. I'm being very careful to show the affection I feel for my children."

As the children approach the teenage years, they become increasingly curious about and interested in sex. A mother found this out in a dinnertime conversation with her two sons, ages ten and nine. They were talking about secret things they think about.

The ten-year-old announced that his secret thoughts were about "sex." "I think about it all the time," he said.

Some children stare at their parents and ask them questions like "Do you have sex when I'm in bed sleeping?"—"How often?"—"Is it fun?"

Children occasionally use babyish voices. It is as if they speak this way to put brakes on or to disguise the momentum and the speed of their growth. Most do want to become teenagers, and in fact they spend a lot of time imitating them, combing their hair in the popular way, copying their clothes. Simultaneously, they don't want to give up the younger parts of themselves, a wish that they articulate with these babyish voices.

In a mother/daughter or father/son relationship, a rivalry can accelerate.

The mother of a nine-year-old girl says, "She wants to dress up and is interested in makeup and her hair style, shoes, and clothing. She's acting like a buddy, but like a rival, too. Like if I'm coming to her school, she says, 'Oh, Mama, could you please wear this?' Or if I'm going out, she says, 'You're not going out with your hair like that, are you?' Once she said to me, 'Why can't you be like the other mothers and take aerobics?' I guess I have to get ready for all these little barbs that are going to keep coming."

The relationships between mothers and sons and fathers and daughters can have sexual overtones. The mother of an eleven-year-old son says, "He comes and hugs me, in almost an exploratory way. I don't know what to do."

Parents do have to figure out what to do. Many parents said that the exploratory behavior made them uncomfortable and they wanted to stop it but without being unloving.

A mother of a twelve-year-old speaks of this dilemma: "Last year Charles [her son] was really provocative and seductive with me. He wanted to lie on top of me and touch me all the time. Although I loved it, I had to find ways to help him stop, without being cruel.

"Charles is a great hulking thing and I would just say, 'You're a big guy and you're too heavy when you do that.' Finally I got to the point where I did say, 'I don't think that's right anymore.'

"He also developed a thing with me when we walked down the street of tucking his arm right underneath my arm so that he could be touching my breast. I would detach him."

Charles can also be childlike and cuddly, but these moments have become rarer. "Now," his mother says, "when he comes and puts his head down in my lap, I think to myself, 'This is going to be the last time'—or 'This is going to be the next-to-the-last time,' or 'How do I know how many more times I can have this?' Cause it's a very special feeling."

ANTICIPATING THE TEENAGE YEARS

These preadolescent years mark the end of childhood per se and the approach of a new stage. Parents think about this coming venture with a mélange of emotions—sorrow, fear, nostalgia, and anticipation. The teenage years, in American culture today, have an awesome reputation. Even during pregnancy, parents-to-be have had foreboding fears; they see themselves cast as the parents of *Rebel Without a Cause*. Some parents, remembering their own teenage years, picture the worst—their children transformed, surly, turning their backs on their parents, ungrateful, speeding dangerously down highways, hot-rodding, hitchhiking, drinking, metamorphosed by drugs, enmeshed in sex. They imagine that the remaining umbilical cords tying their children to them will be severed—not gently, but chopped off, leaving wounds. They have been warned by the parents of teenagers: "You think it's nice (or hard) now—well, just wait."

Parents have the task of forming images about being the parents of teenagers, of rehearsing so that they are ready. And at the same time they look back and evaluate. They review what they have done as parents thus far, hoping that they have prepared their children.

Parents also look at—in fact, study—the experiences of their friends and neighbors. One parent seems to be having an easy time of the teenage years. Why? What has he or she done in the past? What is he or she doing now? What are the causes of this seeming success?

Parents also study the apparent failures. A child was arrested in the seventh grade for drug dealing. Why? Another child ran away from home at fourteen. Why? A father or mother has turned bitter about parenthood. Why?

Sometimes the answers appear clear. The parents seem self-involved—they don't have time for their child. The parents are cruel or overly protective, without reproach paying a child's bail when arrested. Or the parents have ignored the blatant signs that the child is using hard drugs.

But other times, there are no easy answers. The parents seem to care about their child. They have a solid family life. These paradoxes make the parents with soon-to-be-teenagers think harder—until they arrive at an explanation that makes sense to them.

Other parents don't do this kind of exploring—they either have a trust in their child or they have seen other parents handle this era with undue turmoil or they prefer not to look or know. Like some parents during pregnancy, they switch off all thoughts of the impending changes.

But when asked what their daydreams were, most parents in the Interpretive Stage answered something similar to what this parent says:

"I wonder whether we will be able to prepare our children for the kind of world they are going to live in.

"I worry about the drug business.

"I don't know if I have what I need to help them make choices when it comes to experimentation with drugs, and with sex.

"I wonder if I'm as well equipped as I should be to teach them values.

"I wonder whether or not I'll get upset if one of them says, 'I don't really want to go to college.' A couple of years ago I had dreams of them all getting endowments.

"Now I wonder what kind of preparation children need. . . .

"I would want them—and I have thought about this—to have good lives, whatever that is in their day and time.

"These are imponderables—but basically, I think about how well we are attempting to prepare these children for whatever kind of world they'll have to adjust to."

Pondering these imponderables, responding to the children's easy and not-so-easy questions and concerns, causes parents to review what they think, believe, and value. It causes them, whether deliberately or not, to pull together their own philosophy of life, to face their own uncertainties and confusions, translate what they believe to children. A parent cannot pass through this experience unchanged.

V.
The Interdependent Stage

For a long time, people have been saying, "Just wait"

- "Just wait until you are the parent of a teenager."

Then, one day, the parent notices a change.

- A son has thick hair crowding out the silky fine hair that always covered his arms.
- A son and his friend have spent a half an hour listening to a radio program called *Dial-a-Date*.
- A daughter's breasts are no longer flat, but ever so slightly swollen.
- A son has the shadow of a mustache spreading across his upper lip.
- A daughter cups her hand over the phone when she talks, speaking in almost inaudible whispers.
- A son combs his hair in the morning without being asked and, in fact, spends a long time getting his hair to look like his current favorite rock or movie star.
- And a son and a daughter begin to repeat a new phrase: "You don't understand."

PATRICIA SARNOFF

Patricia is a teacher, married and the mother of one son, Justin, soon to be thirteen.

231

"Justin has really never been a testing or a particularly rebellious kid at home. He just somehow hasn't needed to. I've never felt that he was enormously squashed. But now he does test me.

"We had a silly fight last weekend. He had a cold and I'm a vitamin C person and wanted him to take a couple of tablets and he said no. And I was amazed because he'd never said no before.

"I said, 'You really should do it, Justin, because this cold is going to hang on and on and it's just going to be a pain.'

"But he said, 'No, and I don't really want to discuss it anymore!'

"It didn't seem to me to be an issue that was worth pursuing, so I just dropped it. But that's the kind of thing he would never do before.

"Or he will tantalize me. He'll tell me that he has something to tell me but he's not going to tell me, because he knows that that's the kind of thing that will drive me mad.

"And sometimes he will keep it secret and sometimes it will come out. He plays little separation games. He moves away, and then, almost always after an incident like that, he'll be extra specially loving and close. I almost have a feeling that he's crawling back one more time and then he's going to take off again in a separate direction.

"He'll get a phone call and make a point of saying, 'That was a terrific phone call! You want to know who it was?' And depending on the day, I'll either say, 'Yes,' or 'No,' or 'Do you want to tell me?' But his answer is always, 'I don't think I'll tell you.'

"He doesn't rebel in dramatic ways yet, he does it in smaller ways, but they surprise me every time they happen."

Sometimes Images Don't Hold Up

"Surprised." "Shocked." "Unexpected." These are the words that parents often use to describe the change. Even though the children have rehearsed being teenagers, mimicking their clothes, hair styles, dancing, and slang expressions, and even though the parents have tried to prepare themselves, by analyzing other families and projecting themselves into the future, the actual entry into this stage can entail the loss of images.

Images About Timing

A mother notices that one nipple on her daughter seems enlarged. She calls the doctor to find out what's wrong, only to be told, "Your daughter is growing up." Another mother, out to buy fall clothes for her son, holds them up to herself and is amazed that she could wear his polo shirts and pajamas. The daughter hinting or telling her parent that she has found some spots of blood on her underpants can seem too soon.

Parents have images about the timing of life events; they have a schema of what Bernice Neugarten calls the "normal, expectable life-cycle."[1] For the parents who react to the beginning of adolescence with shock, these changes are coming sooner than expected, are contradicting the timing of events as they foresaw them. Several long-term studies, in fact, bear out parents' observations that though children mature at vastly different rates, girls earlier than boys, puberty, as measured by physical changes, is coming earlier and earlier.[2]

The Image That the Child Won't Change

The lowered age for the onset of adolescence and the loss of images are not the only explanation for parents' uneasy response. Throughout parenthood, parents have frequently reacted to changes in their child in this way: The colicky baby who becomes calm, the quiet infant who throws temper tantrums at two, the wild child at four who becomes serious and studious at six all seem to surprise their parents. Parents can never quite prepare or rehearse enough. It is difficult to let go of one's image of a child, say good-bye to the child a parent knows, and get accustomed to this slightly new child inhabiting the known child's body.

One parent summarizes this pattern by saying, "Children do their own growing. They don't do it because you tell them to or in ways that fit what's convenient for you. And there is this miraculous thing. I find that I am never ready. I am always overtaken. It is always a surprise."

The Image That the Parent Has Greatly Improved

There is another reason for this sense of being overtaken. The Interpretive Stage is, in general, not extremely turbulent. The highs are not that far away from the lows. Throughout the Interpretive Stage parents describe themselves as realistic. That realism can become rosier and rosier as the memories of the strife, of the scenes in supermarkets, the crying bouts, the up-all-night nights of early parenthood, fade.

Parents find, as the teenage years begin, that they are transported right back to some of the feelings they had when their child was between two and five.

- A fifteen-year-old boy complains all morning of a stomachache, moping over breakfast, finally falling back into bed. Then a younger sister walks by with a bag of stale candy corn, stored away since Halloween. The sick teenager makes a miraculous recovery, talks his younger sister out of the candy, and eats it all up.
- A fourteen-year-old girl comes into her mother sobbing, saying that she has just ripped a button off the blouse she was going to wear. Her mother says, "Oh, I'm sorry. I'll sew it for you." The daughter turns away, slamming the door, saying, "You don't really care."
- The parents get frantic calls from a neighbor. Their fourteen-year-old son had been hired to do some painting in the neighbor's house, but hasn't shown up. Where is he? The parents realize that their son has forgotten and gone off for the day with some friends.
- A seventeen-year-old girl wants a special pair of boots that "all the kids have." Her parents refuse, saying that the boots are too expensive. The daughter turns up with the boots, saying a friend gave them to her. Later the mother discovers some money missing from her pocketbook.

Episodes such as these stir up strong feelings in the parents. What's more, parents may find that they aren't the parent they thought they were. Old patterns reemerge, and with that some images of themselves may be challenged. A mother who used to slap her son when he was little thought that she had improved because she no longer resorted to slapping. But at thirteen, his sarcasm drove her to the point where she slapped him again—even though, as she says, "he towers over me and it was like a flea swiping at a dog."

It was very discouraging for this mother, as it is for others with a similar experience, to give up some of their images of themselves as parents, to realize that they haven't improved or changed as much as they thought they had. Catherine Chilman writes that whereas teenagers may not remember this earlier stress period, parents do, and they may have a strong "feeling that their son or daughter has, indeed, regressed in many ways to an earlier stage of development. They may have a painful feeling that, as parents, they have succeeded not at all and that the family, as a family, is in an increasingly deteriorating situation."[3]

Parents, in effect, are having to renounce two images—of the child and of themselves. The new selves often seem like the selves they thought they'd outgrown, and so rather than progression, it can seem as if they are going backward.

Moments of Pride, Moments of Pain

This is not to say that being the parent of a teenager is all problematic. There are highs and lows and stretches in between. And the highs can be thrilling.

PATRICIA SARNOFF

"Seeing Justin become an adult is just extraordinary—seeing all these little pieces of strength start to fit together is quite something.

"Last night, his school had a talent show. I was just floored by his self-possession. When did he ever learn self-possession? I don't remember him having it when he was eight or nine. I don't ever remember thinking about self-possession. But, somewhere along the line he has become so comfortable that he was—I don't know—a budding Johnny Carson. He was super."

The low moments, as they have throughout parenthood, have deeply personal connotations.

Patricia says, "I tend to see Justin as more vulnerable than he is. I confuse him with all the vulnerabilities I have. Justin comes out, in my head sometimes, as barely able to walk, when, in fact, he's quite strong. He's really together.

"I know parents who think in terms of the fact that their kids will make friends with kids who they don't consider acceptable or will become involved in drugs. I don't think about those kinds of things. Justin has always been sensible.

"I think the big thing is that I was just a dastardly teenager. I was revolting, and I did it till I was close to thirty. Justin shows these weeny little signs of doing it—nothing big—and it scares me. It scares me to think that he would do the things I did and alienate himself from us. That would make me very sad. I'd miss him terribly.

"I did gross and terribly cruel things to my mother. Of course, I grew up in a different family, and I needed to do some of those things—while I don't think that Justin has to.

"But it would sadden me so terribly if he arrived at my point in life thinking about me the way I think about my mother."

The Things I Hate in My Child

Another mother of a fourteen-year-old daughter says, "She drives me crazy, but sometimes at night, in the deep recesses of my soul, I can see that I've done these things too. The things I hate in my child are the things I hate in myself."

Occasionally, like this mother, parents recognize that their intense response to a teenager's behavior has a ring of familiarity. With the exception of fear about truly dangerous situations, a parent's acute response to a child is often related to whether the parent feels identified with the teenager's behavior. For instance, a mother who had a hard time talking to her own parents as a teenager and who hoped it would be different in the family she formed is driven almost crazy by her teenager's refusal to talk to her. It was crying that bothered another mother. She had always cried easily, and when she saw her fifteen-year-old daughter doing the same, it irritated her. Another mother had always been overly sensitive, almost raw, easily rebuffed by things that didn't seem to bother others. She was distressed that her son was equally vulnerable.

A story that the stepmother of a teenager tells illustrates this point. At two o'clock in the morning, the stepmother and her husband were awakened by a phone call from his ex-wife, who said that their sixteen-year-old son had stolen the car and had taken off for a party. When the police picked him up for speeding, they discovered that he had no license, only a learner's permit.

The father got off the phone, shaking with rage. His wife finally said to him, "I stole the car when I was a teenager. Didn't you ever do anything like that?"

"Yes," he yelled, "but I never got caught!"

As I listened to parents tell stories such as these, I heard them consistently capped with the word "expect." The stepmother of the child who stole the car said, "And I thought this kid was going to be a reasonable teenager. I never expected him to do something like this."

Images rise over parents' feeling about the teenage years, like elusive rainbows. Parents expect their teenager to be reasonable or to be rebellious, to do well academically or not, to avoid smoking or drinking or drugs or to experiment with them, to be able to get a job and bring in some income or to finish school or both.

Just how this process takes hold in parents is depicted clearly by the experience of a single man who had for years been a successful, respected headmaster of a private high school. After serious family problems, he became the legal guardian of his teenage nephew.

"I think that I've become more uptight about academics. [At school] I was very casual. I'd say to parents, 'Don't worry. School will take care of that. We've got five years to work that out.' Now that it's my kid—goddammit—he'd better shape up.

"In every one of these standardized tests that the school gives, he comes home with the ninety-ninth percentile, but he makes D's and C's on his report card. So at that point, I'm uptight.

"The change that becoming a parent has made in me is that I've elevated my expectations. Probably too high."

Against this backdrop of holding onto or changing their images, the tasks that parents confront remain fairly constant throughout parenthood. Parents are once again asking: What kind of authority do I want to be? Who will determine the limits? What are they to be? How will they be enforced? Parents ponder their ability to communicate and their relationship with their child, the degree of distance and of closeness. The same questions are asked because the child's growth often renders the old solution obsolete. New ones have to be found.

In the process of finding solutions to the recurrent tasks of parenthood, parents have the major task of forging a new relationship with this almost adult child.

ADAPTING TO A NEW AUTHORITY RELATIONSHIP

A five-year-old, in trying to make sense of life, became interested in teenagers. "Are all baby-sitters teenagers?" she asked. "Do teenagers live at home?" "Do teenagers go to school?" "Do they drive cars?" "Whose car?" "Do they work?" "Do only teenagers work at McDonald's?" "Can teenage boys have mustaches?" Finally, after a week of intense interrogation, she concluded this study by saying, "Teenagers are half children and half grown-ups."

Many parents, in different words, said the same thing. Of her fourteen-year-old, a mother said, "I was totally taken aback when Alexa recently said that there was a wonderful book that she was reading. She said, 'It has a funny name.' And it was *Dibs!* [an adult book that her mother had loved, too].

"I mean, this was a child who two years ago was reading *Paddington* and *Henry Huggins* and *The Great Brain* and she wasn't really up to reading *Little Women.* Now, suddenly, she's reading adult books.

"Yet, I came in this morning to her room and she was sleeping with her hand rubbing her blanket with the silky edge.

"Teenagers are polarized," this mother says. "They are both mature and still children."

Many of the things teenagers do reflect this mixture of maturity and immaturity.

- A fifteen-year-old has a severe ear infection, goes to the doctor, and is given antibiotics. He goes to the beach, purportedly to sit in the sun and get well, but within a few minutes is in the water, splashing and dunking in a game of "Jaws."
- A sixteen-year-old at a new high school signs up for so many activities that her day begins at six A.M. with track practice and ends at five-thirty P.M. with band. And she has an hour's bus ride in either direction.

Because teenagers are absorbed in themselves, their behavior can be blindly disrespectful.

- A seventeen-year-old spirits away things that belong to others. His mother says, "I'll get up in the morning, having had five combs in a drawer, and I'll have nothing to comb my hair with. He takes anything he likes and uses it in such a way that it becomes his. And he's not concerned about anyone else wanting to use it—all our creams and lotions and Vaseline disappear. I don't know what he uses them for. And it's the kind of thing where he doesn't just use a little. It's gone in a couple of days."

Teenagers can test or disregard their parents.

- A sixteen-year-old boy told his mother that he needed his own car so that he wouldn't always have to be a captive of his friends—that he disliked their fast, uncautious driving, that he also disliked the wild drinking parties his friends always went to. This mother consented, allowing him to buy a cheap used car, and soon learned that he drove very fast and often drove to the very same parties he had professed disliking.

Teenagers can do things that worry and upset their parents.

- A seventeen-year-old boy, always a good student, lost interest in school and his grades began to drop.
- A fifteen-year-old girl became a cheerleader and also began to breeze through her schoolwork in a sloppy and superficial way.

And finally, teenagers can do things that truly frighten their parents.

The mother of a seventeen-year-old says, "One of the things he got into was drinking our liquor. We're not liquor drinkers. We just had some because we had given a big party for my sister's shower, and as it turned out, no one drank it because we made a wine punch. All the liquor bottles were left full. Suddenly the bottles were empty.

"So my husband asked him, 'Did you drink this?' And he said, 'No.'

"I said, 'I'm going to ask you again. Please think about your answer before you answer. Did you drink this?'

"He said, 'Well, I put a little in my tea—because I had a cold.'

"I said, 'Well, that's all right to put a little in your tea. But three empty bottles?'

"Then I remembered that he had been kind of drowsy lately. He'd been falling asleep on the couch very early.

"So we got into this big discussion about liquor with him, and about drugs. That's really my big worry. He's just a prime target for drugs."

Another mother of a sixteen-year-old had what she calls a harrowing experience. Her son, Eric, went off for the day with friends. About ten o'clock in the evening he came home. He warmed up the leftovers from dinner, talked with his mother, and then sprawled out to watch television. She watched with him for a while and went to bed.

At midnight, the phone rang, awakening her. It was the mother of one of the other boys, Jesse. "Is Eric home?" the other mother asked.

"Yes—why?" Eric's mother answered.

"Because Jesse isn't."

"I'll check with Eric and call you back."

Eric was still lying on the couch, watching television. She told him about the phone call. Reluctantly, Eric told what had happened. The boys had gone to the park. Eric and one friend had rented bikes while Jesse and the other friend had gone off to take LSD. Toward the end of the afternoon, Eric and his friend had looked for the other two but had been unable to find them. Finally they overheard someone say that a guy had been taken off to the hospital by an ambulance, suffering from a bad LSD trip.

The two boys then went to the hospital and found their friend in the emergency room. He was so stoned that he was incoherent. Eric tried to find out where the fourth boy, Jesse, was, but the hospitalized boy was delirious and obscene, and Eric and his friend felt embarrassed to be seen with him, so they ducked out. They went back to the park to look for Jesse. He was nowhere. So they went home.

The next morning, Jesse had still not returned. Jesse's mother called Eric angrily. "What are you going to do to find him?" she asked.

Just after that the police called, requesting information.

Eric and his mother made plans to go back to the park to look for Jesse. By then, Eric's mother was visualizing the worst, that Jesse had taken LSD and had died. She pictured finding his body under a tree or beside a pile of rocks.

When they were just about to leave, the phone rang. It was Jesse's mother. Jesse had come home!

Problems Can Seem Foreign

Parents today are fielding many problems that they feel inexperienced in handling. When they were teenagers themselves, there was possibly drinking—beer wrapped in brown paper bags, or cheap bourbon bought by older kids. There may have been parties at homes in which the parents had gone out for the evening. Lights were turned off and the record player, blasting the music of Elvis Presley or the Beatles, drowned out the noises of couples dancing, swaying, then standing still, holding each other. There may have been necking and petting and a few kids who went "all the way," and a few girls who suddenly dropped out of high school for the purported purposes of visiting relatives. There may have been fast cars, Fords and Chevrolets, bought secondhand and painstakingly fixed up, washed and polished until they shone. Glass packs made the mufflers emit a distinctive and menacing rumble. There may also have been playing chicken at stoplights, passing cigarettes from one car to another, cruising, or congregating at drive-in restaurants, and listening for the record requested at the rock 'n' roll station. There may also have been slam or popularity books, calling up pizza restaurants and ordering twenty pizzas to be delivered to the home of a disliked teacher. All of these nostalgic memories, now romanticized by the Golden Oldies and movies like *Grease* and *American Graffiti*, seem a far cry from the world in which teenagers live in today.

A mother from Tennessee with a twelve-year-old and a fourteen-year-old says, "There are outside forces that press heavier and heavier on your children as they get older. We're in the process of realizing that our fourteen-year-old is coming up against young boys drinking and doing other things. You can look at it two ways. You can be judgmental or you can realize that it is a problem that is here. But it's a problem that neither my husband nor I had to face as soon as our son is facing it."

Another parent says that parents nowadays "have to write their own scripts. And there are few guidelines from the past to fall back on."

Parents do have to decide what to say and what to do when their child takes on too many activities, or sneaks off with the car, or sloughs off schoolwork, or drinks up the liquor from the liquor cabinet, or uses drugs, or is silent about such a dangerous experience as a friend's disappearing on an LSD trip.

Parents Have Less Control

The dangers are bigger, and yet parents' power is diminishing. As the children grow older, they become more autonomous. They come and go to school by themselves, stay at home alone, buy their own clothes, cook for themselves. They go off with their friends— to the shopping mall, to movies, to parties.

The father of a fourteen-year-old says, "I feel like the circle of her life is widening away from us."

SUZANNE PROUIX

Suzanne, an educator, is the mother of a seventeen-year-old and a nineteen-year-old.

"My children are very self-directed. I feel like I'm living out their life issues without being a participant. This is very freeing in many ways. Alexander [her son] got a job after school, saved money, went on an American youth hostel trip, wrote me one letter.

"Angelica got herself a job, worked all summer. She zips out of the house at eight o'clock at night on her bike and says, 'I'm staying at Marc's tonight. I took all my clothes for work tomorrow, and yes, I will be home for dinner tomorrow, but not until seven o'clock, because I have to go and do two other things.' Period.

"Now when you have children of this age, you are living with individuals who are making tremendous claims to their separate lives. Nevertheless, they don't live away from you. It isn't really like having grown-up children who are at a distance.

"So you are in the peculiar situation of being close and watching them, and, at least in the case of my children, of being in very clear communication with them.

"I know many parents of adolescents who feel that they've lost their kids for a while—the kids go underground with their lives or they turn out to their peer group. I haven't felt that, but I have felt that my capacity to influence them is diminished. The days of worry, of putting energy into making sure your kids get the right teacher and have the right experiences—that's all over. That's done for.

"There's never a moment that that break happens. You don't know it until, somehow, you find yourself in the next place. And in that place, you have not a less intense relationship, but a different one.

"There is this wonderful joy seeing life open up for them, but also there is this terrible apprehension that you cannot put yourself between them—you can't stand between them and what's going to happen. There's just no way. They've gone into their world. And that's a very powerful experience."

Within this context of more autonomous children living in a changing world, parents face the task of redefining their authority relationship.

Images About Authority Come from Many Sources

The images parents have come from their own years as teenagers, from the experiences in the earlier Authority Stage, and from their adult experiences with teenagers.

JUANITA HARRIS

Juanita is a single parent with three teenagers. She works in an Appalachian women's health clinic. Juanita's images were seeded in her own childhood. "I come from a big family and we were poor. My father was an alcoholic. He'd get drunk at least four or five times a week.

"When we were teenagers, we weren't allowed to do anything. We weren't allowed to date. We couldn't talk on the phone. We couldn't belong to any school activity. We went to school just to study.

"I skipped school every chance I'd get. I wanted to get away from home so bad."

Juanita got away by getting married, but her husband turned out to be a lot like her father. "He never saw a sober day for the first five years we were married. I hated it.

"In the thirteen years we were together, he took me to four, five places at most. The grocery store and the bank were the only places I went, and I had three kids on my hips. He had his fun, but if I asked him to take me to a movie, he'd say, 'You've got your driver's license. Why don't you go yourself?' Only he said it in a lot worse ways than that.

"We fought constantly. It was just like living a replica of what my mother went through. And I didn't want it. So I made up my mind that when my last baby went to school, I was going to get away. I wanted a better life."

After Juanita left her husband, she lived on food stamps for a while, then got a job through a friend. The images acquired from her childhood were reinforced in her time at that job. "I worked at this wholesale house—in security. I worked in disguise. My only job was to see if people were stealing stuff.

"There was a bunch of young kids at this warehouse. They accepted me into their group and would invite me to their pot parties. Most of these kids took dope. I got close to some of them and they would tell me how their parents would never let them do this, never let them do that. They always had to sneak and come around behind their parents' back. That's why they turned out on dope.

"Right away, I realized that I didn't want to do that—tie my kids down to the point where they're going to turn out bad."

And yet, because Juanita is going against what she has lived and seen, the roadway isn't clear. She has decided to spend a lot of time with her kids. "At least once a week I get all my kids and we go to a movie or go swimming or somewhere."

She also tries to keep the lines of communication open. "I've told my oldest son that if he ever wanted to smoke a joint to come in and lay it on the table and we'll all smoke the joint together. I'd want him to smoke at home, rather than behind my back."

Because of the alcoholism in her family, she is far less tolerant about that. "I never have allowed alcohol in my house. There may have been four or five times I've had a six-pack of beer in the refrigerator. I never drink. I can't stand it. I hope that my not having alcohol in my home won't turn my kids on to it."

The Loss of an Image

As always, images turn out to be workable or not. When the latter happens, some parents refuse to budge, trying to keep their ideas afloat.

CAROLYN O'NEAL

Carolyn is unable to be the kind of authority that she had planned: a parent who listens to her children and helps them solve problems. This image comes from her own teenage years.

"We never would have thought of going to our parents to talk about anything. My parents were too busy working. My sister and I were at home. We did our jobs. We did our homework. We listened to the radio. And that was it. There was not that much communication between children and the parents. The father was at the head of the table. We sat down to dinner. We ate our dinner. There was no talking—no communication."

Because, in retrospect, Carolyn felt she had missed out by not being able to talk to her parents, she wanted to be able to communicate with her children. The first step was to be home—not to work. "I am a mother that's here all the time," she says. Now she feels "that's not the solution. They have crises and I can't help them because they won't talk to me.

"The eighteen-year-old, last spring, must have been going through some emotional thing. We really don't, till this day, know what it was. She'd come in crying. She'd always be running upstairs. She never wanted to talk to us. We'd say, 'Well, look, if you don't want to talk with us, would you talk to one of your older brothers or sisters? We'd be glad to pay for a long distance call.' She didn't want any of that. She said, 'I've got somebody I can talk to.' We said, 'Good.' And we found out it was one of the nuns at school.

"It's very, very difficult. You sometimes hear things from their friends, but you never hear from them directly. You know that there is a crisis and you try to get to it, just by asking a simple question, and they won't answer you. And inside you hurt because you want to give them the answer."

Carolyn is also disappointed in her husband. "There's a lot lacking. He's away from the family most of the time. He doesn't really have that much communication with the kids. They never feel that they can talk to him."

When parents have fallen far short of an image, their anger and disappointment can spin out in all directions as they search for a place to thrust the blame. Some put it on themselves—as Carolyn does, in looking through the past to see where she had made mistakes. "You say to yourself, 'Where did I go wrong?' I gave them too much. Maybe that's the reason." Carolyn also attributes part of the blame to her husband.

Because Carolyn is not able to change or achieve her image (perhaps because from my conversation with her, it seems that her idea of communication is telling, more than listening), she often dreams of a reprieve, of going away by herself, of moving, of getting a job, of the kids growing up and leaving home.

Images That Are Revised

The images that parents have are deep-seated, powerful forces.

To change one, a parent often begins by understanding where it came from and why it had such a strong grip on him or her.

DAPHNE ROGERS

Daphne is in the midst of such a process. She has recently sold her half-ownership in a real estate business. She and her husband and their fourteen-year-old daughter and their sixteen-year-old son live in a house filled with the colors of the hilltop outside.

"Children, up until they're around twelve, are almost totally dependent on you. You tell them what to do and where to go. We got along beautifully with both of the children. But when our son reached fourteen, we were shocked and surprised by the changes he went through. It seemed like we could not say anything to him. He was—for the lack of a better word—rebellious.

"He thought any time we said something like 'You need to get a haircut' that we were saying that everyone in his age group wore their hair too long. He did not value our opinion on any subject.

"It was a time when he was trying out beer and things like that. He would say, 'Well, if you have a cocktail, what's wrong with me having a beer?'

"He's an intellectually gifted student. He had never made fantastic grades anyway, but his grades began to fall off.

"My husband and I sat down and talked with him. We told him that we knew this was a troublesome time. We knew how it felt to be that age and ill at ease and insecure.

"That helped momentarily. He had good intentions. But there was the peer-group pressure. And his grades kept declining. So he ran away.

"He left us a note. While he was away, I decided that I had been an overprotective mother. I had told him that he could not go off in a car with teenagers until he was old enough to drive. The restrictions that we had were painful to him. I decided that if we were fortunate enough to have him come back safe, I would change.

"We thought he must have gone to the beach [a favorite place of his], and so we told the Runaway Department. He was picked up there a week later.

"And so when he came back, we all saw a counselor—the three of us together—me, my husband, and my son. She helped me see that when he would get into trouble with some of his friends, I would confront his friends as well as discipline him on the subject. She told me that that was not the thing to do, that that embarrasses him in front of his friends. It makes two problems out of one.

"He was a planned baby. He was just a perfect, beautiful child. He walked at eight months. He was perfect until our daughter was born [when he was twenty-two months old]. I was in the hospital about seven days and my husband's mother stayed with him and pacified him and gave him everything he wanted. He was never the same afterward.

"He cried for the next two straight years. Nothing pleased him.

"My sister had had a little boy, and my cousin had had a boy too—and I thought they were both brats. I thought that when I have one he's going to do all the things he's supposed to. Now I feel we did expect too much out of him too soon.

"I think that my childhood had a lot to do with the way I feel about my children. My parents were killed in an accident when I was seventeen months old. My grandfather and aunt and uncle were all killed at the same time. A train hit the car and killed them all. I lived with my grandmother until I was five or six and then lived with an aunt until I was seventeen.

"As my son was growing up, I would constantly think, 'What would I do if something happened to him?' I didn't feel like I could cope with it. I was not overprotective in the sense that . . . I would let him go down to the lake and swim. It was, I guess, something deeper than that.

"I felt like I wanted to do everything that I could possibly do to make sure that things went well for him."

Daphne wanted to shield her son from the pain and unhappiness she had felt since she was young. Because she was providing him with the kind of childhood she had so sorely wanted she expected him to be happy, to be compliant and conforming.

The times of normal turbulence—following the birth of a baby, the preschool period, and the teenage period, the times when there are frequent mood changes, when the child is stressing his or her own independence—were exceedingly difficult for Daphne. And it is probable that her heightened expectations of her son after the birth of her daughter intensified his distress.

Daphne is now beginning to change her expectations that her son remain tied to her. "I realized that I was making a big mistake. I was depriving him of the things that I enjoyed when I was a teenager: being with other teenagers. I thought that I could keep him from associating with people who would be a bad influence on him by taking him on nice trips and out to dinner. The counselor said, 'Well, if you did that you would finally narrow it down until it was just the four of you. You know—just in your house.' And I said, 'That's exactly what I did!'

"He had this group of friends who were smoking pot. On the other hand, there were about four other kids in the school who were gifted like he is. So some of us parents got together and decided to do fun things for them.

"The more I pushed him toward this group of bright kids, the more he wanted to go with the other group.

"So I decided that these kids that he was associating with are going to be the adults of another generation. And I said to myself that maybe out of the hundred that he's associating with, four will do something with their lives and maybe two or three or four of them will wind up in jail. But the rest of them will be just average citizens.

"I told him that I could not follow him around the rest of his life helping him stay straight, that he would have to make some decisions for himself. I let him hang out with whomever he wants. I let him drive. But I told him that I didn't want any pot smoking or beer drinking in our house until he was an adult."

Daphne's other central image has always been happiness. "The only thing I want in life for him is for him to be happy." Even though she knows that all teenagers have periods of unhappiness, her son, she feels, is more miserable than most. He now seems to judge himself harshly for not being happy.

"He told me that while he was away, that while he was walking on the beach, he said, 'Well, here I am, and I'm not happy. I thought this was what I wanted—to get away.'

"He'd say, 'Well, if I just had some weights . . .' So we'd buy him weights. And he'd be happy for about six weeks, and then it would blow away.

"Then he'd say, 'I believe if I joined the Y, that would give me something to do.' So we'd join the Y. And he'd try hang-gliding. We did everything we felt we could do to make him happy.

"Well, here it is now, almost exactly a year [after he ran away]. He is still not happy. He's doing things that he wasn't doing at this time. He can drive. We let him drive the Volkswagen whenever he needs to. He's allowed to associate with whomever he wants to. He can ask them here. And he's still not happy. I pointed that out to him the other day. I said all the things you ran away for last year— we changed as much as we could. And yet you still feel the same way you did.

"I guess the biggest shock," Daphne says, "is how did this happen to us when we have, all our lives, tried to have a perfect environment for the children to grow?" Then in thinking further, she says, "I probably paid too much attention to his every need when he was tiny. If I had to do it again, it would be to let him be a little more independent."

Daphne is still holding onto her image of happiness for her son, and it has not, in fact, cannot come true. She is using the behavioral changes that she has made as a lever, to bear down on him for not keeping up his side of this unwritten bargain: "I gave. You haven't."

When parents don't get what they feel is a proper return for their investment in a child, they often look back to the child's infancy and regret the giving they have done: "I'm sorry that I gave so much. It wasn't worth it." But it is not the giving per se that is the problem, it is the manner in which it was done.

Daphne feels that she and her son are very much alike. Both are supersensitive people, yet he has had the advantages she never had. He has his parents. She didn't. His parents care for each other, care for their children, hug and kiss them often. Daphne was rarely held as a child. And though she feels that she has the soul of a nonconformist, she pushes herself to comply. She was first in her college graduating class. This is, I feel, the core of her problems. Daphne has given her son everything she once wanted, yet it hasn't worked. The boundaries between him and her, in her mind, are soft. She expects him to be like what she tries to be, but in fact isn't. As children usually do, he has paid more attention to the person she really is than to her cover-up.

She does not totally understand that they are separate. She projects herself onto him, but conversely, she is trying hard to listen: to understand that though she worked hard at school, he may not finish high school. She lives in a genteel and proper way. He wants to go out in the woods and be a recluse.

In the meantime, he has asked for help.

"He told me the other day, 'Why don't you call one of your doctor friends and ask them if being skinny, listless, and with no energy and unable to conform has anything to do with depression?' And I thought, 'Now that's a cry for help, and I'm going to do something about it.'

"So I called the same counselor we went to and said, 'Maybe we need to look at this situation again. My son is more or less asking for help and I know that teenage depression is very dangerous.' She suggested a psychiatric evaluation. And we're going today for the first interview."

Just as some infants cry more than others and some toddlers are more defiant than others, some teenagers have more pain than others. Daphne is not totally responsible for the fix she and her son are in. Their problems are a result of the meshing of their personalities as well as the influences of the rest of the family and the community. One can only hope that this family has skillful psychiatric help.

Images That Are Realized

Some parents, fortunately, do find that their images are more or less realized.

ROBERTA HAHN

Roberta is a single parent, an administrator in a college. She has two children, a daughter, eleven, and a son, fifteen.

"The way I deal with my children is totally different than the way I did years ago.

"It's not just a question of how I deal with them. It's also how I see myself. I didn't know what it meant to be a parent. I had no idea. When I got married and had kids—that's what you were supposed to do. I never thought about whether I wanted kids or liked kids or what it meant to be a mother.

"I was a very unhappy person with a lot of my own problems. I was really a lousy mother because I resented the kids and I didn't know what I wanted to do with my life. Everything I felt about myself got taken out on them.

"I knew absolutely nothing about children. I thought if you were a parent, you diaper your children. You feed your children. You put them to bed at night. You wake them up in the morning. You kiss them and hug them occasionally.

"When I went back to graduate school in education a few years ago, I wouldn't say that I learned as much in classes as I learned being around people who liked children. The excitement that people had when they talked about children—I just felt it. I felt a loving concern about children.

"Then my marriage broke up [her husband moved in with another woman]. In that last year when my marriage was crumbling and in the first few months of my separation, my relationship with my kids went downhill rapidly. And they started showing symptoms of being in a lot of trouble.

"It was during that period when I really examined myself and my role with them. I started being honest. Started being able to laugh with them, to show them that I enjoyed them and appreciated them.

"When I was supportive of their needs, the results were just amazing. There were these constant rewards. Like my son. For a while after the separation he was really down. One day [when he was about twelve], he said to me, 'I used to think when I was a little boy that if you ripped one root out of a tree, the whole tree collapsed. Then I found out that you could rip out a lot of roots and it was okay. The tree still stands!'

"It was amazing. They were withstanding the separation. They were recognizing the changes in me and they appreciated me more.

"I was yelling less. They were yelling less.

"My son has been wanting to go to the *Rocky Horror Show* for a year. For a year, I've been saying, 'No.' I'm not sure why. I was frightened of him being there—at midnight, out on the street. All of his friends and even their younger brothers and sisters had gone. I'd been saying constantly, 'Well, their parents are crazy. I'm the only sane one. I'm taking good care of you.'

"Finally it was the last weekend before it left the neighborhood, and he said to me, 'I want to go.' I said, 'No.' He was very upset and he said, 'Look. You know there are lots of kids in this world that are screwed up. I'm not one of them. And I think you know that. I'm mature. And I'd never do anything that's crazy. I'm responsible and I'm honest with you. I think I can handle this, but your not letting me go is saying to me that you don't think I can handle this. I don't think it's a question of safety anymore. You're really saying I can't handle this.'

"And I stood there, and tears poured down my face and I said, 'You're right. That's what I'd been saying to you—though I don't really feel that way. And, yes, you can go see the *Rocky Horror Show.*'

"I think that that's one of the key things: It's my inability to give up control.

"You know, my daughter wanted an animal desperately. And I really don't like animals. I don't like dogs, and I don't like cats. She worked on me and worked on me, and finally we compromised on a bird. Then it died—about three months ago. But I recognized that she really needs an animal—at this point in her life. And even though I don't want one particularly, I think I need to give her one. So we finally agreed that in September we would get a cat.

"It has to do with my need to control, my need to have my own way, and I have to find a way to let go of that. There's got to be some medium ground.

"When I made a decision five years ago that they couldn't have something, they could stand on their heads and spit wooden nickels. I still would not give in. Now, I'm changing, and they feel that change.

"Once I realized that it was *my* problem and my inability to see what their needs were, it became much easier.

"My mother was a very cold, ungiving person. When she got angry at me, she didn't talk to me. She'd go to bed and stay there. I started to do that a few years ago and I realized I was doing exactly what my mother had done.

"As a child, I got very little support. I was zilch. Nothing I could do or say was good or right. I remember feeling—just ugly—fat—stupid. And I realized that I almost did that to my kids by not giving to them."

Sensing her children's needs. Being able to give. Not Roberta's original image—but the one that she has developed over the years.

At first she didn't live up to her image; now for the most part she does. She has grown. "What's fascinating to me is that it's never too late," Roberta says. "For a while I thought it was. But every day is new to kids. Every single day is new. I'm sure my kids remember some things in my marriage and in my life that were devastating. But at the end of each day now, I can tell that it's okay. Things are good. That relieves the guilt I feel about the years I didn't give them what they needed."

Redefining the authority relationships begins, then, with parents' images of themselves and their children. Carolyn O'Neal, whose image of communication was not realized, remained unhappy. Daphne Rogers realized that some of her images—that her son comply with her wishes and be happy—weren't going to come true, and she was attempting to seek help, search for causes, and build new expectations. Roberta was feeling that her image of being able to listen and respond to her children's needs was now happening.

The images that parents have either collide or converge with reality—and those parents who can understand the underlying expectations, who can listen to what their children are saying, who can adjust their images more realistically, feel that they have grown.

All of the parents of teenagers I interviewed had focused on two facets of redefining the authority relationship: communicating with teenagers, and setting limits and giving guidance.

Communicating with Teenagers

Teenagers run the gamut from ones like Carolyn's, who go off by themselves when in turmoil and refuse to talk, to ones like Roberta's, articulate and vocal about their feelings and problems.

Many parents felt that knowing something about the stage of adolescence was extremely helpful. Roberta, for example, knew that her son's moodiness was normal, and thus when he was unhappy she stayed clear of falling into the trap of blaming herself, of saying, "What did I do wrong?" or of letting him blame her. Even so, she found his periods of pain difficult and coped by "crossing my fingers, knowing that it's normal, knowing that it will pass."

Another help for Roberta was that she got on the phone with the parents of her son's friends on a regular basis. They could talk about problems such as the flagrant drug use in the high school and come to decisions which they all could stand behind, such as "No drugs at school" and "No parties at homes when the parents are out."

Each parent has a different kind of grapevine system—some of which are more entangling and crippling, others of which are more sustaining. When parents had no one to turn to, they felt more bereft. Carolyn O'Neal, for example, had moved away from a group of friends in the East to a new community in the West and she hadn't made close friends. She says, "Each phase of children's growing up is a whole new ball game. At times I really feel that when you get to the preteen and teenager years, there should be some help for parents—someone to talk to.

"I went back East in April, and I was talking to mothers that have eighteen-year-olds. Everyone had a story to tell, and I felt so good knowing I wasn't alone. It's just a phase that all children go through."

Most parents of teenagers felt that opportunities for communicating with other adults about their children had decreased. Parents were more scattered, didn't always know each other, had few chances to meet. Both the parent and the children had moved out to their own spheres, and these spheres didn't necessarily intersect. Those parents who wanted time to mull over issues of being the parent of a teenager with other parents or professionals usually had to take the initiative in making this happen. When they did find people who helped them gain a perspective on what they were doing and thus solve some of their own problems, parenthood was greatly enhanced.

It is, however, unfortunate that this kind of help is far from the reach of many parents of teenagers. This is a facet of our society that, I think, warrants improvement. Immediately needed is a study of the most effective kinds of support for parents of teenagers, a detailing of those factors that seem most and least effective, and developing informal or formal programs based on the information obtained.

One of the reasons that support is necessary now is that many parents find that the communication techniques they have used all along have become less effective. Teenagers don't always come up to their parents and tell them what's on their minds. They are more reserved, seek more privacy.

Old and New Ways of Communicating

Parents found that they had the task of shoring up old ways and developing new ways to facilitate talking together.

"We see less of our daughter time-wise," the mother of a fifteen-year-old says, "but rather than moving away, we've pulled in tighter. Amy will leave home in three years, and time with her is becoming more and more precious.

"It's difficult to schedule this time. I mean, she's not just going to walk in a room and say, 'Mother, yesterday this boy asked me to go to bed with him and I need to talk to you about it.' I mean, they just don't do that.

"You've got to develop a sixth sense about when they want to talk and then leave the door open so if they decide to walk through it, they can.

"That, at least to me, takes an incredible amount of energy and time: just being there without being there.

"It's a hard thing to do—to sit around Saturday afternoon because I know that my daughter has something on her mind. You have to get rid of your agendas and just sort of lay back so the kids feel free to move in with theirs."

STUART CURRAN

Stuart, unmarried, the director of a private high school, has had to start from scratch in attempting to communicate with his brother's thirteen-year-old son, Chris, whose guardian he now is.

"I don't—as the kids say—know where Chris is coming from. We've seen one another and been fond of one another and affectionate—but it's still very different and difficult. Chris is not one to talk about anything personal or about how he feels. He's friendly. He could charm the birds out of the trees. He is handsome and nice. But as far as talking to you about how he feels on a given subject or relaying any inner feelings, he is just the opposite. He will go into an absolute nonverbal state for days on end. I mean, he will speak, but it's 'Yes' and 'No' and 'Maybe.' He will not open up.

"Before I took him, he had run away from home. He was gone for about six months. He had gone to a religious commune. Because he was underage, he had to go to school, so the school down there got in touch with my brother.

"My brother called me and said, 'How shall I handle this?' And I told him to write that he was so happy that Chris had found a good Christian place and perhaps they would be able to do all these wonderful things for Chris and then to request permission to visit.

"Well, of course, they took the bait and my brother went down there and he said, 'Son, do you want to come home?' He said, 'Get me out of here. These people are crazy.'

"Then Chris decided to come to live with me. But he will not say a word about that whole time he was gone.

"I thought that taking Chris was going to be much simpler than it was.

"It's obvious that Chris has some problems that he won't talk about. I tried to talk him into some kind of help. He thinks that if you go to a psychiatrist, you'll be declared crazy and put away. I think that if I push that issue, he'd run away.

"I would say that ninety-nine percent of the kids that I've dealt with at school would talk to me about their feelings. Chris will not.

"That's the part that's made it the most difficult. I had too high expectations.

"How I deal with it is to try to get us in a situation like watching a Dracula film on TV, the kind of situation where we can exchange lines between commercials. I try not to ask him questions, because that makes his defenses go up. So I just talk. Or we will go to an arts-and-crafts fair. Or we'll go to work in the fields for a while. Something that is a together thing, but not verbal. That seems to help the most.

"When things are really uptight, I don't withdraw. I move in, in a nonverbal way. I do something so there's close physical proximity but no questions.

"Then he sort of comes back to having this better feeling about me. That seems the only way to go. But I have to plan that—it doesn't just happen."

Whether parents have to redouble their efforts to communicate, to find new techniques or not, those parents who managed to keep the lines of communication open during the teenage years felt more at ease, pleased, and comfortable about parenthood.

Setting Limits and Giving Guidance

The second facet of redefining the authority relationship is dealing with the results of the communication. *Parents have the task of responding to what the teenager says or doesn't say, and what the teenager does or doesn't do, by setting limits and giving guidance.* Many of the questions parents ask themselves are familiar ones:

Who decides? Who decides what? How are decisions enforced? Some of the questions are new: Is the teenager expected to finish high school, enter college, or go to work? Where is the teenager allowed to go? With whom? By what method of transportation? Staying how long? Returning when? What about smoking, drinking, drugs, and sex?

Money is often at the center of controversies. The costs of parenthood have escalated substantially. It takes more money to keep food in the refrigerator—and sometimes within a matter of hours a full refrigerator has only the dregs left: the milk at the bottom of the carton, the ice cream around the edges of the box. The cabinets fare the same—cereal and cracker boxes with only crumbs remaining.

Teenagers' clothes are as expensive as adults'. The difference is that teenagers are usually more clothes-conscious than adults, constantly wanting the latest jacket or pair of boots.

Pocket money disappears rapidly—for movies, snacks, and magazines.

The prospect of college looms ahead. Is the price of a college education going to continue to rise? How is a parent going to afford it?

Conflicts over money between parent and teenager are, in essence, conflicts over power: The person with the money has the control. If the teenager has earned money, then he or she has more leverage than the teenager who has to depend on others. How parents decide these issues reflects their images as well as their earning ability: Is it important for the parents to pay for the teenager or for the teenager to contribute or pay his or her own way?

Understanding Oneself

The first step in answering these questions is for parents to know what they think, to clarify their own standards and expectations. This is not a once-and-for-all task. Expectations are often not clear until the situation has arisen or until parents have taken a stand and can react to their ensuing feelings.

Understanding the Teenager

The second step is for parents to know their teenager, to know how much guidance he or she seems to need. Parents are using the skill of understanding and responding to the child's cues as they are expressed overtly and covertly.

MARTY DWYER

Marty, a teacher, is the father of two children, a sixteen-year-old daughter and an eleven-year-old son. Last year his daughter, Laura, complained a lot about her high school—that she wasn't learning anything, that it was a warehouse for children, that the teachers were more involved in following the union rules than teaching.

After much discussion, Marty and his wife decided to let Laura apply to a private school, but not before a careful discussion of the family finances and Laura's promise to contribute her baby-sitting money toward this new and quite large family expense.

After Laura was enrolled in the school for several months, Marty noticed that the agreed-on system was slipping. Laura, eager to look like the others in her class, was spending her baby-sitting money on new clothes.

At first Marty didn't say anything. He understood how his daughter felt. But then the tensions at home began to increase. Laura was irritable, and so was Marty—that extra money that Laura had promised to contribute was coming out of his pocket.

Finally, the tension exploded in a fight. Marty realized that Laura was feeling guilty about not putting in money, and they went back to their original plan.

Sometimes parents like Marty "put the lid on" or "stop" their child. Other times they want to encourage their child not to stop but to "go."

One parent says, "My daughter signed up for the track team. Track practice begins at six o'clock in the morning. By the second week of school, she was fizzled out.

"We told her that she had made a commitment to do track. Maybe she'd have to give up other things, but when you make a decision, you stick with it.

"For a week or so, she pouted, and then she decided, 'No. You're right.' And now that she's won several gold medals, she's glad."

Teenagers want room to try their own wings, yet they want a safe, structured place to come back to. They want some choices, and they want guidance. One course of action, laying down rules that cover every occasion, seems to provoke resistance and retreat. The other course, giving teenagers free rein, provokes a feeling of "she (or he) doesn't care what happens to me." Somewhere in the middle range, parents have to find the balance that suits them and their teenager. Parents are not starting with a blank slate. They have a history of a certain kind of relationship—which they build on or attempt to change.

MARY WILLIAMS

Mary and her husband moved out of the city to a farm. Located on a dusty clay road, their house overlooks corn and vegetable fields, a meadow with a pony tied to a stake, and several cars being disassembled and reassembled. Mary has three children, ages sixteen, fifteen, and twelve. They are black.

"When Russell [now sixteen] was in the third grade, our town was desegregated and they began busing. At that age, he said, 'No. I'm not going to be bused.' So I realized that even at an early age, he was capable of thinking for himself and making decisions that would affect his whole life. And I knew that I had to handle him carefully.

"Every day, when he and my other children come home from school, I sit at the table and listen to whatever they have to say, no matter what it is, whether it's good or bad. I don't jump to conclusions. I just listen.

"I think if at an early age I had supported his temper tantrums and his rages in a negative manner, it would have worked out differently.

"He would come in and say, 'Miss Such-and-such-person made us get out of her yard, and I don't think she's fair.' And I would not comment. I would just listen.

"Sometimes we have a meeting. We sit around the table, and we talk. We never leave the table until everybody feels good about a situation. We don't make him feel that he's right or he's wrong, but that he has a problem and we'll help him solve it."

This method, begun when Russell was younger, is continued today. Russell recently had a conflict with a high school teacher, for example, and they talked it out in their family meeting.

Changing as the Teenager Changes

ROBERT BANKS

Robert, a psychiatrist, married and the father of two children, a daughter, fourteen, and a son, seven, sees this kind of family discussion (in his case, based on the method that Rudolph Dreikurs developed)[4] "as a very good device because you learn about yourself and how your behavior affects others." He is using the skill of changing as the child changes.

"Our daughter had gone to the city with some other girls to buy some going-back-to-school clothes. She said, 'I got these slacks and a shirt and so on and it was only $75.'

"My son said, 'Only $75!' His tone was tinged with sarcasm.

"So we pointed out to him that he had come across as 'putting a damper on her enthusiasm.'

"He wasn't ready to look at his resentment.

"So the three of us started putting some pressure on him, not letting him get out of owning up to his feelings of jealousy toward his sister.

"Finally he started crying and getting angry and saying that he always felt that he was second best, that he was given short shrift by the family, that I was always very easy on my daughter but hard on him. Unloving, not doing enough with him.

"Then the criticism shifted to me as not being demonstrative—not risking myself in terms of hugging the wife, hugging the kids.

"It's true. It's easy for me to reciprocate when someone approaches me, but not to venture out on my own.

"One of the criticisms was that I'm a physician—but when the kids hurt themselves, I never make a big deal out of it. My daughter fell at school and broke her nose. I went down to the school and she was all bleeding, and I shifted into my physician's self and examined her eyes, her mouth, and skull and made sure that there were no serious injuries beyond the nose area. I was relieved to see there weren't. I didn't show much sympathy.

"So this week, I've tried to take some corrective action. When they get a little booboo or something, I try to communicate some kind of compassion."

Avoiding a Battle of Wills

A Tennessee mother of four children, fourteen, thirteen, ten, and nine, inadvertently found a way to communicate her values without turning issues into battles. She worked in the hospital as a volunteer and could talk to her children about her experiences, particularly about one pregnant teenager.

"Ruthann, my thirteen-year-old, was very upset—to think that here was a sixteen-year-old who was going to carry a baby and then give it up. She was sad for the girl, but happy for the adoptive parents because she knew how much they wanted it."

This mother felt that to bring her children in on the everyday realities of such things as teenage pregnancy was very instructive for them all.

One reason that these techniques—such as family councils or meetings or discussing a third person's problems—work is that they minimize the chances of a battle of wills between parent and teenager (a skill that has been useful for a long time). These techniques dilute the conflict between parent and child, while pooling the resources of others in the family. At best, communication is open, everyone has a chance to voice an opinion, and a consensus is reached.

Using such techniques does not erase the possibility that there will be times when the parent feels a need to say, "No," or "You can't." Furthermore, these techniques are not always surefire. There are moments that seem almost no-win. One father tells of his daughter coming to him in tears, crying that she had lost a necklace. "I'll help you look; but if we don't find it, we could buy another one."

The daughter's tears stopped. Her face froze as she looked at her father with reproach. "Buy another one! Never. It can never be replaced. It has sentimental value. You really don't understand!" And she fled the room.

A Developmental Irony: Youth vs. Midlife

A series of developmental ironies pervade the relationship between parent and child in the Interdependent Stage. It is ironic that at a point when the parent may be confronting aging, may be feeling more aches and pains and witnessing the illnesses and the deaths of contemporaries or of his or her parents, and thus thinking, "I'm next in line," the child is the very epitome of youth. The child now equals or surpasses the parents in height, is in the prime of physical shape, and may even be able to run faster, work longer hours, excel in sports.

The child's very presence may intensify the discomfort that parents feel as they deal with what Daniel Levinson calls the young/old polarity of midlife:

> A major developmental task of the Mid-life Transition is to confront the Young and the Old within oneself and seek new ways of being Young/Old.[5]

Parents confront this developmental step of their own in many ways. While some dwell on their aging, others cast out thought of becoming old and say that they have never felt younger. They may set up a strict physical regime for themselves, of jogging or tennis or sailing or bowling or exercise. They may want to do things that they didn't allow themselves when they were younger, such as being more sexual, more flamboyant. But in their midst is the teenager, a reminder that the parent is working at something which the teenager has easily in his or her grasp. The parent may be counting every calorie to stay slim and fit, while the teenager splurges on ice cream, looks terrific in a bathing suit, and yet complains, "I'm getting fat."

The result can be a relationship tinged or fraught with envy. Parents' complaints about their teenagers often reveal a stream, narrow or wide, of free-flowing jealousy.

The result can also be a sadness. As one parent spoke of her son's growth, she said, "He makes my own mortality pretty clear to me."

The research that has been done on adult development at midlife has not separated out the effects of children. I wonder, for example, if teenagers are a catalyst for this developmental conflict. Do adults without children feel the same way as adults with children? What about the age of the child? Do adults in their forties with very young children confront this turning point differently from those with teenagers or grown children? Or do they face it later? Conversely, is the parent of a teenager affected differently depending on whether he or she is in the thirties, or forties, or fifties?

Many pressures and tensions seem to converge and band together in the Interdependent Stage. The child has changed and sometimes, it appears, regressed. The parent feels that he or she is letting go of gains made. While the parent might regret these regressions, simultaneously he or she may want to be and act young. But standing there is the teenager, saying, with or without words, "Shape up, be mature, be an adult."

The Parent/Parent Relationship

These pressures can reverberate through or be reflected in the parent/parent relationship. When a father and mother have differing images of themselves, the pressures can be even more intense. The mother who feels that her son needs to be listened to, the father who feels that such listening is indulgence. He thinks that the teenager should be treated strictly, while the mother regards this attitude as cruel. In this family, an action by the son starts waves which crash up into every relationship.

The solution is either to resolve the differences or to accept them, though that is much easier said than done, because parental images are deep-seated.

One mother and father, in an attempt at reconciling their differences, figured out which of their expectations were crucial to them and couldn't be dropped and thus had to be accepted, and which were more superficial and could possibly be changed.

The Parent/Grandparent Relationship

Such issues can permeate the parent/grandparent relationship, too. The world of the teenager, which may seem remote to the parent, may seem actually alien, even threatening, to the grandparent: the deafening sounds of rock music, the street-wise language, the changing morals. Or the grandparents, once removed from responsibility, may appreciate the teenager's experience. In any case, the parent is often "caught in the middle."

Catherine Chilman writes:

> From the viewpoint of the middle-aged parent, one does indeed, seem to be caught in the middle of three generational cycles: between the increasingly complex, costly and disturbing needs of adolescent children who are bursting with desire for entrance into the adult world and the increasing problems and needs of the grandparents who, generally, are bursting with desire not to leave their full status in the adult world. The middle-aged adult, who may feel that his own status is threatened somewhat by his own developmental stage, is apt to feel further threatened by the competing, but somewhat similar claims of both the older and younger generations.[6]

Catherine Chilman continues that the growth struggles of adolescence, by reactivating old pains and joys, failures and hopes, in both the grandparent and parent, can accentuate long-standing impasses.

As one parent says, "I now see I'm still rebelling from my mother. I'm trying to handle my kids' rebellion when here I am doing the same thing with my mother. It's pathetic."

Pathetic? But potentially positive, too. This mother had become so accustomed to the way she acted with her own mother that she was immune to its meaning. When her daughter began to act the same way (criticizing her at every turn, for instance), she started to see that she had never moved beyond the system she had set as a teenager of resisting and rebelling from her own mother. She is now determined to try to be different.

DEALING WITH SEXUALITY

During the teenage years, the child metamorphoses into a fully sexual person. The mother of a son says, "With my son, it was very dramatic. I don't remember any transition. One day his voice was deep. He seemed to have grown five inches. He slimmed down. He was a man."

The beginning of menstruation is a key event for both teenage girls and their parents. A fourteen-year-old from Texas started to menstruate for the first time while spending the night at a friend's house. She called home to tell her mother. The following day, I spoke to her father. He said, "When I saw Adrienne, I was astounded by the fact that she was no longer a child. She is a woman.

"I've had twinges of sadness all day, thinking about losing her as a child.

"I think back to bathing her nude as a child. I think of her as a little baby. But it's a scene that you can't recapture—that childlike innocence.

"I told her that I wanted to take her out to dinner, and she got embarrassed and upset, but then I said maybe we can go to [a very interesting new local restaurant], so she kind of changed her tune. She's considering the idea."

Adrienne, though initially embarrassed with her father, was forthright about menstruation with her mother.

A New York mother of a fourteen-year-old tells a different story. "My daughter," she says, "began menstruating about a year ago. She never told me. I finally found this napkin in the wastebasket. And I said, 'Gee, guess what I found?' I said, 'Is it you?' She said, 'No,' and, of course, I believed her.

"A friend said to me, 'I think she's lying. You should confront her.'

"I said, 'What? What do you mean she's lying?'

"Anyway, that evening, I said [to my daughter], 'I'm upset about a couple of things. One is that you lied to me, and two, I have a feeling you're ashamed to be a girl.'

"She said, 'I don't want to talk about it. Call me tomorrow!'

"And that next night, I said, 'I have three questions: One, when did you get your period? Two, do you know what to do? And three, do you have any discomfort?'

"She didn't answer, so I said something about how she had just started her period and she said, 'What makes you think I *just* started?'

"The whole thing was mind-blowing. She said, 'Why are you making such an issue out of it?' And I said, 'You're the one who's making an issue—you should have told me.' I asked her if she wanted to talk to one of her friends, but she said, 'No. No big deal.'

"She really didn't want to talk, and I didn't press it. I dropped it.

"And the months go by and I buy sanitary napkins and just stick them in her drawer."

The Texas father of the fourteen-year-old describes his daughter as "a woman." The beginning of menstruation means growing up, and growing up means change.

One change that occurs in the teenage years is in the physical relationship between parent and child. The child's body once almost belonged to the parent, like an annexed province perhaps, but one over which the parent held partial sway. The child was there, ready to be wrapped in a large towel as he or she stepped from a warm bath into a chilly room, ready to be held on the parent's lap when a television show became scary, and to cuddle while reading a bedtime story or to sit side by side in the car.

For a while, this relationship has been changing. Teenagers still want affection and attention, but they usually set the rules; they are more likely to decide if and when they want a hug.

Furthermore, the parents are perhaps not the only ones giving and receiving the hugs. There are romances. The child whose eyes once widened and shone when a parent came for pickup at school now may glisten just as brightly for a boyfriend or girlfriend. The child who once walked hand in hand with a parent may now be walking hand in hand with others.

With or without romance, the child is now more sexual than ever before and is looking at everyday events often with erotic eyes, perhaps imagining familiar people without their clothes, conjuring up pictures of the sex lives of people he or she knows.

Parents often find clues to this kind of daydreaming. One mother found a piece of paper folded in the pocket of her son's jeans in the laundry. It was a list that he had made, ranking all of her women friends in order of preference—"Who I would like to sleep with." Another parent overheard her daughter and a friend going over the family's address book, discussing which couples might be sleeping around.

As one part of the major task of defining and redefining their relationship with their child, parents are now dealing with the task of accepting their child's sexuality.

- A mother walks into her twelve-year-old son's room and finds him and another boy naked.
- A girl wants to go over to her close friend's house, a boy, after school. Both of his parents work and there would be no adults at home.
- A father finds stacks of copies of *Playboy* magazine under his son's bed.
- A fifteen-year-old boy begins staying out later and later.
- A sixteen-year-old girl asks many questions surreptitiously that lead up to: "How does a girl know if she is pregnant?"

- An eighteen-year-old boy asks if his girlfriend can move into their house.

Parents may have to deal with situations such as these throughout the teenage years.

Images Form a Mental Guide

Their first question is what to say, when, and how. Parents' images form a mental guide.

ALEXANDRIA STIFEL

Alexandria is the New York parent whose fourteen-year-old didn't want to talk about menstruation. She is divorced, and currently in between jobs.

"My mother," she says, "is a super person on the one hand, but has qualities on the other that are difficult to take. She's very intrusive. Everything always comes back to 'my daughter—she's the greatest.' The sun rises and sets on her Alexandria, but what I know damn well is that it's not me she's bragging about—it's her.

"She has a certain quality where she would sort of—not smother so much as engulf me.

"I call her 'the woodpecker' because when she kisses me, she practically bores a hole in my cheek. That's how I feel. I feel like I've been thrown to the ground.

"She's never separated from me—so that's one reason why I probably tend to go on the other side—to stay aloof from my daughter.

"Sex is a perfect example. If my daughter doesn't want to talk about it, I don't. But on the other hand, if I act so independent, is she going to think that I don't care?

"I hope she knows that I'm interested. But I do tend to be unassertive. I have a horror of asking her too much personal stuff because my mother is that way."

The implications of such feelings are complex. Because Alexandria feels that she has never separated from her mother, in some ways and despite her intention to do the reverse, she has substituted her daughter for her mother:

"Although on the surface I keep my distance because I don't want to intrude, on a deeper level I feel that I am needy of my daughter, that I am dependent on her, on her approval."

LINETTE WOODS

Linette Woods has just the opposite point of view. She was told nothing about sex at all, and when she became pregnant, unmarried, at seventeen, she wasn't sure what was going on. Her mother finally figured it out and took Linette to a doctor, who confirmed the pregnancy but said little, if anything, to Linette. Linette worried all through her pregnancy about how the baby would get out. She was so hysterical with fear during the delivery that she couldn't stop screaming.

That child is now fifteen, and Linette feels she must tell her about sex. She waited for the perfect moment, a time alone with her daughter. When the moment finally arrived, Linette became so nervous that without thinking, she swept the kitchen, then swept it again. But once she began talking, it became easier.

Linette's image is to be different from her own mother, and she has, in fact, been so, but beneath the surface is a deeper similarity to her own upbringing. Linette was not told about sex, to shield and protect her. She has taken the opposite tack but for the same purpose—to protect her daughter. In fact, she keeps her daughter very close, and, only at fourteen, stopped walking her to the inner-city school she attends.

Sexuality and Separation

Both Linette and Alexandria are alike in the kind of ties they have to their mothers. Alexandria Stifel understands that her mother hasn't separated from her, but she also realizes that "I've never separated from her. We'll go into a restaurant and she'll look at the whole menu and order something that's not on it. And I get mad—because I don't like the way she's acting. But that's ridiculous. I mean, she's not me. If she acts in a silly way, what's that got to do with me?"

Both Linette and Alexandria feel similarly connected to their daughters. What I wonder is this: Do parents have to be able to separate—that is, allow and accept differences in their own parents—before they can separate from their children? I have another question—one which is raised in My Mother/My Self. Is it true, as Nancy Friday contends, that a parent cannot accept his or her offspring's sexuality without separating?[7] And are girls and boys treated differently? Creating what advantages and disadvantages?

Sexual Issues: Talking and Taking Action

Linette and Alexandria were in a talking phase. Talking covers a large arena: there is telling the facts of life, but there is also conveying an attitude about sexuality. The celebratory attitude, for example, that the Texas father conveyed about menstruation is far different from the one Alexandria expressed. Are sexual problems broached? Venereal disease? Promiscuity? Prostitution? What do the parents say about childbirth? About common situations that happen to women: cramps, cystitis? What kinds of values do they convey?

Some situations go way beyond telling the facts of life: the son who stays out later and later; the daughter who hints at the question "Am I pregnant?" Or a daughter who either gets a friend or asks her parents to accompany her to a doctor for birth-control protection. There may be brief or sustained romances. There may be pregnancies. There may be homosexuality.

Parents may feel ill equipped to negotiate these issues. Because they probably haven't lived out some of these situations as teenagers years ago, they feel unsure. Granted, perhaps, that the sexual repression of their generation had destructive elements. Granted that women were taught to hold back before marriage, and had a tough time learning to let go, to say yes, to enjoy sex. Granted, too, that they or some of their friends married to have sex and that their marriages may have quickly dissolved. But will the effect of this more open situation lead to a lack of commitment, perhaps even a narcissistic disrespect for themselves? Or perhaps just the opposite, will it lead to relationships formed with much prior thought, a comfort with themselves and their sexuality?

These are both sexual and authority issues, and parents have to find that balance between giving the child guidance and security and letting the child try out his or her ideas.

Figuring out how to achieve that balance, figuring out how to handle sexual issues, grows out of communication between parent and teenager.

JANET WARNER

Janet is a divorced parent with two teenage children. Her daughter, Lisa, had been on a camping trip with friends, both boys and girls, last summer. She recently asked to go again, with one of the boys from the group.

"For me, that meant I had to recognize reality rather than deny it. Lisa is fifteen.

"She has always been terrified of growing up. She used to say to me, 'I want to be like Peter Pan.' But at fifteen, both she and I can't deny that she is growing up.

"Growing up means sex. And she would be sharing a tent with that boy.

"I didn't want to say, 'You can't go because I said you can't,' but I felt very uncomfortable.

"I finally told her that I felt uncomfortable that she would be in a situation that would be stimulating—that we can't pretend that she's ten anymore.

"Lisa denied it and said I was being dramatic. But she'd return to the discussion every day: 'I don't want to get into it, but . . .'

"That was a clue that she wanted me to put the lid on it. We talked about it over several weeks. Finally she said, 'I'm not going to argue with you. I won't go.'

"Two days later, she told me that she wasn't getting along with the boy anymore. I think she was glad I said no, that she secretly felt like it was too much for her to handle.

"She said to me, 'You know why I wanted to go—because I like to wake up in the tent before anyone else is up, when it's still a little dark, get dressed, and run down to the water and watch the sun come up all by myself.'

"It was what she used to do as a child when we went to the beach. She wanted to go back to her childhood."

Parents who are able to keep the lines of communication open, who are able to base their actions on a give-and-take dialogue, remembering that they are the adult and their teenager is younger, that they aren't "buddy-buddies," feel more comfortable and successful in this aspect of parenthood than those for whom the lines of communication are shut down.

The Teenager's Sexuality Affects the Parents' Sexuality

The effect of having another almost-adult in the home can be widespread. The teenager's sexuality can affect the adult's sexuality.

"Having a teenager," a mother says, "makes sex harder. My son never goes to sleep.

"There used to be a time at the end of the day that was ours. And now, it's much more typical for my husband and son to end the day together, because I just flake out about ten-thirty or eleven. That really plays havoc with our sex life—because my husband just isn't in bed. I have to say that is a problem, and both of us actively look for times when he spends the night out."

It is evident, listening to parents talk about their teenagers, that jealousy exists, though it may not be recognized and is often mixed with pride. The father remembers holding his daughter on his lap, her whole body turned into his—but now she has boyfriends. Perhaps this boyfriend is everything the father wished he could have been, or perhaps he is totally mediocre or inferior, an insult as a replacement.

The mother has similar memories with her son. She remembers when he gave her a look that said, "You are the most important person in the world to me." Now those looks are perhaps more infrequent, they are given to others, and they are cut into with looks of disdain: "Oh, Mother, how could you?" The mother and father may remember nights that their child asked to play a game of cards, Monopoly, or Scrabble, or to watch TV together, to go out for ice cream, but the parents were too tired, or busy. Now, the reverse is just as likely to be true. The parents want to do something with the family but the teenager is busy, and the parents may feel guilty or pleased or rejected or saddened by these changes.

The jealousy and pride do not only flow between the parent and the opposite-sex child. They exist, perhaps even more strongly, between mothers and daughters, fathers and sons.

A mother may envy and/or appreciate her daughter's positive features—perhaps her ability to approach life with vigor, her self-confidence. Fathers have a similar range of responses toward their sons. The teenagers have life ahead of them, like a meadow of flowers and thorns without any paths cut across it. The parents have made many inroads and what lies ahead may seem muddy and trampled, or still promising.

A Developmental Irony: The Beginning vs. the Close of the Reproductive Cycle

The issue of sexuality, like that of authority, has an embedded irony. A change of life is most probably occurring for both parents and children, but whereas for children it is a beginning, for parents a midpoint is reached. As the children become physically able to reproduce, women are coming closer to the close of their reproductive cycle. Depending on her age at giving birth, the mother may be far away or close to menopause, but nevertheless the parents I interviewed were thinking about that young/old polarity in terms of reproduction: Am I ever going to be the parent of a baby again or is that part of my life passed?

Parents were asking themselves similar kinds of questions about their own sexuality: Am I young, middle-aged, or old? Am I more or less attractive than I was? Has my sex life peaked or plummeted? Is sex improving for me or not?

ACCEPTING THE TEENAGER'S IDENTITY

It is not a coincidence that almost every interview with parents of teenagers was anchored on the subject of identity. According to Erik Erikson, the major psychosocial task for the adolescent is "identity vs. role confusion." He writes:

> The growing and developing youths, faced with this physiological revolution within them, and with tangible adult tasks ahead of them are now primarily concerned with what they appear to be in the eyes of others as compared with what they feel they are, and with the question of how to connect the roles and skills cultivated earlier with the occupational prototypes of the day. In their search for a new sense of continuity and sameness, adolescents have to refight many of the battles of earlier years, even though to do so they must artificially appoint perfectly well-meaning people to play the roles of adversaries.[8]

Peter Blos writes also that adolescence is like a "second edition of childhood":

> We witness at adolescence a second step in individuation, the first one having occurred toward the end of the second year when the child experiences the fateful distinction between "self" and "non-self." A similar, yet far more complex, individuation experience occurs during adolescence, which leads in its final step to a sense of identity. Before the adolescent can consolidate this formation, he must pass through stages of self-consciousness and fragmented existence. The oppositional, rebellious, and resistive strivings, the stages of experimentation, the testing of the self by going to excess—all these have a positive usefulness in the process of self-definition.[9]

Parents say of their teenagers: "He is acting like he did at four." "She wants so much to stay in step with the group but privately always feels out of step."

Teenagers define themselves by looking at how they are the same as and how they are different from everyone they know or care about—their parents, their relatives, their teachers, their friends, figures from history, modern-day stars. Teenagers can exaggerate both the similarities and differences. If a teenager wants to be like a friend, that friend can do no wrong. If a teenager doesn't want to be like a parent, that parent can do nothing right.

The process of finding out "Who I am" for the teenager usually involves separation from his or her parents—finding and then stressing the ways that teenager is not like the family, and therefore unique. The task for the teenager becomes the task of the parent: *Part of the redefinition of the parent/child relationship is the task of continuing the process of accepting the child's separate identity.*

The word "identity" seems to connote something stolid, static. But the teenager's sense of identity is far from that. It is in flux, alighting here or there, looking for a spot to settle on. Teenagers look toward the future—"the grown-up me."

Images of the Future: The Grown Child

Parents of teenagers also look to this future, attempting to picture the world of the future and their grown-up children in it.

One mother describes her two children:

About her son, age seventeen, she says, "When I think of Alexander, I cannot imagine what he will be like as a grown-up. If you had a crystal ball and told me he was going to be an astronaut, I would say fine. If you told me he was going to go to the Mojave Desert and be a monk, I'd say that's possible. I mean there's no way I could tell you what I think. I feel like he's going to peel his skin about five times and each metamorphosis will be one step along."

About her teenage daughter she says, "I have always felt I knew Angelica quite well. I have a picture of her at twenty-one, give or take all kinds of other experience. She might study Italian. She's crazy about art history. She might be a filmmaker or a writer. That's not to say that I know ultimately what her life will be or what she will work at, but there are certain themes about her that stay the same."

Affinity/Dissimilarity and Identity

Parents' thinking about their child's identity is deeply influenced by their feeling of affinity and dissimilarity to their child. A parent who feels an affinity feels that the child is more known, whereas the dissimilar child is more of a mystery.

On the surface it would seem harder for a parent to separate from a child with whom he or she feels an affinity, easier with a child that is dissimilar, but that is not always the case. "Separate" means that the parent understands the ways in which the child is unique. It doesn't preclude an appreciation of the ways in which the child is similar. In my view, in fact, separateness is always linked with connectedness.

I would like to see a study of affinity/dissimilarity—looking at this process over time and seeing how it influences separation. What other factors come into play? I would also like to look at the process from the vantage point of the child: How do the parents' perceptions of affinity or dissimilarity affect the child as he or she grows into adulthood?

Feelings About Sex Roles

Parents have images about the kind of person they would like their child to be—and these images are based on not only their sense of affinity/dissimilarity but also on their feelings about sex roles.

Popular opinion has it that parents' perceptions on this subject are rapidly changing. However, in a recent book, *Beyond Sugar and Spice,* the authors, Caryl Rivers, Rosalind Barnett, and Grace Baruch, conclude that it hasn't changed much. They feel that a study done in the 1950's by Elizabeth Douvan and Joseph Adelson of the University of Michigan still has much validity. In this study of 3,500 teenage boys and girls, they found that boys were more concerned with achieving a separate identity than girls. Rivers, Barnett, and Baruch feel that many girls today succumb to the "dropping back" syndrome, by devaluating their previous accomplishments and abilities and emphasizing relationships, dating in particular. They write, "The girls who have gotten straight A's, the star athletes, now notice that these accomplishments seem to be less important than they once were." [10]

Parents have images about what their girls and their boys should be like—whether or not their views predate or postdate the women's liberation movement. I hope that those parents who are non-sexist don't just try to push women over into roles that replicate men's. Carol Gilligan from Harvard notes that the end result of growth is often seen as separation (without the connectedness), autonomy, and individuation, devaluing the fact that "women not only define themselves in a context of relationship to others, but judge themselves in terms of their ability to care." [11]

Jessie Bernard hopes for a future in which:

> We would have both men and women, in whatever ratio, at both ends of a rather flat, bell-shaped curve following, at one end, a specialized "feminine" lifestyle and, at the other, a specialized "masculine" lifestyle.
>
> In between we would have an indeterminate number of men and women in whatever ratio who . . . had the dynamism associated with maleness harnessed to the people-oriented, humanitarian achievement values associated with femaleness. Not at all a frightening prospect. [12]

Parents' Images Come from Their Past

Parents' images also grow out of their own past—how their strivings for their own separate identity were handled or how they wish they had been handled.

DAVID WINEBRENNER

David, the father of three children, daughters fourteen and twelve years old and a seven-year-old son, is the director of a nature preserve.

"I was the child of immigrants who for a variety of valid and not so valid reasons learned that your parents were people that you put aside. For a long time my parents wanted to have as little to do with me and my family as possible.

"When my grandmother died, we all got together, and now I think my parents have gotten interested in my children again.

"But when I was a child, they didn't understand or really respect me. I presented one incredible disappointment after another to them. I had all kinds of learning problems. I was the worst goddam student you ever saw. They hoped I would be perfect, and I could hardly spell, let alone that I was no good on the playing field."

In raising his own children, David's image of himself is of a father who is respectful of each of their interests and efforts.

He proudly tells a story in which his fourteen-year-old daughter, Julia, prevailed in making changes in her junior high school.

"Their school is broken up into minischools. About a third of the way into the year, the adults realized that in one minischool there were two classes. One happened to be almost all black, the other predominantly white. The adults then said, 'We're sorry. We have to rearrange the school.'

"So one day, I get a call from Julia at lunch hour. She says, "I may not be home from school on time today because we're sitting in.' I said, 'Where are you?' She said, 'In the principal's office.' "

The kids, including Julia, did not disagree with the necessity of reorganization, but they didn't want the adults to do it, unmindful of the social network that students had spent one-third of the year putting into place.

"The principal wouldn't meet with them. He was always too busy. He was always on the telephone.

"So the students came to the parent-teacher meeting with a clearly thought-through plan. They said they were going to consult with everybody about who they wanted to be with and then sort out the groups, constantly looking at sex, race, economic background, and ability.

"If the principal had done it, he would have just gone down the list and reorganized. He would have come up with the same kind of mix, but he wouldn't have included the kids' friendships.

"The parents really supported the kids' plan, so the principal reluctantly had to agree.

"Julia was one of the chief spokesmen. She knows that that's one of the important things that happened during her time in that school."

David's image of himself is that he allows his children "to be themselves." He feels successful with Julia. He is treating her the way that he wished his parents had treated him.

It is undoubtedly helpful that Julia mirrors David. She is a nonconformist, just as he is. It would be interesting to speculate about whether or not David would be as successful with a child who was conforming, who acquiesced and accepted the status quo.

What is known, however, is that David is not just living out his nonconformist dreams through his daughter. He remains a social activist who, through his job, has been effective in exposing graft and making changes in the local bureaucracies.

Parents Are Engaged in Their Own Evaluations

Parents' images of their children's identity are influenced by their own evaluations. While teenagers are pursuing questions of identity, so are parents. Many are sizing themselves up, seeing how they have measured up to their dreams, how close or how far they are from the marks they set for themselves.

Daniel Levinson writes that some of the forty men in his study did little questioning or searching (for which they paid the price in a later developmental crisis or in a "progressive withering of the self"). Other men, though questioning, did so without much turmoil and pain.

> But for the great majority of men—about 80 percent of our subjects—this period evokes tumultuous struggles within the self and with the external world. Their Mid-life Transition is a time of moderate or severe crisis. Every aspect of their lives comes into question, and they are horrified by much that is revealed. They are full of recriminations against themselves and others. They cannot go on as before, but need time to choose a new path or modify the old one.[13]

Lillian Rubin entitles her study of 160 midlife women (which she defines with a broader age range than Levinson does—from thirty-five to fifty-four) *Women of a Certain Age: The Midlife Search for Self.* She writes:

> The issue of identity—a troubling one for women at any age—is brought to center stage at midlife . . . The midlife transition is . . . a time often filled with turmoil and self-doubt, a time when old roles are being shed and the shape of new ones not yet apparent; a time of reordering long-held priorities, of restructuring daily life.[14]

The women that Lillian Rubin interviewed had spent some time staying home with children, so their midlife transition involved moving out in the world. Gail Sheehy has noted that many women and men are at a dissonant point at midlife—with women often on the first phases of a job, eager to push ahead, while men are retreating, wanting to put more time into their families.[15] Since the U.S. Department of Labor figures show that more and more women are returning to work when their children are young, it's important to study how women who have been employed for a while fare at midlife, as opposed to those just returning to work.[16]

Lillian Rubin finds that one trigger for women's search for identity is the child's growing up.[17] Is this true for men? For working mothers? And then a question I've been asking throughout this section of the book: How do chronological age and the circumstances of life (being the parent of a teenager, for example) intersect in influencing the midlife transition?

Teenagers Are Also Evaluating Parents

Not only are the parents evaluating themselves and their children, teenagers are also casting a critical eye at the parents: "Why did you stick out a nine-to-five job that you dislike?" "How can you talk about conserving energy and have a car that's a gas guzzler?" "Why do you ask me to be successful when you never have been?" Teenagers can often detect the hypocrisies between dreams and life as it is lived, and voice them.

To look at oneself through one's teenager's point of view changes a parent. To face up to the subtle and not so subtle criticism and praise, to have to take stock of and defend one's life, is a transforming experience.

Robert Coles and Jane Hallowell Coles tell of a woman, Hannah Morgan, going through this phase of life. Hannah says:

> My daughter was twelve, and she was already a woman, and she was asking me all these questions—I near went mad. I told her to stop. But she said if she stopped, she'd still ask them of herself, and I knew she was right. So I listened, and I tried to give answers, if I could think of some. The main thing on her mind was where she would be living when she was older, and whether she would have a job, and what kind.

In the course of their conversations, the daughter says she doesn't want to follow her parents' course, settling for many children and poverty. These conclusions prompt Hannah to look back to her own dreams: "I guess I wanted a different life, too—just like my daughter does. My mother was wrong not to see what was on my mind."

But, at the same time, she resents her daughter's questioning. "I began to realize that there are mountains between us—as high as the mountains back home. My daughter will never be part of Harlan County the way I am. She has dreams of her own."

She feels that her daughter has turned against her origins, that she has lost her, and she begins to pick on her for sloppy clothes, poor posture, laziness.

The changing nature of her feelings reaches a climax during a bus ride one morning when Hannah is on the way to work. She missed her stop, but when she reached up to pull the cord, she was unable to do so: "I thought I was sick. I couldn't move. I couldn't lift my arm to pull that cord. . . . I felt as if I was no longer me! I felt as if I was watching myself and watching the others on the bus and watching the world go by through the window.

"I had a strange idea—a *crazy* idea; I wondered if it was like that to die—your soul leaving your body behind, like they tell you in church. I wasn't even nervous at the thought of dying. I remember thinking to myself that I'd had enough of life, and I would just as soon find out what was ahead of me in the next world."

The bus finally stopped and the driver had to call, "Last stop— last stop," many times before she came to her senses. She got herself back to work, but all that day a series of pictures flashed through her mind. The question she asked herself was, "What am I doing here?"

At the core of this question—"What am I doing here?"—is a changing relationship between mother and daughter.

Hannah says, "I think I was too close by far to Pauline. She was my first child, my first daughter, and I couldn't stop myself from telling her what was on my mind. I don't know if a mother should do that with her child. I'll be looking at Pauline now, and I'll want to run away from her. She gets me angry. She's so sure of herself, it seems to me. Then I'll leave the room, and I'll miss seeing her, and I'll wish it could be like in the old days, when we'd sit and talk." [18]

FORMING NEW BONDS WITH THE ALMOST-GROWN CHILD

Separation is a gradual process. It is like a pendulum which swings back and forth, except that the span of this pendulum does not stay constant. I can almost visualize a giant, grinning child swinging such a pendulum—unevenly—faster, slower, with an ever-widening arc, on one side separateness, on the other connectedness.

Teenagers move back and forth—from family to friends. They don't need their parents in the same ways they once did. They are fully capable of surviving on their own, though in greater or lesser degrees they accept care: money, cooked meals, clean laundry, a place to live, attention, and affection. Parents may feel that their children have become "boarders," at times "companions."

Most teenagers spend large amounts of time away from home—at school or work, at sports practice, at after-school activities or lessons, or hanging out with friends. Even at home they may insist on privacy.

There are key events in this separation, perhaps none so pivotal as the teenager's getting a driver's license. A teenager who can drive may have to wait for a turn with the car, may have to buy a car, may have to ration the use of gasoline, but once inside the car, with a tank of gas, he or she can go . . . and go. Cars often become symbolic, to both parents and teenagers, of this newfound distance between them.

Parents have the task of dealing with the distance between them and their child while creating new ties.

Separateness Brings Feelings of Envy

Parents have many feelings about the separateness. Envy is one. Many parents voiced the thought that everyone else has a better relationship with their child than they.

A wife says of her husband and teenage son, "I see them watching television together and it looks really lovely, but I guess I'm jealous that my husband has that and I don't."

Parents can also resent the bonds between their children and their friends. They see their child coming home from school in a group, or in a group at the drugstore or next to the entrance to the movie house or by the side of the road—wherever the gathering spot is. Laughter and conversation seem to come from the group like clouds of frosty breath on a chilly day, shooting out, lingering above, dissipating, both illusive and elusive to the parent.

It is fascinating that often unbeknownst to both of them, the teenager and the parent may be undergoing parallel feelings. The parents want to feel connected to the teenager, want to feel that they have meaningful ties to each other, but the tensions between them keep that vision dim. Teenagers also want to feel a part of their group, want their chosen friendships to be meaningful, but rivalries, rejections, and hurts intervene. Teenagers use their friends as a sanctuary, a safe refuge to belong to as they move away from their families. They also use them as reflectors: I must be popular or smart or political or athletic or attractive or rebellious because those are the kinds of kids that I hang out with. Even though they so want to feel in harmony, they, like their parents, have feelings of dissonance.

Separateness Also Stirs Up Fears

Another feeling that can emanate from this growing separateness is fear. No longer able to protect their child, to stand between their child and the car coming too fast, or the dangers of life, parents can be fearful—afraid of the influence of other kids, afraid of hearing the siren go by.

When the phone rings while a teenager is out, parents talk about having an instantaneous crackle of fear, like lightning: Something has happened. Part of this fear comes from their own memories. They may remember themselves or their friends taking dangerous risks as a teenager: driving a hundred miles per hour, riding on a motorcycle over the snow-slippery streets without a crash helmet, taking crazy dares, and then remaining silent or lying to their parents about these adventures.

The film *Saturday Night Fever* comes to mind. Clearly it is told from the hindsight of adults—one of the kids balancing on the bridge railing falls to a cold, dark death in the river. Teenagers would be more likely to hope at least that they are invincible, indestructible. Adults know better, and they worry.

Thoughts of death do tend to accumulate and become accentuated when separations are occurring: before birth, before sending one's child off to school, and now when the child is growing up. Separation is a symbolic kind of death.

Separateness Creates Hostilities, Pride, and Regret

Another feeling that accompanies this changing parent/child relationship is hostility. As Hannah Morgan, the mother from Harlan County in *Women in Crisis*, says of her daughter, "She gets me angry. She's so sure of herself."

There is pride, too. Pride that one's own child can do or say or think what he or she does. Looking at the almost grown child, parents often feel aglow.

Pride can mix with nostalgia and regret, a longing for times passed, for cuddling this person, once a small child, or for opportunities missed or mistakes made. Parents of teenagers used the phrase "if only." This wouldn't be happening "if only" we lived here instead of there, if my child went to this school instead of that, if the father or mother spent more time with the child. Some of these "if onlys" may be true, but some may be in regret of a time passed.

All of the feelings that surround the increasing separateness between parent and child are common. Some parents find themselves taking them out on the child, picking on the child, blaming, castigating—while other parents feel them no less intensely but are less likely to act on them. The difference, in part, seems to be an understanding, continuously accrued throughout parenthood, that "I am not my child and my child is not me. We may be alike, but we are not the same person."

Parents do begin to gather up their images about the way they want to handle this increasing separation. One woman who felt that she had no emotional privacy when she was a teenager is eager to try to provide privacy for her son. On the other side is a mother whose parents seemingly didn't care about whom she went off with and what she did. She wants to emphasize her involvement with her two teenage children. That hub called the family may be seen as separate strands, as the slightest threads hung together, or as a tightly bound entity.

The Teenager's Travels Are a Portent

The teenager may leave home, for short or long periods, frequently or infrequently—going to camp or for visits to their grandparents or their friends. Some teenagers go away to boarding school or work away from their families during summer vacations.

These earlier leavings are meaningful for parents because they are a sign of changes to come.

PATRICIA SARNOFF

Patricia, a teacher, has a twelve-year-old son, Justin.

"I have the sense that my husband and I are preparing to spend the bulk of our lives together, sharing things in a way that we haven't over the last twelve years.

"The first time we faced it in a monumental way was when Justin went to camp, and it was very, very hard. Justin left for camp on a Saturday and I was just distraught that he wasn't in the house and wouldn't be for a whole month. In the next three or four days, Charles [her husband] and I had the worst time personally that we'd ever had in our whole married life. Everything fell down around us. We couldn't handle that at all. Charles said perfectly absurd and outrageous things. We had an awful time, the two of us.

"We finally came out of that, and I was really sorry when it was time for Justin to come home because we were having such a good time.

"Interestingly, some of our good friends who sent their boy to camp for the first time decided to separate in that month. And I remember thinking to myself: 'Are they responding to the same kinds of pressures that we were?'

"There have been times when I have really been feeling arid about Charles—and maybe he's been been feeling arid about me—where it has struck me that I have depended too much on Justin as a kind of conversational gambit. There's always something about a child that is worth talking about. But I find it offensive when I do it—trotting these gambits out to make up for what I feel is a hole in our own relationship."

Images of the Future: The Parent Without Children

Parents, fathers and mothers, may feel distress or pleasure at these leavetakings, though most likely it is a combination of both. It is as if parents are looking at the approaching land from the window of an airplane. The closer the plane dips toward earth, the more the landscape changes from an abstract pattern of color, line, and shape into cars and roads and trees and houses. With each of their children's trips away from home, parents begin to see the shape of the future more clearly: that each child's departure will bring a change to their family, to their marriage if they are married, and to themselves.

When a child first leaves, time seems momentarily empty—a void is created. If parents have not reestablished their relationship with each other, then the void is all the more chafing. The mother of an eighteen-year-old says, "My husband and I didn't live together before our marriage, and we were only married a year before our child came. Our children have been our common endeavor. I don't know if I would stay married if I didn't have the children. I love my husband—but it's different. It's sort of a new term."

Parents see that they themselves will change, and they try to propel themselves into the future to see what this change will mean.

MARY WILLIAMS

Mary Williams is a full-time mother of three children, ages sixteen, fifteen, and twelve.

"My husband really wanted children, and we had them exactly

the way he wanted them, boy, girl, boy. Each time I became pregnant, I wasn't ready. I saw it as an interference. But during pregnancy, he built me up and said, 'Look. This is a miracle. Seeing you developing like this.' And he taught me to understand—birth, living, and giving, and then I began to see the beauty, I now still think it's great to have a baby and see it develop and love it and take care of it.

"And now sometimes I feel my children don't need me and I'm so sad. I see them growing away from me. Russell, my oldest, has his driver's license and I don't have to drive him anyplace. In fact, he takes the other children where they have to go.

"I have to work on myself.

"I'm getting more involved in children at the community center. I've been giving cooking lessons. If I also get involved in adult classes, that will help me not to lose myself—because I've been wrapped up in my family for so long."

Those parents, almost always women, who have devoted themselves solely to their families confront the prospect of a more abrupt transition in their lives than those women and men who have other involvements. And they, like Mary, either have to begin to stretch their inside-the-home interests beyond the family or to find other interests or work. Some don't. Like Lillian in Ellen Goodman's *Turning Points*, they assume that the active part of their life is over (temporarily, at least).[19]

But whether the parents are men or women, employed or not, they feel their child's growing up will bring a change. The father of teenage daughters says, "I need my children for nourishment. Without them, I would have been very much involved in my own feelings. So I tend to want to hold onto them. And I think that's bad. Then I say to myself, 'Why is that bad? It's very nice.'

"I would like *always* to be close to them. I would like always to be a part of their life. That can't be. I can't keep them from flying off to different places and doing different things. One part of me says I would like to be free of them. The other part of me says, 'No!' "

Parents try to remember back to that self that they were before they had children—almost to peel away the changes they have made to find that inner kernel of self, but because that self has changed in the course of parenthood, they are not sure what it will be. *Preparing for the changes to the self and family is the one final task of redefining one's relationship with the teenager.*

This impending change to the self is comparable to the time before birth. Parents know that they will change, and the lifetime reserve of feelings that they have accrued about change rises up. They approach it more eagerly or less eagerly, and they form images of themselves as the parent of an adult. They also form images of how they will handle this loosening of the reins of parenthood.

One mother who in her own youth was marked as the one "to stay home to take care of aging parents" is determined not to revisit that prescription on her oldest daughter. A father who strayed far from his family, his Italian heritage, and his church, now that he has recently "sealed the lid on both of his parents' coffins," forms images of his children staying closer to home.

In this time preceding departure, parents think back to their decisions about family size. Sometimes they are pleased that they decided not to or didn't happen to have any more children. Conversely, with the heavy scent of change, like that from fading flowers hanging over the air, they may feel sad and wish they had had more children.

Parents do begin to probe back to the very beginnings of their family life. In my interviews with parents, I found them once again talking about their pregnancies, their children as babies, not only trying to find that long-ago self, that self before children, that self now altered, but beginning the process that will be a focus in the next stage of parenthood: a counting up of the score, a search for answers to the query: Was the investment worth it?

Amid thoughts of partings, however, come new unions, new times of togetherness, new meetings of the mind. It may never be the way that the parent once imagined it: the reproduction of an equal, a compatriot who, having been helped to walk, can now walk straight beside the parent, along a common path.

In actuality, parents find that they can reach out to teenagers from across different paths, accepting the time and age distance between them. That distance doesn't preclude closeness. They can share memorable moments—perhaps with a parent recounting his or her life, perhaps in discussing issues of present-day life, perhaps in intimate talks about love and life. The two worlds, the one inhabited by the adult and the one inhabited by the teenager, can intersect in a way that can truly enliven and enlarge the perspective of both.

A Developmental Irony: Idealism vs. Realism

Even so, parents feel the ironic bite of this situation: that just at the point when the child is almost an adult, he or she is pushing away; that just at the point when the parent is once again having to grapple with and shed images of perfection for him or herself and the child, the child is bathing in the reflected glow of idealism.

The Interdependent Relationship

The major task of this stage has been redefining the parent/child relationship. The new relationship is welded together with elements that may seem like polar opposites: distances and closeness, separateness and connectedness. This relationship is also pervaded by bitter developmental ironies that at times make parents feel out of synch with this child. Why does the parent, facing midlife, need a youthful reminder at the breakfast table every day, or, facing self-evaluations, need another voice—what's more, the voice of idealism—while trying to be more realistic?

How the parent emerges from this stage is very individual. Bruised, confused, rueful, pleased, better or worse for it all, but nonetheless changed. The parent who squares away his own sense of identity with those professed by the almost grown child is changed.

A teenage son had been away for the summer. Upon his return, his mother says, "At first, I didn't recognize him. Who was this person? The second time I got close, I recognized him. But he looks like a young man—a man who's young.

"And what is this like for me? I'm a parent, but I no longer have a proprietary claim like I did when my children were small: 'Look at my children. They're small and I'm their mother.'

"Now they're big. And it's a different relationship. They're as big as I am. They're people. They are my people. My children—people."

VI.
The Departure Stage

For as long as parents can remember, they have been thinking about their children's eventual departure. Even when holding a baby, staring at the baby's face close up, the parent is overcome with a picture of that baby as a grown-up, leaving home. A four-year-old's threat to run away—"I am going to go away from you; you are never going to see me again"—brings an opposite reaction: The parent thinks, "Not a bad idea. No more smart talk, smudges on the wall, hassles in the morning, and bedtime stallings." A ten-year-old makes a perceptive observation or asks an intelligent question and the parent suddenly sees that child in an office, directing business transactions. Each small departure—the child leaving on the school bus, spending the night away from home, spending a week away from home—portends a final one, an event which is anticipated with pride, sorrow, relief, and pleasure.

As the time comes closer, parents' thoughts move to the meaning of this new phase. *That, in essence, is the major task of the Departure Stage: Parents take stock of the whole experience of parenthood. They have the related tasks of preparing for the departure, then adjusting their images of this event with what actually happens, redefining their identities as parents with grown-up children, and measuring out their accomplishments and failures.*

PREPARING FOR THE DEPARTURE

In my interviews with parents, I found a definite dividing line that I came to see as the beginning of the Departure Stage.

283

Parents became less concerned with the here and now, the daily details, and focused more on the past and the future. They began scanning back to their own lives and pulling out memories of how their parents had dealt with their growing up. One woman, for example, feels that she was in effect pushed out of the nest too soon. Because sex was forbidden, except in marriage, she got married at twenty. She is in favor of the more relaxed attitude her children have about sex and is vowing to keep her home a comfortable, permissive place so that the children can stay as long as they like. A man, in contrast, feels that he was held in, kept close to home for much too long. And he is promising himself to let his children go.

As they ponder what to do and what to expect, parents also look to the experiences of their friends, neighbors, and relatives. One parent sees that a neighbor is driving his children away by battling with them. Another that her sister is trying to prevent her son from leaving by doing everything for him—picking up after him and making all of his meals. The result is that her son is chafing to get away and is making plans to go to a distant college.

Parents are anticipating and preparing themselves for their children's departure in the same way that they coped with the task of readying themselves for birth and for every other predictable change in parenthood. They are forming and re-forming images. Whether these images are clearly understood or unconsciously assumed, they cover every aspect of departure: when the children are supposed to go, how far they will go, and what their new parent/child relationship will be like.

The research of Bernice Neugarten has emphasized the importance of the concept of time: that every parent has a preconception of the right age for his or her children to grow up and move away from home.[1] For some, departure is supposed to happen after high school, for others after employment or college or marriage.

Interestingly, most of the research that was done first on what psychologists call "the empty nest" obliterated the importance of this self-set standard by fixing the boundary between the full and the empty nest at the point when the youngest child graduated from high school. In a recent study by Elizabeth Bates Harkins, only 1.3 percent of the mothers in her sample of 318 chose this time as the event that signified leaving home.[2]

The earliest research on the empty nest was also skewed in another way. These studies were done mainly on a clinical population, those people who were in psychiatric treatment, and consequently the empty nest became almost synonymous with crisis.[3] In an effort to right this emphasis, the most current research has been done on the general population, some of it comparing parents before, during, and after their youngest child leaves home. These studies have indicated that this time is not a crisis but a passageway between two eras in parents' lives.[4] In correcting this stress on crisis, it seems to me that some of the researchers have gone too far in the other direction by playing down the fact that any separation can have its turbulent, its sad, its poignant moments.

Anticipating an Ending

MICHAEL YANNIS

It is toward the end of the summer that Michael sees as the last time his whole family will be together. Soon his youngest son will go off to college and his two oldest daughters will move into an apartment together.

This impending ending brings back memories of his oldest child as a baby. "At first it was strange to have children. Lauren [his wife] took right over. I was not used to her as a mother, and I felt slighted. I didn't really understand what had happened to me.

"I didn't become interested in the children until they were two-year-olds, until they developed a personality that I could respond to.

"Increasingly, I've become sorry that I missed those early years.

"What scares me now," he says, "is that I am so attached that I'm afraid of what I'll be like without my children.

"We're a family. Everybody that's included in our children's lives is included in our lives. And I feel that we [he and his wife] don't really have an identity of our own. Not a strong identity. Not as strong as our identity as a family."

Every evening, when he walks into the house, there is activity. Kids—sitting around the kitchen table talking, perhaps cooking dinner or listening to music. He joins them or one or more of them come with him for a walk into the woods at dusk, watching the moon rise over the far hills. Perhaps they all pile into the car together and go to the movies.

From the midst of this activity, he finds it hard to imagine coming home to a childless house, to contemplate walks or films or going out for dinner without his children.

"But I also go through times when I wish they would be gone," says Michael, "when I say to myself, 'This is enough.' I would like to experience a little more of myself without them."

His wife, Lauren, also sees this summer as an ending. "It's all going to go zap soon," she says, "and then the kids will really be gone."

Michael finds himself harkening back to memories of the person he was before he had children: "a loner." Lauren is doing the same. "I was the kind of person who would do anything for a dare." She both wants and doesn't want to rediscover this spirited self. "In some ways I can't imagine the children not being here—in this house. It will seem like a totally useless place, except for them to come back to."

Parents' perceptions of their homes are telling: Lauren and Michael assume their home will seem empty, void, whereas another mother, Joan Buckley, suspects that her home will be a quiet refuge.

JOAN BUCKLEY

Joan and her husband have six children. The last is about to leave home.

Her response differs from Lauren's. She says, "The nest doesn't seem to empty . . . I suspect because I'm so eager for it to happen.

"My children have been slow in moving out. I think that this is a change among a number of people. We moved out because we had to go to test ourselves. We were not allowed sexual freedom. Certainly we felt an eagerness to get out.

"Partly because we are more relaxed than our parents were, our children are much more comfortable with us and find it less necessary to leave. So I've been awaiting a little peace and quiet which it seems that I'm about due for.

"My youngest child is in college, but one of the older ones is at home and he cannot quite seem to get on his way. He threatens to and perhaps he will, but it's been eighteen months since he graduated from college and he's still here. When he does go, I'm confident that I'm going to feel, first, relief. It will be nice to come home to quiet. Of course the children are all grown up and theoretically I shouldn't worry about getting meals and so forth, but I do. It's hard to break out of that pattern. I can't really imagine that I'm going to be bereft."

The departure for Lauren and Michael is following their images—it looks as if it will be on time—whereas for Joan, the empty nest is past due. She is ready to have reality catch up with her expectation.

A frequent theme in current research on the empty-nest phase is that being on or off time is the most significant variable. Harkins, after examining many other factors, states that "the only threat to well-being may be in having a child who does not become successfully independent when it is expected."[5] Bernice Neugarten and Nancy Datan, in a paper entitled "The Middle Years," say that "it may more often be the *timing* of the life event, not its occurrence, that constitutes the problematic issue."[6]

I would argue that it is not timing per se that is the critical variable, but that timing is one instance of the larger principle: When an image (whatever its content) is not being realized, the parent may become very distressed.

I found that parents became upset over many other images left unfulfilled. One mother had an image of her daughter staying close to home during college. She had planned to stay in touch with her by calling her weekly on the telephone and visiting her for football weekends. Her daughter, on the contrary, was deciding to go two thousand miles away. And the mother, to use her words, was "taking it very hard."

There is a popular notion that if a parent is happy with the other aspects of life, if he or she, for example, has other satisfying commitments or work, the empty-nest time will be easier. That notion has not been adequately studied. I found that there is a mixture of feelings, including sadness, that accompany a coming separation. In addition, when an important expectation is unrealized, that disappointment can momentarily at least override other satisfactions.

The mother whose daughter decided to go far away for college was very pleased with her work as a writer/editor for a local magazine. Her own happiness at her job was for the time being palling because her image and reality were so far out of kilter.

The prospect of children's growing up, leaving home, signals a change in parents' lives that is most difficult when it doesn't happen when and where and how parents think it should. This coming event also points to a change in parents' identity, and new questions begin to be asked: How will I use my time when there will be more of it to spare? What will my priorities be?

These periods of change, when one's sense of self seems dislodged or uprooted, bring thoughts of more final endings or death. That was true in the Image-Making Stage and is true now. Parents think, "Perhaps I am getting old."

Both of Michael Yannis's parents have recently died, and he is particularly involved with the specter of death. He says, "I realize that I'm leading the procession, that I'm next in line, the next to drop off."

His wife, Lauren, has similar feelings. She continually discusses the way she sees life as "ephemeral": "I am very much aware of how ephemeral this particular existence is."

Recalling Beginnings

This changing sense of self also precipitates thoughts of beginnings—particularly the child's beginnings. Sitting at the dinner table, the child starts to laugh and a memory comes back to a father—of an afternoon years before, when he and his child got the giggles and couldn't stop. Or another child says the word "hamburger" and the parent flashes back to when, as a four-year-old, that child said "hangaburger" or "maglazine" for "magazine."

For some parents and their almost-grown children, talking about these recollections can cause discomfort. The child feels as if the parent is trying to push him or her back into childhood. References to old idiosyncrasies or episodes are embarrassing. In other families, they are enjoyed, like a verbal scrapbook, collected together.

Parents can find that they have a new appreciation for other people's little children, that they nostalgically stare at a two-year-old taking forever to trudge up the steps on a bus, or a chubby baby digging in the sand on the beach. They enjoy catching a child's eye in a crowd and smiling, or talking to the young children they know.

"A friend," Lauren Yannis says, "came over last night with his young son, Gabey, and I got out the small chair we have. I looked at Gabey in that chair and I started to cry. My God, you blink and it's all gone by. Once my son was climbing in that chair.

"It's funny because I never thought I'd be the kind of woman who would look at a baby and go 'Oooh.' It's funny the way things turn out.

"When Gabey left, there were these little tiny handprints all over the windows, and it was another interesting thing—I usually would be bothered by smudges on the windows. When I saw those little fingerprints, I went, 'Oh, aren't they cute.' "

Recently a friend of Michael's and Lauren's, a woman in her forties with teenage children, had a baby. "When our friend had that baby," Lauren says, "I was devastated. I wanted one. Everyone in the neighborhood felt that way—the same people whom I've heard say, 'No more children!' "

Fantasizing About Babies

Even without the stimulus of a new child in the neighborhood, many parents of almost-grown children are surprised to find themselves daydreaming about having a new baby, thought not necessary giving birth. In these reveries, the baby often arrives in *deus ex machina* fashion.

In her story of a family in therapy, Claire Pomeroy, the mother, writes that her husband "told me he had a recurring fantasy that he would have another son some day, not a drop-out bike-freak like Glen, but a son who would carry on his work." After considerable discussion, Claire exclaimed, "You've got six kids."

"I know. I know," he said, "but still I just can't believe—it's really all over." [7]

"I hate things to end," a mother of a twenty-two-year-old and a twenty-one-year-old said. "Like there's no going back. There isn't another child.

"I wanted another child—and we talked about adopting a child. I think it came from the feeling that I could do things better now. Maybe I wanted to prove that to myself."

A North Carolina mother of five grown children who works as a teacher says, "When my baby son married and left, my husband and I sat down together and he said, 'I can't stand this lonely house anymore.' And I made a joke, 'Let's go out and adopt a child.' He said, 'You're trying to be funny—but it would be nice to have someone else around here.' It was just dull.

"Your children sometimes create these frustrating problems and you say, 'Mercy. I'll be so glad when I get them out of my hair. That will be a great day.'

"But it isn't a great day, because then you feel kind of useless. You feel like—what do I do now?"

ADAPTING TO THE DEPARTURE

Most often this time of departure spans a long period of time—beginning when the oldest child begins to drift back and forth, to home, away from home, and ending when the youngest child leaves. With each child, there can be an event that parents signify as "departure," a moment that even years later parents remember vividly.

They recall their child in a car, then the car pulling away and their child's size receding, becoming smaller and smaller—until their child was just a dot that disappeared. Or they remember their child climbing up the steps into a train, legs going up and up, then the child turning the corner, disappearing, reappearing momentarily at the window before streaking away. Perhaps their child left in an airplane. The parents waved good-bye in the crush of people at the gate, and driving home, saw a pencil-thin line of silver glinting in the sun, and a jet trail of smoke that divided the sky. The parents wondered if that was the plane that was carrying their child away.

Sometimes it is the parents who do the leaving, driving away from their son or daughter at college or at a new apartment or home.

For a while, the absence of the child is jarring. The parents half expect to hear his or her voice when they come home. The empty bed and untouched room seem somehow ominous, too neat, too still, too silent.

Parents find themselves staring at their child's possessions—the stuffed animal that sits limply on the top of a shelf, a stamp or postcard collection forgotten in a drawer, a box filled with models of prancing horses, or a bedside-table tableau of pink china poodles bought with a child's allowance at the dime store. The basketball hoop, the pack of baseball's ten-year-ago heroes on bubblegum cards, wrinkled posters of the Beatles and the BeeGees, and a high school yearbook stand out. Parents will come across a scrap of paper with their child's handwriting, or a family photograph, and that will bring back memories of the leavetaking once again.

Although seeing the child's possessions can be upsetting, it can also be a reassuring reminder that the child was just in their midst. One mother, after her son had married, said to him: "If you see something in your room you want, take it." One day after work, she found that he had accepted her offer: "He had taken everything in the room. Even the carpet off the floor. Practically all that he had left was a [toy] tanker truck.

"The room appeared empty—just that tanker truck in the corner. Nobody was here, and I could cry, and I did."

Redefinitions of Identity

Once the sharper, more strident feelings subside, and what was unusual becomes everyday, normal, parents face the task of redefining their own sense of identity.

When the place of parenthood is decreased in the definition of self, parents look at what's left.

Elena Gerwitz

The last of Elena's four children has just left home. With her youngest son away at college. Elena describes herself as being caught up in a struggle. "Someone was in the house a few weeks ago and she looked around and saw pictures of everyone in the family. She said, 'You know, I don't see a picture of you.'

"That stayed in my mind. I was totally directed outward, I disregarded myself. Now I have to start building and concentrating on myself.

"I am even beginning to get angry that I haven't done it—to put myself back into focus."

Elena is left with a blurry, unclear definition of herself, one that has a missing piece, almost like a puzzle with one large part knocked out.

This task of redefining the self hinges on how crucial parenthood is to the jigsaw puzzle that is self-concept. For Elena, parenthood has been central, even though she has a career as a doctor.

Equally important is how parents feel about the other pieces of the puzzle, how meaningful or peripheral the other sources of their identity are. When the children leave, it is as if a bright light is suddenly cast on what was formerly in shadows, revealing all the loose or crumbling pieces, the cracks, as well as the strengths in the structure of their own lives.

Now that parents have more time, where will they put it? Into work? But what if, like Elena Gerwitz's, one's job seems meaningless? Elena did, in fact, decide to a shift, moving into the public-health field.

Unlike Elena, women who have little else left face the most abrupt transition. When their children leave home, their job as well as a prime source of identity evaporates. When they were young mothers, there was a cultural constraint to stay home. Now that trend is reversed with economic and social pressure mounting on the other side: Go out and work. But at what? What have their years of motherhood prepared them for? To start back at the beginning of the career ladder? That can be a painful thought, especially when their friends (men and women) who have stayed in the job market are rungs ahead, seemingly reaching the pinnacle of success.

These women can feel that all of the giving they have done is adding up to very little. They want to be given to, but by whom? Some women express this need in daydreams, perhaps of a glittering affair with a man who showers them with love, attention, and gifts, who gives and gives and gives.

Social service, nursing, and educational institutions need to help with this transition out of parenthood, especially for the at-home mother. Some educational institutions are offering counseling services, but the major roadblock is economic—not enough jobs for every person in our society. I wish, however, that more services could be provided, because their absence is costly in human terms.

Some women do find exciting work. One woman enrolled in a master's degree program in "Future Studies" says, "I felt my commitments as a parent were fulfilled and it was time for me to do what I had put aside when I became a parent and take it as seriously as I did parenting."

Another turned her volunteer position in a religious agency into a paid job.

A third woman obtained a job in her husband's firm and finds herself "engrossed"—"I work ten hours a day with great enthusiasm and interest."

Finding work that excites people this way can obviously happen—or not happen—at any point in the adult years. When parents do have meaningful work or commitments, their new sense of self as the parent of a grown child falls into place with more ease.

Parents Reexamine Their Other Important Relationships

Looking at what's left, what makes up the other pieces of their definition of themselves, parents also reexamine their other significant relationships.

If the parent is a single parent, the children's leaving underscores the aloneness, and the parent reconsiders its meaning: Is it anxiety-producing or comforting? Does the parent want to remain single or seek out companionship?

If they are married or involved in a long-term relationship, parents work on a task: to redefine their identity as a couple. The dinner table is no longer filled with young people clamoring for attention or even sitting sullenly or silently. The evenings and weekends and early mornings are also quiet—the parents are back together. Alone.

As in every situation, parents have many different responses to this change—from pleasure to surprise. Old patterns, somewhat muffled by the noise of the larger family, can slide back into prominence. One woman says, "My husband doesn't talk much. I seem to do most of the talking. So we'll try to talk, but he's buried under a book. Now, I read a lot, too."

The research on this subject, the change in the couple relationship, is mixed, with some studies concluding that couples are happier, others that they are less so.[8] What the researchers and writers have agreed upon is the potential for a discontinuity in development between men and women at this phase of life. This was the conclusion in Gail Sheehy's *Passages*, and is cited in Daniel Levinson's study as well.[9] Bernice Neugarten and Nancy Datan describe this discontinuity when they write: "Most of the women interviewed feel that the most conspicuous characteristic of middle age is the sense of increased freedom . . . middle age marks the beginning of a period in which latent talents and capacities can be put to use in new directions." These changes in women come at the same time that "their husbands are reporting increased job pressures or—something equally troublesome—job boredom." [10]

Lillian Rubin writes: "When, for the first time in a couple's life, *her* work, *her* interests interfere with *his* life, it's an especially troubling shift for him—which, of course, means for her as well." Rubin states that husbands often shift from alarm to anger to reaching back to old ploys: gifts, promises that previously would have made a wife happy, but which now don't. "Over and over, that's the story. Husbands offer goods their wives once cherished only to find them rejected now for reasons the men don't clearly understand." And this lack of understanding leads them to "a fear of being out of control in a world they thought they knew." [11]

It is to be noted that Rubin's study of 160 women intentionally focuses on women who took marriage and motherhood as their principal job. There is a need, in view of the changing times, for a study comparable to Rubin's that includes long-employed women as well. Do they, for example, face the same kinds of discontinuities in their relationships, the same kind of misunderstandings and jealousies?

CHANGING IMAGES

When parents have settled into the routine of being the parents of grown-up children, they find that they have accumulated many images of how this part of life is supposed to go. *They have the task of integrating these images with reality.* Perhaps as far back as the first sleepless night with an infant, many parents have thought to themselves, "I can't wait until I'm free of the job of parenthood." This wish is reinforced through the years: when the toddler refuses to budge and it's time to go somewhere; when the five-year-old looks at the parent with disdain and says, "I wish that Daniel's mommy were my mommy—she's so nice"; when the parent has, in anger at a child's minor offense, proclaimed, "You aren't going to the birthday party," and now has to decide whether to enforce the punishment or not; when the teenager fills the house with gangs of friends who, like locusts, make every bit of food in the house disappear, leaving in its place a mess. At these times, parents look forward to being free of their children.

The Image That Parenthood Is Over

That wish builds and builds into an image for many parents: that there will be a day, somewhere in the future, when the parent can return to the carefree, daring, impulsive, indulgent person he or she remembers being—the kind of person who can sleep all day Saturday or spend an outrageous amount of money on something luxurious or jump into a swimming pool with his or her best clothes on. Not that people don't do these kinds of things throughout parenthood, but they may do them with the thought that their children are looking over their shoulders, almost like chaperons, judging them.

Then the dreamed-of day comes, the chaperon moves away, and the parent is supposed to be free of the job of parenthood. The parent finds that this image will never totally come true.

"When the children got married," one mother said, "I said, 'Well, this one or that one's off my hands.' But that's not right. You don't just forget them. Whatever problems they may be having, you worry about them. My mother used to tell me, 'You can get them off your hands, but you can never get them off your heart.' "

Parents do remain involved in their children's lives. There is a scene in a play by John Guare, *Bosoms and Neglect*, which epitomizes these feelings to me. The mother, hospitalized with cancer, considering suicide, tells her son why she doesn't want to die. She tells him that his life is like a book. She wants to stay around to find out what's going to happen next.[12]

One of the mothers I interviewed tells of coming to this realization while traveling thousands of miles away from home.

"I remember when I had my first child. I had gone to town by myself and I missed the train back. I was in a rage. I realized that I wasn't the same—the freedom, the lack of responsibility, the daring were gone."

Now, even with her children out on their own, she couldn't shed this parent self, like an old skin. She realized, on this trip, that she was permanently changed. "The parent's career is never-ending because there is a continuum of involvement. You see that you are never going to be the same again. And you never are! You may be in Europe, traveling, but you still are thinking, 'What are they doing?' "

The parents of a son who moved out felt that they worried less with their son away from home. If he was out until three or four in the morning, they, at least, didn't know about it. Yet their concern was merely diminished rather than removed.

Many parents of grown children told of a fear—that the telephone will ring in the night and an anonymous official voice will say that the child has been hurt or even killed.

Parents do not stop caring, being concerned, worrying, and thinking about their children. But because many expected to, they may have the suspicion that "something is wrong with me" or "I'm different" or any of the other distresses that occur when an image conflicts with reality. Then parents either change their image, or continue to think, "Something must be wrong with me—maybe I am overinvolved."

The Image That the Grown Child Will Be Settled

Another image frequently clashes with reality: that when a child leaves home, that child will be grown up and that he or she will be settled. "Settled" was a word that I heard over and over, usually as a lament.

Today the initiation into adulthood takes a longer time than it did in the past. Some young people aren't sure what they want to do. Many stop, drop out, take time off, take time-killing jobs. For others, career preparation is long and arduous, and even then, after years of training, they have to try to find a job, to set up their own business or practice.

"Settled" can also mean married. But there are some people who are wary of long-term commitments. They live together, move in and out of relationships, or perhaps marry and then divorce.

For others, being "settled" may mean their children have children. But perhaps their children reject this idea or postpone it.

Whatever the parent's images of "settled," some find these expectations realized, others don't. And those parents end up with a misfit between the way that things are supposed to go and what is actually happening.

The Image That the Grown Child Has Left for Good

One of the most common instances of such a gap is when the grown children, for one reason or another, return home. Growing up for most parents means leaving home. It doesn't include coming back. That may seem like a regression, an admission of failure.

Yet children often do ask to come back. They have to move out of their apartment or they are caught in a money crunch or they are deciding what to do next or a marriage or a romance has broken up.

ROSE WILLIAMS

Rose runs a social agency in the South. Her three daughters are twenty-seven, twenty-six, and twenty-three. Recently the middle daughter's marriage broke up and she is "back at home, hopefully temporarily.

"First of all, I didn't want her to come home. I still don't. I felt that I've been a good parent. I've done everything that I ought to have done. And I'm finished.

"Parenting is a long hard job and I just want to get out of this business of parenting.

"And then here she comes, impinging on my life when I felt I'd finished. It's hard."

It's hard financially. It's hard to share again. "She had to borrow my car for the summer, and you know the situation in the South—you need a car. What's happened is that I had to use my husband's car or get a friend to pick me up, and I resent that."

Rose's response to this situation is to look for a place to pin the blame. Maybe it is her daughter's fault. Maybe it's because she's "lazy." "I said to her, 'If you'd gone out to work you and your husband might not have broken up.' I used all kinds of excuses."

Rose also blamed herself. "I feel guilty because I spoiled her. I never really made her autonomous. She knew that she could always have a place to go if some problem came up, and so she didn't try too hard in terms of her life or her marriage to be an independent person.

"My husband says, 'I told you so. You should have made her more independent.' "

Rose's anger has deeper roots. This daughter reminds Rose of herself, the disliked side of herself. "I don't listen very much to what other people have to say, and neither does she. One of the reasons we don't get along is because she makes me feel uncomfortable about who I am."

Rose is angry because her grown daughter has returned home. That wasn't supposed to happen. She didn't expect it. She didn't want it, and she still doesn't. Because she hasn't given up her image and she hasn't changed reality (told her daughter to find another place to live), she is caught in a contradiction, a contradiction which is compounded by her sense of affinity to her daughter.

Another family had their daughter, after several years on her own, decide to come with them when the father changed jobs and they moved to a new city. This family, though they didn't expect her return, enjoyed having her back almost immediately—enjoyed going back to the family traditions of decorating the Christmas tree, a family New Year's Eve party, and summers of sailing together.

One crucial factor in how the grown child's return home turns out is the quality of the parent/child relationship that has been established over the years.

The Image That the Relationship Was Close to Perfect

Sometimes when a child leaves home, a troubled relationship can take on a nostalgic gleam, can be remembered more the way parents wish it had been than the way it actually was. But when the grown child comes back home, the reality of the relationship returns, scattering these fantasies.

ROGER MORGAN

Roger is the director of a Midwestern private school. He and his wife have two children, ages twenty-two and twenty-one. Recently the twenty-one-year-old, a son, Ben, arrived back at home.

"The apartment that he had with his friend was in a building that got sold. Then he moved to a new apartment, but it was broken into just as he was moving. And so we suggested that that wasn't a good place to live.

"He came back—but at first he wasn't really here. He never unpacked. And then he had a party, and he unpacked for it, and I guess he's here to stay. It's never really been discussed. That was six months ago.

"He does make noises about getting his own place, but it's cheaper here."

Ben began college, then dropped out. Three weeks ago, he told his parents that he had signed up for a few college courses. They felt that two of the courses would be useful, English and Business, but that the third, The History of Comedy in Films, wasn't.

"I said, 'Ben, you spent money on that. Why? What can that course lead to?' "

His wife, Bonnie, continues, "Ben said, 'What do you think I should have taken?' He got angry and defensive. And then Roger started hollering because Ben had said something nasty to him. We had a conflict situation when there didn't need to be one. We should have congratulated him on signing up for courses, for spending his own money, for taking the initiative."

Roger says, "I knew we had done the wrong thing, and I talked to Ben and said, 'I'm sorry. I shouldn't have done that. If you need help in making other choices'—I had to get that little lick in—'I'll be glad to sit down with you and go through what's available and maybe discuss them and you can do what you want.'

"But then—even knowing that I'd made a mistake—I made the same damn mistake a few days later. The business course was canceled and he decided to take Intermediate Algebra. I said, 'Intermediate Algebra. You're going to take that with English? Do you know how tough that will be?'

"Then I thought to myself, 'Here I go again.' And I stopped.

"I find myself drifting back into things that I don't want to do—things that I would advise parents not to do—things that are totally inappropriate."

For Roger, the image that is unrealized is not that his son would stay away from home. It is the image of himself as a father who doesn't interfere, doesn't criticize, doesn't engage in knock-down, drag-out battles. It is the image of a father/son relationship that is better in fantasy—or when the son is away from home—than it is in actuality. Roger, like Rose Williams, feels the discomfort of an image unmet.

Also like Rose, Roger's son reminded him of aspects of himself that he dislikes. "He's bullheaded. I am, too."

"This is very disturbing to me. It's like going through my own growth all over again." Old conflicts are stirred up, conflicts which Roger would prefer to remain fallow.

Images About the Post-Departure Relationship

All parents have images about their post-departure relationship with their children. These images have been developed since childhood and run the gamut from the parent who expects to launch a child out into his or her own life, to the parent who expects the child to care for the parent in old age.

Susan Thayer

Susan is a parent who expected to launch her three children. In fact, that's the very word she used.

"I think that it's unnatural after you've raised your children to build your whole life around their coming back home to visit you. I think that if parents have done a good job, they launch their children into life."

According to her, the children are like "little birds—they fly away.

"You say good-bye to them and if you are an interesting person, they'll want you around. If they want to come back to visit, okay, and if not, that's okay, too.

"I always felt that it was a drag that we felt so obligated to go and visit our parents. We didn't want to go sometimes. Eventually, I broke those strings with my parents. Although it was painful, I felt in the long run I was much better for it than the people who lived in the same town as their parents and every Sunday they went over and had dinner with them.

"It's not that I feel that we are rootless. I feel that my children are very rooted in our family, and even though they go away, the roots are long and will come up in other parts of the ground."

The ties between Susan and her own parents were expected to be tight and became constrictive. She had to cut them to become independent. Susan had formed a different image, one of a loose, elastic connection, an acceptance of her grown children's individuality and independence.

Her image, even though it was built in opposition to the way she had been raised, has remained steady. And it has been borne out. Her children do have their own lives, but also do seek her out.

Images Can Be at Odds

Sometimes, however, images that are built in opposition to one's experience or cultural background can become shaky as the time approaches to compare them to reality.

GRACE CALDERON

Grace, a teacher, has one daughter. The day before I talked to her in her Texas home, she and her husband had driven their eighteen-year-old daughter, Ana, to college.

The conflict for Grace is primarily a cultural one. In her Mexican-American background, the family stays together. Yet she, as a young mother, moved 140 miles away and established a separate life. Her image has always been that her daughter would do the same. But now, she is less sure.

"Ana's not that far, about eighty miles away. She wanted to go to the East, and we compromised by saying, 'Stay in Texas for a year or two and let's get used to being away from each other and then if you still want to leave the state, we'll talk about it again.'

"I'm really hoping that she'll like it so much that she'll want to stay. I don't want her to go that far away because I'm afraid that she'll marry up there.

"Culturally our people are very dependent on each other and we stay close. We don't leave home.

"I did leave and I handled it, but there are certain traditions and feelings that are still there. I don't want her to get too far away. It's difficult to readjust your life so that it's not the way that you grew up.

"I do want her to be close enough so that when I feel like seeing her or when I need her or she needs me, we can get to each other without too much trouble. But I don't want to smother her. I want to give her freedom to develop herself, to make her own life."

The dilemma is compounded by the conflict of dual cultures—the Mexican one and the American one.

"We wanted to give her both. She loves Mexican food and Mexican music, up to a point, and she dances. She understands Spanish, but she will not speak it.

"But her ways, a lot of her ways, are very much into the American way of life. Especially because we once lived in Washington, D.C., where everybody came from all different places.

"When we came back to Texas, my daughter was immediately identified as a Mexican-American, and she thought she should run around with the Mexican-American children. And yet she couldn't identify with them because they spoke the language and she didn't. Yet the Anglo children looked at her name, looked at her, and thought, 'Well, she's not one of us,' so she felt lost. She didn't know what she was or who she was."

Grace solved this problem by putting her daughter in a small, more congenial parochial school. But this pull between the Mexican and the American way of life has a deeper source for Grace. She feels her own culture does not accept adoption, and this daughter is adopted.

"When my daddy knew he was dying, the last thing he did was to get everyone together. He said to me, 'This house is yours.' Everyone gave their consent to his wish.

"Soon after Daddy died, about nine months or so, I adopted my baby. When she was about two or three, we were sitting on the porch of my family's house with my mother and my aunt. My mother said, 'I can't leave you anything because everything I leave you would go to Ana.'

"I was stunned. I was shocked. My mother had never, never let on that she had felt that way. She always had a Christmas gift and a birthday gift for Ana. She always greeted her and loved her and kissed her.

"My aunt was sitting there. When my aunt said nothing I knew that the two of them had been discussing this.

"I got up. I could not say anything. I started running down the street. I didn't know where I was going. Thanks to God, I looked up about a block away and saw my husband in his car. I stopped him and said, 'Take me away from here.'

"So he drove me away and I had the biggest cry in my life. I had never been hurt like this. I just never expected this.

"It doesn't really matter now, because Ana is well provided for—

but the hurt did matter because I thought my family had accepted her fully.

"Because of that, we decided that we'd better raise her to be very self-sufficient, very independent, so that if anything happens to us, she could carry on with her life without the need of anybody. And she is just that—very independent."

Now that Ana has left, this earlier image, of a close family, has surfaced. Grace is fighting it—telling her husband that they can't visit her on every football weekend, remembering acquaintances that have smothered their children by being too possessive.

These two images, the older one and the newer one, are temporarily in conflict, but Grace has no doubt that the newer one will win out. "Now that I am letting go, I am finding it more convenient to be the old way. But the other part of me comes in and I say, 'That's not the way of life that we are living in today. That's not in my daughter's interest.'"

Unfulfilled Images

MARLENE FRIEDMAN

Grace Calderon's difficulty is caused by images that are at odds with each other. For Marlene Friedman, the parent of a grown child and a teenager, however, a problem arose when her image of her relationship with her grown-up child was not achieved. She felt that if she stayed home while her children were young, they would have the compatibility that she and her own mother lacked. But the oldest daughter is rebelling.

"Harriet is at a university in Israel right now. She went to a university here and then transferred. We want her to stay one year, and she wants to stay indefinitely.

"I had prepared myself for Harriet's leaving. I felt that it was the right thing to do because she had her heart set on it. But for me, not to be able to call her, not to know anything about what she's doing, not to know who her friends are, has been hard.

"Mail takes two weeks. If I really want to know something, if I ask her and she answers me immediately, it would take a month. It's hard to keep up meaningful communication under those circumstances.

"This was really a big adjustment for me. It was a much harder wrench than what I expected.

"She has a boyfriend there. She actually met him here in the United States and he was going back to Israel. He had a lot to do with her going—she had always wanted to go there, but she went a year sooner than we had planned.

"Harriet has gone into Orthodox Judaism—maybe that's a rebellion on her part. It sounds mild compared to the Moonies, but you'd be surprised at how much Orthodox Judaism isolates her from people that aren't observant. There's a whole thing about modest dressing. She won't go swimming in a public pool. In some ways, she has cut herself off from what I consider to be normal living.

"These are things that Harriet is working through. If she wants to do things like observe rituals, there's nothing wrong with that. I think it's kind of nice, actually. But if she's going to be fanatic about it, that's what I don't like: to get deeper and deeper into things that I think are kind of pointless. But at this stage, I don't have any control over what's going on. I'm kind of washing my hands of it.

"The school that she is at is a school for religious students. It's not a yeshiva but is an academic university. It's a good compromise—a place where she can be religious but still be in an intellectual environment.

"Harriet's boyfriend hasn't had the advantage of a formal education. It sounds like he's an intelligent person, but it also sounds like his family is in the lower strata socially. I don't know if I'm right or not about this, but if I am, it disturbs me.

"Even though I think it's important for people to choose each other for personal qualities, I'm not a romantic enough to think that economics don't make a difference.

"I want my kids to be free to do things, which is why I let Harriet go to Israel. But at the same time, it's hard for me because my instinctive reaction is, 'Don't go that far.' I want more control."

Marlene had thought that if she gave to her children, if she was home, available to her children, she might avoid the kind of situation she is in now—completely cut off from one of her children. Her image hasn't worked. Of course, it may work in the future—but now she and her daughter aren't in touch the way Marlene wishes they were and her daughter has a boyfriend that Marlene disapproves of.

If, however, nothing changes—that is, if Marlene sticks to her image of closeness, yet her daughter stays away—it is likely that Marlene will stay depressed and angry, for these two emotions are the almost inevitable result of tightly held but unfulfilled images.

Pauline Bart came to a similar conclusion in her comprehensive study of depression. By using cross-cultural measures as well as an examination of the records of 533 hospitalized women who had no previous hospitalization for mental illness and in-depth interviews with twenty patients, she uncovered a pattern: that these depressed women had lost their most important role when their children left home. These women were, in Bart's analysis, overprotective, conventional martyrs. They were the women who were "doing what was expected of them by their families, their friends, and the mass media"—that is, devoting themselves selflessly to their children.

Bart states: "If one's satisfaction, one's sense of worth comes from other people rather than from one's own accomplishments, one is left with an empty shell in place of a self when such people depart." And depression (in psychoanalytic terms, depression is anger turned to the self in response to a loss) is the result.

Bart makes a further point that since these women had behaved in the way that they thought they were supposed to throughout motherhood—in other words, they had been good—they expected to be rewarded. Perhaps that reward was that they would be cared for by their grown children.

"When asked what their children owed them, all the women say 'nothing,' even though, in fact, they are apparently dissatisfied with their present situation and want more from their children. Much as some of the mothers want to live with their children, they cannot openly state this as a legitimate demand." [13]

When these rewards are not realized, when these women's images fall far short of their experiences, they become depressed.

Donald Spence and Thomas Lonner, in a study of the empty-nest transition for twenty-seven women, found that those mothers who have a more difficult transition to the postparental stage are "lacking in clear-cut cultural expectations." [14] Bart makes the same point when she says, "there are no guidelines, no rites de passage for the mother herself to guide her through this transaction." [15]

While it is true that the cultural norms are changing and unclear, is it the case that these women have no expectations, no images, or that their images prove conflicted or unrealistic? That is a question that needs more probing, but I would suspect that the latter is true: that the parents who have the most difficult time with departure transition expected their relationship with their grown children to stay the same or expected certain kinds of relationships which never materialized.

Parents also have expectations about the kind of "new" family that their children should form, the kind of people that their children should live with or not live with, marry or not marry. If the child chooses someone who counters the parents' expectations, who seems too different or unfamiliar, or who seems to pull the grown child away from his or her parents, the parents feel many things, not the least of which are apprehension, anger, and envy. This situation has the potential for being the most problem-laden one for this stage, because if the hurt continues, it can drive parent and grown child apart.

LOOSENING CONTROL

The "old," "original" family has changed, the children have grown, moved away, and the parents' roles have changed, and most parents search for new ways to say that they are still a family.

Often this definition of the changed family comes through ritual. Many parents in the Departure Stage described customs that still connected them to their children: the regular dinners or Sunday-morning telephone call, the letters written once a week, the celebration of birthdays, holidays, or family events.

The mother of two grown children says that her husband, grown children, and their families "sit down as a family on Sunday and we have dinner. People say that it takes a lot to prepare dinner in the dining room, but I feel much better when I do it. I think it takes away from the individualism that I feel develops in most families where everybody does his own thing. It's important to take the time and do the things that pinpoint you as a family."

A mother of three grown children says, "I do believe that one of the important things in rearing children is the ritualization of life events. I learned that from the church, but I don't think the church should carry all the rituals. I think the family needs to do it, too. So, when anything happens, our family still comes back together to celebrate it. That celebration is not only a happy occasion—the birth of a grandchild—it can be a sad occasion—like when my husband went to the hospital for a bypass operation.

"And when my mother was eighty, we had a big party for her. We gave her Maurice Chevalier's record *Gigi*, and we asked questions about her early life and put her answers on tape.

"Then when my son got married, I gathered together everything I could find about his life from birth on and put it in a scrapbook and gave it to his wife. Symbolically, what I was saying was that I was giving him up. I wonder sometimes why in the marriage ritual they don't build that in: The father gives the daughter away, but the mother also gives the son up, too. That's what has to happen psychologically."

Separateness/Connectedness

Giving the child away, giving the child up—every interview with a parent in this stage touched upon this theme. Marlene Friedman was finding it hard to give up control, yet she knew that her daughter needed freedom. Roger Morgan was in the middle of the same internal battle. The "correct way" to deal with his son, he felt, was to say, "The decisions are yours to make. If you want help, I'm here and I'd be glad to help." He tries to stand back and allow the mistakes to take place. However, this intellectual conviction doesn't always filter down to the way he acts—as when he criticized his son's college-course choices.

Even though parents do use the words "giving up" or "giving away" and these words do parallel the image that the job of parenthood will be finished when the child leaves home, these words and this image do not fit their feelings. They are still the parents, they care what happens. The authority relationship that they've had with their child has been continuously changing—moving away, notch by notch, from more control to less control. *In the Departure Stage, parents have the task of loosening their control even more because their grown-up child is responsible for himself or herself.* This task sets out a complex path to follow: of caring, of being available, of helping without controlling. And obviously, while it is a step that not all parents make, many do. One is Clara Patterson.

CLARA PATTERSON

Clara has two grown children and lives in the South. Her daughter, Eva, has just begun graduate work in a Northern college, where she is the only black person in one of her classes.

"Eva made ninety on her first test and eighty on the second and then things caught up with her, and she called me one night saying, 'People don't know how hard it is being the only black in a situation. I should be concentrating on what I'm doing. I know that—but nobody has even come over to talk to me!'

"People in the North aren't as hospitable as we are in the South. We would not let a stranger come without saying, 'Hey,' or sitting with them, but that's not the Northern pattern of life.

"Eva says that she listens to the teacher, but she's not hearing. She made sixty-eight on the next test. She finally said that she felt like dropping the course to give her time to pull herself together. So I said, 'Fine. I don't want you to worry about the money, because you have learned from the experience, and that's what education is all about.'

"I don't want her to have pressure saying, 'Hey, you gotta pass because it's too much money.' I think she probably will do well after this, after she gets over this hump.

"When Eva calls, I don't give her an opinion unless she asks for it. I always say, 'What do you think?' Even though I've had experiences in growing up myself, I try to see the world as my daughter or my son would, so I always say, 'What do you think?'

"And if their thoughts are not so good, I don't tell them what to do. I try to give them a couple of alternatives. I say, 'Did you think about this?' or 'Have you thought about that?' And I wait. And usually what they come up with will be all right."

Accepting the Grown Child's Separate Identity

RACHEL LITTLE

When I was talking to Rachel Little, the mother of grown children, one of her daughters, there for a visit, began edging closer and closer into the room. Rachel was talking about her regrets. One was that she felt she continued to make decisions for her children beyond the point where it was helpful. "That's an area that I'd handle differently now."

Her daughter Deborah, left her listening post against the door-frame and sat down on the sofa next to her mother.

"When I went to college," Deborah said, "the rules and regulations were worse than they were at home. So I was still sheltered.

"Then I moved to California [from the East], and I still was dependent on my parents. I was on the phone so much it was ridiculous. Collect.

"I finally realized how naive I was. I had to be in that position to realize what it takes to deal with the events that come up day to day. It took me in all honesty a good six months to say, 'I'm twenty-three years old. It's high time I stopped being so dependent on my parents, who are three thousand miles away,' to really start taking care of myself."

As I listened to this mother and grown daughter talk to each other through me, I heard about an underlying struggle in the daughter's growing-up years. She had wanted to be a dancer. Her mother and father felt that dancing wasn't a safe profession and insisted instead that she get a degree in physical education. That way Deborah would always have a job.

Deborah had gone along with her parents' plan and had entered college in physical education, then dropped out, moved to California, married, had two children, and ended up with a job in an actuarial firm.

Even though she says that she feels that she is finally independent, she has a strong current of distrust of her own decisions. This distrust is symbolized to her by her lack of a college degree and her fear of returning to get one. "I still feel incomplete, and probably that incomplete feeling comes from the fact that I know my parents would have wanted me to have my degree by now."

Her parents want that. "My mother," Deborah says, "has even asked me am I afraid that I'm going to fail. I say that probably is it."

When asked what her dreams are, Deborah wants her own children to "be individuals, to have thoughts of their own. To do what they want to do, then have the guts to go after it."

In essence, she wants what she didn't have—independence—but she also wants something else that she didn't have. "I want my daughter to dance, and she has expressed some desire. Then I question myself: 'Has she only expressed this because I've brainwashed her?' But I can just see her as a prima ballerina."

That later wish, while coming from the same source as the first, contradicts it. If this daughter is really an independent thinker, she may decide not to be a ballerina.

The twin-edged desire in Deborah illustrates that when parents have trouble accepting their own children's separate identity, the children, in turn, may have the same kinds of problems.

This task of the Departure Stage, of accepting one's grown child's separateness and individuality, while maintaining the connections, is a very familiar one. Because parents draw up their overall master plans for child-rearing *as if* they were his child, they continue to have to differentiate themselves from their child.

This task calls for a dual empathy—what the mother Clara Patterson calls seeing the world through one's own and one's children's eyes, while being cognizant they are two separate visions. Empathizing can stir up old ghosts in parents, memories perhaps long forgotten. That happened with Clara Patterson when her daughter began having trouble in the all-white class.

"I was once in that same situation, the only black in a class. But I knew that I had to pass. I challenged myself to make an A because I *was* the only black."

Clara doesn't tell her daughter, "Well, when I was your age . . ." She listens, understanding that "this affected my daughter differently than it did me."

Problems from the Past Can Resurface

Some of these old ghosts can be particularly painful. Roger Morgan, an educator, found it upsetting that his son initially rejected education.

ROGER MORGAN

"I often feel like the barber whose children go without a haircut or the shoemaker whose children go without shoes.

"In high school, Ben felt as if he couldn't do as well as we would like him to do, and he stopped trying. He would sleep late. Skip school. He was suspended many times. I think he felt that he couldn't be blamed for not getting good grades if he just didn't try." Ben finally quit college and became a gardener.

Roger says that Ben "felt as if he couldn't do as well *as we would like him to*." They, as parents, had very high expectations. And these expectations were based on Roger's feeling of affinity, of being like, of identifying with his son.

Yet, years ago, when he was in Ben's position, there was a different outcome. "I was in college and decided to quit the end of my first year. And then I went back the next year to a different school and managed to do fairly well, even though I really didn't like it." High expectations, like those that Roger has for his son, can be an important incentive to children, yet at best they should be balanced with a realistic appraisal of the child and an understanding that the parent and the child are separate.

Roger, because he has been trained in working with parents, feels that he should accept the fact that he and his son are different. "If it had been any other parent or child, I would counsel them how to deal with this situation in a quite different way than I was doing. But with Ben, I kept getting sucked in."

Roger had two images that were in conflict—one that his son would turn out like him, a financially successful, educated person, and the other that he as a father would deal with problems in an objective, accepting manner rather than being sucked into hurtful arguments. Because neither of his images was coming true, he felt "embarrassed"—"these problems eat you up."

When one's child reminds the parents of the part of the self that he or she likes least, the separation may be more difficult. If the parent, like Roger, wants the child to turn around and become the best part of the self, or the self one wishes for, there can be problems, too. For no child, no matter how similar, is just like a parent, and in our culture, as children become adults, as they "pull up roots," they emphasize their uniqueness.[16]

Whether or not it is easier for a parent to separate from a child who is dissimilar, this relationship poses many other issues. The parent has to learn to seemingly understand foreign needs, and, in the words of a mother, "learn to live with people who are very different from you."

Learning to Live with People Who Are Different

CHRISTINE FREDERICKS

Christine, a craftsperson, is married and the mother of a daughter, twenty-three, and a son, twenty-four.

"We've had years and years of struggle, of pulling and tugging, because each one of our children is different from each other and from us. They're all strong-minded. Now we all get along, but it took us that long.

"Lucy was always a good child who didn't do things wrong, but she did them slowly, irritating everybody. At fifteen and sixteen, she suddenly changed from being this very passively rebellious but pleasant, agreeable person to a nasty person who hated everyone. When she was eighteen, she left home, left school, and went to live with a group of her friends. It wasn't until she had no structure for a long time that she decided that she really did like structure, classes, hard work, and all those things. Now she is struggling with herself over lateness.

"Peter has a lot of energy and a lot of aggressiveness. He's the one that's the most different from us. He's not somebody who enjoys reading. He has an active mind and lots of ideas, but he's not an intellectual. He prefers to spend his time working hard, playing sports.

"When I got interested in meditation, he really thought that was crazy. He feels like there's a split, that we are so different, that I wouldn't understand anything that's important.

"When he's in the house, it's like having an elemental force here. All of this energy bursts up and bursts out. It's interesting—having one's children turn out to be people that I wouldn't ordinarily have chosen to live with. Because I never would have gotten beyond their surface mannerisms. Being a parent has made me able to live with people who are very different from myself."

Christine is a contemplative person, a person who likes sitting alone in the garden on a warm day, or being curled up with a book on cold days, who likes to talk about theoretical ideas. What has made it possible for her to become friends with her determined, energetic, noncontemplative children, to bridge what she calls a "misfit," is that she mostly stopped feeling responsible for how they turned out, instead understanding and accepting her children's differing needs. They then mostly stopped rebelling and blaming her for their problems.

TAKING STOCK OF SUCCESSES AND FAILURES

Grown children, as they look forward to the kinds of lives they want, also examine the past, their parents' lives, and their upbringing. Sometimes, the conclusions that the children come to are surprising.

A mother tells a story about her married daughter's being asked to describe her family: "I thought she was going to say all these glowing things about us," the mother said, "that we were the model family in the Episcopal Church, we were involved in school things and the PTA.

"But my daughter said, 'I didn't grow up with very much security.'

"I thought, 'Oh my God, I failed.' But I said, 'What did you mean by that?'

"She said, 'Well, I never had the security of knowing what was right or wrong when you discussed political, sociological, or theological issues because you and Dad seldom agreed. But,' she said, 'what happened in the process of hearing both sides of everything was that I was forced to think for myself, and that was good.' "

Not a condemning statement at all, but a novel viewpoint for this family.

The grown child's perspective can also seem uncomfortably familiar, like a repeat of a performance, only now the child is playing the part that the parent once played: the idealistic, anything-is-possible, and I-won't-fall-prey-to-hypocrisies young adult.

"I look back at the way I looked at my parents," the father of three grown-up children says, "and now I look at the similar way my children look at me, and it's a cliché come true."

Evaluating Images

Parents are likewise reviewing the past. *The major task for parents in the Departure Stage is to evaluate, to see how they and their children have lived up to the images they have accumulated during their years of parenthood.*

Just as Bernice Neugarten has observed that the stories of the old are qualitatively different from the stories of the middle-aged, so too are the stories of parents in the Departure Stage.[17] What they say (like old people) has more of a beginning, a middle, and a conclusion. One parent even verbalized it. She started by saying, "Do you want to hear my story?" and she began. Hours later, well into the night, she said, "That's my story," and she stood up. Time to leave. Not that her life with her children won't go on and on, that there won't be more chapters in their saga together. The conclusion that parents speak of is not one of severing a relationship, but of measuring how far or how close to the mark they have come in fulfilling their images.

Bruno Bettelheim writes: "If we hope to live not just from moment to moment, but in true consciousness of our existence, then our greatest need and most difficult achievement is to find meaning in our lives." [18]

Parents do search for meaning, but not meaning per se; they compare the hoped-for meaning against the meaning that has accrued. This process of looking back, measuring up, assessing, is an experience from which parents emerge changed.

Susan Thayer

Of Susan's three children, two have left home, and one has returned temporarily after a divorce.

"I was probably a lot more permissive than parents of my time. It's not that I didn't say no, but I said it over very important issues. I believed in very strict discipline, very little punishment. I usually told my children what I expected of them. In any new social situation, I helped them fantasize what was going to happen. If they were going to the hospital or if I were going to have a party, I'd tell them what to expect.

"I was always interested in giving them choices, the freedom to make decisions for themselves. Little things—like when Carolyn [her youngest daughter] was in kindergarten, I would let her choose her clothes.

"I always had a costume closet, and they were interested in play-acting. I wanted to let them develop their imaginations. I read them fairytales, too.

"My son, Eric [the middle child], had reading problems. He was held back in kindergarten and in third grade. The schools couldn't teach him to read. My sister, who's a speech therapist, finally did teach him.

"Eric couldn't read well, but he loved hamsters. We turned the whole garage over to him for his nature club. He used the hamster manual three years in a row for his book reports.

"No doctor could diagnose what was wrong with him. Finally, when he entered the university, I went to a doctor who was doing

some work in dyslexia, and he said, 'Your son is a chronic dys-
lexic.' He also said to me, 'Your son is fortunate because you
haven't punished him or compared his grades with his sisters'.
You've also found other ways for him to excel.'

"At the university, he worked with this doctor. He had him tape
all of his classes. He could learn that way, and he graduated. He's
now in business with his father.

"Carolyn, the youngest, majored in drama. She's now the pro-
ducer of a television show.

"Nicole, the oldest, is very sensitive to other people. She saw *The
Miracle Worker* on television four times, and that influenced her.
She teaches mentally retarded children and adults.

"She went through a sad divorce, and she's currently living with
me until she gets her financial life together."

Susan's life has not been all smooth. She and her husband have
separated. Eric's schooling was scarred by his inability to read, and
now Nicole is divorced.

Susan's assessment of her parenthood is that it is a success. This
discrepancy between life as it is lived and as it is perceived led
George Vaillant, the most recent director of the Grant study of 268
healthy undergraduates (a study which has now gone on for over
thirty-five years), to conclude that mental health is adaption. He
titled his book reporting on the study *Adaption to Life*, stating that
soundness is a way of responding to difficulty, not an absence of
difficulty itself.[19]

Susan's success comes from more than the ability to adapt. It
comes from having achieved an important image: imbuing her children with the capacity to think and make choices for themselves.
Nicole might seem a contradiction. She is back living at home.
Susan, however, sees this as a very short refueling stop.

Most parents find in these overall evaluations that they have
achieved some of their images for their children and not others. For
reasons not entirely understood, some dwell on their successes.
One parent had a son wrongly accused of stealing from the store
where he was employed. Another had a son rightly accused of drug
dealing who was imprisoned for several years. Yet both of these
parents, some time later, felt good. These hurts had healed, and in
general, they had lived up to their images.

Others dwell on their failures. One mother, a factory worker at a
Southern peanut plant, had hoped that her children could all be
educated. Four of her children had college degrees. The fifth had
dropped out of school. Talking to me, she traced, step by step, how

she handled his truancy, his lack of interest. It was a still-raw disappointment.

In comparing those parents who had an overall sense of accomplishment with those who had a comparable feeling of failure, one difference, however, does stand out. Those parents who were the most satisfied had accepted that their children were separate. When they wanted something for their children, it was for the children, not for the parent. That is, of course, a hard line to draw.

Does a parent who wants a child to be well educated want it for the child or for the parents, or (most probably) both? Ultimately this measure is a matter of degree.

When images are not reached in reality, parents look for a place to put the blame: "I gave too much," "I didn't give enough," and "The schools didn't give enough" are the three explanations that I heard most frequently.

The idea of giving is significant. In practically no other venture do people give so much—money, time, effort, thought, love. And when parents take stock, they ask themselves: Was it worthwhile?

This is one reason that parents often deplore their grown children's saying, "Maybe I won't have children of my own." Not only are these young people seemingly denying the parent the human form of immortality, they are also deriding the parent's investment.

Facing the Death of a Child

It was difficult to know where in this book to discuss this subject, because death, as everyone knows, can happen at any time. The fear of a child's dying is one that is always with parents.

The parent of an infant checking to see if the baby is still breathing is really wondering, "Is my baby still alive?" The parent touching the young child's feverish head, watching the child's temperature rise, is scared. The parent saying, "Be careful," to the child setting off on a bike or driving off in a car, has the specter of an accident lurking in his or her mind. The parent watching the child walk into woods for a hike has to push aside the pictures of venomous snakes and rock slides. This fear, always with parents, whether stirred up or still, is perhaps the single factor that most differentiates parents from nonparents.

Yet if death happens, if death, as one parent put it, "snuffs out the life of my child," there is no way to comprehend it, no way to understand how this vital presence, who has infused the parents' life, filled up the parents' waking thoughts and nighttime dreams, is gone. Though the possibility of death is always with parents, the reality of death is inconceivable. Death contradicts one of parents' most entrenched images: that children are the link to humanity, the tie to the future; that the child will outlive the parent.

The disbelief eventually turns to anger and guilt and then to sorrow, one gray seamless day following another and another, until finally the sun begins to shine a little and the sky seems a little blue.

But even that blue sky and sunshine remind parents of the child. Certain seasons, certain days, certain sounds or smells bring back the pain, fully back. And even when parents get to a point at which they have to stop and count how old the child would have been or count how many years since the death, the pain, though dulled, is there.

Whenever parents who have faced the death of a child find themselves evaluating, whether it's when another child is about to be a teenager or when the children are grown and gone, memories of the child who has died return. They wonder once again if there wasn't something they could have done to prevent it. They evaluate the meaning of this event: what possible good it has brought, what it has taught them, how it has made them grow. For even an occurrence as terrible as the death of a child can and often does lead to enormous growth.

Altered Images

Parents say that growth comes from replacing an unreal, untenable image with one that is real and tenable, thus reducing the rubbing, chafing, grating feeling that one has when there is dissonance between fantasy and reality. For most people, fortunately, this is not facing death.

JOAN BUCKLEY

The last of Joan's six children is soon to leave. Her oldest, Beth, thirty-one, has a one-year-old. That one-year-old just had what they all call "her first blood." She fell, cut her face, and bled for the first time.

"We went to visit shortly after the baby's fall and I told Beth and her husband that the nearest I ever came to divorce was the time that one of my sons fell." He had climbed out onto a porch and fallen off of it.

"My husband, as usual, was not around. In fact, he was out of town, and that evening, I picked him up at the train. I told him about my grueling day and he said, 'Why did *you* let that happen?'

"Beth and her husband turned toward each other, because evidently those were the words they'd used when their baby was hurt.

Not 'How did it happen?' but 'Why did *you* let that happen?'

"I think that the determination they both have to make every-thing perfect for that baby is not just a fault of their generation. I was that way, too.

"I remember Christmastime letters from friends. My son had just built a boat in the backyard. Another child was schlepping through school—while my friend's letter says that her son has just gotten a scholarship to Oxford and is studying with Professor Whosis. Or another whose son has a wonderful job with Whatchamacallit.

"It's not as if you don't want your child to be building a boat. You want your child to be the best so you can look better.

"It does persist, just niggardly little things. If your children are making candles and exploring alternative life-styles, you could be happy with that except for that little bit of competition.

"But do I wish that they were doing anything different? *Now* I don't. I really don't believe I do.

"Mark is a carpenter. He shares a large farm with other people. He's married. And he and his wife have a baby. They built their house out of logs on the land. They're trying to keep their life simple and uncluttered, and they're doing so. Their life is self-selected and they're pleased with it."

Although that edge of competition, that wish for success, is in us all, Joan has pushed it down, altering her image, being gratified by what her son wants.

Her pleasure comes from somewhere else, too. "When Mark and his wife are here, I get no sense that they are rejecting us and our values—only that ours are different. There was never any hint that they thought that we were wallowing in materialism and that they were off to something pure, but simply that we do things differently. I think that's kind of remarkable. They have great generosity of spirit."

Daydreams of Reunions

Several days after she had given birth to her first child, I asked a mother about her daydreams. She said that she pictured herself on a porch, sitting on a glider. Her hair was gray and long, bound around her head in thick braids. And a circle of her children and grandchildren enveloped her.

The father of recently grown children, when asked about his fantasies, saw himself buying a house on a Caribbean island, a place where his grown children could join him for sailing, sunning, and fishing.

Ten years after her last child has left, a mother had a similar daydream: going to the beach with her children and grandchildren.

It is interesting that many of these fantasies take place at vacation sites—they are kept safely at a distance from home, yet throughout parenthood, people return to this theme: that their child will leave, but return, as equal, as friend, companion. The child will return home—not in reality, but in the domain of a different adult-to-adult relationship.

These dreams—or images—have come true for Joan Buckley and her son Mark. When one's children do transcend the adolescent rebellion and parents transcend the desire for perfection, when in fact both can accept each other's foibles as well as abilities, it is indeed what Susan calls "remarkable."

Frequently this reunion happens when one's children become parents and can empathize with the emotions their parents once had.

These moments of reunion do not necessarily signal the dawn of utopia, for most relationships swing back and forth. There are moments when the parent and grown child are together, when they talk or even share silence in the spirit of near-perfect communion. They may be traveling together, going shopping or to a movie together, playing golf or visiting each other's home. But then the next time they see each other, one says something that sets the other off (a you-should-lose-weight or not-smoke or buy-some-new-clothes or move-to-a-smaller-place statement), and a coldness creeps into the relationship.

Like seasonal cycles, there are thaws and frosts. Yet there are many moments which validate parenthood. They reveal the meaning of separation: that to accept separateness implies the beginning of a new connection.

Epilogue

Parents ask, "What have I gained and what have I lost in being a parent?" They also pose a corollary question to themselves: "Have I changed?"

That was one of the questions that I asked when I began my study. The answer is yes.

Parenthood has changed us. We all have probably had the experience of being with a group of adults when the subject of children came up. Inevitably, an invisible curtain is drawn and the group separates into camps—those who have children and those who don't.

The differences are large. The people without children can resent the absorption parents have in their children. The people with children can likewise resent the self-absorption of the others.

Taking care of a small, dependent, growing person is transforming, because it brings us in touch with our baser side, it exposes our vulnerabilities as well as our nobility. We lose our sense of self, only to find it and have it change again and again. We learn to nurture and care. We struggle through defining our own rules and our own brand of being an authority. We figure out how we want to interpret the wider world, and we learn to interact with all those who affect our children. When our children are teenagers, we redefine our relationships, and then we launch them into life.

Often our fantasies are laid bare, our dreams are in a constant tug of war with realities. And perhaps we grow. In the end, we have learned more about ourselves, about the cycles of life, and humanity itself. Most parents describe themselves as more responsible, more accepting, more generous than before they had children.

A nonparent can look at a parent and child in a screaming match with condemnation and intolerance. A parent never can. We can dislike this parent's solution, but we understand.

We look at a pregnant woman, fat, uncomfortable, lost in reveries, and we understand.

We look at a father, carrying his baby and at the same time saddled with far too much equipment, and we understand.

We look at a mother saying, "Eat your vegetables and then you can have dessert," and we remember.

317

A parent towing a tired child home from an outing brings back memories. As does a parent drilling a child on the multiplication tables.

- A mother bemoans the fact that her preteen daughter doesn't like the shape of her nose or the texture of her hair.
- A father walks down the street with a teenager ten paces behind. The teenager pretends he doesn't know his father.
- Two parents are teary yet proud at the wedding of their child.

All of these bring a familiar feeling. We will probably always feel the rush of adrenaline when a baby, even a stranger's baby, cries.

We are not the same, and I think we are richer for the difference.

Appendix

I made contact with parents through a network approach, one person suggesting another. I also met parents through professional channels such as parent education groups, day-care centers, schools, child-advocacy groups, councils for adoptive parents, and single-parent organizations. I met with them in living rooms and kitchens, at backyard picnic tables, beside swimming pools, in playgrounds and parks, in the playroom of a commune, in the emergency room of a hospital, in a women's health center, in schools, and in offices.

I devised an in-depth biographical interview form, which I revised after testing it with ten parents. It is:

1. When you have time to think (whether it's when you are driving or riding or walking or taking a bath or shower or falling asleep at night), when you listen to that voice that is always going in your head, what is it saying about being a parent? What are the things you think about?
2. What are the parts of being a parent that you enjoy most? What do you find the hardest? Why?
3. Do your children remind you of yourself and/or someone else in your family? In what ways? How does this affect you?
4. How has having children affected your relationship with your _____ (wife, ex-wife, girlfriend/husband, ex-husband, boyfriend)?
5. How has having children affected your relationship with your parents?
6. Do you remember yourself as a child of your children's age? What were you like? How does this memory affect you?
7. What from the way your parents raised you do you want to do with your children? What don't you want to do and why?
8. How has having children affected your work and the rest of your life?

9. If you want advice and help, whom do you turn to? Whom have you learned the most from?

10. What have you learned in being a parent? Have you changed? How? If you were going to start over, would you do anything differently?

11. What are your worries about yourself and your family?

12. What are your daydreams about yourself and your family?

Notes

Introduction

1. Philippe Ariès, *Centuries of Childhood: A Social History of Family Life,* trans. Robert Baldick (New York: Vintage, 1962).
2. Sigmund Freud, *The Basic Writings of Sigmund Freud,* trans. and ed. A. A. Brill (New York: Modern Library, 1938).
3. Erik H. Erikson, *Childhood and Society,* 2nd ed. (New York: Norton, 1950);Jean Piaget, *The Language and Thought of the Child,* trans. Marjorie Gabain (New York: New American Library, 1955); Benjamin Spock, *Baby and Child Care* (New York: Pocket Books, 1945); Bruno Bettelheim, *Love Is Not Enough* (New York: Collier, 1950); Robert Coles, *Children of Crisis* (New York: Delta, 1964); Selma H. Fraiberg, *The Magic Years* (New York: Scribner's, 1959); Jerome Kagan, *The Growth of the Child* (New York: Norton, 1978); T. Berry Brazelton, *Infants and Mothers: Differences in Development* (New York: Delacorte, 1969).
4. Gail Sheehy, *Passages: Predictable Crises of Adult Life* (New York: Dutton, 1976); Erikson, op. cit., pp. 247–274.
5. Daniel J. Levinson et al., *The Seasons of a Man's Life* (New York: Knopf, 1978); Roger L. Gould, *Transformations: Growth and Change in Adult Life* (New York: Simon and Schuster, 1978).
6. Lillian B. Rubin, *Women of a Certain Age: The Midlife Search for Self* (New York: Harper & Row, 1979); Iris Sanguiliano, *In Her Time* (New York: Morrow, 1978).
7. E. E. LeMasters, *Parents in Modern America: A Sociological Analysis,* rev. ed. (Homewood, Ill.: Dorsey, 1970); Alice Rossi, "Transition to Parenthood," in *Family in Transition,* eds. Arlene S. Skolnick and Jerome H. Skolnick (Boston: Little, Brown and Company, 1971), pp. 331–342; Jessie Bernard, *The Future of Motherhood* (New York: Penguin, 1974); Grete L. Bibring et al., "A Study of the Psychological Process in Pregnancy and of the Earliest Mother-Child Relationship," in *The Psychoanalytic Study of the Child,* ed. Ruth S. Eissler et al., Vol. 16 (New York: International Universities Press, Inc., 1961), pp. 9–72; Helene Deutsch, *The Psychology of Women, Vol. II: Motherhood* (New York: Bantam, 1945); E. James Anthony and Therese Benedek, eds., *Parenthood: Its Psychology and Psychopathology* (Boston: Little, Brown, 1975); Group for the Advancement of Psychiatry, *Joys and Sorrows of Parenthood* (New York: Scribner's, 1975); Urie Bronfenbrenner, *The Ecology of Human Development: Experiments by Nature and Design* (Boston: Harvard University Press, 1979); Rhona and Robert N. Rapoport et al., *Fathers, Mothers, and Society* (New York: Basic Books, 1977).

8. Jane Lazarre, *The Mother Knot* (New York: Laurel, 1976); Angela Barron McBride, *The Growth and Development of Mothers* (New York: Barnes & Noble, 1973); Boston Women's Health Book Collective, *Ourselves and Our Children* (New York: Random House, 1978).

9. B. L. Neugarten, "Continuities and Discontinuities of Psychological Issues into Adult Life," *Human Development*, Vol. 12 (1969), p. 125; Levinson, op. cit., p. 91.

10. Donald W. Winnicott, *Playing and Reality* (New York: Basic Books, 1971); Barbara Biber, *Play as a Growth Process* (New York: Bank Street College of Education, 1951); Millie Almy, "Spontaneous Play: An Avenue for Intellectual Development," in *Early Childhood Play: Selected Readings Related to Cognition and Motivation*, ed. Millie Almy (New York: Associated Educational Services Corporation, 1968), pp. ALM 1C-14C; Eveline Omwake, "The Child's Estate," in *Early Childhood Play*, pp. OMW 1A-18A.

11. Klaus F. Riegel, "The Dialectics of Human Development," *American Psychologist*, Vol. 31 (October 1976), pp. 689–700.

12. R. Gould, op. cit.

13. Brandt I. Steele and Carl B. Pollock, "The Battered Child's Parents," in *Family in Transition*, pp. 356–365.

14. Erikson, op. cit.; Robert J. Havighurst, "History of Developmental Psychology: Socialization and Personality Development Through the Life Span," in *Life Span Developmental Psychology: Personality and Socialization*, eds. Paul B. Baltes and K. Warner Schaie (New York: Academic Press, 1973), pp. 3–24.

I. The Image-Making Stage

1. Sigmund Freud, *The Basic Writings of Sigmund Freud*, trans. and ed. A. A. Brill (New York: Modern Library, 1938); Erik H. Erikson, *Childhood and Society*, 2nd ed. (New York: Norton, 1950); Jean Piaget, *The Language and Thought of the Child*, trans. Marjorie Gabain (New York: New American Library, 1955).

2. John Munder Ross, "Toward Fatherhood: The Epigenesis of Paternal Identity During a Boy's Decade," *International Review of Psychoanalysis*, Vol. 4 (1977), pp. 327–347.

3. Sigmund Freud, "On Narcissism: An Introduction," in *Standard Edition*, ed. J. Strachey, Vol. 14 (London: Hogarth Press, 1957).

4. Lois Hoffman and Martin Hoffman, "The Value of Children to Parents," in *Psychological Perspectives on Population*, ed. J. T. Fawcett (New York: Basic Books, 1973).

5. Myra Leifer, "Psychological Changes Accompanying Pregnancy and Motherhood," *Genetic Psychology Monographs*, Vol. 95 (1977), p. 68.

6. E. E. LeMasters, "Parenthood as Crisis," in *Sourcebook in Marriage and the Family*, 2nd ed., ed. Marvin B. Sussman (Boston: Houghton Mifflin, 1963), p. 196.

7. Shirley L. Radl, *Mother's Day Is Over* (New York: Warner, 1973), p. 18.

8. Ibid., p. 19.

9. Ellen Peck, *The Baby Trap* (New York: Pinnacle, 1971).

10. Ruth Davidson Bell, "Considering Parenthood," in *Ourselves and Our Children*, the Boston Women's Health Book Collective (New York: Random House, 1978).

11. Virginia Barber and Merrill Maguire Skaggs, *The Mother Person* (New York: Schocken, 1975); Angela Barron McBride, *The Growth and Development of Mothers* (New York: Barnes and Noble, 1973); Jane Lazarre, *The Mother Knot* (New York: Laurel, 1976); Radl, op. cit.; Eliot A. Daley, *Father Feelings* (New York: Morrow, 1978); the Boston Women's Health Book Collective, *Ourselves and Our Children* (New York: Random House, 1978).

12. Daniel J. Levinson et al., *The Seasons of a Man's Life* (New York: Knopf, 1978), p. 91.

13. Adrienne Rich, *Of Woman Born: Motherhood as Experience and Institution* (New York: Norton, 1976), p. 39.

14. Suzanne Arms, *A Season to be Born* (New York: Harper/Colophon, 1973), pp. 9, 13.

15. Arthur Colman and Libby Colman, *Pregnancy: The Psychological Experience* (New York: Bantam, 1971), p. 36.

16. Carol Gilligan, "In a Different Voice: Women's Conceptions of Self and Morality," *Harvard Educational Review*, Vol. 47 (1977).

17. Grete L. Bibring et al., "A Study of the Psychological Processes in Pregnancy and of the Earliest Mother-Child Relationship," in *The Psychoanalytic Study of the Child*, eds. Ruth S. Eissler et al., Vol. 16 (New York: International Universities Press, Inc., 1961), pp. 9–72.

18. Phyllis Chesler, *With Child: A Diary of Motherhood* (New York: Crowell, 1979), p. 7.

19. James A. Levine, *Who Will Raise the Children: New Options for Fathers (and Mothers)* (Philadelphia: Lippincott, 1976).

20. Lucie Jessner et al., "The Development of Parental Attitudes During Pregnancy," in *Parenthood: Its Psychology and Psychopathology*, eds. E. James Anthony and Therese Benedek (Boston: Little, Brown, 1970), pp. 209–244.

21. Ibid.

22. Therese Benedek, "The Psychobiology of Pregnancy," in Anthony and Benedek, op. cit., p. 147.

23. Albert J. Solnit and Mary H. Stark, "Mourning and the Birth of a Defective Child," in *The Psychoanalytic Study of the Child*, eds. Ruth S. Eissler et al., Vol. 16 (New York: International Universities Press, 1961), pp. 523–537.

24. Leifer, op. cit., pp. 72–73.

25. Ibid., p. 91.

26. Nora Ephron, "Having a Baby After 35," *New York Times Magazine* (Nov. 26, 1978), p. 28.

27. Roger L. Gould, *Transformations: Growth and Change in Adult Life* (New York: Simon and Schuster, 1978), p. 11.

28. Jane E. Brody, "Miscarriage: Myths Often Add to Grief," *New York Times*, March 5, 1980, Section C, pp. 1, 14.

29. Tracy Hotchner, *Pregnancy and Childbirth* (New York: Avon, 1979).

30. Nancy Friday, *My Mother/My Self* (New York: Delacorte, 1977), p. 402.

31. Chesler, op. cit., p. 6.

32. Ephron, op. cit., p. 29.

33. Lois Wladis Hoffman, "Effects of the First Child on the Woman's Role," in *The First Child and Family Formation*, eds. Warren B. Miller and Lucile F. Newman (Chapel Hill, N.C.: Carolina Population Center, 1978), pp. 340–367.

34. Levinson, op. cit., p. 197.

35. Gail Sheehy, *Passages: Predictable Crises in Adult Life* (New York: Dutton, 1976).
36. Pamela Daniels and Kathy Weingarten, *Sooner or Later: The Timing of Parenthood in Adult Lives* (New York: Norton, in press).
37. Felix Boehm, "The Femininity Complex in Men," *International Journal of Psychoanalysis*, Vol. II, p. 456.
38. John Munder Ross, "Paternal Identity: The Equations of Fatherhood and Manhood," in *On Sexuality: Psychoanalytic Observations*, eds. Toksoz B. Karasci and Charles W. Socarides (New York: International Universities Press, 1979), pp. 73–97.
39. Lazarre, op. cit., pp. 36–37.
40. Therese Benedek, *Psychosexual Functions in Women* (New York: Ronald, 1952), p. 413.
41. John G. Loesch and Nahman H. Greenberg, "Some Specific Areas of Conflict Observed During Pregnancy: A Comparative Study of Married and Unmarried Pregnant Women," *American Journal of Orthopsychiatry*, Vol. 32 (July 1962), p. 634.
42. Mabel Blake Cohen, "Personal Identity and Sexual Identity," *Psychiatry*, Vol. 29 (February 1966), p. 9.
43. Robert A. Fein, "Consideration of Men's Experiences and the Birth of a First Child," in Miller and Newman, eds., op. cit., pp. 327–339.
44. Marshall H. Klaus and John H. Kennell, "Parent-to-Infant Attachment," in *Mother/Child Father/Child Relationships*, eds. Joseph H. Stevens, Jr., and Marilyn Mathews (Washington: National Association for the Education of Young Children, 1978), p. 9.
45. Jessner et al., op. cit., p. 224.
46. McBride, op. cit., pp. 23, 24.
47. Bibring et al., op. cit., pp. 12–13; Grete L. Bibring et al., "Some Considerations of the Psychological Processes in Pregnancy," in *The Psychoanalytic Study of the Child*, eds. Ruth S. Eissler et al., Vol. 14 (New York: International Universities Press, 1959), p. 119.
48. Alice Rossi, "Transition to Parenthood," in *Family in Transition*, eds. Arlene S. Skolnick and Jerome H. Skolnick (Boston: Little, Brown, 1971), pp. 331–342; Rhona and Robert N. Rapoport et al., *Fathers, Mothers, and Society* (New York: Basic Books, 1977), pp. 152–161.

II. The Nurturing Stage

1. Adrienne Rich, *Of Woman Born: Motherhood as Experience and Institution* (New York: Norton, 1976), pp. 193.
2. Klaus F. Riegel, "The Dialectics of Human Development," *American Psychologist*, Vol. 31 (October 1976), pp. 689–700.
3. Albert J. Solnit and Mary H. Stark, "Mourning and the Birth of a Defective Child," *The Psychoanalytic Study of the Child*, eds. Ruth S. Eissler et al., Vol. 16 (New York: International Universities Press, 1961), pp. 523–537; Marshall H. Klaus and John H. Kennell, "Parent-to-Infant Attachment," in *Mother/Child Father/Child Relationships*, eds. Joseph H. Stevens, Jr., and Marilyn Mathews (Washington: National Association for the Education of Young Children, 1978), pp. 5–29.
4. Klaus and Kennell, op. cit., p. 24.
5. Marshall H. Klaus and John H. Kennell, *Maternal-Infant Bonding* (St. Louis: C. V. Mosby, 1976), pp. 209–239.
6. Klaus and Kennell, "Parent-to-Infant Attachment," pp. 11, 12.

7. Peter Wolff, "Observations on Newborn Infants," *Psychosomatic Medicine*, Vol. 21 (1969), pp. 110–118.
8. M. M. Desmond et al., "The Transitional Care Nursery: A Mechanism of Preventive Medicine," *Pediatric Clinics of North America*, Vol. 13 (1966), pp. 651–668.
9. T. Berry Brazelton et al., "The Origins of Reciprocity—The Early Mother-Infant Interaction," in *The Effect of the Infant on Its Caregiver*, eds. Michael Lewis and Leonard A. Rosenblum (New York: Wiley, 1974), pp. 49–76.
10. Klaus and Kennell, "Parent-to-Infant Attachment," pp. 11–12.
11. Martin Greenberg and Norman Morris, "Engrossment: The Newborn's Impact upon the Father," *American Journal of Orthopsychiatry*, Vol. 44 (1974), pp. 520–531.
12. Marshall H. Klaus and John H. Kennell, "Mothers Separated from Their Newborn Infants," *Pediatric Clinics of North America*, Vol. 17 (November 1970), pp. 1015–1037.
13. Greenberg and Morris, op. cit.
14. Klaus and Kennell, *Maternal-Infant Bonding*, pp. 99–166.
15. Stella Chess et al., *Your Child Is a Person* (New York: Viking, 1965), pp. 24–34.
16. Richard Q. Bell, "Stimulus Control of Parent or Caretaker Behavior by Offspring," *Developmental Psychology*, Vol. 4 (January 1971), pp. 63–72; Sibylle Escalona, *The Roots of Individuality* (Chicago: Aldine, 1968); Lois Barclay Murphy and Alice E. Moriarty, *Vulnerability, Coping, and Growth: From Infancy to Adolescence* (New Haven: Yale University Press, 1976).
17. Lewis and Rosenblum, eds., op. cit., p. xv.
18. Louis W. Sander, "Issues in Early Mother-Child Interaction," in *Infant Psychiatry: A New Synthesis*, eds. Eveoleen V. Rexford et al. (New Haven: Yale University Press, 1976), pp. 131–132.
19. David Steinberg, *Fatherjournal: Five Years of Awakening to Fatherhood* (New York: Times Change, 1977), pp. 13-14.
20. Louise J. Kaplan, *Oneness and Separateness: From Infant to Individual* (New York: Simon and Schuster, 1978).
21. Helene Deutsch, *The Psychology of Women*, Vol. 2: *Motherhood* (New York: Bantam, 1945) p. 226.
22. Jane Lazarre, *The Mother Knot* (New York: Laurel, 1976), pp. 51–52.
23. John Bowlby, *Attachment and Loss*, Vol. 1, *Attachment* (New York: Basic Books, 1969); Leon J. Yarrow and Frank A. Pedersen, "Attachment: Its Origins and Course," *Young Children*, Vol. 27 (June 1972), p. 302.
24. Mary D. Salter Ainsworth, "The Development of Infant-Mother Attachment," in *Review of Child Development Research*, Vol. 3, eds. Bettye M. Caldwell and Henry N. Ricciuti (Chicago: University of Chicago Press, 1973), p. 1.
25. Marsha Weinraub, Jeanne Brooks, and Michael Lewis, "The Social Network: A Reconsideration of the Concept of Attachment," mimeographed paper (Princeton, N.J.: Educational Testing Service, 1977), p. 1.
26. Ross D. Parke and Douglas B. Sawin, "Fathering: It's a Major Role," *Psychology Today* (November 1977), p. 109.
27. M. Kotelchuck et al., "Infant Reaction to Parental Separations When Left with Familiar and Unfamiliar Adults," *Journal of Genetic Psychology*, Vol. 126 (1975), pp. 255–262.

28. Parke and Sawin, op. cit., p. 111.
29. Ernest L. Abelin, "The Role of the Father in the Separation-Individuation Process," in *Separation-Individuation*, eds. John B. McDevitt and Calvin F. Settlage (New York: International Universities Press, 1971), p. 232.
30. Michael E. Lamb, "Fathers: Forgotten Contributors to Child Development," *Human Development*, Vol. 18 (1975), pp. 245–266; idem, "Father-Infant and Mother-Infant Interaction in the First Year of Life," *Child Development*, Vol. 48 (1977), pp. 167–181.
31. Reported in Parke and Sawin, op. cit., p. 111.
32. Lois Wladis Hoffman, "Effects of the First Child on the Woman's Role," in *The First Child and Family Formation*, eds. Warren B. Miller and Lucile F. Newman (Chapel Hill, N.C.: Carolina Population Center, 1978), pp. 340–367.
33. Carolyn Pape Cowan, "How a Couple Become a Family," *Redbook Magazine* (September 1978), p. 156.
34. Dorothy Dinnerstein, *The Mermaid and the Minotaur: Sexual Arrangements and Human Malaise* (New York: Harper Colophon, 1977); Nancy Chodorow, *The Reproduction of Mothering: Psychoanalysis and the Sociology of Gender* (Berkeley: University of California Press, 1978).
35. John Munder Ross, "Paternal Identity: The Equations of Fatherhood and Manhood," in *On Sexuality: Psychoanalytic Observations*, eds. Toksoz B. Karasci and Charles W. Socarides (New York: International Universities Press, 1979), p. 85.
36. Jean Curtis, *Working Mothers* (New York: Doubleday, 1976).
37. René A. Spitz, "Hospitalism," *The Psychoanalytic Study of the Child*, Vol. 1 (1945), pp. 54–117.
38. Selma Fraiberg, *Every Child's Birthright* (New York: Basic Books, 1977).
39. Erik H. Erikson, *Identity, Youth and Crisis* (New York: Norton, 1968).
40. Lazarre, op. cit., pp. 52–53.
41. Lillian Breslow Rubin, *Worlds of Pain* (New York: Basic Books, 1976), pp. 81–82.
42. Steinberg, op. cit., p. 15.
43. Rubin, op. cit., p. 82.
44. Chodorow, op. cit., p. 201.
45. Carolyn Pape Cowan et al., "Becoming a Family: The Impact of a First Child's Birth on the Couple Relationship," in Miller and Newman, eds., op. cit., pp. 302, 306–307.
46. Rubin, op. cit., p. 80.
47. E. E. LeMasters, "Parenthood as Crisis," in *Sourcebook in Marriage and the Family*, 2nd ed., ed. M. Sussman (Boston: Houghton Mifflin, 1963), pp. 195–196, 197.
48. Everett D. Dyer, "Parenthood as Crisis: A Re-Study," *Marriage and Family Living*, Vol. 25 (May 1963), pp. 196–201: Daniel F. Hobbs, Jr., "Parenthood as Crisis: A Third Study," *Journal of Marriage and the Family*, Vol. 27 (August 1965), pp. 367–372; Daniel F. Hobbs, Jr., and Sue Peck Cole, "Transition to Parenthood: A Decade Replication," *Journal of Marriage and the Family*, Vol. 38 (November 1976), pp. 723–731.
49. Rich, op. cit., pp. 222–223.
50. Muriel K. Taylor and Kate L. Kogan, "Effects of Birth of a Sibling on

Mother-Child Interactions," *Child Psychiatry and Human Development*, Vol. 4 (1973), pp. 55, 58.

51. Jessie Bernard, *The Future of Motherhood* (New York: Penguin, 1974), p. 9.

52. Barbara K. Schwartz, "Easing the Adaptation to Parenthood," *Journal of Family Counseling*, Vol. 2 (Fall 1974), pp. 32–39.

53. Frank A. Pedersen and Kenneth S. Robson, "Father Participation in Infancy," *American Journal of Orthopsychiatry*, Vol. 39 (April 1969), pp. 466–472.

54. Robert H. Fein, "Consideration of Men's Experiences and the Birth of a First Child," in Miller and Newman, eds., op. cit., pp. 327–339.

55. Richard E. Gordon et al., "Factors in Postpartum Emotional Adjustment," *Obstetrics and Gynecology*, Vol. 25 (1965), pp. 158–164.

56. F. T. Melges, "Postpartum Psychiatric Syndromes," *Psychosomatic Medicine*, Vol. 23 (1968), pp. 520–525.

57. Bertram J. Cohler et al., "Child-Care Attitudes and Emotional Disturbances Among Mothers of Young Children," *Genetic Psychology Monographs*, Vol. 82 (August 1970), p. 33.

58. Donald W. Winnicott, "The Mother-Infant Experience of Mutuality," in *Parenthood: Its Psychology and Psychopathology*, eds. E. James Anthony and Therese Benedek (Boston: Little, Brown, 1970), pp. 245–256.

59. Sander, op. cit., p. 135.

60. Margaret S. Mahler, "On the First Three Subphases of the Separation-Individuation Process," *International Journal of Psychoanalysis*, Vol. 53 (1972), p. 334.

61. Daniel J. Levinson et al., *The Seasons of a Man's Life* (New York: Knopf, 1978), p. 54.

62. Daniel Stern, *The First Relationship: Infant and Mother* (Cambridge, Mass.: Harvard University Press, 1977).

63. Yarrow and Pedersen, op. cit.

64. Bell, op. cit., p. 68.

65. Erik K. Erikson, *Childhood and Society*, 2nd. ed. (New York: Norton, 1950) p. 247.

66. Rich, op. cit., pp. 35–36.

67. Steinberg, op. cit., pp. 18–19.

68. Stern, op. cit., p. 20.

69. Erikson, op. cit., p. 251.

70. Philip and Carolyn Cowan, interview, Berkeley, Calif., September 1978.

71. Cowan, op. cit., p. 159.

72. Therese Benedek, "Parenthood During the Life Cycle," in Anthony and Benedek, eds., op. cit., pp. 185–206.

73. Marilyn French, *The Women's Room* (New York: Jove/HBJ, 1977), pp. 108, 110, 113–114.

74. U.S. Department of Labor, Employment Standards Administration, Women's Bureau, *Working Mothers and Their Children* (Washington, D.C.: U.S. Government Printing Office, 1977), p. 5.

75. Ellen Hock, "Working and Nonworking Mothers and their Infants: A Comparative Study of Maternal Caregiving Characteristics and Infant Social Behavior," mimeographed paper (Columbus: Ohio State University, 1979); Ellen Galinsky, "Infants and Toddlers in Day Care: How Do They Turn Out," *Working Mother* (May 1980), pp. 97, 147–150; Sandra

Sohn Jaffe and Jack Viertel, *Becoming Parents* (New York: Atheneum, 1979), pp. 34–41.

76. Richard Ruopp et al., *Children at the Center* (Cambridge, Mass., Abt Books, 1979).
77. Fraiberg, op. cit.
78. Henry N. Ricciuti, *Effects of Infant Day Care Experience on Behavior and Development: Research and Implications for Social Policy* (Washington, D.C.: HEW, 1976), pp. 26–27.
79. Bettye Caldwell et al., "Infant Day Care and Attachment," *American Journal of Orthopsychiatry*, Vol. 40 (1970), pp. 397–412.
80. Jerome Kagan et al., *Infancy: Its Place in Human Development* (Cambridge, Mass.: Harvard University Press, 1978), pp. 175–293.
81. Ricciuti, op. cit.; Alfred J. Kahn and Sheila B. Kamerman, *Child Care, Family Benefits and Working Parents* (New York: Columbia University Press, 1980).
82. Ricciuti, op. cit., p. 40.
83. Sheila B. Kamerman, *Parenting in an Unresponsive Society: Managing Work and Family Life* (New York: Free Press, 1980); Urie Bronfenbrenner, "Reality and Research in the Ecology of Human Development," *Proceedings of the American Philosophical Society*, Vol. 119 (December 1975), p. 468.
84. Arlene Skolnick, interview, Berkeley, Calif., September 1978.
85. Alice S. Rossi, "The Transition to Parenthood," in *Family in Transition*, eds. Arlene S. Skolnick and Jerome H. Skolnick (Boston: Little, Brown, 1971), pp. 331–342.

III. The Authority Stage

1. Adrienne Rich, *Of Woman Born: Motherhood as Experience and Institution* (New York: Norton, 1976), p. 224.
2. Ibid., p. 23.
3. Roger L. Gould, *Transformations: Growth and Change in Adult Life* (New York: Simon and Schuster, 1978), p. 11.
4. E. Mavis Hetherington et al., "The Aftermath of Divorce," in *Mother/Child, Father/Child Relationships*, eds. Joseph H. Stevens, Jr., and Marilyn Mathews (Washington, D.C.: National Association for the Education of Young Children, 1978), p. 174.
5. Jessie Bernard, *The Future of Motherhood* (New York: Penguin, 1974), p. 9.
6. Leigh Minturn and William L. Lambert, *Mothers of Six Cultures: Antecedents of Child Rearing* (New York: Wiley, 1964).
7. Elaine Heffner, *Mothering: The Emotional Experience of Motherhood after Freud and Feminism* (Garden City, N.Y.: Doubleday, 1978).
8. Erik H. Erikson, *Childhood and Society*, 2nd ed. (New York: Norton, 1950), p. 255.
9. Gould, op. cit., pp. 109–111.
10. Daniel J. Levinson et al., *The Seasons of a Man's Life* (New York: Knopf, 1978), 97–101.
11. Rudolph Dreikurs and Vicki Soltz, *Children: The Challenge* (New York: Hawthorn, 1964); Thomas Gordon with Judith Gordon Sands, *P.E.T. in Action* (New York: Wyden, 1976); Haim G. Ginott, *Between Parent and Child* (New York: Macmillan, 1965); Lee Salk with Rita

Kramer, *How to Raise a Human Being: A Parent's Guide to Emotional Health from Infancy through Adolescence* (New York: Random House, 1969); Jean Illsley Clarke, *Self-Esteem: A Family Affair* (Minneapolis: Winston, 1978); Ben F. Feingold, *Why Your Child Is Hyperactive* (New York: Random House, 1975); Lendon H. Smith, *Feed Your Kids Right* (New York: McGraw-Hill, 1979).

12. Brandt I. Steele and Carl B. Pollock, "The Battered Child's Parents," in *Family in Transition*, eds. Arlene S. Skolnick and Jerome H. Skolnick (Boston: Little, Brown, 1971), pp. 361, 362, 363.

13. Angela Barron McBride, *The Growth and Development of Mothers* (New York: Barnes & Noble, 1973), p. 59.

14. Margaret S. Mahler et al., "The Mother's Reaction to her Toddler's Drive for Individuation," in *Parenthood: Its Psychology and Psychopathology*, eds. E. James Anthony and Therese Benedek (Boston: Little, Brown, 1970), pp. 257–274.

15. D. W. Winnicott, "Transitional Objects and Transitional Phenomena," in *Collected Papers* (London: Tavistock, 1958), p. 238.

16. Hannah L. Frisch, "The Effect of Designated and Actual Sex of Infant on Adult-Infant Play," Ph.D. dissertation, University of Chicago, 1976.

17. Sigmund Freud, *The Basic Writings of Sigmund Freud* (New York: Modern Library, 1938); E. James Anthony, "The Reactions of Parents to the Oedipal Child," in *Parenthood: Its Psychology and Psychopathology*, eds. E. James Anthony and Therese Bendek (Boston: Little, Brown, 1970), pp. 275–288.

18. Nancy Chodorow, "Perspectives on Family Structure," paper presented at Children and Family in a Changing World Conference, Sarah Lawrence College, Bronxville, N.Y., May 12, 1979.

19. Jerome Kagan, "The Child in the Family," *Daedalus*, Vol. 106 (Spring 1977), pp. 50–54.

IV. The Interpretive Stage

1. Daniel J. Levinson et al., *The Seasons of a Man's Life* (New York: Knopf, 1978), p. 49.

2. Angela Barron McBride, *The Growth and Development of Mothers* (New York: Barnes & Noble, 1973); Jane Lazarre, *The Mother Knot* (New York: Laurel, 1976); Shirley L. Radl, *Mother's Day Is Over* (New York: Warner, 1973).

3. Erik H. Erikson, *Childhood and Society*, 2nd ed. (New York: Norton, 1950) p. 259.

4. Erikson, *Identity, Youth and Crisis* (New York: Norton, 1968), p. 96.

5. Reported in L. Joseph Stone and Joseph Church, *Childhood and Adolescence: A Psychology of the Growing Person*, 3rd edition (New York: Random House, 1957), p. 365.

6. Judith S. Kestenberg, "The Effect on Parents of the Child's Transition into and out of Latency," in *Parenthood: Its Psychology and Psychopathology*, eds. E. James Anthony and Therese Benedek (Boston: Little, Brown, 1970), p. 290.

7. Kenneth Keniston, "Psychological Development and Historical Change," in *Rethinking Childhood*, ed. Arlene Skolnick (Boston: Little, Brown, 1970), p. 196.

8. Catherine S. Chilman, "Families in Development at Mid-Stage of the

Family Life Cycle," *Family Coordinator,* Vol. 17 (October 1968), p. 308.

9. Jean Piaget, *The Language and Thought of the Child,* trans. Marjorie Gabain (New York: New American Library, 1955); Lawrence Kohlberg, "Development of Moral Character and Moral Ideology," in *Review of Child Development Research,* Vol. 1, eds. M. Hoffman and L. Hoffman (New York: Russell Sage Foundation, 1964), pp. 383–431.

10. Patricia Minuchin, "Transition to Peer Group Life," *Lucy Sprague Mitchell Memorial Conference,* 5th, ed. Charlotte B. Winsor (New York: Bank Street College of Education, 1978).

11. Kohlberg, op. cit.

12. Eliot A. Daley, *Father Feelings* (New York: Morrow, 1978), pp. 36–38, 39.

13. Jerome Kagan, "The Child in the Family," *Daedalus,* Vol. 106 (Spring 1977), p. 34.

14. John Condry and Michael L. Siman, "Characteristics of Peer- and Adult-Oriented Children," *Journal of Marriage and the Family,* Vol. 36 (August 1974), pp. 543–554.

15. Anne Morrow Lindbergh, *Gift from the Sea* (New York: Vintage, 1955), p. 81.

16. Kenneth Keniston and the Carnegie Council on Children, *All Our Children* (New York: Harcourt Brace Jovanovich, 1977), pp. 17, 18.

V. The Interdependent Stage

1. B. L. Neugarten, "Continuities and Discontinuities of Psychological Issues into Adult Life," *Human Development,* Vol. 12 (1969), p. 125.

2. L. Joseph Stone and Joseph Church, *Childhood and Adolescence: A Psychology of the Growing Person,* 3rd ed. (New York: Random House, 1957), p. 421.

3. Catherine S. Chilman, "Families in Development at Mid-Stage of the Family Life-Cycle," *Family Coordinator,* Vol. 17 (October 1968), p. 303.

4. Rudolph Dreikurs and Vicki Soltz, *Children: The Challenge* (New York: Hawthorn, 1964).

5. Daniel J. Levinson et al., *The Seasons of a Man's Life* (New York: Knopf, 1978), p. 210.

6. Chilman, op. cit., p. 307.

7. Nancy Friday, *My Mother/My Self: The Daughter's Search for Identity* (New York: Delacorte, 1977), pp. 254–293.

8. Erik H. Erikson, *Childhood and Society,* 2nd ed. (New York: Norton, 1950), p. 261.

9. Peter Blos, *On Adolescence: A Psychoanalytic Interpretation* (New York: Free Press, 1962), p. 12.

10. Caryl Rivers, Rosalind Barnett, and Grace Baruch, *Beyond Sugar and Spice: How Women Grow, Learn, and Thrive* (New York: Putnam's, 1979), p. 179.

11. Carol Gilligan, "Woman's Place in Man's Life Cycle," talk at Harvard Alumni College, August 1977, revised October 1978, p. 17.

12. Jessie Bernard, *Women, Wives, Mothers: Values and Options* (Chicago: Aldine, 1975), p. 67.

13. Levinson, op. cit., p. 199.

14. Lillian B. Rubin, *Women of a Certain Age: The Midlife Search for Self* (New York: Harper & Row, 1979), pp. 42, 24.
15. Gail Sheehy, *Passages: Predictable Crises of Adult Life* (New York: Dutton, 1976), pp. 285–303.
16. U.S. Department of Labor, Employment Standards Administration, Women's Bureau, *Working Mothers and Their Children* (Washington, D.C.: U.S. Government Printing Office, 1977).
17. Rubin, op. cit., pp. 13–40.
18. Robert Coles and Jane Hallowell Coles, *Women of Crisis: Lives of Struggle and Hope* (New York: Delacorte, 1978), pp. 85, 93, 90, 98–99, 100, 97.
19. Ellen Goodman, *Turning Points: How People Change, Through Crisis and Commitment* (Garden City, N.Y.: Doubleday, 1979), pp. 11–13.

VI. The Departure Stage

1. B. L. Neugarten, "Continuities and Discontinuities of Psychological Issues into Adult Life," *Human Development*, Vol. 12 (1969), pp. 121–130.
2. Elizabeth Bates Harkins, "Effects of Empty Nest Transition on Self-Report of Psychological and Physical Well-Being," *Journal of Marriage and the Family*, Vol. 40 (August 1978), p. 553.
3. Lillian B. Rubin, *Women of a Certain Age: The Midlife Search for Self* (New York: Harper and Row, 1979).
4. Harkins, op. cit.; Norval D. Glenn, "Psychological Well-Being in the Post-parental Stage: Some Evidence from National Surveys," *Journal of Marriage and the Family*, Vol. 37 (February 1975), pp. 105–110.
5. Harkins, op. cit., p. 555.
6. Bernice L. Neugarten and Nancy Datan, "The Middle Years," in *American Handbook of Psychiatry*, 2nd ed., ed. Silvano Arieti (New York: Basic Books, 1974), p. 605.
7. Claire Pomeroy, *Fight It Out, Work It Out, Love It Out: The Story of a Family in Therapy* (Garden City, N.Y.; Doubleday, 1977), p. 190.
8. Boyd C. Rollins and Harold Feldman, "Marital Satisfaction over the Family Life Cycle," *Journal of Marriage and the Family*, Vol. 26 (February 1970), pp. 20–28; Boyd C. Rollins and Kenneth L. Cannon, "Marital Satisfaction over the Family Life Cycle: A Reevaluation," *Journal of Marriage and the Family*, Vol. 36 (May 1974), pp. 271–282; Peter C. Pineo, "Disenchantment in the Later Years of Marriage," *Marriage and Family Living*, Vol. 23 (February 1961), pp. 3–11; Graham B. Spanier et al., "Marital Adjustment over the Family Life Cycle: The Issue of Curvilinearity," *Journal of Marriage and the Family* (May 1975), pp. 263–275.
9. Gail Sheehy, *Passages: Predictable Crises of Adult Life* (New York: Dutton, 1976); Daniel J. Levinson et al., *The Seasons of a Man's Life* (New York: Knopf, 1978).
10. Neugarten and Datan, op. cit., p. 598.
11. Rubin, op. cit., pp. 181–183.
12. John Guare, *Bosoms and Neglect* (New York: Dramatists Play Service, 1980).
13. Pauline B. Bart, "Depression in Middle-Aged Women," in *Woman in*

Sexist Society, eds. Vivian Gornick and Barbara K. Moran (New York: Basic Books, 1971), p. 115, 116, 107, 103.

14. Donald Spence and Thomas Lonner, "The Empty Nest: A Transition within Motherhood," *Family Coordinator,* Vol. 20 (October 1971), p. 369.
15. Bart, op. cit., p. 103.
16. Sheehy, op. cit., pp. 34–81.
17. Neugarten, op. cit., p. 124.
18. Bruno Bettelheim, *The Uses of Enchantment: The Meaning and Importance of Fairy Tales* (New York: Vintage, 1976), p. 3.
19. George E. Vaillant, *Adaption to Life* (Boston: Little, Brown, 1977), pp. 3–4.

Bibliography

Abelin, Ernest L. "The Role of the Father in the Separation-Individuation Process." In *Separation-Individuation*, eds. John B. McDevitt and Calvin F. Settlage. New York: International Universities Press, 1971.

Ainsworth, Mary D. Salter. "The Development of Infant-Mother Attachment." In *Review of Child Development Research*, Vol. 3, eds. Bettye M. Caldwell and Henry N. Ricciuti. Chicago: University of Chicago Press, 1973.

Almy, Millie. "Spontaneous Play: An Avenue for Intellectual Development." In *Early Childhood Play: Selected Readings Related to Cognition and Motivation*, ed. Millie Almy. New York: Associated Educational Services Corporation, 1968.

————, ed. *Early Childhood Play: Selected Readings Related to Cognition and Motivation*. New York: Associated Educational Services Corporation, 1968.

Anthony, E. James. "The Reactions of Parents to the Oedipal Child." In *Parenthood: Its Psychology and Psychopathology*, eds. E. James Anthony and Therese Benedek. Boston: Little, Brown, 1970.

————, and Therese Benedek, eds. *Parenthood: Its Psychology and Psychopathology*. Boston: Little, Brown, 1970.

Ariès, Philippe. *Centuries of Childhood: A Social History of Family Life*. Trans. Robert Baldick. Paperback. New York: Vintage, 1962.

Arms, Suzanne. *A Season to Be Born*. New York: Harper/Colophon, 1973.

————. *Immaculate Deception: A New Look at Women and Childbirth in America*. Paperback. Boston: Houghton Mifflin, 1975.

Bailyn, Lotte. "Career and Family Orientations of Husbands and Wives in Relation to Marital Happiness." *Human Relations*, Vol. 23, No. 2 (April 1970), pp. 97–113.

Bane, Mary Jo. *Here to Stay: American Families in the Twentieth Century*. Paperback. New York: Basic Books, 1976.

————. "Marital Disruption and the Lives of Children." *Journal of Social Issues*, Vol. 32, No. 1 (1976), pp. 103–117.

Barber, Virginia, and Merrill Maguire Skaggs. *The Mother Person*. Paperback. New York: Schocken, 1975.

Bart, Pauline B. "Depression in Middle-Aged Women." In *Woman in Sexist Society*, eds. Vivian Gornick and Barbara K. Moran. New York: Basic Books, 1971.

Bell, Richard Q. "Stimulus Control of Parent or Caretaker Behavior by Offspring." *Developmental Psychology*, Vol. 4 (January 1971), pp. 63–72.

Bell, Ruth Davison. "Considering Parenthood." In *Ourselves and Our Children*, the Boston Women's Health Book Collective. New York: Random House, 1978.

Benedek, Therese. "The Emotional Structure of the Family." In *The Family: Its Function and Destiny*, Science and Culture Series, Vol. 5, ed. R. N. Anshen. New York: Harper, 1949.

———. "Parenthood as a Developmental Phase." *Journal of the American Psychological Association*, Vol. 7 (1959), pp. 389–417.

———. "Parenthood During the Life Cycle." In *Parenthood: Its Psychology and Psychopathology*, eds. E. James Anthony and Therese Benedek. Boston: Little, Brown, 1970.

———. "Psychobiological Aspects of Mothering," *Psychoanalytical Investigations*. New York: Quadrangle/New York Times, 1973.

——— "The Psychobiology of Pregnancy." In *Parenthood: Its Psychology and Psychopathology*, eds. E. James Anthony and Therese Benedek. Boston: Little, Brown, 1975.

———. *Psychosexual Functions in Women*. New York: Ronald, 1952.

———. "The Psychosomatic Implications of the Primary Unit: Mother-Child," *Psychoanalytic Investigations*. New York: Quadrangle/New York Times, 1973.

Bernard, Jessie. *The Future of Motherhood*. Paperback. New York: Penguin, 1974.

———. *Women, Wives, Mothers: Values and Options*. Chicago: Aldine, 1975.

Bettelheim, Bruno. *Love Is Not Enough*. Paperback. New York: Collier, 1950.

———. *The Uses of Enchantment: The Meaning and Importance of Fairy Tales*. Paperback. New York: Vintage, 1976.

Biber, Barbara. *Play as a Growth Process*. New York: Bank Street College of Education, 1951.

Bibring, Grete L. "Some Considerations of the Psychological Processes in Pregnancy." In *The Psychoanalytic Study of the Child*, Vol. 14, eds. Ruth S. Eissler, et al. New York: International Universities Press, 1959.

———, et al. "A Study of the Psychological Process in Pregnancy and of the Earliest Mother-Child Relationship." In *The Psychoanalytic Study of the Child*, Vol. 16, ed. Ruth S. Eissler, et al. New York: International Universities Press, 1961.

Bigner, Jerry J. *Parent-Child Relations*. New York: Macmillan, 1979.

Blos, Peter. *On Adolescence: A Psychoanalytic Interpretation*. Paperback. New York: Free Press, 1962.

Boehm, Felix. "The Femininity Complex in Men." *International Journal of Psychoanalysis*, Vol. 11 (1930), pp. 444–469.

The Boston Women's Health Book Collective. *Ourselves and Our Children*. New York: Random House, 1978.

Bowlby, John. *Attachment and Loss*, Vol. 1, *Attachment*. New York: Basic Books, 1969.

Brazelton, T. Berry. *Infants and Mothers: Differences in Development*. New York: Delacorte, 1969.

———, et al. "The Origins of Reciprocity—The Early Mother-Infant Interaction." In *The Effect of the Infant on Its Caregiver,* eds. Michael Lewis and Leonard A. Rosenblum. New York: Wiley, 1974.

Broderick, Carlfred B. "Beyond the Five Conceptual Frameworks: A Decade of Development in Family Theory." *Journal of Marriage and the Family,* Vol. 33, No. 1 (February 1971), pp. 139–159.

Brody, Jane E. "Miscarriage: Myths Often Add to Grief." *New York Times,* March 5, 1980, Section C, pp. 1, 14.

Brody, Sylvia. *Patterns of Mothering: Maternal Influence During Infancy.* Paperback. New York: International Universities Press, 1956.

Bronfenbrenner, Urie. *The Ecology of Human Development: Experiments by Nature and Design.* Boston: Harvard University Press, 1979.

———. "Reality and Research in the Ecology of Human Development." *Proceedings of the American Philosophical Society,* Vol. 119 (December 1975), pp. 439–469.

———. *Two Worlds of Childhood: U.S. and U.S.S.R.* Paperback. New York: Pocket Books, 1973.

Broussard, Elsie K., and Miriam Sergay Sturgeon Hartner. "Further Considerations Regarding Maternal Perceptions of the First Born." In *Exceptional Infants: Studies in Abnormalities,* Vol. 2, ed. J. Hellmuth. New York: Brunner/Mazel, 1971.

Burck, Frances Wells. *Babysense.* New York: St. Martin's, 1979.

Burke, Ronald J., and Tamara Weir. "Some Personality Differences Between Members of One-Career and Two-Career Families." *Journal of Marriage and the Family* (August 1976), pp. 453–459.

Caldwell, Bettye M. "Aggression and Hostility in Young Children." *Young Children* (January 1977), pp. 4–13.

———, et al. "Infant Day Care and Attachment." *American Journal of Orthopsychiatry,* Vol. 40 (1970), pp. 397–412.

Callahan, Sidney Cornelia. *Parenting: Principles and Politics of Parenthood.* Paperback. Baltimore: Penguin, 1973.

Campbell, Joseph, ed. *The Portable Jung,* trans. R. F. C. Hull. Paperback. New York: Viking, 1971.

Caplan, Gerald. "Patterns of Parental Response to the Crisis of Premature Birth." *Psychiatry,* Vol. 23, No. 4 (November 1960), pp. 365–374.

Chesler, Phyllis. *About Men.* New York: Simon and Schuster, 1978.

———. *With Child: A Diary of Motherhood.* New York: Crowell, 1979.

Chess, Stella, et al. *Your Child Is a Person.* New York: Viking, 1965.

Chilman, Catherine S. "Families in Development at Mid-Stage of the Family Life-Cycle." *Family Coordinator,* Vol. 17, No. 4 (October 1968), pp. 297–312.

Chodorow, Nancy. "Perspectives on Family Structure." Children and Family in a Changing World Conference, Sarah Lawrence College, Bronxville, N.Y., May 12, 1979.

———. *The Reproduction of Mothering: Psychoanalysis and the Sociology of Gender.* Berkeley: University of California Press, 1978.

Clarke, Jean Illsley. *Self-Esteem: A Family Affair.* Minneapolis, Minn.: Winston, 1978.

Cohen, Mabel Blake. "Personal Identity and Sexual Identity." *Psychiatry*, Vol. 29 (February 1966), pp. 1–14.

Cohler, Bertram J., et al. "Child-Care Attitudes and Emotional Disturbances Among Mothers of Young Children." *Genetic Psychology Monographs*, Vol. 82 (August 1970), pp. 3–47.

Coles, Robert. *Children of Crisis*. Paperback. New York: Delta, 1964.

———, and Jane Hallowell Coles. *Women of Crisis: Lives of Struggle and Hope*. New York: Delacorte, 1978.

Colman, Arthur, and Libby Colman. *Pregnancy: The Psychological Experience*. Paperback. New York: Bantam, 1971.

Condry, John, and Michael L. Siman. "Characteristics of Peer-and-Adult Oriented Children." *Journal of Marriage and the Family*, Vol. 36 (August 1974), pp. 543–554.

Cowan, Carolyn Pape. "How a Couple Become a Family." *Redbook*, September 1978, pp. 20–22, 154–159.

———, et al. "Becoming a Family: The Impact of a First Child's Birth on the Couple Relationship." In *The First Child and Family Formation*, eds. Warren B. Miller and Lucile F. Newman. Chapel Hill, N.C.: Carolina Population Center, 1978.

Cowan, Philip, and Carolyn Cowan. Interview by Ellen Galinsky. Berkeley, Calif., September 1978.

Curtis, Jean. *Working Mothers*. New York: Doubleday, 1976.

Daley, Eliot A. *Father Feelings*. New York: Morrow, 1978.

Daniels, Pamela, and Sara Ruddick, eds. *Working It Out*. New York: Pantheon, 1977.

———, and Kathy Weingarten. *Sooner or Later: The Timing of Parenthood in Adult Lives*. New York: Norton, to be published.

de Mause, Lloyd, ed. *The History of Childhood*. Paperback. New York: Harper Torchbooks, 1974.

———, ed. *The New Psychohistory*. New York: Psychohistory Press, 1975.

Desmond, M. M., et al. "The Transitional Care Nursery: A Mechanism of Preventive Medicine." *Pediatric Clinics of North America*, Vol. 13 (1966), pp. 651–668.

Deutsch, Helene. *The Psychology of Women*, Vol. II, *Motherhood*. Paperback. New York: Bantam, 1945.

Devor, Geraldine M. "Children as Agents in Socializing Parents." *Family Coordinator*, Vol. 19, No. 3 (July 1970), pp. 208–212.

Dinnerstein, Dorothy. *The Mermaid and the Minotaur: Sexual Arrangements and Human Malaise*. New York: Harper/Colophon, 1977.

Dreikurs, Rudolph, and Vicki Soltz. *Children: The Challenge*. New York: Hawthorn, 1964.

Drotar, Dennis, et al. "The Adaptation of Parents to the Birth of an Infant with a Congenital Malformation: A Hypothetical Model." *Pediatrics*, Vol. 56, No. 5 (November 1975), pp. 710–717.

Dullea, Georgia. "Vast Changes in Society Traced to the Rise of Working Women." *New York Times*, Nov. 29, 1977, pp. 1, 28.

Dyer, Everett D. "Parenthood as Crisis: A Re-Study." *Marriage and Family Living*, Vol. 25 (May 1963), pp. 196–201.

Ephron, Nora. "Having a Baby after 35." *New York Times Magazine*, Nov. 26, 1978, pp. 28–29, 86–88.

Erikson, Erik H. *Childhood and Society*, 2nd ed. New York: Norton, 1950.

———. *Identity, Youth and Crisis*. New York: Norton, 1968.

Escalona, Sibylle. *The Roots of Individuality*. Chicago: Aldine, 1968.

Escalona, Sibylle K. "Some Determinants of Individual Differences." *Transactions of the New York Academy of Sciences*, Series 2, Vol. 27, No. 7 (May 1965), pp. 802–816.

Fallaci, Oriana. *Letters to a Child Never Born,*, trans. John Shepley. Paperback. Garden City, N.Y.: Anchor, 1978.

Featherstone, Joseph. "Family Matters." *Harvard Educational Review*, Vol. 49 (February 1979), pp. 20–52.

Fein, Robert A. "Consideration of Men's Experience and the Birth of a First Child." In *The First Child and Family Formation*, eds. Warren B. Miller and Lucile F. Newman. Chapel Hill, N.C.: Carolina Population Center, 1978.

Feingold, Ben F. *Why Your Child Is Hyperactive*. New York: Random House, 1975.

Feldman, Harold, and Margaret Feldman. "The Family Life Cycle: Some Suggestions for Recycling." *Journal of Marriage and the Family*, Vol. 37, No. 2 (May 1975), pp. 277–284.

Ferreira, Antonio J. "The Pregnant Woman's Emotional Attitude and Its Reflection on the Newborn." *American Journal of Orthopsychiatry*, Vol. 30, No. 3 (July 1960), pp. 553–561.

Fraiberg, Selma. *Every Child's Birthright*. New York: Basic Books, 1977.

———. *The Magic Years*. New York: Scribner's, 1959.

Freeling, Nelson W., Stanley Kissel, and Louis Sargent. "Parenting for Foster Parents." *Child Psychiatry and Human Development*, Vol. 6 (4) (Summer 1976), pp. 244–250.

French, Marilyn. *The Women's Room*. Paperback. New York: Jove/HBJ, 1977.

Freud, Sigmund. *The Basic Writings of Sigmund Freud*, trans. and ed. A. A. Brill. New York: Modern Library, 1938.

———. "On Narcissism: An Introduction." *Standard Edition*, Vol. 14, ed. J. Strachey. London: Hogarth, 1957.

Friday, Nancy. *My Mother/My Self*. New York: Delacorte, 1977.

Friedan, Betty. *The Feminine Mystique*. New York: Norton, 1963.

———. "Feminism Takes a New Turn." *New York Times Magazine*, Nov. 18, 1979, pp. 40, 92, 94, 96, 98, 100, 102, 106.

Frisch, Hannah L. "The Effect of Designated and Actual Sex of Infant on Adult-Infant Play." Ph.D. dissertation, University of Chicago, 1976.

Galinsky, Ellen. *Beginnings*. Boston: Houghton Mifflin, 1976.

———. "Infants and Toddlers in Day Care: How Do They Turn Out." *Working Mother*, May 1980, pp. 97, 147–150.

———, and William H. Hooks. *The New Extended Family: Day Care That Works*. Boston: Houghton Mifflin, 1977.

Gilligan, Carol. "In a Different Voice: Women's Conception of Self and Morality." *Harvard Educational Review*, Vol. 47 (1977), pp. 481–517.

———. "Woman's Place in Man's Life Cycle." Talk at Harvard Alumni College, August 1977. Revised October 1978.

Ginott, Haim G. *Between Parent and Child*. New York: Macmillan, 1965.

Glazer-Malbin, Nona, ed. *Old Family/New Family*. Paperback. New York: D. Van Nostrand Co., 1975.

Glenn, Norval D. "Psychological Well-Being in the Post-Parental Stage: Some Evidence from National Surveys." *Journal of Marriage and the Family*, Vol. 37 (February 1975), pp. 105–110.

Goode, William J. *The Family: Foundations of Modern Sociology Series*. Englewood Cliffs, N.J.: Prentice-Hall, 1964.

Goodman, Ellen. *Turning Points: How People Change, Through Crisis and Commitment*. Garden City, N.Y.: Doubleday, 1979.

Gordon, Richard E., et al. "Factors in Postpartum Emotional Adjustment." *Obstetrics and Gynecology*, Vol. 25 (1965), pp. 158–164.

Gordon, Thomas, with Judith Gordon Sands. *P.E.T. in Action*. New York: Wyden, 1976.

Gould, Roger L. "The Phases of Adult Life: A Study in Developmental Psychology." *American Journal of Psychiatry*, Vol. 129, No. 5 (November 1972), pp. 521–531.

———. *Transformations: Growth and Change in Adult Life*. New York: Simon and Schuster, 1978.

Green, Maureen. *Fathering*. New York: McGraw-Hill, 1976.

Greenberg, Martin, and Norman Morris. "Engrossment: The Newborn's Impact upon the Father." *American Journal of Orthopsychiatry*, Vol. 44 (1974), pp. 520–531.

Greenberg, Selma. *Right from the Start: A Guide to Non-Sexist Child Rearing*. Boston: Houghton Mifflin, 1978.

Greenblat, Cathy S., et al. *The Marriage Game*, 2nd ed. New York: Random House, 1974.

Greenfeld, Josh. *A Child Called Noah: A Family Journal*. New York: Holt, Rinehart, and Winston, 1972.

———. *A Place for Noah*. New York: Holt, Rinehart, and Winston, 1978.

Group for the Advancement of Psychiatry. *Joys and Sorrows of Parenthood*. New York: Scribner's 1975.

Guare, John. *Bosoms and Neglect*. New York: Dramatists Play Service, 1980.

Hagood, Margaret Jarman. *Mothers of the South: Portraiture of the White Tenant Farm Woman*. Paperback. New York: Norton, 1977.

Harkins, Elizabeth Bates. "Effects of Empty Nest Transition on Self-Report of Psychological and Physical Well-Being." *Journal of Marriage and the Family*, Vol. 40 (August 1978), pp. 549–556.

Harper, Lawrence V. "The Scope of Offspring Effects: From Caregiver to Culture." *Psychological Bulletin*, Vol. 82, No. 5 (1975), pp. 784–801.

Havighurst, Robert J. "History of Developmental Psychology: Socialization and Personality Development Through the Life Span." In *Life Span Development Psychology: Personality and Socialization*, eds. Paul B. Baltes and K. Warner Schaie. New York: Academic Press, 1973.

Hawke, Sharryl, and David Knox. *One Child by Choice.* Paperback. Engle-wood Cliffs, N.J.: Prentice-Hall, 1977.

Heath, Douglas H. "Competent Fathers: Their Personalities and Mar-riages." *Human Development,* Vol. 19, No. 1 (1976), pp. 26–39.

Heffner, Elaine. *Mothering: The Emotional Experience of Motherhood After Freud and Feminism.* Garden City, N.Y.: Doubleday, 1978.

Heinstein, Martin I. "Expressed Attitudes and Feelings of Pregnant Women and Their Relations to Physical Complications of Pregnancy." *Merrill-Palmer Quarterly,* Vol. 13, No. 3 (July 1967), pp. 217–236.

Hetherington, E. Mavis, et al. "The Aftermath of Divorce." In *Mother/Child, Father/Child Relationships,* eds. Joseph H. Stevens, Jr., and Marilyn Mathews. Washington, D.C.: National Association for the Education of Young Children, 1978.

Hill, Reuben, and Donald A. Hansen. "The Identification of Conceptual Frameworks Utilized in Family Study." *Marriage and Family Living,* Vol. 22, No. 4 (November 1960), pp. 299–311.

Hilton, Irma. "Differences in the Behavior of Mothers Toward First- and Later-Born Children. *Journal of Personality and Social Psychology,* Vol. 7, No. 3 (1967), pp. 282–290.

Hobbs, Daniel F., Jr. "Parenthood as Crisis: A Third Study." *Journal of Marriage and the Family,* Vol. 27 (August 1965), pp. 367–372.

———, and Sue Peck Cole. "Transition to Parenthood: A Decade Replica-tion." *Journal of Marriage and the Family,* Vol. 38 (November 1976), pp. 723–731.

Hock, Ellen. "Working and Nonworking Mothers and Their Infants: A Comparative Study of Maternal Caregiving Characteristics and Infant Social Behavior." Mimeographed paper. Columbus: Ohio State Univer-sity, 1979.

Hoffman, Lois Wladis. "Effects of the First Child on the Woman's Role." In *The First Child and Family Formation,* eds. Warren B. Miller and Lucile F. Newman. Chapel Hill, N.C.: Carolina Population Center, 1978.

———, and Martin Hoffman. "The Value of Children to Parents." In *Psy-chological Perspectives on Population,* ed. J. T. Fawcett. New York: Basic Books, 1973.

———, and Ivan F. Nye. *Working Mothers.* San Francisco: Jossey-Bass, 1975.

Hotchner, Tracy. *Pregnancy and Childbirth.* Paperback. New York: Avon Books, 1979.

Howard, Jane. *Families.* New York: Simon and Schuster, 1978.

Howe, Louise Kapp, ed. *The Future of the Family.* Paperback. New York: Touchstone, 1972.

Hunt, J. McV. "Parent and Child Centers: Their Basis in the Behavioral and Educational Sciences." *American Journal of Orthopsychiatry,* Vol. 41 (1) (January 1971), pp. 13–38.

Jaffe, Sandra Sohn, and Jack Viertel. *Becoming Parents.* New York: Athe-neum, 1979.

Janeway, Elizabeth. *Man's World, Woman's Place.* Paperback. New York: Delta, 1971.

Jessner, Lucie, et al. "The Development of Parental Attitudes During Pregnancy." In *Parenthood: Its Psychology and Psychopathology*, eds. E. James Anthony and Therese Benedek. Boston: Little, Brown, 1970.

Kagan, Jerome. "The Child in the Family." *Daedalus*, Vol. 106 (Spring 1977), pp. 33–56.

———. *The Growth of the Child*. New York: Norton, 1978.

———. *Understanding Children: Behavior, Motives, and Thought*. Paperback. New York: Harcourt, Brace Jovanovich, 1971.

———, et al. *Infancy: Its Place in Human Development*. Cambridge, Mass: Harvard University Press, 1978.

Kahn, Alfred J., and Sheila B. Kamerman. *Child Care, Family Benefits and Working Parents*. New York: Columbia University Press, 1980.

———. *Not for the Poor Alone: European Social Services*. Paperback. New York: Harper/Colophon, 1977.

Kamerman, Sheila B. *Parenting in an Unresponsive Society: Managing Work and Family Life*. New York: Free Press, 1980.

———, and Alfred J. Kahn, eds. *Family Policy: Government and Families in Fourteen Countries*. New York: Columbia University Press, 1978.

Kaplan, Louise J. *Oneness and Separateness: From Infant to Individual*. New York: Simon and Schuster, 1978.

Keniston, Kenneth. "Psychological Development and Historical Change." In *Rethinking Childhood*, ed. Arlene Skolnick. Boston: Little, Brown, 1970.

———, and the Carnegie Council on Children. *All Our Children*. New York: Harcourt Brace Jovanovich, 1977.

Kennell, John H., et al. "Maternal Behavior One Year After Early and Extended Post-partum Contact." *Developmental Medicine and Child Neurology*, Vol. 16, No. 2 (April 1974), pp. 172–179.

Kestenberg, Judith S. "The Effect on Parents of the Child's Transition into and out of Latency." In *Parenthood: Its Psychology and Psychopathology*, eds. E. James Anthony and Therese Benedek. Boston: Little, Brown, 1970.

Klaus, Marshall H., and John H. Kennell. *Maternal-Infant Bonding*. St. Louis: C. V. Mosby, 1976.

———. "Mothers Separated from Their Newborn Infants." *Pediatric Clinics of North America*, Vol. 17 (November 1970), pp. 1015–1037.

———. "Parent-to-Infant Attachment." In *Mother/Child, Father/Child Relationships*, eds. Joseph H. Stevens, Jr., and Marilyn Mathews. Washington, D.C.: National Association for the Education of Young Children, 1978.

Klaus, Marshall H., Mary Ann Trause, and John H. Kennell. "Does Human Maternal Behavior After Delivery Show a Characteristic Pattern?" In *Parent-Infant Interaction*, Cina Foundation Symposium 33 (new series). Amsterdam, Holland: ASP, 1975.

Klemesrud, Judy. "Child Custody: Separate but Equal." *New York Times*, Feb. 2, 1978, pp. 17, C6.

Knox, David, and Kenneth Wilson. "The Differences Between Having One and Two Children." *The Family Coordinator*, January 1978, pp. 23–25.

Kohl, Herbert. *Growing into Parenthood.* Boston: Little, Brown, 1978.

Kohlberg, Lawrence. "Development of Moral Character and Moral Ideology." In *Review of Child Development Research,* Vol. 1, eds. M. Hoffman and L. Hoffman. New York: Russell Sage Foundation, 1964.

Komarovsky, Mirra. *Blue Collar Marriage.* Paperback. New York: Vintage, 1967.

Kotelchuck, M., et al. "Infant Reaction to Parental Separations When Left with Familiar and Unfamiliar Adults." *Journal of Genetic Psychology,* Vol. 126 (1975), pp. 255–262.

Lamb, Michael E. "Father-Infant and Mother-Infant Interaction in the First Year of Life." *Child Development,* Vol. 48 (1977), pp. 167–181.

————. "Fathers: Forgotten Contributors to Child Development." *Human Development,* Vol. 18 (1975), pp. 245–266.

Lasch, Christopher. *The Culture of Narcissism.* New York: Norton, 1978.

Lazarre, Jane. *The Mother Knot.* Paperback. New York: Laurel, 1976.

Leifer, Myra. "Psychological Changes Accompanying Pregnancy and Motherhood." *Genetic Psychology Monographs,* Vol. 95 (1977), pp. 55–96.

LeMasters, E. E. "Parenthood as Crisis." In *Sourcebook in Marriage and the Family,* 2nd ed., ed. Marvin B. Sussman. Boston: Houghton Mifflin, 1963.

————. *Parents in Modern America: A Sociological Analysis,* rev. ed. Homewood, Ill.: Dorsey, 1970.

Levine, James A. *Day Care and the Public Schools: Profiles of Five Communities.* Paperback. Newton, Mass.: Education Development Center, Inc., 1978.

————. *Who Will Raise the Children? New Options for Fathers (and Mothers).* Paperback. New York: Bantam, 1976.

LeVine, R. A. "Parental Goals: A Cross-Cultural View." In *The Family as Educator,* ed. H. J. Leichter. New York: Columbia Teachers College Press, 1974.

Levinson, Daniel J. "Growing Up with a Dream." *Psychology Today,* January 1978, pp. 20–31, 89.

————, et al. *The Seasons of a Man's Life.* New York: Knopf, 1978.

Levy, Judith M., and Richard K. McGee. "Childbirth as Crisis: A Test of Janis's Theory of Communication and Stress Resolution." *Journal of Personality and Social Psychology,* Vol. 31, No. 1 (1975), pp. 171–179.

Lewis, Jerry M., et al. *No Single Thread: Psychological Health in Family Systems.* New York: Brunner/Mazel, 1976.

Lewis, Michael, and Leonard A. Rosenblum, eds. *The Effect of the Infant on Its Caregiver.* New York: Wiley, 1974.

Lewis, Oscar. *Five Families: Mexican Case Studies in the Culture of Poverty.* Paperback. New York: Science Editions, 1959.

Lidz, Theodore. *The Person: His and Her Development throughout the Life Cycle.* New York: Basic Books, 1968.

Lindbergh, Anne Morrow. *Gift from the Sea.* Paperback. New York: Vintage, 1955.

Loesch, John G., and Nahman H. Greenberg. "Some Specific Areas of Conflict Observed during Pregnancy: A Comparative Study of Married and Unmarried Pregnant Women." *American Journal of Orthopsychiatry*, Vol. 32 (July 1962), pp. 624–636.

Loevinger, Jane. "Patterns of Parenthood as Theories of Learning." *Journal of Abnormal and Social Psychology*, Vol. 59, No. 1 (July 1959), pp. 148–150.

Logan, Margaret. *Happy Endings*. Boston: Houghton Mifflin, 1979.

Lott, Bernice E. "Who Wants the Children?" *American Psychologist*, July 1973, pp. 573–582.

Lynn, David B. *The Father: His Role in Child Development*. Monterey, Calif.: Brooks/Cole, 1974.

Lytton, Hugh, Dorice Conway, and Reginald Sauvé. "The Impact of Twin-ship on Parent-Child Interaction." *Journal of Personality and Social Psychology*, Vol. 35, No. 2 (1977), pp. 97–107.

McBride, Angela Barron. *The Growth and Development of Mothers*. Paperback. New York: Barnes & Noble, 1973.

———. *Living with Contradictions: A Married Feminist*. Paperback. New York: Harper/Colophon, 1976.

Maddox, Brenda. *The Half-Parent*. Paperback. New York: Signet, 1975.

Mahler, Margaret S. *Of Human Symbiosis and the Vicissitudes of Individuation*, Vol. 1 *Infantile Psychosis*. New York: International Universities Press, 1968.

———. "On the First Three Subphases of the Separation-Individuation Process." *International Journal of Psycho-analysis*, Vol. 53 (1972), pp. 333–338.

———, et al. "The Mother's Reaction to Her Toddler's Drive for Individuation." In *Parenthood: Its Psychology and Psychopathology*, eds. E. James Anthony and Therese Benedek. Boston: Little, Brown, 1970.

Mead, Margaret. "Selections from Culture and Commitment." In *Family in Transition*, eds. Arlene S. Skolnick and Jerome H. Skolnick. Boston: Little, Brown, 1971.

———. "Some Theoretical Considerations on the Problem of Mother-Child Separation." *American Journal of Orthopsychiatry*, Vol. 24, No. 3 (July 1954), pp. 471–483.

Melges, F. T. "Postpartum Psychiatric Syndromes." *Psychosomatic Medicine*, Vol. 23 (1968), pp. 520–525.

Minturn, Leigh, and William L. Lambert. *Mothers of Six Cultures: Antecedents of Child Rearing*. New York: Wiley, 1964.

Miller, Warren B., and Lucile F. Newman, eds. *The First Child and Family Formation*. Chapel Hill, N.C.: Carolina Population Center, 1978.

Minuchin, Patricia. "Transition to Peer Group Life." *Lucy Sprague Mitchell Memorial Conference*, 5th, ed. Charlotte B. Winsor. New York: Bank Street College of Education, 1978.

Minuchin, Salvador. *Families and Family Therapy*. Cambridge, Mass.: Harvard University Press, 1974.

Moss, Howard A. "Sex, Age, and State as Determinants of Mother-Infant Interaction." *Merrill-Palmer Quarterly*, Vol. 13 (1967), pp. 19–36.

———, Kenneth S. Robson, and Frank Pedersen. "Determinants of Maternal Stimulation of Infants and Consequences of Treatment for Later Reactions to Strangers." *Developmental Psychology*, Vol. 1, No. 3 (1969), pp. 239–246.

Murphy, Lois Barclay, and Alice E. Moriarity. *Vulnerability, Coping, and Growth: From Infancy to Adolescence.* New Haven: Yale University Press, 1976.

Mussen, Paul. *The Psychological Development of the Child*, 2nd ed. Englewood Cliffs, N.J.: Prentice-Hall, 1973.

Neal, Arthur E., William J. Ivoska, and H. Theodore Gruat. "Dimensions of Family Alienation in the Marital Dyad." *Sociometry*, Vol. 39, No. 4 (December 1976), pp. 396–405.

Neubauer, Peter B., ed. *The Process of Child Development.* Paperback. New York: Meridian, 1976.

Neugarten, B. L. "Continuities and Discontinuities of Psychological Issues into Adult Life." *Human Development*, Vol. 12 (1969), pp. 121–130.

———, and Nancy Datan. "The Middle Years." In *American Handbook of Psychiatry*, 2nd ed., ed. Silvano Arieti. New York: Basic Books, 1974.

Nordheimer, Jon. "The Family in Transition: A Challenge from Within." *New York Times*, Nov. 27, 1977, pp. 1, 74.

Omwake, Eveline. "The Child's Estate," *Early Childhood Play: Selected Readings Related to Cognition and Motivation*, ed. Millie Almy. New York: Associated Educational Services Corporation, 1968.

Osofsky, Joy D. "Neonatal Characteristics and Mother-Infant Interaction in Two Observational Situations." *Child Development*, Vol. 47, No. 4 (December 1976), pp. 1138–1147.

Parke, Ross D., and Douglas B. Sawin. "Fathering: Its Major Role." *Psychology Today*, November 1977, pp. 109, 111–112.

Peck, Ellen. *The Baby Trap.* Paperback. New York: Pinnacle, 1971.

Pedersen, Frank A., and Kenneth S. Robson. "Father Participation in Infancy." *American Journal of Orthopsychiatry*, Vol. 39 (April 1969), pp. 466–472.

Piaget, Jean. *The Language and Thought of the Child*, trans. Marjorie Gabain. Paperback. New York: New American Library, 1955.

Pineo, Peter C. "Disenchantment in the Later Years of Marriage." *Marriage and Family Living*, Vol. 23, No. 1 (February 1961), pp. 3–11.

Pomeroy, Claire. *Fight It Out, Work It Out, Love It Out: The Story of a Family in Therapy.* Garden City, N.Y.: Doubleday, 1977.

Price, Jane. *How to Have a Child and Keep Your Job.* New York: St. Martin's, 1979.

Putney, Snell, and Gail J. Putney. *The Adjusted American: Normal Neuroses in the Individual and Society.* Paperback. New York: Harper/Colophon, 1966.

Quindlen, Anna. "Relationships: Independence vs. Intimacy." *New York Times*, Nov. 28, 1977, pp. 1, 36.

Radl, Shirley L. *Mother's Day Is Over.* Paperback. New York: Warner, 1973.

Rapoport, Rhona, and Robert N. Rapoport *Dual-Career Families Re-examined.* Paperback. New York: Harper/Colophon, 1976.

———, et al. *Fathers, Mothers, and Society.* New York: Basic Books, 1977.

Rapoport, Robert. "Home and School at the Launch: Some Preliminary Observations." *Oxford Review of Education*, Vol. 1, No. 3 (1975), pp. 277–286.

Reinhold, Robert. "The Trend Toward Sexual Equality: Depth of Transformation Uncertain." *New York Times*, Nov. 30, 1977, pp. 1, B4.

Ricciuti, Henry N. *Effects of Infant Day Care Experience on Behavior and Development: Research and Implications for Social Policy.* Washington, D.C.: HEW, 1976.

Rich, Adrienne. *Of Woman Born: Motherhood as Experience and Institution.* New York: Norton, 1976.

Richards, M. P. M., J. F. Dunn, and B. Antonis. "Caretaking in the First Year of Life: The Role of Fathers, and Mother's Social Isolation." *Child: Care, Health, and Development*, Vol. 3 (1977), pp. 23–36.

Riegel, Klaus F. "The Dialectics of Human Development." *American Psychologist*, Vol. 31 (October 1976), pp. 689–700.

Rivers, Caryl, Rosalind Barnett, and Grace Baruch. *Beyond Sugar and Spice: How Women Grow, Learn, and Thrive.* New York: Putnam's, 1979.

Robbins, Lillian Cukier. "The Accuracy of Parental Recall of Aspects of Child Development and of Child Rearing Practices." *Journal of Abnormal and Social Psychology*, Vol. 66, No. 3 (1963), pp. 261–270.

Rollins, Boyd C., and Kenneth L. Cannon. "Marital Satisfaction over the Family Life Cycle: A Reevaluation." *Journal of Marriage and the Family*, Vol. 36 (May 1974), pp. 271–282.

Rollins, Boyd C., and Harold Feldman. "Marital Satisfaction over the Family Life Cycle." *Journal of Marriage and the Family*, Vol. 26 (February 1970), pp. 20–28.

Rosen, Jacqueline L. "Matching Teachers with Children." *School Review*, Vol. 80, No. 3 (May 1972), pp. 409–431.

Ross, John Munder. "Paternal Identity: The Equations of Fatherhood and Manhood." In *On Sexuality: Psychoanalytic Observations*, eds. Toksoz B. Karasci and Charles W. Socarides. New York: International Universities Press, 1979.

———. "Toward Fatherhood: The Epigenesis of Paternal Identity during a Boy's Decade." *International Review of Psychoanalysis*, Vol. 4 (1977), pp. 327–347.

Rossi, Alice S. "The Transition to Parenthood." In *Family in Transition*, eds. Arlene S. Skolnick and Jerome H. Skolnick. Boston: Little, Brown, 1971.

———, Jerome Kagan, and Tamara K. Hareven, eds. *The Family.* New York: Norton, 1978.

Rothman, Sheila M. *Woman's Proper Place.* New York: Basic Books, 1978.

Rubin, Lillian Breslow. *Women of a Certain Age: The Midlife Search for Self.* New York: Harper & Row, 1979.

———. *Worlds of Pain.* New York: Basic Books, 1976.

Ruopp, Richard, et al. *Children at the Center.* Cambridge, Mass.: Abt Books, 1979.

Salk, Lee, with Rita Kramer. *How to Raise a Human Being: A Parent's*

Guide to Emotional Health from Infancy through Adolescence. New York: Random House, 1969.

Sander, Louis W. "Issues in Early Mother-Child Interaction." In *Infant Psychiatry: A New Synthesis,* eds. Eveoleen V. Rexford et al. New Haven: Yale University Press, 1976.

Sanguiliano, Iris. *In Her Time.* New York: Morrow, 1978.

Satir, Virginia. *Peoplemaking.* Palo Alto, Calif.: Science and Behavior Books, 1972.

"Saving the Family." *Newsweek,* May 15, 1978, pp. 63–75.

Schlesinger, Benjamin, and Rubin Todres. "Motherless Families: An Increasing Societal Pattern." *Child Welfare,* Vol. 55, No. 8 (September/October 1976), pp. 553–558.

Schwartz, Barbara K. "Easing the Adaption to Parenthood." *Journal of Family Counseling,* Vol. 2 (Fall 1974), pp. 32–39.

Segal, Julius, and Herbert Yahraes. *A Child's Journey.* New York: McGraw-Hill, 1979.

Sheehy, Gail. "Hers Column." *New York Times,* Feb. 7, 1980, p. C2.

———. *Passages: Predictable Crises of Adult Life.* New York: Dutton, 1976.

Skolnick, Arlene S. *Intimacy, Family, and Society.* Boston: Little, Brown, 1974.

———. *The Intimate Environment.* Boston: Little, Brown, 1973.

———, ed. *Rethinking Childhood.* Boston: Little, Brown, 1976.

———. Interview by Ellen Galinsky. Berkeley, Calif., September 1978.

———, and Jerome H. Skolnick *Family in Transition.* Boston: Little, Brown, 1971.

Smith, Lendon H. *Feed Your Kids Right.* New York: McGraw-Hill, 1979.

Solnit, Albert J., and Mary H. Stark. "Mourning and the Birth of a Defective Child." *The Psychoanalytic Study of the Child,* Vol. 16, eds. Ruth S. Eissler, et al. New York: International Universities Press, 1961, pp. 523–537.

Spanier, Graham B., et al. "Marital Adjustment over the Family Life Cycle: The Issue of Curvilinearity." *Journal of Marriage and the Family,* May 1975, pp. 263–275.

Spence, Donald, and Thomas Lonner. "The Empty Nest: A Transition Within Motherhood." *Family Coordinator,* Vol. 20 (October 1971), pp. 369–375.

Spitz, René A. "Hospitalism." *The Psychoanalytic Study of the Child,* Vol. 1 (1945), pp. 54–117.

Spock, Benjamin. *Baby and Child Care.* Paperback. New York: Pocket Books, 1945.

Spradley, Thomas S., and James P. Spradley. *Deaf Like Me.* New York: Random House, 1978.

Steele, Brandt I., and Carl B. Pollock. "The Battered Child's Parents." In *Family in Transition,* eds. Arlene S. Skolnick and Jerome H. Skolnick. Boston: Little, Brown, 1971.

Steinberg, David. *Fatherjournal: Five Years of Awakening to Fatherhood.* New York: Times Change, 1977.

Stephens, William N. *The Family in Cross-Cultural Perspective.* Paperback. New York: Holt, Rinehart and Winston, 1963.

Stern, Daniel. *The First Relationship: Infant and Mother.* Cambridge, Mass.: Harvard University Press, 1977.

Stevens, Joseph H., Jr., and Marilyn Mathews, eds. *Mother/Child, Father/Child Relationships.* Washington, D.C.: National Association for the Education of Young Children, 1978.

Stone, L. Joseph, and Joseph Church. *Childhood and Adolescence: A Psychology of the Growing Person,* 3rd ed. New York: Random House, 1957.

Taylor, Muriel K., and Kate L. Kogan. "Effects of Birth of a Sibling on Mother-Child Interactions." *Child Psychiatry and Human Development,* Vol. 4 (1973), pp. 53–58.

Tracy, Russel L., Michael E. Lamb, and Mary D. Salter Ainsworth. "Infant Approach Behavior as Related to Attachment." *Child Development,* Vol. 47, No. 3 (1976), pp. 571–578.

Trotter, Robert J. "Changing the Face of Birth." *Science News,* Vol. 108, No. 7 (Aug. 16, 1975), pp. 106–108.

Tulkin, Steven R., and Jerome Kagan. "Mother-Child Interaction in the First Year of Life." *Child Development,* Vol. 43, No. 1 (1972), pp. 32–41.

U.S. Department of Labor, Employment Standards Administration, Women's Bureau. *Working Mothers and Their Children.* Washington, D.C.: U.S. Government Printing Office, 1977.

Vaillant, George E. *Adaption to Life.* Boston: Little, Brown, 1977.

Walters, James, and Nick Stinnett. "Parent-Child Relationships: A Decade Review of Research." *Journal of Marriage and the Family,* February 1971, pp. 70–111.

Weinraub, Marsha, Jeanne Brooks, and Michael Lewis. "The Social Network: A Reconsideration of the Concept of Attachment." Mimeographed paper. Princeton, N.J.: Educational Testing Service, 1977.

Weiss, Robert S. "The Emotional Impact of Marital Separation." *Journal of Social Issues,* Vol. 32 (1976), pp. 135–145.

Whiting, Beatrice B., and John W. M. Whiting. *Children of Six Cultures: A Psycho-Cultural Analysis.* Cambridge, Mass.: Harvard University Press, 1975.

Winnicott, Donald W. *The Child, the Family, and the Outside World.* Paperback. Middlesex, England: Penguin, 1964.

———. "The Mother-Infant Experience of Mutuality." In *Parenthood: Its Psychology and Psychopathology,* eds. E. James Anthony and Therese Benedek. Boston: Little, Brown, 1970.

———. *Playing and Reality.* New York: Basic Books, 1971.

———. "Transitional Objects and Transitional Phenomena," *Collected Papers.* London: Tavistock, 1958.

Wolfenstein, M. "Fun Morality: An Analysis of Recent American Child-training Literature." In *Childhood in Contemporary Cultures,* eds. Margaret Mead and Martha Wolfenstein. Chicago: University of Chicago Press, 1955.

Wolff, Peter. "Observations on Newborn Infants." *Psychosomatic Medicine,* Vol. 21 (1969), pp. 110–118.

Yarrow, Leon J., and Frank A. Pedersen. "Attachment: Its Origins and Course." *Young Children*, Vol. 27 (June 1972), pp. 302–310.

Zajone, R. B. "Family Configuration and Intelligence." *Science*, Vol. 192 (April 1976), pp. 227–236.

Zemlick, Maurice J., and Robert I. Watson. "Maternal Attitudes of Acceptance and Rejection During and After Pregnancy." *American Journal of Orthopsychiatry*, Vol. 23, No. 3 (July 1953), pp. 570–584.

Index